T0205341

Formal Approaches to Computing and
Information Technology

Springer
London
Berlin
Heidelberg
New York
Barcelona
Hong Kong
Milan
Paris
Santa Clara
Singapore
Tokyo

Also in this series:

Proof in VDM: A Practitioner's Guide
J.C. Bicarregui, J.S. Fitzgerald, P.A. Lindsay, R. Moore and B. Ritchie
ISBN 3-540-19813-X

The B Language and Method
K. Lano
ISBN 3-540-76033-4

A Theory and Practice of Program Development
D. Andrews
ISBN 3-540-76162-4

Constructing Correct Software: *the basics*
J. Cooke
ISBN 3-540-76156-X

Formal Methods in Human-Computer Interaction
P. Palanque and F. Paternò (Eds)
ISBN 3-540-76158-6

Proof in VDM: Case Studies
J.C. Bicarregui (Ed.)
ISBN 3-540-76186-1

Program Development by Refinement
E. Sekerinski and K. Sere (Eds)
ISBN 1-85233-053-8

High-Integrity System Specification and Design
Jonathan P. Bowen and Michael G. Hinchey
ISBN 3-540-76226-4

Michael G. Hinchey and Jonathan P. Bowen (Eds)

Industrial-Strength Formal Methods in Practice

Springer

Michael G. Hinchey, BSc, MSc, PhD
Department of Computer Science, University of Nebraska-Omaha,
College of Information Science and Technology, 6001 Dodge Street, Omaha,
NE 68182-0500, USA

Jonathan P. Bowen, BA, MA
Department of Computer Science, University of Reading, P.O. Box 225, Whiteknights,
Reading, Berkshire, RG6 6AY, UK

Series Editor
S.A. Schuman, BSc, DEA, CEng
Department of Mathematical and Computing Sciences
University of Surrey, Guildford, Surrey GU2 5XH, UK

ISBN 1-85233-640-4 Springer-Verlag London Berlin Heidelberg

British Library Cataloguing in Publication Data
A catalogue record for this book is available from the British Library

Library of Congress Cataloging-in-Publication Data
Industrial strength formal methods in practice / Michael G. Hinchey
    and Jonathan P. Bowen, [editors].
        p.   cm.   –   (Formal approaches to computing and information
    technology)
      ISBN 1-85233-640-4 (alk. paper)
      1. Formal methods (Computer science)   I. Hinchey, Michael G.
    (Michael Gerard), 1969-   . II. Bowen, J. P. (Jonathan Peter),
    1956-   . III. Series.
    QA76.9.F67I53   1999   99-33669
    005.13'1 – dc21   CIP

Apart from any fair dealing for the purposes of research or private study, or criticism or review, as
permitted under the Copyright, Designs and Patents Act 1988, this publication may only be reproduced,
stored or transmitted, in any form or by any means, with the prior permission in writing of the
publishers, or in the case of reprographic reproduction in accordance with the terms of licences issued
by the Copyright Licensing Agency. Enquiries concerning reproduction outside those terms should be
sent to the publishers.

© Springer-Verlag London Limited 1999
Printed in Great Britain

The use of registered names, trademarks etc. in this publication does not imply, even in the absence of a
specific statement, that such names are exempt from the relevant laws and regulations and therefore free
for general use.

The publisher makes no representation, express or implied, with regard to the accuracy of the
information contained in this book and cannot accept any legal responsibility or liability for any errors
or omissions that may be made.

Typesetting: Camera ready by editors
Printed and bound at the Athenæum Press Ltd., Gateshead, Tyne & Wear
34/3830-543210 Printed on acid-free paper SPIN 10733477

Mathematicians are very happy to discuss things that don't exist, but engineers are very unhappy about it.

— Maurice V. Wilkes (10 May 1999)

Preface

Computer design is an engineering discipline, not a mathematical one.

— Maurice V. Wilkes[1] (10 May 1999)

It is jokingly said that in any report one should address all of the thorny issues straight away, and ignore them thereafter, whether they have been resolved or not. Therefore, in this collection, we will make the sole mention of Y2K and the so-called Millennium Bug here in the preface.

This book is not about the problems that will/could/might occur on 1 January, 2000, and was never intended to be. However, concerns over that event do make the publication of this collection particularly timely. The amount of publicity that the "Y2K problem" has attracted has brought to people's attention that much of software development has, in the past, been rather *ad hoc*, often careless, and has taken place without consideration for the longevity of software, and the influence that software systems have on so many aspects of our lives. (For technical details on the specification and design of high-quality software, the reader is referred to *High-Integrity System Specification and Design* (Bowen and Hinchey, 1999), also in the FACIT series.)

Many would argue that software is never truly "engineered" in the sense that buildings, bridges, chemical plants, and, even, hardware systems are. Although they have been available for three decades now, formal methods are still too often seen as a mathematical "toy" exercise for academics. We dispute this fact, however, and we hope that the papers in this collection will help to convince sceptics that formal methods can indeed be applied at a scale suitable for industrial practice. That "proof of concept" was the goal of a previous collection, *Applications of Formal Methods* (Hinchey and Bowen, 1995). This collection goes further, however, in that rather than trying to illustrate that formal methods can be used in industrial practice, chapters in this collection aim to guide the reader in actually applying formal methods to industrial scale projects.

---

[1] On the occasion of the 50th anniversary of the EDSAC computer at a British Computer Society Computer Conservation Society (BCS-CCS) meeting held at the Science Museum, London.

Chapter 1, by ourselves, the editors, highlights several "sins" often committed by those attempting to apply formal methods. The chapter aims to give some general guidelines that should help in the real-life application of formal methods.

In Chapter 2, Bernard and Laffitte describe their experiences using the B-Method, a tool-supported formal software development approach, to automate systems used in conducting the French Census of Population in 1990. The system was critical in that the statistical data would be used in making political decisions. Based on their experiences, the authors discuss the relevance of B for industrial practice.

Anderson, in Chapter 3, describes a very interesting example of the use of formal methods, namely the application of the BAN logic (developed by Burrows, Abadi and Needham, to help in the formal reasoning about authentication) to an electronic payment system where security considerations are paramount. The result was a highly successful system and an example of how necessary formal methods can be in particular circumstances.

Chapter 4, by Lano, Sanchez and Goldsack, describes experiences with applying the B-Method in the development of chemical process control systems. It describes the authors' experiences in applying the method, including how it can be made industrially relevant, and gives excellent guidelines for large-scale application of formal methods in process control environments.

Hardware is the focus of Chapter 5, by Brock and Hunt, which describes the application of ACL2 (A Computational Logic for Applicative Common Lisp) to the verification of the Motorola DSP Complex Arithmetic Processor (CAP). This involves a high level of assurance through the use of automated theorem proving techniques and tool support, a key issue for formalisation.

Chapter 6, by Kesten *et al.*, describes an application of formal methods to Internet security. A combination of techniques was used, which exploits the benefits of model-checking, an increasingly important issue in formal methods.

The topic of tool support is continued in Chapter 7, as Leveson, Heimdahl and Reese describe a successful CAD environment used in the development of safety-critical software systems.

The railway industry provides the application domain for Chapter 8, as Bjørner, George and Prehn report on experiences with applying the RAISE tool-supported formal development approach to the Chinese railway system. This was a particularly large project spanning over a long period of time, and involving collaboration between the railway authorities and Fellows at the United Nations University.

Jacky, in Chapter 9, reports on a large-scale critical system using the Z formal specification notation, namely University of Washington's experiences with the formal specification and development of a radiation therapy machine.

Chapter 10, by Hall, is a fascinating paper, first published in *IEEE Software*, describing experiences in the development of an air traffic control system for the London airports, and pointing out many issues that anyone embarking on using formal methods would be wise to consider.

The use of formal methods in tandem with other (less formal) notations is a growing area of interest for the formal methods community. Chapter 11, by Semmens and Bryant, describes their success in using the Rigorous Review Technique, whereby formal methods (specifically the Z notation) are used to enable great insights into specifications and designs produced using structured analysis techniques and notations.

Z is also the focus of Chapter 12. Craigen, Meisels and Saaltink describe the use of the Z/EVES tool for analysing Z specifications and proving properties of them. While Z can be used simply as a notation to capture specifications unambiguously, in practical industrial use, tool-support is required to check and reason about these formal descriptions in order to help avoid human errors when large specifications are involved.

Moore, Klinker and Mihelcic describe, in Chapter 13, how to approach formal specification and verification in such a way that those certifying systems will be convinced of the validity of the approach.

Chapter 14, by Ardis and Mataga, addresses the importance of domain engineering and describes how to the tackle the ever-difficult problem of technology transfer.

Verification, and in particular tool-supported verification, is also the subject of Chapter 15, by Borälv and Stålmarck, who report on their many years of successful application of formal methods in a variety of industries.

Finally, Chapter 16, by Linger and Trammell, presents the Cleanroom approach to software engineering. The approach places high emphasis on quality, with components that fail to meet strict criteria being discarded.

Our thanks to all those who contributed to this collection, especially when one of us tormented them over PostScript figures, deadlines, and other issues that, at the end of the day, seem so trivial. And our special thanks to Michael Jackson for kindly agreeing to write a foreword to the collection and to Maurice Wilkes for permission to quote him at the start of the book.

We are very grateful to all at Springer-Verlag for their assistance and patience during the preparation of this book. In particular we would like to thank Rebecca Mowat, Karen Barker, and, especially, Rosie Kemp. Additionally, Jane Bowen kindly proofread Chapter 1 for us.

We hope that the collection will prove to be useful to you, the reader, whether you are a student, an academic, or an industrialist wanting to know more about formal methods or how to put formal methods into practice on an industrial scale. Relevant information about this book will be kept up to date online at:

http://www.fmse.cs.reading.ac.uk/isfm/

M.G.H.   J.P.B.
Omaha   Reading

Contents

Foreword

Henry Buckle, the nineteenth-century English historian, asked himself why historians had been unable to discover general laws, principles and calculi of the kind and quality that mathematicians, physicists and chemists had found with such spectacular success. He concluded that historians were simply inferior to the scientists, "...no one having devoted himself to history who in point of intellect is at all to be compared with Kepler, Newton, or many others ...", but he also believed that within another century history would assimilate the methods and principles of natural science and would itself become a respectable science.

The earliest and most impassioned advocates of formal methods sometimes sounded like Buckle. Software development practitioners, they implied, were simply the intellectual inferiors of the researchers and academics who had devised mathematically sound development methods; practitioners should learn and adopt formal methods and their difficulties would melt away. But these advocates, like Buckle, had failed to understand the nature of the work.

Certainly, many aspects of software development, as of history, can profitably draw on formal reasoning and calculation. But serious software developments are about the real world, and there is more in heaven and earth than is dreamt of in the philosophy of mathematical formalisms. The formal system embodied in the computer and its software must interact with the inherently informal world of human beings and physical nature, where its whole purpose resides. A very large part of the software engineering task is to analyse and describe that inherently informal world, and the system's purpose within it, well enough to ensure the practical achievement of that purpose. This is not a work of formal reasoning or refinement or calculation: it is a work of formalisation and description — the necessary prelude to the formal parts of the work.

Today's advocates of formal methods understand this much better than their impassioned predecessors, and their work is correspondingly more convincing and more valuable. The editors themselves write in their introductory chapter: "One of the most difficult aspects [in the application of formal techniques] is learning to model reality with sufficient accuracy". They recognise that "Often it is best to use formal methods with a light touch, applying them only when extra assurance is required for the development of a difficult part of a large system", and that "The process of producing the formalisation is as important as, or perhaps even more important than, the resulting specification itself ...".

This, then, is not a book of dogma. It is a fruit of many substantial and successful applications of formal methods to serious and often safety-critical developments. The application areas include process control, population census, railway signalling, air traffic control, telecommunications and radiotherapy. The methods used include B, Z, VDM and CSP. Customers for the systems include large organisations already possessing a large store of software development experience.

The authors of the contributed chapters show a wide appreciation of the range of factors that may be important in a development. They recognise that development must be supported by convincing justification of the formal model; that formal reasoning must be made intelligible to the customer; and that in a world that is informal — not bounded *a priori*— testing is absolutely necessary and can never be dispensed with in favour of complete reliance on formal proofs. They also recognise that the development process itself is subject to human error, and that the resulting systems must therefore be analysed, like the products of established engineering disciplines, for their potential modes of failure.

In short, both experience and advocacy of formal methods are coming of age. This book is a rich record of much that has been learned in the progression from the *naïveté* of childhood to the practical common sense of more mature years.

Michael A. Jackson
London, June 1999

List of Contributors

Ross J. Anderson, University of Cambridge Computer Laboratory, Cambridge, UK

Mark Ardis, Software Production Research Department, Bell Laboratories, Lucent Technologies, NJ, USA

Pascal Bernard, Philips Consumer Communications, Le Mans, France

Dines Bjørner, Technical University of Denmark, Department of Information Technology, Lyngby, Denmark

Arne Borälv, Prover Technology AB, Stockholm, Sweden

Jonathan P. Bowen, The University of Reading, Department of Computer Science, Reading, UK

Bishop C. Brock, IBM Corporation, Austin, TX, USA

Tony Bryant, Leeds Metropolitan University, Leeds, UK

Chris George, United Nations University, International Institute for Software Technology, Macau

Stephen Goldsack, Imperial College, Department of Computing, London, UK

Dan Craigen, ORA Canada, Ottawa, Ontario, Canada

Anthony Hall, Praxis, Bath, UK

Mats P.E. Heimdahl, University of Minnesota, Department of Comptuer Science and Engineering, Minneapolis, MN, USA

Mike Hinchey, University of Nebraska-Omaha, Department of Computer Science, Omaha, NE, USA

Warren A. Hunt, Jr., IBM Corporation, Austin, TX, USA

Jonathan Jacky, University of Washington, Department of Oncology, Seattle, WA, USA

Yonit Kesten, Ben Gurion University, Department of Communication Systems, Beer-Sheva, Israel

Amit Klein, Perfecto Technologies Limited, Herzelia, Israel

J. Eric Klinker, Naval Research Laboratories, Washington DC, USA

Guy Laffitte, Institut National de la Statistique et des Études Èconomique (INSEE), Nantes, France

Kevin Lano, Imperial College, Department of Computing, London, UK

Nancy G. Leveson, Department of Aeronautics and Astronautics, Massachussetts Institute of Technology, Cambridge, MA, USA

Richard C. Linger, Software Engineering Institute, Carnegie Mellon University, Pittsburgh, PA, USA

Peter Mataga, Software Production Research Department, Bell Laboratories, Lucent Technologies, NJ, USA

Irwin Meisels, ORA Canada, Ottawa, Ontario, Canada

David M. Milhelcic, Naval Research Laboratories, Washington D.C., USA

Andrew P. Moore, Naval Research Laboratories, Washington D.C., USA

Søren Prehn, TERMA Elektronik AS, Birkerod, Denmark

Amir Pnueli, Weizmann Institute of Science, Rehovot, Israel

Gil Raanan, Perfecto Technologies Limited, Herzelia, Israel.

Jon D. Reese, Safeware Engineering Corporation, Seattle, WA, USA

Mark Saaltink, ORA Canada, Ottawa, Ontario, Canada

Arturo Sanchez, Imperial College, Department of Chemistry, London, UK

Lesley Semmens, Leeds Metropolitan University, Leeds, UK

Gunnar Stålmarck, Prover Technology AB, Stockholm, Sweden

Carmen J. Trammell, CTI-PET Systems, Inc., Knoxville, TN, USA

CHAPTER 1

It's Greek to Me: Method in the Madness?

Jonathan P. Bowen and Michael G. Hinchey

1.1 Prologue

(προλογος)

> *Plato is dear to me, but dearer still is truth.*
>
> — Aristotle (384–322 B.C.)

The use of formal methods is fraught with difficulties, any one of which could cause the downfall of a project depending on their use. We enumerate a number of pitfalls which should be avoided in order to help make sure a formal methods project is successful, together with some guidance on the use of formal methods in the overall design process. While this cannot ensure favourable results, it will help to avoid failure, which is all too easy an outcome (see, for example (Neil *et al.*, 1998)).

1.2 Madness — Seven Deadly Sins

> *How about 'Cloudcuckooland'?*
>
> — Aristophanes (c.444–c.380 B.C.)

Any scientifically-based activity requires a level of responsibility and it is important that those involved understand the moral questions (Sagan, 1997). Science has developed technology such as nuclear fission and fusion which has the potential for great harm as well as good. When developing high integrity systems, it is even more important than normal in software development to ensure that the system is as dependable as possible.

In this section, a number of undesirable practices which should be avoided in order to help ensure success in a software development project are presented (Bowen and Hinchey, 1995a). While these considerations cannot ensure favourable results, they may help to avoid failure, which is all too easy an outcome in software-based projects, especially those attempting to use a more formal approach.

1. Epideictic (επιδεικτικος) — used for effect

Formal methods should not be applied merely as a means of demonstrating one's ability, nor to satisfy company whim, or as a result of peer pressure (Bowen and Stavridou, 1994). Just as the advent of "object-orientation" saw many firms incur possibly needless expense as they unnecessarily converted their systems to object-oriented implementations, there is a possibility that some could unnecessarily adopt formal methods. Realistically, the first thing that must be determined before a formal development is undertaken is that one *really* does need to use formal methods, whether for increased confidence in the system, to satisfy a particular standard required by procurers, or to aid in conquering complexity, etc.

There are, however, occasions where formal methods are not only desirable, but positively required. A number of standards bodies have not only used formal specification languages in making their own standards unambiguous, but have strongly recommended them and in the future may mandate the use of formal methods in certain classes of applications (Bowen, 1993; Bowen and Hinchey, 1994).

2. Hyperbole (υπερβολη) — exaggeration

Formal methods are not a panacea; they are just one of a number of techniques that, when applied correctly, have been demonstrated to result in systems of the highest integrity, and one should not dismiss other methods entirely (Bowen and Hinchey, 1995a,b). Formal methods are no guarantee of correctness; they are applied by humans, who are obviously prone to error.

Various support tools such as specification editors, type-checkers, consistency checkers and proof checkers should indeed reduce the likelihood of human error ... but not eliminate it. System development is a human activity, and always will be. Software engineering will always be subject to human whim, indecision, the ambiguity of natural language, and simple carelessness.

3. Pistic (πιστικος) — too trusting

One must be careful not to place too much trust in techniques and tools that have not been demonstrated to be "correct". While the use of formal methods should certainly reduce the number of anomalies in system development, inexperience and carelessness can result in specifications that reduce to *false*, and are as ambiguous as natural language specifications.

Similarly, no proof should be taken as definitive. Hand-proofs are notorious in not only admitting errors as one moves from one line to the next, but also at making gigantic leaps which are unfounded. From experience of machine checking proofs, most theorems are correct, but most hand-proofs are wrong (Rushby, 1995). Even the use of a proof checker does not guarantee the correctness of a proof. While it does aid in highlighting unsubstantiated jumps, and avoidable errors, proof should never be considered an alternative to testing, although it may reduce the required amount of testing, and in particular unit testing.

4. Oligarchy (ολιγαρχια) — rule by a few

The formal methods community tends to be very introspective. However, there has been considerable investment in existing software development techniques and it would be foolhardy to replace these *en masse* with formal methods. Instead it is desirable to integrate formal methods into the design process in a cost-effective manner (Faser *et al.*, 1994). One way to do this is to investigate how an existing formal method can be combined effectively with a structured method already in use within industry.

In addition, novice formal developers must ensure that they have access to expert advice. The majority of successful formal methods projects to date have had access to at least one consultant who is already expert in the use of formal techniques. It appears to be very difficult to learn to use formal methods successfully without such help until sufficient local expertise has been built up to make this unnecessary.

5. Ephemeral (εφημερος) — transitory

The application of formal methods to the development process should not be seen as "re-inventing the wheel". Rather, exploiting reuse in formal development can (at least in theory) aid in offsetting some of the set-up costs (e.g., tools, training and education) of the development.

Formal methods (or formal specification languages, specifically) provide a means of unambiguously stating the requirements of a system, or of a system component. In this way, formally specified system components that meet the requirements of components of the new system can easily be identified. Thus components that have been formally specified *and sufficiently well documented* can be identified, reused and combined to form components of the new system.

It is important however not just to focus on the reuse of code that has been developed using a formal approach, but rather to reuse the formal specifications themselves also.

6. *Epexegesis* (επεξηγησις) — *additional words*

Formal specifications *can* be made intelligible and acceptable to non-technical personnel (Hall, 1990), but only provided that they are augmented with sufficient amounts of informal explanation, diagrams, etc.

The formal specifier must not use a formal specification as a means of demonstrating his/her own ability, but rather must be willing to rework specifications to make them more intelligible to others. Similarly, abstraction should be used to hide unnecessary detail, making a specification suitable for different audiences.

7. *Maiandros* (Μαιανδρος) — *meandering*

The use of formal methods radically changes the cost structure of system development (Bowen and Hinchey, 1995b). Inexperience with cost-estimation has resulted in a number of formal developments running considerably over-budget and behind schedule. However, a large number of projects have come in on-time and within budget (see, for example, projects previously reported in (Hinchey and Bowen, 1995)).

Moreover, most of the successful applications of formal methods have employed formal methods from the early stages of development, replacing natural language and informal specification. Indeed, most projects have reported the greatest savings at these early stages, where formal specification techniques have highlighted errors that could be corrected before the programming phase.

1.3 Method — Philosophical Considerations

> But, my dearest Agathon, it is truth which you cannot contradict; you can without any difficulty contradict Socrates.
> — Plato (c.429–347 B.C.)

The origins of western philosophy and scientific thinking can be traced back to the Greeks. Indeed, it has been said by John Burnet in his book on *Early Greek Philosophy* (Burnet, 1892; van Doren, 1992) that:

> It is an adequate description of science to say that it is "thinking about the world in the Greek way." That is why science has never existed except among peoples who came under the influence of Greece.

This may be overstating the case somewhat, but certainly ancient Greece provided the catalyst for much early advancement of knowledge in the European sphere of influence. Socrates (469–399 B.C.), then Plato (c.429–347 B.C.) and Aristotle (384–322 B.C.) developed philosophical research in a manner far advanced for their time. This was made possible by the Greek way of life, which left time to ponder more abstract questions, at least for a proportion of the population. Their influence is still very much with us today, and their ideas are still under active discussion in philosophical research circles (see Crivelli (1996) discussing false beliefs).

Aristotle was a great teacher and left many notes. Among these were those for his lectures on ethics, developed over the course of several years. While these were never finished in the form of a complete book, they are of sufficient interest to be the subject of continued study, and to have been reworked into book form by much more recent researchers (Aristotle, 1976).

Aristotle's *Nicomachean Ethics* has had a profound and lasting effect on western philosophical thinking since its origins in the 4th century B.C. It has been both supported and rejected subsequently, but never ignored. It is inevitably flawed by its very nature, being working notes for lectures. It starts with the object of life (aiming at some good), and proceeds via morals, justice, intellectual virtues, pleasure, and friendship to happiness, the ultimate goal, even if it is difficult to define. Here we concentrate on Book VI concerning *Intellectual Virtues* (Aristotle, 1976). We use some of the headings to discuss some issues in the use of formal method for computer-based system development, especially for software.

What is the right principle that should regulate conduct?

In some systems, failure is unlikely to result in catastropic disasater. However, this is not the case in a safety-critical system (Storey, 1995). Here the developer should aim to avoid the loss of human life or serious injury by reducing the risks involved to an acceptable level. This is an overriding factor. The system should always aim to be safe, even if this affects its availability adversely. It is the responsibility of the software engineering team and the management of the company involved to ensure that suitable mechanisms are in place and are used appropriately to achieve this goal for the lifetime of the product.

It is sensible to follow certain guidelines when developing any software-based artifact, and especially if there are safety concerns. Most professional bodies such as the ACM (Association for Computing Machinery, USA), IEEE (Institute of Electrical and Electronics Engineers, Inc., USA), BCS (British Computer Society, UK) and IEE (Institution of Electrical Engineers, UK) provide codes of conduct for members which it is wise for them to follow. Most of these codes which come from an engineering background place a very high priority on safety aspects.

For example, the IEEE *Code of Ethics* (1990) commits its members to the following, listed first out of ten points of ethical and professional conduct:

> *1. to accept responsibility in making engineering decisions consistent with the <u>safety</u>, health and welfare of the public or the environment.*

Codes of conduct from a computer science background tend to place slightly less emphasis on safety and consider other losses such as information as well, although safety is still an important factor. The first two *General Moral Imperatives* for ACM members are:

    1.1   Contribute to society and human well-being.
    1.2   Avoid <u>harm</u> to others.

"Harm" is considered to mean injury or other negative consequences such as undesirable loss of information. The points are elaborated further. For example, 1.1 goes on to say *"An essential aim of computing professions is to minimize negative consequences of computing systems, including threats to health and safety."*

In the UK, there is guidance specifically for engineers and managers working on safety-related systems (see Figure 1.1, extracted from (Hazards Forum, 1995)). This code of practice is intended for use by professional engineering institutions such as the IEE, who may wish to augment the code further with sector-specific guidance on particular techniques. For example, in 1995 the IEE held a workshop on the role of formal methods in the development of safety-related systems, as reported in Thomas (1996). The results of this workshop and other similar discussion forums could form the basis for more detailed guidance.

Contemplative and calculative intellect

There are two types of thought process, the irrational and the rational. Obviously the professional engineer should aim to use rational lines of thought in the reasoning about and development of a safety-critical system. Unfortunately development can depend on the personal, possibly unfounded, preferences of the personnel involved, especially those in a management role.

Within the rational part of the mind, Aristotle makes a further distinction. In science, theory and practice are two very important aspects, each of which can help to confirm support the other. Without a firm theoretical basis, practical applications can easily flounder; and without practical applications, theoretical ideas can be worthless. To quote from Christopher Strachey, progenator and leader of the Programming Research Group at Oxford:

> *It has long been my personal view that the separation of practical and theoretical work is artificial and injurious. Much of the practical work done in computing, both in software and hardware design, is unsound and clumsy because the people who do it do not have any clear understanding of the fundamental principles underlying their work. Most abstract mathematical and theoretical work is sterile because it has no point of contact with real computing.*

It is highly desirable to ensure that the separation between theory and practice is minimised, although achieving this is a lengthly process (Glass, 1997). Some perceive formal methods as a difficult technique being foisted on them by academia (Heitmeyer, 1997). However it is certainly extremely important to ensure theory and practice are both combined in an effective manner for the development of critical systems. A good theoretical and mathematical underpinning is essential to ensure the maximum understanding of the system being designed. If this understanding is not achieved, serious problems can easily result (Neumann, 1995).

Engineers and managers working on safety-related systems should:

- *at all times take all reasonable care to ensure that their work and the consequences of their work cause no unacceptable risk to safety*
- *not make claims for their work which are untrue, or misleading, or which are not supported by a line of reasoning which is recognised in the particular field of application*
- *accept personal responsibility for all work done by them or under their supervision or direction*
- *take all reasonable steps to maintain and develop their competence by attention to new developments in science and engineering relevant to their field of activity; and encourage others working under their supervision to do the same*
- *declare their limitations if they do not believe themselves to be competent to undertake certain tasks, and declare such limitations should they become apparent after a task has begun*
- *take all reasonable steps to make their own managers, and those to whom they have a duty of care, aware of risks which they identify; and make anyone overruling or neglecting their professional advice formally aware of the consequent risks*
- *take all reasonable steps to ensure that those working under their supervision or direction are competent; that they are made aware of their own responsibilities; and that they accept personal responsibility for work delegated to them*

Anyone responsible for human resource allocation should:

- *take all reasonable care to ensure that allocated staff will be competent for the tasks to which they will be assigned*
- *ensure that human resources are adequate to undertake the planned tasks*
- *ensure that sufficient resources are available to provide the level of diversity appropriate to the intended integrity.*

Figure 1.1. Code of practice for engineers and managers

(from (Hazards Forum, 1995), reproduced with permission)

Both kinds of intellect aim at truth, but the calculative faculty aims at truth as rightly desired by the exercise of choice

In practical applications, there is nearly always a choice of which techniques to use. The decision may be influenced by many considerations, including ethical issues. It is important to recognise the choices available, and assess their relative merits in as objective a manner as possible.

Five modes of thought or states of mind by which truth is reached

The mind of man — how far will it reach? Where will its daring impudence find limits?
                                                            — *Hippolytus*, Euripides (480–406 B.C.)

There are various ways to help ensure the correctness of a system. The background and expertise of the engineers involved is an extremely important contributing factor to the success of a project. Here five important aspects of the personnel involved are considered.

1. Science or scientific knowledge
(επιστημη — **epistēmē**)

It is important to have the basic theoretical groundwork on which to base practical application. This is typically achieved through initial education, topped up with specialist training courses. Modern comprehensive software engineering textbooks and reference books normally include a section or chapter on both safety-critical systems and formal methods (e.g., see McDermid (1991), Pressman (1997), Sommerville (1996)). Subsequent professional development is also crucial to keep up to date with changes in the state of the art.

   There are now a number of courses available specifically for safety-critical systems, especially at Master of Science level. For example, the University of York in the UK runs a modular MSc in *Safety Critical Systems Engineering* (University of York, 1997) and Diploma / Certificate short courses. The teaching is split into intensive one week taught modules, which have been found to be much more convenient for industrial employees taking the course part-time. It is easier to take a week off work every so often rather than being committed to a particular day of the week for a much longer period.

The course content is agreed and monitored by a panel of experts, many from industry to ensure the relevance of the material. Introductory modules comprise an Introduction to Safety, Mathematics for Safety and Introduction to Project Management. Mandatory modules consist of Requirements Engineering, Formal Methods, Safety and Hazard Analysis, Dependable Systems Analysis and Management of Safety Critical Projects. There are a number of other optional modules. The course includes a significant mathematical content, especially in the areas of probability and discrete mathematics for software development using formal methods. The MSc normally lasts one year if done full-time, and three years for part-time students, including a project for half the time.

2. Art or technical skill
(τεχνη — technē)

The life so short, the craft so long to learn.
— *Aphorisms*, Hippocrates (5th century B.C.)

Once the educational groundwork has been covered, much further expertise is gained in the actual application of the techniques learned. Applying mathematical skills can be even harder than acquiring them in the first place for some.

One of the most difficult aspects is learning to model reality with sufficient accuracy (Bowen and Hinchey, 1997). Abstraction is a skill that only comes with practice. Unfortunately many existing programmers have to un-learn their natural tendency to become bogged down in implementation detail when considering the system as a whole. Instead, only the pertinent aspects should be included at any given level of abstraction.

3. Prudence or practical wisdom
(φρονησις — phronēsis)

It is essential to take great care in the development of high integrity systems in order to avoid undesirable consequences. New techniques (including formal methods) should be used with great caution and introduced gradually. It is best for new approaches to be used on non-critical systems first to gain confidence, even if they look promising theoretically and are understood by the development team.

Once sufficient experience has been gained, and the benefits have been assessed, then a technique may be recommended and adopted for use in critical applications. For this reason, any prescriptive recommendations in standards should be updated regularly to ensure they remain as up to date as possible.

Every engineer has his/her limitations, and it is important that individuals recognise their own limitations, as well as those of others, and keep within their bounds of expertise. However competent a person is, there will always be tasks which cannot reasonably be tackled. If the constraints on the development of a high integrity application are impossible to meet, there should be mechanisms to allow this to be expressed at all levels in a company.

A well-known example where such mechanisms were not effective is the Therac-25 radiation therapy machine where several fatal radiation overdoses occurred due to an obscure malfunction of the equipment, the first of its type produced by the company involved to include software (Leveson and Turner, 1993). It should be remembered that software by itself is not unsafe; it is the combination with hardware and its environment to produce an entire system that raises safety issues (Leveson, 1995).

4. Intelligence or intuition
(νους — nous)

I have hardly ever known a mathematician who is capable of reasoning.
— Plato (c.429–347 B.C.)

The highest quality of personnel should be employed in the development of critical applications. The engineers involved should be capable of absorbing the required toolkit of knowledge and also accurately apprehending the required operation of computer-based systems.

Specialist techniques, including the use of mathematics, are important in producing systems of the highest integrity. Formal specification helps reduce errors at low cost, or even a saving in overall cost (Hill, 1991). Formal verification (Henzinger, 1996), while expensive, can reduce errors even further, and may be deemed cost effective if the price of failure is extremely high (e.g., involving loss of life). For the ultimate confidence, machine support should be used to mechanise the proof of correctness of the software implementation with respect to its formal specification. For example, the B tool has been used to support the B method (Abrial, 1996, 1997) in a number of safety-critical applications, especially in the railway industry (Dehbonei and Mejia, 1995).

For mathematicians, proofs are a social process, taking years, decades or even centuries to be generally accepted. The automation of proof is regarded with suspicion by many traditional mathematicians (MacKenzie, 1995). A critical aspect of proofs is seen by many to be their surveyability, leading to understanding of *why* a proof is valid, and explaining why the theorem under consideration is true.

An automated proof may have millions of (very simple) steps, and be extremely difficult to follow as a result. In addition, any "proofs" undertaken in the software engineering world must be performed several orders of magnitude faster than in traditional mathematics. However they are far shallower than most proofs of interest to professional mathematicians. Hence intuition about why a program is correct with respect to its specification is difficult to obtain in all but the simplest of cases. Unfortunately this problem will not disappear easily and much research remains to be done.

Collaborations such as the European **ProCoS** project on "Provably Correct Systems" (Bowen *et al.*, 1996) have attempted to explore formal techniques for relating a formal requirements specification, through various levels of design, programming, compilation and even into hardware using transformations based on algebraic laws. Unifying theories for these different levels are needed to ensure consistency. However it is often difficult to guarantee compatibility of the models used at the various levels without unduly restricting flexibility.

> *Quod erat demonstrandum.* (Translated from the Greek.)
> Which was to be proved.
>
> — Euclid (c.300 B.C.)

5. Wisdom
(σοφια — sophia)

With experience comes wisdom. It is safest to aim for very modest ambitions if possible to ensure success. Unfortunately software tends to encourage complexity because of its flexibility. This should be resisted in high integrity applications. The critical aspects of the software should be disentangled from less critical parts if possible. Then more effort can be expended on ensuring the correctness of the critical parts of the system.

Resourcefulness or good deliberation
(ευβουλια — euboulia)

Impulses should be avoided in critical system development and all choices should be carefully considered. This is why formalising the system early is recommended since this allows much more informed and reasoned choices to be made, and for the consequences to be assessed.

Understanding
(συνεσις — sunesis)

A formal specification significantly aids in the comprehension of a system (German, 1996). The process of producing the formalisation is as important as, or perhaps even more important than, the resulting specification itself in helping with this understanding (Hall, 1990). The construction of proofs for theorems concerning the system can bring an even greater depth of knowledge about why the system works the way it does. Modelling, animation and rapid prototyping are also complementary aids to understanding (Bowen and Hinchey, 1997).

Judgement (γνωμη — gnōmē) *and consideration*

Choosing appropriate techniques requires good judgement, which can be built up with experience, but also requires a decisive managerial approach. Often it is best to use formal methods with a light touch, applying them only when extra assurance is required for the development of a difficult part of a large system (Jones, 1996).

Choices also occur in the design process itself; otherwise it could all be done by computer. It may be necessary to refine a non-deterministic specification to a deterministic implementation by gradually reducing the design space until just one choice is left. It is important to ensure the number of choices is not reduced to zero (i.e., no implementation), which can be easily done by accident if a formal approach is applied without due care. Fortunately formality allows the possibly of checking from such errors in a rigorous manner, something that is not possible if only an informal specification such as natural language or diagrams is available.

General comments on the various states of mind

The programming profession has traditionally had many of the attributes of a crafts-man, such as artistry, but has often lacked foundational knowledge, such as mathe-matical underpinning of the concepts involved (Hoare, 1983). This is not so impor-tant for programs which are not critical for the operation of a system, where errors will not produce disastrous results. However if safety is of prime importance, such an approach is no longer practical, and in fact is downright unethical.

Personnel involved in critical application development should possess a balance of high-quality skills with regard to all the aspects outlined earlier in this section. Those that cannot demonstrate the right mix of expertise should be restricted to non-critical applications.

Currently no special qualifications are required for personnel developing or maintaining software for safety-critical systems. This contrasts with the more es-tablished engineering professions where regulations, certification and accreditation often apply more strictly.

Standards can apply to both hardware and software, but are often more *au fait* with the problems and solutions associated with hardware rather than software. However, standards for software are being introduced across a wide range of in-dustrial sectors with an interest in safety-critical applications such as aviation, the nuclear industry, railways, etc. Some standards are prescriptive, recommending par-ticular approaches such as formal methods (Bowen and Stavridou, 1993; Bowen and Hinchey, 1994). As well as standards, legislation is likely to play an increasing role in safety-critical systems, as and when accidental death and injury caused by computer-controlled systems do occur.

The faculty of cleverness
(δεινοτης — deinotēs)

Finally, it is advisable not to be too "clever" in critical applications. This is best left to researchers developing new ideas. It is more sensible to use the simplest and most obviously correct solution possible to reduce the chances of error. To quote Professor C.A.R. Hoare:

> *There are two ways of constructing a software design. One way is to make it so simple that there are obviously no deficiencies. And the other way is to make it so complicated that there are no obvious deficiencies.*

We recommend the former approach, although unfortunately the latter has been widely adopted in practice.

1.4 Epilogue

(επιλογος)

> *The unexamined life is not worth living.*
>
> — Socrates (469–399 B.C.)

Some of the words in the section headings in this chapter may be unfamiliar to some readers. The same problem occurs when new methods are used, especially ones employing mathematical symbols such as formal methods. In the past, the necessary grounding for the use of sound techniques like formal methods has not been taught adequately on computer science courses, resulting in many software engineers, and even more managers, shying away from their use because they feel they are out of their depth. Fortunately many undergraduate courses (at least in Europe, and particularly in the UK), do now teach the requisite foundations to software engineering. Courses also normally give a grounding in mathematics, often at the behest of professional bodies who may not accredit the course otherwise.

However, the teaching of formal aspects of software engineering is often rather unintegrated with the rest of the syllabus. More coordinated courses (e.g., see (Dean and Hinchey, 1996), (Garlan, 1995)) in which the mathematical foundations are subsequently applied to practical problems will help to produce more professional software engineers for the future. The use of formal methods is promising, but also potentially problematic (Luqi and Goguen, 1997). Clear ideas on future directions are required to avoid future pitfalls (Clarke and Wing, 1996; Woodcock, 1996).

It is hoped that the examples of the use of formal methods presented in the rest of this book will help to demonstrate that the bridging of the chasm between formal methods theoreticians and practitioners is underway. These emphasise the variety of applications where formal methods are being applied at an industrial level. Other books have presented specific standard case studies using a variety of formal approaches which may also be of interest to readers (Abrial *et al.*, 1996; Lewerentz and Lindner, 1995). Previous examples of the applications of formal methods may be found in Hinchey and Bowen (1995) and a selection of recommended articles and papers on high-integrity system specification and development is presented in (Bowen and Hinchey, 1999).

Further general information on formal methods maintained by one of the authors of this book is available as part of the World Wide Web (WWW) Virtual Library under the following URL (Uniform Resource Locator):

```
http://www.comlab.ox.ac.uk/archive/formal-methods.html
```

I've got it! (Ευρηκα — Eureka!)

                 — Archimedes (287–212 B.C.)

Acknowledgement

We are grateful to Jane Bowen for proofreading this chapter.

CHAPTER 2

The French Population Census for 1990

Pascal Bernard and Guy Laffitte

2.1 Introduction

The Population Census is a snapshot of France at a certain date. The information is gathered through smaller censuses covering all of France. This information concerns those people living in France on that date, and it provides the primary data which are eventually used to obtain various statistics. For example, it permits the comparison of proportions of single people in urban and rural areas.

A computer system needed to be designed to support the collection of data and to organise the data for statistical analysis. Every application program which calculates specific statistics has to access data from the census. This organisation was a critical step in the whole census. It involved the collection procedure as well as every eventual application program providing specific statistical analysis. It was decided that both the collection of and access to the data were to be based on the structure of the French administration (such as counties, regions, etc.): *the administrative geography* (hereafter called geography). This structure is large and complex. J.-R. Abrial was a consultant at the INSEE[1]. He suggested adopting the B notation in order to describe this structure and to extract its properties. Moreover, it was essential that statisticians, collectors and programmers associated the same meanings with the same words. The B method was also adopted for the implementation. This chapter presents both the specification and the implementation.

One problem was to specify the organisation for programmers in a clear and unambiguous way. Some properties must hold for the structure to make sense while others are simply expected to hold. For instance, it was important to know if there was a hierarchy covering the whole country. Another problem, therefore, was to check such properties. We had to specify verification procedures in order to check

---

[1] Institut National de la Statistique et des Etudes Economiques

that these properties actually held. Last but not least, the organisation had to be completed for data access performance and optimisation.

Our solution was to define two sets of procedures. The first set was given to the programmers in order to retrieve information about the geography. We carried out the specification of these procedures in order to explain to the programmers what they were for and to know what had to be implemented. The second set of procedures enabled the construction of a representation of the geography from the data which were provided and was used to check the properties. We carried out the specification of these procedures in order to make a reliable implementation. Reliability was very important since the results of statistical analysis would affect political decisions. If the system were not correct, all other applications developed by the programmers would give meaningless results. In short, a failure of our design would have cost a lot of money.

This chapter describes the method followed and choices made for the design. It gives an example of an actual development using B (Abrial, 1994, 1997) for both the specification and the implementation. In conclusion we evaluate the benefits obtained from our design. The computer system produced has been in use for a few years now. We will also draw conclusions about the contribution of specifications to the solution of the original problems.

Section 2.2 presents the French geography informally. Section 2.3 defines the set constructions we used in order to give a set theoretic model of the geography. The notation used is that of B, as we use B for the formal specification.

Section 2.4 presents the specification of a part of the geography. This is the specification of an abstract machine which provides a set theoretic modelling of the geography, states the properties of the geography and the semantics of data retrieval procedures in terms of this modelling. This specification, together with the comments associated with it, serves as a very precise manual of the procedures, and is provided to the programmers for retrieving information about the geography.

In Section 2.5 we give the specification of an abstract machine which takes as its input the existing description of the geography and builds up another representation. This representation follows the previous modelling. The properties are checked in tandem with the construction process.

Section 2.6 describes how the specification was used to build actual implementations.

In conclusion, we give our answer to the question : "Does this experiment qualify the B method for industrial usage?".

2.2 The Case Study

We give a simplified version of the geography. However, it is not clear whether the informal description will help the reader to understand the formalisation, or if the converse is true. We do not believe that the only reason for this is that our English is very coarse. The structure is complex enough to make it difficult to describe it in an informal way. But the informal description relates the dummy identifiers of the

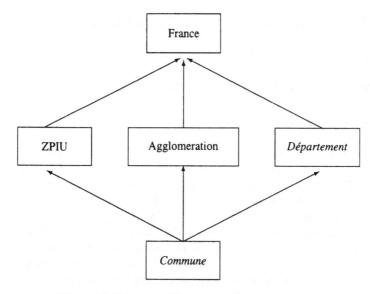

Figure 2.1. Structure of French Geography

formal specification to real life entities. Figure 2.1 is intended to aid in reading this section. Section 2.4 gives the formalisation.

For this presentation, we will consider that the small censuses cover what is called a *commune* in French. A *commune* is a part of the territory administered by the council of a village or a town. Wherever one is in France, one is on some territory administered by one and only one *commune* council. In other words, the set of *communes* forms a partition of France. *Communes* are grouped into *départements* which are like British counties. The set of *départements* also forms a partition of the territory. There is, in addition, the set of French regions which is discarded for the sake of clarity. Finally, there is the country itself, which covers the entire territory.

Communes may also be grouped into *agglomerations*. These may spread over several *départements*, but they generally do not contain all of the *communes* of a *département*. Statistics sometimes refer to larger groupings called ZPIU[2]. When belonging to a ZPIU, all the *communes* of an agglomeration must be in the same ZPIU.

There are two kinds of *département*: metropolitan and overseas *départements*. All the *communes* which are part of an agglomeration are also part of a ZPIU if and only if they belong to a metropolitan *département*. Moreover, no *commune* of an overseas *département* belongs to a ZPIU.

---

[2] Zone de Peuplement Industriel et Urbain (economical interest)

2.3 Structuring the Data: Some Useful Techniques

The set constructions which were used to formalise the geography are explained here. They are introduced in a section of their own because the same techniques may be used in many other cases. The remaining sections illustrate their usage.

2.3.1 Groups and Hierarchies

Let S be a set; elements of S can be grouped by considering a subset of S. But very often, while grouping, one wants to create a new entity which has its own properties[3]. For instance, the staff of a company is a group of persons which has a director. It should also be noticed that, even if all the staff join the same choir, the choir and the staff are not the same thing. To solve these problems, we can introduce a set G of groups over S and a membership relationship between S and G.[4] This is a much more flexible technique. Groups can be grouped themselves. For instance, one may consider the group of groups which have a director. In object-oriented design, classes gather together objects which have the same kind of feature on which the same operations apply. The design decision of grouping objects within a class is an important one: the class itself cannot be considered as an object on its own and the gathered objects are tied in this class (they cannot be grouped with other objects in another class). Set theoretic modelling, while making use of the presented technique, allows the designer to structure the specification without committing himself to premature decisions. However it does not prevent the specifier from using object-oriented design (see, for example, (Hall, 1994)).

If the elements of S all belong to at most one group, the membership relation is a function. This function is total if all the elements of S are in a group. In this case, it gives rise to a partition of S. Two elements of S are in the same part if they belong to the same group.

Trees whose leaves are at the same level are called **hierarchies**. Each level is a set of nodes and each non-terminal node (a node which is not a leaf) groups nodes (the children) of the following level. The membership relation of these groupings is a function (is_child_of) which is total from the set of nodes of one level to the set of nodes of the preceding level. Except for the root of the tree, this childhood relationship gives rise to a partition of the set of nodes of one level. The previous technique applies for modelling hierarchies. This will be illustrated with the country–*département*–*commune* hierarchy.

2.3.2 Direct Product of Functions

Given two functions f and g, it is possible to construct a new set by taking the range of their direct product (see Abrial (1997) §I.2.4.2 and §I.2.6). Given three sets S, U

---

[3] Notice that what is termed a "group" here has nothing to do with the well-known algebraic structure

[4] In fact, this is how "users" are organised under UNIX systems for access rights to files.

and $\mathcal{V}$, two binary relations f and g such that "$f \in \mathcal{S} \leftrightarrow \mathcal{U}$" and "$g \in \mathcal{S} \leftrightarrow \mathcal{V}$", the direct product of f and g, denoted $f \otimes g$, is defined by:

$$\{(x,(y,z)) \mid (x,(y,z)) \in \mathcal{S} \times (\mathcal{U} \times \mathcal{V}) \wedge (x \mapsto y) \in f \wedge (x \mapsto z) \in g\}$$

If f and g are functions, then $f \otimes g$ is also a function. Here we are only concerned with the direct product of functions. From this definition, we can deduce that:

$$(u \mapsto v) \in \mathbf{ran}(f \otimes g) \Leftrightarrow \exists s.(s \in \mathcal{S} \wedge u = f(s) \wedge v = g(s))$$

This equivalence is quite interesting for two reasons. The first one is a matter of style. It provides a means of avoiding quantified formulae which are difficult to understand. The second reason is related to the technique given for grouping. Let $\mathcal{U}$ and $\mathcal{V}$ be sets of groups of elements of $\mathcal{S}$. If f is the membership relation between elements of $\mathcal{S}$ and groups of $\mathcal{U}$ and g is the membership relation between elements of $\mathcal{S}$ and groups of $\mathcal{V}$, then $u \mapsto v$ is in $\mathbf{ran}(f \otimes g)$ if and only if u and v have a common element of $\mathcal{S}$. Moreover, we have:

$$\mathbf{dom}(f \otimes g \rhd \{u \mapsto v\}) = \{s \mid s \in \mathcal{S} \wedge u = f(s) \wedge v = g(s)\}$$

This gives a construction of the intersection of groups for our modelling technique. It can be noticed that $\mathbf{ran}(f \otimes g)$ is a relation between $\mathcal{U}$ and $\mathcal{V}$. This relation is satisfied for pairs of groups which have a non-empty intersection. The set of groups of $\mathcal{U}$ that have a non-empty intersection with a group $g2$ of $\mathcal{V}$ is constructed by $\mathbf{dom}((\mathbf{ran}(f \otimes g)) \rhd \{g2\})$. Similarly, the set of groups of $\mathcal{V}$ that have a non-empty intersection with a group $g1$ of $\mathcal{U}$ is constructed by $\mathbf{ran}(\mathbf{ran}(\{g1\} \lhd (f \otimes g)))$. The direct product will be used for stating the invariant of our system.

2.4 Formalisation of the Geography

In the previous description, we did not state the actual geography, but only what it looks like. Categories were introduced for the different entities (*communes*, *départements*, ...), and properties governing these entities were stated (e.g., every *commune* belongs to a *département*). The formalisation will give a set theoretic modelling of administrative geography together with procedures for retrieving information about an actual geography. As we are using B for this specification, it means that we define an abstract machine whose invariant states what the geography looks like and whose operations consist of those necessary to retrieve information about the actual geography.

The informal specification will be extended during the formalisation process. In this way Section 2.2 serves as a good introduction while details are introduced progressively.

2.4.1 The Context

The informal presentation of the geography is a rather refined presentation compared to that which was obtained originally. Nevertheless, modelling the geography requires further analysis. Let us take the example of the *départements*. They are introduced as groupings of *communes*. But they are also entities in their own right which may be named and have properties, such as being metropolitan or overseas. They cannot just be sets of *communes*. Figure 2.2 gives the context part of the abstract machine: it introduces the deferred sets (termed basic types in (Spivey, 1992)).

SETS
 COM;
 DEP;
 AGG;
 ZPIU

Figure 2.2. The context (first machine)

We use our grouping technique of Section 2.3 by introducing sets of groups for *départements*, agglomerations and ZPIU. They are called DEP, AGG and ZPIU, respectively. The set of *communes* is called COM.

As the root of the country–*département*–*commune* hierarchy is a singleton, it is not worth representing the grouping of all the *départements* into the one and only country. One level of the hierarchy therefore disappears.

2.4.2 The Variables

We now have the sets of elements of the actual geography and the functions for grouping. The introduction of variables is presented in Figure 2.3. *Com* is the set of actual *communes*. *Dep* is a set of groups, the set of actual *départements*. Similarly, *Agg* is the set of actual agglomerations and *Zpiu* is the set of actual ZPIUs. *Com2Dep*, *Com2Agg* and *Com2Zpiu* are the actual membership relations between the *communes* and the different sets of groups. *OverSeas* is the subset of *Dep* which contains the overseas *départements*.

The variables *KeyCom*, *KeyDep*, *KeyAgg* and *KeyZpiu* are functions relating the entities of the geography to keys which will be used to identify them. To simplify matters, we will replace keys by natural numbers.

2.4.3 The Invariant

We give some definitions which will simplify the expression of the invariant. Then we state the invariant for an actual geography.

> **VARIABLES**
> *Com*, *Dep*, *Agg*, *Zpiu*,
> *Com2Dep*, *Com2Agg*, *Com2Zpiu*,
> *OverSeas*,
> *KeyCom*, *KeyDep*, *KeyAgg*, *KeyZpiu*

Figure 2.3. The variables

Definitions. Definitions are like macros. They are composed of two parts separated by the symbol $\mathrel{\widehat{=}}$. The part on the left-hand side is an identifier and the part on the right-hand side is an expression. In the invariant, the identifiers which are bound to a definition are to be taken as abbreviations for the corresponding expressions.

> **DEFINITIONS**
> $DefInZD \mathrel{\widehat{=}} \mathbf{ran}(Com2Zpiu \otimes Com2Dep) \mathbin{\stackrel{\circ}{\circ}}$
> $DefInAD \mathrel{\widehat{=}} \mathbf{ran}(Com2Agg \otimes Com2Dep) \mathbin{\stackrel{\circ}{\circ}}$
> $DefAgg2Zpiu \mathrel{\widehat{=}} \mathbf{ran}(Com2Agg \otimes Com2Zpiu)$

Figure 2.4. The definitions of group intersections

The definitions for our case study are given in Figure 2.4. *DefInZD* is a relation between *ZPIU* and *DEP* whose instances are pairs $z \mapsto d$ where z is a ZPIU and d is a *département* having some *commune(s)* in common (Cf Section 2.3). The other definitions are similar. *DefInAD* denotes the intersection of agglomerations with *départements*. *DefAgg2Zpiu* denotes the intersection of agglomerations and ZPIUs. The invariant will force this set to be the graph of a function which associates a *commune* with its *ZPIU*.

The Invariant. The invariant states the constraints that the values of variables must satisfy in order to represent a geography. These constraints are the properties of the geography. They are presented in Figure 2.5. They can be read as follows:

- *Com* is a subset of the set of all possible *communes*, etc.;
- *département*s keys are natural numbers, each *département* is identified by one key (the function *KeyDep* is total and injective);
- all the overseas *département*s are *département*s;
- agglomerations are identified by their keys;

INVARIANT

$Com \subset COM \wedge Dep \subset DEP \wedge Agg \subset AGG \wedge Zpiu \subset ZPIU \wedge$

$KeyDep \in Dep \rightarrowtail \textbf{NAT} \quad \wedge$
$OverSeas \subset Dep \quad \wedge$
$KeyAgg \in Agg \rightarrowtail \textbf{NAT} \quad \wedge$
$KeyZpiu \in Zpiu \rightarrowtail \textbf{NAT} \quad \wedge$

$KeyCom \in Com \rightarrow \textbf{NAT} \quad \wedge$
$Com2Dep \otimes KeyCom \in Com \rightarrowtail (Dep \times \textbf{NAT}) \quad \wedge$
$Com2Agg \in Com \twoheadrightarrow Agg \quad \wedge$
$DefInAD \rhd OverSeas \in Agg \nrightarrow Dep \quad \wedge$
$Com2Dep \in Com \twoheadrightarrow Dep \quad \wedge$

$Com2Zpiu \in Com \twoheadrightarrow Zpiu \quad \wedge$
$DefInZD \rhd OverSeas = \emptyset \quad \wedge$
$DefAgg2Zpiu \in Agg \nrightarrow Zpiu \quad \wedge$
$\textbf{dom}(DefAgg2Zpiu) = \textbf{dom}(DefInAD \rhd OverSeas)$

Figure 2.5. The invariant of an actual geography

- ZPIUs are identified by their keys;
- all the *communes* have a key;
- the *communes* of a *département* have different keys. The key of a *commune* is local to its *département*;
- some *communes* are in agglomerations, but a *commune* can be in at most one agglomeration (*Com2Agg* is a partial function). Each agglomeration contains at least one *commune* (the function is surjective);
- all the *communes* belonging to overseas *département*s and belonging to the same agglomeration are in the same *département*. Overseas *département*s are islands or group of islands. Agglomerations are sets of contiguous towns. This is why it is impossible to have agglomerations spreading over two overseas *département*s;
- every *commune* is in a *département* and every *département* has a *commune* belonging to it (constraint between two levels of a hierarchy);
- *communes* belong to at most one ZPIU, and each ZPIU contains at least one *commune*;
- there is no ZPIU spreading over overseas *département*s;
- agglomerations cannot spread over two ZPIUs;
- all the agglomerations spreading over metropolitan *département*s spread over a ZPIU.

2.4.4 Initialization

The initialization is a procedure which must establish the invariant. The machine we are defining does not modify the geography. The geography will be constructed through the refinement of the initialization, importing the second machine. The constructed geography will thus satisfy the invariant. The initialization of this machine consists in setting the variables with the actual geography (Figure 2.6). The proofs that the provided geography exists and satisfies the invariant are carried out by the refinement of the machine importing the second machine.

2.4.5 The Operations

The specification of data retrieval procedures can be done in terms of the modelling. Figure 2.7 gives an example of the specification of an operation which fetches the set of *communes* of overseas *départements*. The specification of the other procedures is of no interest for the purposes of this chapter.

2.5 Building a Representation

The second machine specifies the procedures for constructing a representation of the geography. The refinement of the first machine will import the specification of this machine. The data retrieval procedures access data in a structure which is built by procedures specified in this section. This cooperation is enforced by taking the same model of the geography and the same implementation for the structure with both machines.

The geography is given by several files containing respectively:

1. the keys of the *départements*;
2. the keys of the agglomerations;
3. the keys of the ZPIU;
4. the local keys of the *communes* associated with the key of their *départements*;
5. the association of *communes* to agglomeration by the triplets (key of the *département*, key of the *commune*, key of the aggomeration);
6. the association of *communes* to ZPIU by the triplets (key of the *département*, key of the *commune*, key of the ZPIU).

To each file we associate the task (with the same number) of loading the file in order to construct the geography. From the contents of the files, it can be seen that tasks 1,2 and 3 can be done in any order or even in parallel. They should precede task 4. Task 4 should precede tasks 5 and 6.

In order to improve the performance of the sytem, the intersections defined in Section 2.4.3 are computed. The state of the machine contains three variables to hold these values. To help the design of a procedure which computes incrementally the intersection of agglomerations with ZPIU, we have to choose an order for tasks 5 and 6. Our choice is to perform task 5 before task 6.

INITIALIZATION
   ANY
        $ActCom, ActDep, ActAgg, ActZpiu,$
        $ActCom2Dep, ActCom2Agg, ActCom2Zpiu,$
        $ActOverSeas,$
        $ActKeyCom, ActKeyDep, ActKeyAgg, ActKeyZpiu$
   IN
        $ActCom \subset COM \land ActDep \subset DEP \land$
        $ActAgg \subset AGG \land ActZpiu \subset ZPIU \land$

        $ActKeyDep \in ActDep \rightarrowtail \mathbf{NAT} \quad \land$
        $ActOverSeas \subset ActDep \quad \land$
        $ActKeyAgg \in ActAgg \rightarrowtail \mathbf{NAT} \quad \land$
        $ActKeyZpiu \in ActZpiu \rightarrowtail \mathbf{NAT} \quad \land$

        $ActKeyCom \in ActCom \rightarrow \mathbf{NAT} \quad \land$
        $ActCom2Dep \otimes ActKeyCom \in$
                $ActCom \rightarrowtail (ActDep \times \mathbf{NAT}) \quad \land$
        $ActCom2Agg \in ActCom \twoheadrightarrow ActAgg \quad \land$
        $ActDefInAD \rhd ActOverSeas \in ActAgg \nrightarrow ActDep \quad \land$
        $ActCom2Dep \in ActCom \twoheadrightarrow ActDep \quad \land$

        $ActCom2Zpiu \in ActCom \twoheadrightarrow ActZpiu \quad \land$
        $ActDefInZD \rhd ActOverSeas = \emptyset \quad \land$
        $ActDefAgg2Zpiu \in ActAgg \nrightarrow ActZpiu \quad \land$
        $\mathbf{dom}(ActDefAgg2Zpiu) =$
                $\mathbf{dom}(ActDefInAD \rhd ActOverSeas)$
   THEN
        $Com := ActCom \;\|\; Dep := ActDep \;\|$
        $Agg := ActAgg \;\|\; Zpiu := ActZpiu \;\|$
        $Com2Dep := ActCom2Dep \;\|$
        $Com2Agg := ActCom2Agg \;\|$
        $Com2Zpiu := ActCom2Zpiu \;\|$
        $OverSeas := ActOverSeas \;\|$
        $KeyCom := ActKeyCom \;\|\; KeyDep := ActKeyDep \;\|$
        $KeyAgg := ActKeyAgg \;\|\; KeyZpiu := ActKeyZpiu$
   END

Figure 2.6. The initialization

```
OPERATIONS
     scod ⟵ Over_Com
          BEGIN
               scod := dom(Com2Dep ▷ Overseas)
          END
 . . .
```

Figure 2.7. Example of data retrieval operation

2.5.1 The Context

The properties of a completed geography may be stronger than those of pieces of a geography being constructed. We introduce a variable "Stage" which gives the stage of the construction. The greater the value of this variable, the stronger the constraints of the invariant over the other variables. The significant stages, given the tasks and given the invariant of the first machine are:

- the keys of all groups are loaded. The groups are created and it makes it possible to attach *communes* to them;
- the *communes* are attached to their *départements* and their local keys are defined. *Communes* can be grouped into agglomerations and ZPIU;
- the contents of agglomerations are defined. It is possible to define the contents of ZPIU while constructing the intersection of ZPIUs and agglomerations;
- the contents of ZPIUs are defined. The actual geography is ready for use.

GREATER introduces an order over stages. The other constants are stages. It should be noticed that our specification may be extended easily. It may be enriched by new stage constants which can be "inserted" in between the existing ones. One common mistake is to take numbers instead of such constants. It makes it impossible to enrich the specification with new inserted stages. The problem can be overcome by taking symbolic constants instead of actual values, and by stating the orderings to which they must comply.

OVERKEYS is a set of natural numbers which contains the keys of overseas *départements*.

2.5.2 The Variables

Stage is the current stage of construction of the geography by the machine. The variables *InZD*, *InAD* and *Agg2Zpiu* are introduced to hold the values of the intersections.

SETS

$\ldots$

$STAGE = \{Scratch, GroupsLoaded, CDepLoaded,$
$\qquad\qquad CAggLoaded, CZpiuLoaded\}$

CONSTANTS

$GREATER, OVERKEYS$

PROPERTIES

$GREATER = \{(GroupsLoaded \mapsto Scratch),$
$\qquad\qquad (CDepLoaded \mapsto GroupsLoaded),$
$\qquad\qquad (CAggLoaded \mapsto CDepLoaded),$
$\qquad\qquad (CZpiuLoaded \mapsto CAggLoaded)\}^* \wedge$
$OVERKEYS \subset \mathbf{NAT}$

Figure 2.8. The context (second machine)

VARIABLES

$\ldots,$

$Stage, InZD, InAD, Agg2Zpiu$

Figure 2.9. The variables

2.5.3 The Invariant

During the construction of a geography, the variables of the machine will satisfy a weaker invariant. We state a general invariant which has to hold at all stages of the construction.

On the last block of the invariant (Figure 2.10), the values of *InZD, InAD* and *Agg2Zpiu* are constrained to correspond to the respective definitions. The rest of the invariant concerns the same variables modelling the geography as for the first machine. It is almost a carbon copy of the invariant machine. But it has been altered in order to take into account the temporary states of the representation under construction.

INVARIANT
$Com \subset COM \wedge Dep \subset DEP \wedge Agg \subset AGG \wedge Zpiu \subset ZPIU \wedge$

$KeyDep \in Dep \rightarrowtail \mathbf{NAT} \quad \wedge$
$OverSeas \subset Dep \quad \wedge$
$KeyAgg \in Agg \rightarrowtail \mathbf{NAT} \quad \wedge$
$KeyZpiu \in Zpiu \rightarrowtail \mathbf{NAT} \quad \wedge$

$KeyCom \in Com \rightarrow \mathbf{NAT} \quad \wedge$
$Com2Dep \otimes KeyCom \in Com \rightarrowtail (Dep \times \mathbf{NAT}) \quad \wedge$
$Com2Agg \in Com \twoheadrightarrow Agg \quad \wedge$
$DefInAD \triangleright OverSeas \in Agg \nrightarrow Dep \quad \wedge$
$Com2Dep \in Com \rightarrow Dep \quad \wedge$
$(GREATER(Stage, CDepLoaded) \Rightarrow$
$\qquad Com2Dep \in Com \twoheadrightarrow Dep \quad) \wedge$
$(GREATER(Stage, CAggLoaded) \Rightarrow$
$\qquad Com2Agg \in Com \twoheadrightarrow Agg \quad) \wedge$

$Com2Zpiu \in Com \nrightarrow Zpiu \quad \wedge$
$DefInZD \triangleright OverSeas = \emptyset \quad \wedge$
$DefAgg2Zpiu \in Agg \nrightarrow Zpiu \quad \wedge$
$\mathbf{dom}(DefAgg2Zpiu) \subset \mathbf{dom}(DefInAD \triangleright OverSeas) \quad \wedge$
$(GREATER(Stage, ZpiuLoaded)$
$\qquad \Rightarrow \mathbf{dom}(DefAgg2Zpiu) = \mathbf{dom}(DefInAD \triangleright OverSeas)$
$\qquad \wedge Com2Zpiu \in Com \twoheadrightarrow Zpiu) \wedge$

$InZD = DefInZD \wedge$
$InAD = DefInAD \wedge$
$Agg2Zpiu = DefAgg2Zpiu$

Figure 2.10. The invariant of a geography for all stages

2.5.4 Initialization

Initialization consists of setting an "empty" geography to which the entities given by the files will be added. The first line of the initialization (see Figure 2.11) states that there is no entity of any kind. The variable *State* is set to *Scratch* in order to allow the addition of new entities. The rest of the variables are set to be empty in order to satisfy the invariant[5].

INITIALIZATION
   BEGIN
       $Com, Dep, Agg, Zpiu := \emptyset, \emptyset, \emptyset, \emptyset \parallel$
       $Com2Dep, Com2Agg, Com2Zpiu := \emptyset, \emptyset, \emptyset \parallel$
       $OverSeas := \emptyset \parallel$
       $KeyCom, KeyDep, KeyAgg, KeyZpiu := \emptyset, \emptyset, \emptyset, \emptyset \parallel$
       $InZD, InAD, Agg2Zpiu := \emptyset, \emptyset, \emptyset \parallel$
       $State := Scratch$
   END

Figure 2.11. The initialization

2.5.5 The Operations

For each task, we specify a procedure for introducing an atomic datum. For instance, the procedure *Add_Dep* takes a key as input and creates a *département* associated with this key. The precondition of these procedures states that they must be called at the right stage of the construction. For each stage, we specify a validation procedure which checks the progression of the invariant, prevents the call of procedures of the current stage and authorises the calls of procedures for the following stage.

A selection of specifications of these procedures is given in Figures 2.12 and 2.13. It is representative of the whole set. When f is a function $f(x) := u$ means $f := f <+ \{(x \mapsto u)\}$. The operator $<+$ represents the overriding of the function by another.

– *Add_Dep*(*dk*) creates a new *département* identified by the key *dk*. This procedure may only be called at the first stage of the construction: the loading of groups.

---

[5] In a similar specification with Z, these settings would have been enforced by the invariant. We prefer the B policy. In Z, if settings are not enforced by the invariant, they have to be explicitly constrained. With B, no setting changes unless otherwise specified. In order to make sure the invariant is established, the setting of the other variables has to be constrained to the only possible value.

The key must be a natural number which has not already been associated with an existing *département*. This ensures that *KeyDep* remains injective;

- *Set_GL* validates the stage of the loading of groups. The variable *Stage* is set to *GroupsLoaded*. Therefore the preconditions of procedures for adding groups will no longer hold;

- *Add_Com*(*clk*, *d*) creates a new *commune* identified by the local key *clk* within *département* *d*. This procedure may only be called at the second stage of the construction. *d* must be an existing *département*, and *clk* is not associated with another *commune* of the same *département*;

- *Add_CZ*(*c*, *z*) incorporates the *commune* *c* in the ZPIU *z*. The *commune* *c* is not already in a ZPIU, it does not belong to an overseas *département*. If *c* is in an agglomeration and if a *commune* of this agglomeration already is in a ZPIU, then this ZPIU must be *z*;

- *Set_ZL* is the last validation. It succeeds when the last part of the invariant is satisfied.

2.6 Implementation

As shown in Figure 2.14 the system was specified with three abstract machines. The first and second machines are the machines of the previous sections. The third machine, the DB machine, relates the logical view of the relations introduced so far to their physical representation. The design of this machine will be presented in detail. In order to understand the way it has been designed, we will take a closer look at the overall project.

2.6.1 The Overall Project

The first machine is a very small part of the overall system, but it is its core. The collection of the data of the census and the organisation of these data are based on the geography. This means that every application computing some statistics will access the data through the geography. Moreover, their results are usually structured following the geography (such as the total population of the *communes* for each *département*). All of these applications will be based on top of a refinement of the first machine in order to access the data of the geography. More precisely, they will be designed like the first machine which was built on top of the second machine by the refinement outlined in Figure 2.15[6].

For the two machines specified, the main problem of the implementation consists in finding a suitable representation of relations. There is quite a large number of them and many possibilities for their implementation. The design of one representation is tedious and error prone. Most of the other applications have the same

---

[6] This features a FOR loop instead of a WHILE loop as provided by B. This is just to make it more readable.

OPERATIONS
    Add_Dep(dk) =
        PRE
            Stage = Scratch $\wedge$
            dk $\in$ **NAT** $\wedge$ *dk* $\notin$ **ran**(*KeyDep*)
        THEN
            ANY *d* **IN** $d \in (DEP - Dep)$
            THEN
                Dep := *Dep* $\cup$ {*d*} ||
                KeyDep(d) := *dk* ||
                IF *dk* $\in$ *OVERKEYS* **THEN**
                    Overseas := *Overseas* $\cup$ {*d*}
                END
            END
        END
   . . .

    Set_GL =
        PRE
            Stage = Scratch
        THEN
            Stage := *GroupsLoaded*
        END

    Add_Com(clk, d) =
        PRE
            Stage = GroupsLoaded $\wedge$
            d $\in$ *Dep* $\wedge$ *clk* $\in$ **NAT** $\wedge$
            $(d \mapsto clk) \notin$ **ran**(*Com2Dep* $\otimes$ *KeyCom*)
        THEN
            ANY *c* **IN** $c \in (COM - Com)$
            THEN
               Com := *Com* $\cup$ {*c*} ||
               Com2Dep(c) := *d* || *KeyCom(c)* := *clk*
            END
        END
   . . .

Figure 2.12. Examples of construction operations

$\ldots$

$Add\_CZ(c, z) =$
    PRE
        $Stage = AggLoaded \wedge$
        $c \in Com \wedge$
        $z \in Zpiu \wedge$
        $c \notin \textbf{dom}(Com2Zpiu) \wedge Com2Dep(c) \notin Overseas \wedge$
        $(c \in \textbf{dom}(Com2Agg) \wedge Com2Agg(c) \in dom(Agg2Zpiu)$
            $\Rightarrow Agg2Zpiu(Com2Agg(c)) = z)$
    THEN
        $Com2Zpiu(c) := z \parallel$
        $InZD := InZD \cup \{(z \mapsto Com2Dep(c))\} \parallel$
        IF $c \in \textbf{dom}(Com2Agg)$ **THEN**
            $Agg2Zpiu(Com2Agg(c)) := z$
        END
    END

$\ldots$

$Set\_ZL =$
    PRE
        $Stage = AggLoaded \wedge$
        $\textbf{ran}(Com2Zpiu) = Zpiu \wedge$
        $\textbf{dom}(DefInAD \rhd OverSeas) \subset \textbf{dom}(DefAgg2Zpiu)$
    THEN
        $Stage := ZpiuLoaded$
    END

Figure 2.13. Examples of construction operations (continued)

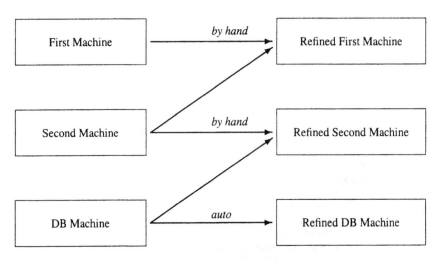

Figure 2.14. Implementation

problem. This is why a tool was developed to generate such representations from a concise description.

The census is a snapshot. Once the data is gathered, it will not be updated. The results computed by the applications are deduced from this fixed data. In the overall project, any data is computed once and for all by an application. Once it is computed, it will be made available for other applications and will not change. This is important because it means that there is no concurrent access to data except read-only access. This simplifies the procedures which manipulate the data. The real problems are to save space and to allow fast access. The generating tool was designed to tailor an efficient database which does not support concurrent access.

Even when the development is rigorous, the programs obtained should be tested. In the project, the programs had to run on a mainframe (IBM under MVS). This system is not appropriate for program development. This is why the tests were performed on SUN workstations under UNIX. The generating tool was able to provide implementations of the databases for both systems. There was no problem of portability because both systems had compatible compilers except for file handling. The latter is under the control of the application builder. The compilers had to allow separate compilation in Pascal and to code integers on 32 bits.

The next section presents the database generator. It shows how it permits one to develop applications keeping a logical view of the data and how the database can be finely tuned. Its output is used by the application builder. The application builder provides a package of procedures for handling the data from the bases. It is presented just after the database generator.

REFINEMENT
    RefinedFirstMachine
REFINES
    FirstMachine
IMPORTS
    SecondMachine
SETS
    *File*1, *File*2, *File*3, *File*4, . . .
PROPERTIES
    *File*1 $\in$ **iseq**(**NAT**) $\wedge$ *File*2 $\in$ **iseq**(**NAT**)
    $\wedge$ *File*3 $\in$ **iseq**(**NAT**) $\wedge$ *File*4 $\in$ **iseq**(**NAT** $\times$ **NAT**)
    $\wedge$ **ran**(*File*4; **prj1**) $\subset$ **ran**(*File*1) . . .
INITIALIZATION
    VAR i, dl, lck **IN**
        FOR i **IN** **dom**(*File*1) **DO**
            Add_Dep(*File*1(i))
        END $\stackrel{\circ}{\scriptstyle 9}$
        FOR i **IN** **dom**(*File*2) **DO**
            Add_Agg(*File*2(i))
        END $\stackrel{\circ}{\scriptstyle 9}$
        FOR i **IN** **dom**(*File*3) **DO**
            Add_ZPIU(*File*3(i))
        END $\stackrel{\circ}{\scriptstyle 9}$
        Set_GL $\stackrel{\circ}{\scriptstyle 9}$
        . . .
        Set_ZL $\stackrel{\circ}{\scriptstyle 9}$
END

Figure 2.15. Part of the refinement

2.6.2 The Database Generator

All our relations are partial or total functions. As we have seen before, this is a good principle to follow when trying to get quantifier-free specifications. Such specifications are more easily readable (with some training) and proof obligations are more simple. This is why the database generator only implements functions. The reader will see that it is obviously not a constraint anyway.

A database consists of a set of tables. Typically, a table corresponds to a set which is the source of some function. Each element of the table is made of fields. Each field corresponds to a function. The source of the function is the set. Thus, an element of the table (which corresponds to an element x of the set), contains in its field f the image of x by f, $f(x)$. Choosing the same name for the field and the function makes it clear what it corresponds to in the specification. If the value of the function is in some other basic set, then the value of the field is the index of the image in the corresponding table. If the value of the function is a subset of values of a basic set, then the value of the field is an integer denoting a set. Implementation of these sets is described later. Let us first study the piece of database described in Figure 2.16.

The figure shows three tables corresponding to the sets *Dep*, *Com* and *Agg* of the specification. For the sake of clarity, we will forget about *Zpiu* in this section. Elements of these tables are like objects: their attributes (or fields) contain the values of images for the corresponding functions. Some of the functions are total, the others are partial. The same applies to the fields. We can find *Com2Dep* and *Com2Agg* which are variables from the specification. The keys are implemented as integers. Some procedures have been written by hand for converting actual keys (strings) of the end-user to internal keys and vice versa. Finally, the set *Overseas*, which is a subset of *Dep*, is implemented as a Boolean function (overseas *départements* have a key greater than some given key). This was possible because this database was not going to be modified once it was built.

All the variables from the specification have their counterpart in the implementation. The implementation being a **refinement**, it may contain more information. The names of the *communes*, *départements* and agglomerations have been added. They are useful for the applications to display their results in a human oriented way. Adding information can also be used to store some redundant data which will speed up access. The table corresponding to the set *InAD* is shown in Figure 2.17. This permits one to add the relations between *InAD*, *Com* and *Dep*[7]. These relations are the functions *Com2InAD*, *InAD2Agg* and *InAD2Dep*. We have also added the inverse of *Com2Dep* which we called *Dep2Com*. Finally, a new set of one element (France) was introduced in order to have access by key to *départements* and agglomerations through *Fra2Dep* and *Fra2Agg*. The invariant of the refined machine is stronger than the invariant of the specification: it must contain the definitions of newly introduced functions. These can be easily listed[8]:

---

[7] Recall that $InAD \mathrel{\widehat{=}} \mathbf{ran}(Com2Agg \otimes Com2Dep)$.

[8] *Fr* denotes the element of the set France

```
BASE geo IS

   TABLE
     Dep
   TOTAL
     KeyDep   : 0 .. 120
   PARTIAL
     DepName  : STR(20) ;
     Dep2Com  : OSET(KeyCom)(500) ;
     Dep2InAD : OSET(KeyAggInAD)(20)
   IMPL
     array, mtay(101)
   END ;

   TABLE
     Com
   TOTAL
     KeyCom   : 0 .. 999 ;
     Com2Dep  : 0 .. 101
   PARTIAL
     ComName  : STR(20) ;
     Com2Agg  : 1 .. 2000 ;
     Com2InAD : 1 .. 2040
   IMPL
     DELAYED
   END ;

   TABLE
     Agg
   TOTAL
     KeyAgg   : 0 .. 131000
   PARTIAL
     AggName  : STR(10) ;
     Agg2InAD : OSET(KeyDepInAD)(2)
   IMPL
     array, mtay(2000)
   END ;
 ...
```

Figure 2.16. Description of the database Geo

$$Com2InAD \; = \; Com2Agg \otimes Com2Dep$$
$$InAD2Agg \; = \; InAD \triangleleft \mathbf{prj1}(Agg, Dep)$$
$$InAD2Dep \; = \; InAD \triangleleft \mathbf{prj2}(Agg, Dep)$$
$$Dep2Com \; = \; Com2Dep^{-1}$$
$$Fra2Dep(Fr) \; = \; Dep$$
$$Fra2Agg(Fr) \; = \; Agg$$

```
TABLE
  InAD
TOTAL
  KeyAggInAD : 0 .. 131000 ;
  KeyDepInAD : 0 .. 120 ;
  InAD2Agg    : 0 .. 2000 ;
  InAD2Dep    : 0 .. 101 ;
  InAD2Com    : SET(10)
IMPL
  array, mtay(2040)
END ;

TABLE
  France
TOTAL
  Fra2Dep   : OSET(KeyDep)(101) ;
  Fra2Agg   : OSET(KeyAgg)(2000)
IMPL
  array, mtay(1)
END ;
```

Figure 2.17. Database Geo (continued)

The database generator checks the syntax of the description and sets the database implementation for the application builder.

The description contains information about the size of the tables and the ranges of the fields. This enables the data in the table elements to be compressed and the size of the files containing the tables to be computed. The creation of files of fixed length prevents "file system full" exceptions. It is also required under MVS in order to have direct access to the files.

Let us take the example of the table Com (Figure 2.16). The generator produces the following mapping:

```
Map of Table : Com

Used Words : 3
  Lost bits : 23
```

```
ComName   : PARTIAL ; STR(20) ; Full Word 0

KeyCom    : TOTAL   ; (0 .. 999) ; Word 1 ; Bits 2 To 11 ;
                                            Length 10
Com2Dep   : TOTAL   ; (0 .. 101) ; Word 1 ; Bits 12 To 18 ;
                                            Length 7
Com2Agg   : PARTIAL ; (1 .. 2000) ; Word 1 ; Bits 19 To 29 ;
                                            Length 11
Com2InAD  : PARTIAL ; (1 .. 2040) ; Word 2 ; Bits 2 To 12 ;
                                            Length 11
```

Only one word of 32 bits is used for three fields. It is sometimes possible to reorder the fields in the description to improve data compression. A field is always contained within one word. There are two ways of implementing a table:

1. as an array of integers of the application which is stored and restored to/from a file, or
2. as a file. The application has access to pages from the file through buffers. Modified buffers are saved to a log file. The file is updated at validation.

The database produced is equipped with management procedures by the application builder. These procedures allow for recovery in case of system failure (double commit).

The table Dep is implemented by an array of size 101. The implementation of the table Com is *delayed*. It is described in another file. Different files will be used for the testing version and the actual system. Here is an example of implementation:

```
TABLE
  Com
IMPL
  memdiff, mtay(36666), ptay(100), nbuf(4), ratio(40)
END
```

The size of the table is 36666, there are 4 buffers. Each buffer contains a page of 100 elements. The size of the log file is 40% of the size of the file.

Sets are implemented following the B method. They use a *basic* machine: SEQUENCE[INTEGER]. This machine can also be implemented by an array or a file. We have similar implementation clauses for the machine used for representing sets and the machine used for strings.

There is a special kind of set. Ordered sets (denoted OSET) permit access by key which is more efficient. The field Dep2Com of table Dep holds an ordered set of elements of the table Com. The invariant of the specification ensures that KeyCom is a key for the set of *communes* of a *département*. We have to refer to the specification to prove that the implementation is sound. The size given for sets is a hint which is used at their creation to limit memory management.

This approach to implementation allows constant reference to the specification for correctness. At the same time, it allows for very fine tuning of data representation.

We now present the application builder which generates the procedures for managing the data.

2.6.3 Application Builder

An application may access several databases, each of them in one of two modes: read-only or update. We denote *system* to be a set of databases associated with one of these modes. The application builder generates a package of Pascal procedures and macros for the three levels: system, table, and field. The following gives the name and meaning of the procedures generated at each of these levels. Name clashes are prevented using prefixes. The prefix at the table level is composed of the name of the database followed by the name of the table. At field level the prefix consists of the name of the database followed by the name of the field. Within a database two fields with the same name cannot exist. The prefixes are discarded in what follows, but they reappear in the example at the end of this section. Procedures marked with an asterisk are generated only when the database is in update mode.

At the system level we have:

- **ini** logically empties all the tables and sequence machines of the bases in update mode;
- **openSession** opens a session, loading files in the arrays;
- **vld** validates updates;
- **rlb** rollback;
- **closeSession** closes the session, updating files.

At the table level we have:

- **make*** creates a new element in the table. It takes as arguments values to initialise total scalar fields. The order is the same as the order of the fields in the implementation description. Partial fields are initially undefined. Total fields holding sets are initialised with empty sets. It returns the index of the newly created element.
- **nbr** returns the number of elements in the table.

Indices range between 1 and **nbr**. It is not possible to garbage an element.

The field level is more complex. Fields can be partial. There are different possibilities for the type of a field. All the procedures at field level have as their first argument the index of the element in the table.

If the field is partial we have:

- **def** Returns true if the field is defined;
- **rem*** Turns the field undefined. If the field value refers to a set or a string, the refered set or string is garbaged.

The value of a field is obtained by a call to **val** when it is defined. It is modified by a call to **mod** whose second argument is the value to assign. The procedure **mod** should not be used with fields holding sets or strings. We will give just a few procedures which are available on these data types.

For strings, we have:

- **length** returns the string length;
- **value** returns the value of the *i*th character of the string. The position *i* is given as second argument;
- **clear** empties the string;
- **push** adds the character given as the second argument to the end of the string;
- **assign** copies into the string the contents of the string referred to by the second argument ...

For sets we have **card** for the cardinality, **add** to add an element, etc. In ordered sets, search by key is implemented by binary search. So we have for example:

- **bsearch** takes a key as its second argument. It returns the index of the element corresponding to the key when it is a member of the set. Otherwise it returns the value **OBJbad**,
- **binsert** for adding an element. The second argument of this procedure is the index of the element in its table. The procedure fetches the key by looking in the table.

The application builder also generates macros for spanning sets and tables. It has been run on the small example of Figures 2.16 and 2.17. It produced more than 4000 lines of comment-free code. The application builder has been used by all the developers of the project with much larger schemas. It was worth writing 14 000 lines of code for the database generator and the application builder. The use of these tools reduces the debugging effort considerably, while producing the most efficient code.

Higher level procedures were written by hand, following the specification, the invariant of the implementation and the naming convention of the application builder. Figure 2.18 shows the code of the implemention of *Add_Dep* (specified in Figure 2.12). This implementation has a somewhat weaker precondition than its

```
#define FR     1

procedure Add_Dep(dk :   integer) ;
var
  dep :  integer
begin
  dep := geo_Fra2Dep_bsearch(FR, dk) ;
  if dep <> OBJbad then
  begin
    writeln('*** Already known Dep ; key : ', dk:3) ;
    halt
  end ;
  dep := geo_Dep_make(dk) ;
  geo_Fra2Dep_binsert(FR, dep)
end ;
```

Figure 2.18. Application procedure

specification. It checks that no *département* has been registered with the same key. It is not defined on a wider domain, but its call to a wider domain is harmless. The application building the geography cannot work if the files given in the input are not correct. The implementation extension of the invariant shows that if a *département* is added, Fra2Dep has to be extended too. Adding a *commune* to an agglomeration (i.e., adding a new element to Com2Agg) may have more dramatic consequences. This can easily be traced by looking at each "clause" of the invariant.

2.6.4 Evaluation of the Approach

Because of a lack of time, most of the proof obligations have not been carried out. Nevertheless, the construction resulted in code in which we can have great confidence. In fact, the system has been used intensively for several years now, and no problem has arisen with the geography[9]. In any case, all the ingredients are available for performing the proofs (the specifications, their refinements and the logical system of Abrial (1997)).

The tool for refining databases was designed with respect to the philosophy of the B method. The main features of this software are:

- each database system is the implementation of an abstract machine;
- idiosyncrasies of the operating systems have been encapsulated in technical abstract machines;
- the lowest level of the implementation consists of the implementations of the abstract machine which is a portable virtual memory. It offers an example of several refinements of the same specification. It provided an opportunity to test the whole system on small databases during the development phase on the workstation;
- the system has been designed to save storage space and to be portable.

The specification of the whole system resulted in 65 pages of B. The invariant occupies 8 pages. It was derived within two weeks by a B expert and an expert on the geography[10]. The refinement and the implementation took 2 months and resulted in 14,000 lines of Pascal. The system was then tested and transferred to the mainframe. This took another two weeks. The size of the resulting database is 40Mbytes. These figures do not take into account any training in B nor the time spent in developing the tool-generating databases.

The time spent improving the expression of the invariant was not wasted. This resulted in a relatively easy specification of the required procedures which, in turn, resulted in a quick and reliable implementation. Indeed, we believe that spending extra time on improving the invariant is *always* a good policy. This extra time is easily compensated for by the rapidity with which the implementation is achieved. A carefully designed invariant makes it unlikely that special cases are omitted during the design of operations. Therefore there is a gain in both time and reliability.

---

[9] That is, a part of the census which has been entirely specified with B.

[10] Namely, G. Laffitte and J.-P. Faur.

2.7 Conclusion

The development of a *real-life application* following the B method has been presented. Powerful techniques have been used for both the specification and the implementation. The outcome was not only a reliable core of the system supporting the census — it also provided the rest of the project with a clear definition of the organisation of the data and with a tool for implementing databases.

A significant example of specification for program development has been given. The specification was not carried out *a posteriori*. Part of it was extracted for the purpose of this chapter. It constitutes a case study on a specification development method and on specification language evaluation.

We have presented the method followed in order to achieve the specification:

- a technique for modelling groupings of different kinds, and hierarchies, and the use of a direct product for stating the relationships between the groups;
- the modelling of local keys using a direct product;
- the specification of a construction. We started from the modelling of the final object to design the dynamics of the system: stage decomposition is obtained by taking the final invariant as a target and by considering the atomic steps of the construction. We have tried to be as close as possible to the final invariant during the construction. It resulted in well-defined and minimal tests.

The implementation is based on the abstract specification. Data retrieval efficiency is built from properties found in the specification. *The implementation is reliable because it is driven by the specification.* It can be checked by performing the proof obligations provided by the B method. The tedious part of the implementation is automated. The tool designed for this purpose produced implementations of basic abstract machines. It enables the development of the system within the framework of the method. The implementations of the databases can be easily verified and tested. They provide the same recovery services as the best database management systems.

The system supporting the census has been running for a few years and is still in use. It proves that our solution was adequate. The benefits of our approach are:

- **for the system development:** a quick and reliable implementation. The ultimate goal was stated clearly right from the beginning;
- **for the users of the system:** a clear and concise definition of the services provided by the system. The specification supplemented by comments, as it is presented in this chapter, proved to be a very effective way to explain the geography. This was important since the whole geography is very complex;
- **for the programmers:** writing applications for producing statistics, a well documented library of efficient routines for spanning the geography and a tool for generating their own databases.

The B method proved to be effective for the development of the system supporting the census. The method requires that all the people involved in the project have or get some background in mathematics (set theory and first-order predicate calculus). This is the price to be paid in order to make wide and complex projects manageable.

Although it is difficult to draw general conclusions from one example, it seems that the development of different kinds of systems should also benefit from the B method.

CHAPTER 3

The Formal Verification of a Payment System

Ross J. Anderson

3.1 Introduction

UEPS, the Universal Electronic Payment System, was an electronic funds transfer product designed for use in developing countries, where poor telecommunications make offline operation necessary. It was built around smartcard-based electronic wallet functions: money is loaded from the bank, via bank cards, to customer cards, to merchant cards, and finally back to the bank through a clearing system (Anderson, 1992).

This architecture is very demanding from the point of view of security, and its protection involves a combination of factors such as the tamper-resistance of the smartcards used; a back-end accounting system that settles transactions reported by customers and merchants within a few days and can thus detect imbalances resulting from card alteration or forgery; and a fall-back processing mode in which, even if the electronic security systems are penetrated, the cards can still be used under the existing system of bank card controls (such as merchant floor limits and hot card lists).

Recently, tampering has been much in the news. In a recent paper (Anderson and Kuhn, 1996), we showed how many common smartcards and security processors could be broken using a variety of attacks. However, many of the most devastating attacks did not involve any physical penetration of the device, but rather a failure of the protocol that the device implemented. This is by no means a new phenomenon; protocol failures have been known for many years, and yet they still regularly cause failures in banking systems and elsewhere.

For example, one British bank adopted a system whereby customers' Personal Identification Numbers (PINs) were encrypted and written on the magnetic strip of their debit cards. The idea was to support offline operation and thus improve customer service and cut costs. However, criminals found that they could replace the account number on their own card (whose PIN they knew) with a number found, for example, on a discarded cash machine slip; they could then draw money from that account (Anderson, 1994). The failure of course was that the account number should have been encrypted along with the PIN, and VISA protocols now support this (VISA, 1986).

In another case, a prepayment electricity meter system used tokens to convey an enciphered value of electricity from a shop to a meter in the customer's home; however, the cryptography did not protect the electricity tariff, and tokens could be produced with a tariff of a fraction of a cent per kilowatt hour (Anderson and Bezuidenhoudt, 1996). Very recently, a cinema ticket vending system was broken by organised criminals; the system designers had arranged for the smartcard issued to the customer to check that the vending machine was authentic, but not vice versa. Many other systems have fallen to protocol attacks, and an introductory article on the subject can be found in (Anderson and Needham, 1995).

As a result, researchers began to appreciate that unaided human intuition was not adequate when designing such protocols, and began to look for a better way. The seminal work of Burrows, Abadi and Needham (1989) provided a "logic of authentication"; this enables one to reason formally about the beliefs of the participants in a security protocol, and follow the chain of reasoning that establishes the genuineness and the freshness of authentication messages (or fails to) (Burrows *et al.*, 1989). We will describe this logic in more detail below.

As far as we are aware, UEPS is the first live financial system whose underlying protocol suite was designed and verified using such formal techniques. We used an extension of the BAN logic, and our work raised some interesting scientific questions. Firstly, logics like BAN had been thought limited in scope to verifying mutual authentication or key sharing (e.g., by Gligor *et al.*, 1991); we showed that this was not so. Secondly, we found a bug in another extension of BAN (Gong, 1990). Thirdly, we highlighted the need for a formalism to deal with cryptographic chaining. Fourthly, this type of formal analysis turns out to be so useful and indeed straightforward that we argued it should be routine "due diligence" for financial and security critical systems. Our results were first published in (Anderson, 1992); in this chapter, we have updated them and presented them in a manner aimed at the general formal methods community rather than at security and banking system specialists.

3.2 The Application

Developed countries have many sophisticated networks which cater for cash machines, the use of credit and debit cards at the point of sale, interbank payments, and various other kinds of transaction. As the telecommunications infrastructure becomes ever faster and more reliable, these systems are increasingly online and centralised, and their existence can weaken the motive for introducing new crypto technologies such as smartcards.

The opening up of the formerly centrally-planned economies of Eastern Europe, India, Latin America and Africa created a sudden demand for modern banks and their associated payment systems. However, telecommunications are a serious problem: decades of neglect had left many of these countries with abysmal telephone networks, and villages are often without any connection at all. The lines that do exist are often not good enough to support modem communications: manual exchanges are still widespread. Transactions must often be carried out offline, and the risk of fraud with forged cards is such that the standard ISO magnetic stripe card with its associated PIN management techniques (Visa, 1986) cannot be used.

However, the flip side of this problem was an opportunity: for these countries to leapfrog two generations in electronic payment technology, and go straight from manual ledger systems to distributed processing based on smartcard electronic wallets. Such systems might not only integrate retail banking and shopping functions but also provide the payment side of utility and government networks. Slashing transaction costs by an order of magnitude could promote economic growth and eliminate a major bottleneck in economic development.

This was the opportunity perceived by our client, the Net 1 group, which secured a contract from a building society in South Africa (now part of Nedcor Bank) to design and build a national eftpos system. This institution had the largest card base in the country with some 22% of the market, and most of its accounts were simple savings accounts. It had the largest base of black customers of any financial institution in the country and, with political change, plans were made to provide a full range of banking services.

The poor telecommunications in homelands and townships, plus the requirement to keep costs down, led naturally to an electronic wallet approach. Money is transferred between bank cards, customer cards and merchant cards using offline terminals, which can be made portable if necessary.

3.3 Design Philosophy

The security of UEPS is based on two levels of authentication. The basic payment instrument is an electronic cheque which is generated by the client card, passed to the retailer card and then through a central clearing system to the customer's bank. The cheque carries two authentication codes: one generated with a key known only to the issuing bank's security module and the customer card, and one generated with a key which is controlled by the clearing house and loaded to the card before it is supplied to the bank. The latter code is checked before funds are credited to the retailer presenting the cheque, while the former is only checked in the event of a dispute. Both these codes are calculated using the standard banking encryption algorithm (ANSI DES MAC (Schneier, 1996)) on amount, payee and date.

Had public key technology been available in low cost smartcards, it would have been possible for the merchant to check a digital signature generated on the cheque by the customer's smartcard. This was not an option at the time, and so we had to design a transaction protocol to minimise the likelihood that bad cheques would get into the system. This uses a challenge-response protocol by which both cards in any transaction verify each other and carry on a secure session. In effect, the merchant trusts an application that runs in the customer smartcard (but is hopefully beyond most customers' ability to tamper with); this vouches for the authenticity of the electronic cheque. (The merchant is not trusted with the clearing house's key or the bank's key, and so cannot verify the cheque's authentication code directly.)

Similar transaction protocols are employed between the bank and the customer, and between the customer and the clearing house, and the use of independent security mechanisms (authentication codes and challenge response protocols) enables us to meet resilience requirements: the whole system should not be exposed to fraud through the compromise of any one key or device.

That is the theory: however, in reality there is always the possibility that a design blunder might leave open a hole that an attacker could discover by chance and exploit opportunistically. Most actual banking system failures have happened in this way (Anderson, 1994). A decision was therefore taken to use formal methods to verify the most security critical parts of the system. The choice of the BAN logic was a matter of circumstance; we had just become aware of it, and thought that it might be suitable for the job.

3.4 Authentication Protocols

In order to make the verification of the UEPS protocol easy to understand, we will digress to describe basic authentication protocols and the BAN logic.

A typical application for an authentication protocol is when two principals, whom we will conventionally call Alice and Bob, wish to communicate privately for the first time. They do not share a key with each other, but each of them shares a key with some third party, conventionally called Sam, who will act as an introducer. They might proceed as follows:

1. Alice first calls Sam and asks for a key for communicating with Bob;
2. Sam responds by sending Alice a pair of certificates. Each contains a copy of a key, the first encrypted so only Alice can read it, and the second encrypted so only Bob can read it;
3. Alice then calls Bob and presents the second certificate as her introduction. Each of them decrypts the appropriate certificate under the key they share with Sam and thereby get access to the new key.

We will simplify the discussion by ignoring the encryption algorithm details and using the following notation: if P is the plaintext and K the key, then the ciphertext is given by:

$$C = \{P\}_K$$

We will assume that this gives integrity as well as secrecy — cut-and-paste attacks on encrypted blocks do not work. (One may think of the encryption operation as a variable-length block cipher with the property that any change to the plaintext will cause a change to the ciphertext, and vice versa, that is completely unpredictable to anyone who does not know the key.)

We will also use the notation N_A to mean a "nonce" (number used once) generated by Alice. Such nonces may be random numbers or serial numbers, depending on the application; they are used in cryptographic protocols to help ensure that messages are fresh.

With this notation, we can describe one of the first authentication protocols to be published, by Needham and Schroder in 1978. It formalises the protocol that we described in general terms above.

$$A \longrightarrow S: \quad A, B, N_A$$
$$S \longrightarrow A: \quad \{N_A, B, K_{AB}, \{K_{AB}, A\}_{K_{BS}}\}_{K_{AS}}$$
$$A \longrightarrow B: \quad \{K_{AB}, A\}_{K_{BS}}$$
$$B \longrightarrow A: \quad \{N_B\}_{K_{AB}}$$
$$A \longrightarrow B: \quad \{N_B - 1\}_{K_{AB}}$$

Here Alice takes the initiative, and tells Sam that she wants to talk to Bob. Sam provides her with a session key, and with a certificate to convey this key to Bob. She passes it to him, and he then does a challenge-response to check that she is present and active.

There is one flaw in this protocol — Bob has no way of knowing that the key K_{AB} from Sam is fresh: Alice could have waited a year between steps 2 and 3. In many applications this may not be important; but if Charlie ever got hold of Alice's key, he could use this to set up session keys with many other principals, and could continue to use these even after Alice had set up a new K_{AS} with Sam. In other words, revocation is problematic.

The majority of crypto protocols published in the almost twenty years since then have turned out to have some such subtle flaw. This is quite remarkable when one considers that an authentication protocol is just a program of typically 3–5 lines and that one would expect to get such a small program right after starting at it for a while. Anyway, as mentioned above, the persistence of such protocol flaws led to the development of the BAN logic, which we will now describe briefly.

3.5 The BAN Logic

The BAN logic provides a formal method for reasoning about the beliefs of principals in cryptographic protocols. Its underlying idea is that we will believe that a message is authentic if it is encrypted with a relevant key and it is also fresh (that is, generated during the current run of the protocol). This is formalised using a notation which includes:

$A |\equiv X$ *A believes X*, or more accurately that A is entitled to believe X;
$A |\sim X$ *A once said X* (without implying that this utterance was recent or not);

$A \mid\Rightarrow X$ *A has jurisdiction over X*, in other words A is the authority on X and is to be trusted on it;

$A \triangleleft X$ *A sees X*, i.e. someone sent a message to A containing X in such a way that he can read and repeat it;

$\sharp X$ *X is fresh*, that is, contains a current timestamp or some information showing that it was uttered by the relevant principal during the current run of the protocol;

$\{X\}_K$ *X encrypted under the key K* — a notation we explained above;

$A \leftrightarrow^K B$ *A and B share the key K*, in other words it is an appropriate key for them to communicate.

There are further symbols dealing, for example, with public key operations and passwords, that need not concern us here; the reader should consult (Burrows *et al.*, 1989) for the full description.

These symbols are manipulated using a set of postulates which include:

- the message meaning rule states that if A sees a message encrypted under K, and K is a good key for communicating with B, then he will believe that the message was once said by B (we assume that each principle can recognise and ignore his own messages).

  Formally, $\dfrac{A \mid\equiv A \leftrightarrow^K B, A \triangleleft \{X\}_K}{A \mid\equiv B \mid\sim X}$

- the nonce-verification rule states that if a principal once said a message, and the message is fresh, then that principal still believes it.

  Formally, $\dfrac{A \mid\equiv \sharp X, A \mid\equiv B \mid\sim X}{B \mid\equiv X}$

- the jurisdiction rule states that if a principal believes something, and is an authority on the matter, then he should be believed.

  Formally, we write that $\dfrac{A \mid\equiv B \mid\Rightarrow X, A \mid\equiv B \mid\equiv X}{A \mid\equiv X}$

There are a number of further manipulation rules for dealing with concatenated statements. These are as one would expect; For example, if A sees a statement then he sees its components provided he knows the necessary keys, and if part of a formula is known to be fresh, then the whole formula must be.

Given this machinery, we can now set about attempting to verify the soundness of cryptographic protocols. Very often, we get stuck; and given the sparsity of the BAN postulates, it is usually pretty clear what is missing when this happens. For example, in the Needham-Schroder protocol referred to above, it is straightforward for A and B to deduce that K_{AB} is a key that they share (S being an authority on this) but it is necessary to add the assumption that B accepts the key as new in order to show that it is a good key. This "hole" in the chain of trust makes the replay attack on Needham–Schroder obvious; again, the interested reader is referred to (Burrows *et al.*, 1989) for full details.

3.6 The UEPS Transaction Protocol

The transaction protocol is used to ensure the integrity of each step of the cash path, from bank to customer to merchant to clearer to bank. At each step, each transaction is made unique by random challenges, sequence numbers or both.

Our first task, in view of our requirement for double encryption, was to implement a way of doing this which satisfied the security requirements of the client within the technical constraints of the card. In view of growing bank concern about the strength of DES (Garon and Outerbridge, 1991), we had to use double encryption; we decided to combine this with key chaining in order to get a compact implementation. Given a run of a protocol between two cards A and B, using a key pair K1 and K2, and a series of message blocks A1, B1, A2, B2, ... we proceed as follows:

$$A \longrightarrow B: \quad \{\{A1\}_{K2}\}_{K1}$$
$$B \longrightarrow A: \quad \{\{B1\}_{K3}\}_{K1} \text{ where } K3 = \{A1\}_{K2}$$
$$A \longrightarrow B: \quad \{\{A2\}_{K4}\}_{K1} \text{ where } K4 = \{B1\}_{K3}$$

In effect, the intermediate product of each double encryption is used as the second key in the following encryption. In this way each block doubles as an authenticator of all the previous messages in the protocol and information can be exchanged efficiently.

This is because one normally includes redundancy within each message, in the form of a fixed pattern or an already known variable, in order to check that the encryption has been performed with the right key. As our security requirements dictated four bytes of redundancy, and our communications protocol (dictated by the limitations of the available terminal equipment) exchanged eight byte ciphertext blocks, a naive design would have resulted in half of each message being redundant. However, by key chaining we need only have one redundant data block, namely in the last message (which is the one which causes value to be credited in the recipient card).

During the development process we had been using the BAN logic to check the correctness of the authentication structure, and it proved its value by highlighting several subtle errors and redundancies in the first draft of our protocol specification (the proof was a constantly evolving multicolour document covering several whiteboards in the Net 1 boardroom). We found, however, that while the BAN logic supports conventional block chaining operations, it cannot deal with key chaining.

We will illustrate this by the exchange which takes place between a customer card C and a retailer card R when goods are purchased. The other transactions, whether bank to and retailer to, are essentially similar, but each transaction type uses different keys to prevent splicing attacks (e.g., in which a customer card is manipulated in order to appear to be a merchant card).

Let C be the customer's name, N_C a nonce generated by him (a random number), R the retailer's name, N_R a nonce generated by him (the transaction sequence number), and X the electronic cheque. Then we can idealise the purchase transaction as:

$$C \longrightarrow R: \quad \{C, N_C\}_K \quad (=L)$$
$$R \longrightarrow C: \quad \{R, N_R\}_L \quad (=M)$$
$$C \longrightarrow R: \quad \{X\}_M$$

In this protocol, the client card debits itself after step 2, while the retailer card only credits itself after step 4. The system is therefore failsafe from the bank's point of view: if anyone tampers with the protocol the only result they are likely to achieve is to increase the bank's float, by debiting the customer card without crediting any retailer.

In order to see how such a protocol can be validated, let us first consider a simplified protocol where the information is accumulated without chaining.

$$C \longrightarrow R: \quad \{C, N_C\}_K$$
$$R \longrightarrow C: \quad \{R, N_R, C, N_C,\}_K$$
$$C \longrightarrow R: \quad \{C, N_C, R, N_R, X\}_K$$

This can be analysed in a straightforward way using BAN. The trick is to start from the desired result and work backwards; in this case, we wish to prove that the retailer should trust the cheque, ie $R \mid\equiv X$ (the syntax of cheques and cryptographic keys is similar for our purposes here; a cheque is good if and only if it is genuine and fresh).

Now $R \mid\equiv X$ will follow under the jurisdiction rule from $R \mid\equiv C \mid\Rightarrow X$ (R believes C has jurisdiction over X) and $R \mid\equiv C \mid\equiv X$ (R believes C believes X). The former condition follows from the hardware constraint, that no-one except C could have uttered a text of the form $\{C, \ldots\}_K$. The latter, that $R \mid\equiv C \mid\equiv X$, must be deduced using the nonce verification rule from $\sharp X$ (X is fresh) and $R \mid\equiv C \mid\sim X$ (R believes C uttered X). $\sharp X$ follows from its occurrence in $\{C, N_C, R, N_R, X\}_K$ which contains the sequence number N_R, while $R \mid\equiv C \mid\sim X$ follows from the hardware constraint.

The BAN logic turns out to be easy to use because of the sparsity of its inference rules. When working back from a goal statement, it is rare for there to be more than one possible way to proceed. However, it provides no mechanism for dealing with the key chaining used in the actual protocol. In effect, we have to find a way of unravelling $\{X\}_{\{R, N_R\}_{\{C, N_C\}_K}}$ to $\{C, N_C, R, N_R, X\}_K$.

During the design of UEPS, we solved this problem by adding a further postulate. The existing message meaning rule says that if P believes that the key K is shared with Q and sees a message X encrypted under K ($P \mid\equiv Q \leftrightarrow^K P, P \triangleleft \{X\}_K$), then he will believe that Q once said X ($P \mid\equiv Q \mid\sim X$). To this we added a symmetrical rule to the effect that if P tries a key K to decrypt a block, and recognises the result as coming from Q ($P \mid\equiv Q \leftrightarrow^X P, P \triangleleft \{X\}_K$), then he will believe that Q in fact used K ($P \mid\equiv Q \mid\sim K$).

It has since been suggested that we might rather use the existing extension of the BAN logic by Gong and others (Gong, 1990; Gong *et al.*, 1990), which formalises recognisability in a different way. However, there always remains the nagging doubt that logics which reason about belief and implication in the same calculus may fall foul of the transitivity paradoxes (Hesse, 1974); and in the specific case of that particular BAN extension, we found a significant bug. It turns out that axioms F4 and F14 (in (Gong, 1990): F2 and F7 in (Gong *et al.*, 1990)) together imply a strange result: that someone who possesses a recognisable text X and a fresh key K may conclude that X is fresh by deducing first that $\{X\}_K$ is fresh, and then that X is. This is clearly undesirable and we prefer our original single-postulate extension of BAN.

Quite apart from the soundness aspects, there are pragmatic reasons to prefer a small set of rules: we found it more tedious to work with the large extension of BAN defined in (Gong, 1990; Gong *et al.*, 1990), as there are many more rules which have to be considered at each stage. It is much preferable to use a lightweight, specialised tool where possible; a more complex, general purpose tool would probably have to be supported by proof checking software. While some useful work in this direction has been done (e.g., (Paulson, 1996)), a system that can be learned in an hour or less and deployed effectively without mechanical help will remain more attractive to the working engineer.

To return now to UEPS, we find that the validation, however it is performed, shows that the customer does not receive any confirmation of the transaction, but merely the knowledge that a valid retailer card is present. The value of this knowledge is to rule out a denial-of-service attack by a false terminal; but if the client bank is prepared to tolerate such attacks, then the first message of the protocol could be omitted.

One could also add a confirmation message from the retailer's card, but this would not solve the problem of an interruption after step 2, at which time the customer card has already committed to the transaction and debited itself, while the retailer has still not got the cheque. As we have seen, no financial benefit can be gained by doing this, and accidents are sufficiently rare that they can be dealt with manually. The procedure is to refund to the customer any missing amount which remains unbanked after 21 days; but if the money were to be banked, the dispute would be resolved by comparing the two card records, or inspecting the paper tally roll printed by the merchant terminal (which shows the transaction plus a MAC). No dispute was reported during the pilot.

3.7 Conclusions

The UEPS system was a commercial success. During the pilot stage, the average float of about ten days turned out to be sufficient to cover the capital costs. It offered the bank the same level of information and control as on a cheque account, but cleared two days sooner and cost about a tenth as much to run (these savings were largely passed on to the customer). No fraud losses were recorded in the first year of the pilot period, and the pilot was extended to the other three major banking groups in South Africa. The system was then sold in Namibia and Russia; and finally in 1996 it was adopted by VISA as the COPAC electronic purse. It is expected to be rolled out in Latin American and other parts of the world as a fully supported VISA product during 1998 (CWI, 1996).

It may owe this success in some small part to the fact that we used formal methods to verify its prototype. This may have helped prevent its running into the same kind of opposition and reservations on security grounds as, for example, Mondex (Martin, 1994) (it may be of note that Mondex have just hired one of our recent formal methods PhDs).

Quite apart from the commercial effects that our exercise may have had on the product and on the repute of formal methods within the banking industry, there were scientific benefits. We have showed that the BAN family of logics is not restricted to verifying mutual authentication and key exchange, but are a practical and helpful tool in the design of working crypto protocols, even for substantial and complex systems. Once a modicum of familiarity has been obtained with their use, this is straightforward; so much so that a failure to verify a cryptographic protocol using BAN or one of its competitors could well be construed as a failure of due diligence.

The BAN logic was also useful as a general design discipline. In addition to helping us tighten up the security aspects, it pointed out redundant fields in the messages, allowing the protocol to be made more efficient; it made clear the security dependencies; it provided intellectual stimulation at meetings with designers and programmers who were forced to examine and defend their assumptions; and finally, it greatly strengthened the client's confidence in the system.

Acknowledgements

A number of people contributed to this work in various ways, including Roger Needham, who introduced me to the BAN logic; Serge Belamant, André Mansvelt and Gavin Shenker of Net1, who supplied the problem; and a number of protocol researchers including Cathy Meadows, Ralf Hauser and the members of the Cambridge University Computer Laboratory who provided useful feedback following the first publication of this work in (Anderson, 1992).

CHAPTER 4

Specification of a Chemical Process Controller in B

Kevin Lano, Stephen Goldsack and Arturo Sanchez

4.1 Introduction

This chapter shows the combined use of formal methods with techniques developed in control engineering for the design and development of automation systems for discrete-event processes. On the one hand, formal methods guarantee the correct implementation of a given specification. On the other, control engineering techniques are used to develop a specification which is guaranteed to satisfy operational and safety requirements.

Discrete-event processes are common in industrial practice. Flexible manufacturing systems and multipurpose-multiproduct batch chemical plants are some examples. Operational aspects are studied in disciplines such as control science, operations research and mechanical, electrical and chemical engineering. These disciplines focus on the design of process operation and ways of operating and controlling them where automation frequently plays a key role. A recently proposed paradigm, Procedural Control Theory, or PCT, (Sanchez, 1996b), for the synthesis of control devices at a high level (i.e., abstract design of behavioural specifications), termed *procedural controllers*, has demonstrated its applicability in the synthesis of control devices for process systems (i.e., chemical, pharmaceutical industries). PCT builds upon standard control engineering methods. Based on a model of the process to be controlled and a theoretical framework to support the synthesis activities, "control laws" are designed for making the event-driven process behave in an expected and safe manner (e.g. rejecting unexpected perturbations, following state trajectories). One of the great benefits of using a solid mathematical machinery to design a control law, if it exists, is that it is possible to guarantee, by means of mathematical proofs, that the process will behave as expected within certain boundaries, thus avoiding the need for extensive testing. In PCT the control law thus synthesised takes the form of a finite state machine (FSM) that can be used as the specification of the process behaviour (i.e., the logic) to be achieved by the automation system.

This chapter illustrates the benefits of incorporating process control synthesis tools to formal specification and development (i.e., formal) methods. Among them are:

- using modelling techniques from control engineering helps in the understanding of the process being automated. It focuses not only on obtaining ways of guaranteeing that the desired process behaviour is achieved, but allows an understanding of how the process behaves under unconstrained (i.e. open-loop) conditions, thus allowing the systems designer to take provisions for unexpected or not yet considered behaviour. It also helps in defining the operational goals in an unambiguous fashion;
- the fact that PCT guarantees that a given specification, if it exists, will be correct and will consider safety and operational constraints, permits the system engineers to focus on the important issues at the operational level (i.e. what to do to achieve a given operational goal);
- the formal method can help in the discovery of *variants* — natural number expressions which are strictly decreased by each action along a path starting from a given state. This can support proofs that certain states are eventually achieved;
- the formal method supports *animation* and validation at an early development stage;
- the executable implementation produced by B can be a useful complement to simulations such as gPROMS (Barton *et al.*, 1991) as an early prototype of the automation system, and addresses how real-world events are detected and communicated to the control system.

In general, rigorous analysis of a system using a formal method such as B enables design errors and unintended behaviour to be identified at an early development stage, thus enhancing the quality of the final system.

We will assume knowledge of the B notation. Books by Abrial (1997) and Lano (1996) describe the notation and its tool support in detail.

4.1.1 Method Used

The method used follows a general "specification-refinement-implementation" approach.

The specification stage is divided into two parts. First an abstract specification of the process behaviour is performed. Based on a discrete-event model of the process under consideration, a procedural controller (in the form of a finite state machine) is synthesised (Sanchez, 1996b; Rotstein *et al.*, 1997). The procedural controller is mathematically guaranteed to describe the desired operation and goals to be achieved in a safe manner and never reach forbidden situations. This abstract specification is then captured in B. In order to discharge proof obligations it is necessary to build in B a model equivalent to that used for the procedural controller synthesis.

Once the procedural controller has been transformed into a B specification, refinement and implementation steps are carried out, including the discharging of proof obligations to verify and achieve a correct implementation.

A simple but realistic example taken from the process industries is used to illustrate the method.

We begin by presenting PCT in a synthetic manner and its use for specifying the behaviour to be imposed upon the process by the automation system. It is shown how it can be guaranteed that the procedural controller (i.e., the specification of the process behaviour) is provably correct. Since this is a technique taken from control engineering, special emphasis is placed on explaining the concepts within a software engineering context. The section closes with a synthesis method for procedural controllers. The following section explains how the process specification is done and how the control specification is used within refinement and implementation steps performed with support tools for B.

The B development starts with the construction of a model of the process in B notation that maps to the model used for the synthesis of the procedural controller. The refinement takes this information and through a series of refinement steps, an executable implementation in C code is obtained. Verification and simulations along the development process are also included. Section 4.4 presents an example to illustrate the development method. The process chosen is a metering tank, common in the chemical industries. These tanks are frequently of very large capacity being impractical to use continuous level sensors to measure delivered amounts of liquid. Instead, either flow totalizers or discrete level switches or both are used. Given some behaviour requirements, a procedural controller that satisfies the requirements is obtained. The FSM representing this procedural controller is then used as the starting point for the refinement-implementation steps. The obtained implementation is tested in Section 4.7. Finally some conclusions are given.

4.2 Controller Specification Using Procedural Control Theory

Procedural Control Theory is a formal framework for the specification analysis and synthesis of feedback model-based control mechanisms, termed procedural controllers, targeted to discrete-event sequential systems (Sanchez, 1996b; Rotstein *et al.*, 1997). Currently, PCT has been applied to chemical processes (Alsop *et al.*, 1996). Two key components of PCT are the notions of procedural controller and controllability. A *procedural controller* is a mathematical representation which describes the behaviour the process must fulfil in order to achieve desired goal states in a safe manner and never reach forbidden situations. A procedural controller is represented by an FSM in which each state either has: (i) a unique transition leaving it, representing an output from the controller to the controlled system, i.e. a control command; or (ii) process responses that can be issued in the current process state. Procedural control theory gives sufficient conditions of existence for a procedural controller fulfilling safety properties. That is, if a procedural controller exists for a given specification, it can be guaranteed that the process behaviour will be kept by the controller within desired boundaries, avoiding any hazardous or unsafe operation by issuing control commands.

The synthesis of a procedural controller comprises the following stages (Sanchez and Macchietto, 1995):

1. **Identification and input-output modelling of elementary process components (e.g. valves, timers, switches)** They are usually modelled as state-transition structures in which transitions are classified as process responses (uncontrollable transitions from the controller point of view) or control commands (controllable transitions from the controller point of view). The latter will correspond to events issued by the controller whilst the former will usually form the list of events to which the controller must respond.

2. **Identification of important states that must be reached during operation**. These are states of particular significance for the system such as the initial state, a state of desired activity, etc., that must be reached during operation driven by the *procedural controller*. They are termed *marked* states.

3. **Prescription of forbidden states**. States that must be avoided during operation must be declared as forbidden. Logical invariants are used to model the avoidance of these states.

4. **Prescription of dynamic specifications**. Desired dynamic behaviour to be imposed upon the process by the procedural control must be declared. These include normal, abnormal and emergency operation. They can be captured as temporal logic (RAL (Lano *et al.*, 1997), LTL (Sanchez, 1996b)) formulas.

5. **Process modelling**. Given the input-output model for each elementary component, a model of the unconstrained (open-loop) behaviour is built using FSM operators (Sanchez, 1996b). This model will serve as a basis for the synthesis of the closed-loop (constrained) behaviour and the procedural controller realising such behaviour.

6. **Procedural controller superstructure synthesis**. This superstructure represents the maximal feasible closed-loop behaviour that avoids all forbidden states. It is synthesized by first eliminating forbidden states from the process model and then deriving the maximal structure realising controllable behaviour (Rotstein *et al.*, 1997).

7. **Procedural controller synthesis**. Given the dynamic specifications and the controller superstructure, closed-loop behaviour is found which satisfies the dynamic specifications and is controllable (Rotstein *et al.*, 1997). This comprises the sequences of controllable transitions in response to uncontrollable transitions occurring from each reachable state. The FSM realising such behaviour is termed a procedural controller. Methods for its synthesis are given elsewhere (Rotstein *et al.*, 1997). Modularity issues have also been addressed (Sanchez, 1996b).

Each of these steps is partly tool supported. Note that it is possible that no procedural controller exists satisfying the stated specifications. This becomes a design problem in which either the process equipment or the specification must be modified. Animation of this class can also assist in enhancing the models before controller synthesis. A model-checking system such as SMV (Burch *et al.*, 1992) can also help to determine if the procedural requirements are consistent.

4.3 Specification, Refinement and Implementation Using B

This involves the following steps:

- process model specification;
  - specification of elementary components: expressing the FSM models of these components as B machines;
  - actuators specification: aggregation of the machines modelling actuators, together with invariants expressing the static constraints which the actuators must satisfy;
- procedural controller specification;
  - high level controller specification: derivation of a B machine expressing, abstractly, the desired effect of the procedural controller operations;
  - refinement: implementation of this specification, using some strategy for polling sensors or otherwise detecting input events;
  - testing: execution of test scenarios using the generated C code of the system.

Using the synthesised procedural controller, the first step is to define the controller specification in B. The specification of the controller can be derived from the procedural controller by abstraction of groups of states into high-level controller states. The actuators effected by the controller will be modelled by a machine which contains the static constraints that the states of these actuators must satisfy. The following verifications can then be carried out:

1. that the actuator operations preserve the static constraints, if they are executed within their preconditions (internal consistency of the actuator machines);
2. that the high-level controller implementation invokes the actuator operations only in situations where their preconditions hold (part of the refinement proof of this implementation);
3. that the characterisation of the abstract states in the controller specification are correct (part of the internal consistency proof of the controller);
4. that the controller implementation obeys its specification (this should be automatically true, but is confirmed by the refinement proof of the implementation);
5. that additional invariants of the high-level controller, stronger than the required static constraints, hold (part of internal consistency proof of the controller).

Ultimately we will need to make assumptions about the accuracy of the controllers model of the state of its environment, i.e., how up-to-date its record of the state of the physical components is, and hence about the frequency of sampling required.

The following validation steps can be carried out:

1. symbolic execution of the controller specification;
2. testing of the controller implementation;

3. checking that the order of invocations of actuator operations by the controller implementation meets the dynamic constraints – this check is automatable in principle, but is not supported by the current B tools;
4. checking that eventuality requirements in the dynamic constraints are met, by defining suitable variants for the high-level controller specification – in principle the check that these are variants could also be tool supported.

Having validated and verified the system, an executable implementation in C can be automatically generated from the B implementation.

4.4 Case Study Description

The tank case study is described in (Sanchez, 1996a). A schematic diagram of the system is shown in Figure 4.1. It consists of a tank with a level measuring device with four level switches to indicate when the tank is empty, at the proper discharge level (normal level), above the discharge level (high level) or at its maximum. Liquid is fed into the tank using the on/off valve FV and discharged through on/off valve EV. These two valves are prone to fail while either opening or closing. Each valve is also able to send responses to the controller indicating if it has opened or closed successfully or it is stuck closed or open. Also, once the valve has been repaired after being stuck, it emits a signal indicating its availability. To cope with the eventual failure of any of these two valves and to adjust the liquid to the proper discharge level if required, the on/off valve RV is provided. Valve RV has been designed to handle the maximum expected upstream flow-rate when the tank is at its maximum level in order to avoid spilling. It is connected to a dump tank where the liquid can be collected for reuse. To reduce the size of the model and make it more tractable, it is assumed that this valve does not fail and only takes two possible states, open or closed. An on/off switch is provided to start and stop the process. The initial and final states of the operation are when all the valves are closed, the tank is empty and the on/off switch is in the off position. To start the operation, the switch takes the on position and to terminate, it changes to off. Once the switch is off, the process must reach a safe state (i.e. level empty and all valves closed). The purpose of this system is to deliver a measured quantity of fluid through the exit valve (i.e. the level measurement must indicate normal level before starting the discharge). If either FV or EV fails, the controller must signal for the repair crew to service the faulty valve and await acknowledgement that the repair has been effected. If FV fails to close, the controller must use RV to avoid spillage while FV is being repaired. Also, RV must be used to remove from the metering tank any excess of liquid. There are a large number of static and dynamic constraints on the operation of the system. For example, the feed valve and relief valves must be closed if the exit valve is open, in order that a precise quantity of fluid is delivered. Moreover the system must react to failures in the feed or exit valves, or situations where the level of fluid becomes too high. We will only consider a few of these constraints in this chapter to illustrate each step of the specification process. The interested reader is referred to Lano and Sanchez (1997), where the full set of constraints is addressed.

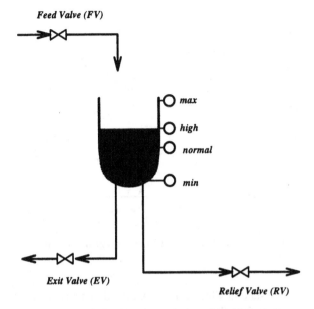

Figure 4.1. Schematic structure of tank system

A data and control flow diagram of the system is shown in Figure 4.2.

The synthesis of the procedural controller is carried out following the steps mentioned in Section 4.2. Due to space restrictions, a description of each step is given below. A detailed account can be found in Sanchez (1996a).

4.4.1 Synthesis of the Procedural Controller

Identification and input-output modelling of elementary process components. The process is divided into five elementary process components: level measurement, valve FV, valve EV, valve RV and on/off switch. The FSMs for each component are described in Table 4.4.1. The level measurement is modelled as the FSM M_1. Its state variable *level_status* takes four different values, giving rise to four *states*, each corresponding to a level switch in the tank. *States* 1 and 2 in which state variable *level_status* takes the value of empty or normal are marked. The transitions connecting the states are uncontrollable. Valves FV and RV are modelled as M_2 and M_3 respectively with seven states as illustrated in Figure 4.3 in which the state variable *valve_status* can take the following values: valve open or closed, in the process of opening or closing, stuck opened or closed and under repair. If the valve is open, a control command is issued to close the valve. Afterwards, the valve may uncontrollably either fail to open or fulfil the control instruction. If it fails and becomes stuck open, the next control command will drive the valve to the repair state but with the valve still open. Following repair, the valve returns to the closed state. The same behaviour occurs when the valve is closed. If the valve fails to execute the opening

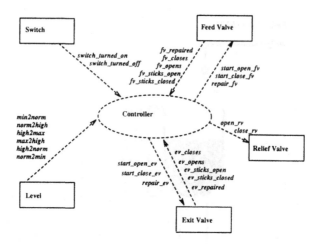

Figure 4.2. Data and control flow diagram of tank

action, it will reach a state in which it is stuck closed and a control command must be issued to repair it, eventually reaching the closed state again.

Note that control actions (controllable transitions) are modelled together with the responses of the elementary component (the uncontrollable transitions). Valve RV is modelled by M_4. It can only be open or closed and it changes its status in response to the controllable transitions (control commands) "open valve" or "close valve". The only marked state in each of the three valves is when it is closed. In this way, only circumstances in which there is no change in the liquid level are considered as possible states in which the operation can be terminated or held. The on/off switch is modelled as the FSM M_5. Both states are marked. Transitions are uncontrollable because we consider the change in the switch as an nondeterministic external action (e.g., an operator changes the switch position to off unexpectedly due to problems in the process upstream).

Identification of important states that must be reached during operation. The following states are defined as marked

– initial/final state. State-variable values: FV, EV and RV closed, level minimum and button off;
– end of filling in normal mode. State-variable values: FV, EV and RV closed, level normal and button either on or off.

Prescription of forbidden states. In order to simplify the operation of the process (for safety considerations), restrictions are imposed on the functioning of the valves. These are modelled as Predicate Logic (PL) statements. 10 PL statements describe different situations identified as forbidden (Sanchez, 1996a). For instance, valves FV and EV must not change position simultaneously. This is modelled by the following PL statements in terms of the component states (the order of the elementary

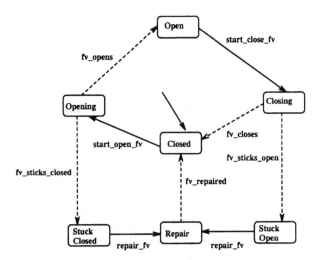

Figure 4.3. FSM of feed valve

Table 4.1. Elementary *FSMs* of the metering system (* = uncontrollable transition)

elementary component	FSM	state-variable desc.	state-variable value	state label	transition label	transition description	from	to
level switch	M_1	level status	min	1	11*	min to norm	1	2
			norm	2	12*	norm to high	2	3
			high	3	13*	high to max	3	4
			max	4	14*	max to high	4	3
					15*	high to norm	3	2
					16*	norm to min	2	1
fill valve FV	M_2	valve status	closed	1	21	comm to open	1	2
			opening	2	22*	opening	2	3
			open	3	23	comm to close	3	4
			closing	4	24*	closing	4	1
			s/open	5	25*	get stuck open	2	5
			s/closed	6	26*	get stuck closed	4	6
			u/repair	7	27	comm to repair	5, 6	7
					28*	end repair	7	1
exit valve EV	M_3	valve status	closed	1	31	comm to open	1	2
			opening	2	32*	opening	2	3
			open	3	33	comm to close	3	4
			closing	4	34*	closing	4	1
			s/open	5	35*	get stuck open	2	5
			s/closed	6	36*	get stuck closed	4	6
			u/repair	7	37	comm to repair	5, 6	7
					38*	end repair	7	1
discharge valve RV	M_4	valve status	closed	1	41	comm to open	1	2
			open	2	42	comm to close	2	1
on/off switch	M_5	switch status	off	1	51*	comm to go on	1	2
			on	2	52*	comm to go off	2	1

state variables in each state is: (level status, FV status, EV status, RV status, switch status)):

$$q : (\infty_1, 1, 3, \infty_4, \infty_5) = \text{FALSE} \tag{4.1}$$

$$q : (\infty_1, 3, 1, \infty_4, \infty_5) = \text{FALSE} \tag{4.2}$$

The rest of the forbidden states and their corresponding PL statements can be found in Sanchez (1996a).

Prescription of dynamic specifications. The dynamic behaviour, including normal and emergency, to be imposed is captured in 15 temporal logic (TL) formulas, ranging from operational sequences to eventuality constraints. An example of an operational sequence is the operation start-up. If the switch is turned on, the level is minimum and the other components are de-energised, the next action must be to open FV. This is captured in the following TL formula:

$$(0, 0, 0, 0, 0) \rightarrow \bigcirc (\tau = 21) \tag{4.3}$$

An example of a liveness constraint is the necessity that the process terminates. That is, if the on/off switch is turned off, then FV must never open again. This is captured by the following TL formula:

$$(\infty_1, \infty_2, \infty_3, \infty_4, 1) \wedge (\tau = 52) \rightarrow \Box (\tau \neq 21) \tag{4.4}$$

The rest of the operational behaviour specification and its corresponding TL formulas can be found in Sanchez (1996a).

The dynamic constraints are of two types (1) operational obligations, asserting that input event occurrences lead to certain sequences of output response events; (2) eventuality and liveness constraints, asserting that a goal state must be eventually reached.

Constraint 4.3 above is an example operational obligation, which can be expressed using the B names for component state variables as follows:

level = *minimum* $\wedge$ *fvstate* = *fv_closed* $\wedge$
evstate = *ev_closed* $\wedge$ *rvstate* = *rv_closed* $\wedge$
switch_turned_on $\Rightarrow$ $\bigcirc$ *start_open_fv*

"If the switch is turned on and the other components are de-energised, the next action must be to open the feed valve".

An eventuality constraint that is needed to show the overall system goal that the discharge through the exit valve always corresponds to the difference between the minimum and normal levels is:

level = *normal* $\wedge$ *evstate* = *ev_opening* $\Rightarrow$
    (*evstate* $\neq$ *ev_closed*) $\mathcal{U}$ (*level* = *minimum*)

"Once the exit valve is opened with the level at normal, it is not closed again until the level becomes minimum".

An example liveness constraint is:

$$cstate = filling \implies \diamond (cstate \neq filling)$$

"The filling process must terminate."

Each of these can be captured in a B specification, although with certain limitations, due to the sequential nature of the language. Specifically:

- permission constraints are expressed as operation preconditions in the controller specification — theoretically it is more accurate to model them as guards (Abrial, 1996), but using preconditions gives rise to more useful proof obligations for validation of the model — callers of the controller operations must ensure these preconditions, i.e., send events to the controller only when these event occurrences are valid given our model of the system and its current state;
- operational obligations are expressed as operation definitions in the controller implementation;
- eventuality "Until" constraints are expressed via flags which signal that the obligation in the first argument of the $\mathcal{U}$ must hold in the current state;
- liveness constraints are expressed via variant functions which are decreased by actions until they reach zero, characterising the goal state.

Process modelling. Given that the set of transitions of the five elementary models are disjoint, a model considering all the possible behaviour is obtained by the *asynchronous product* (Sanchez, 1996b) of the five elementary models. The obtained structure contains 784 states. Due to the size of the structure, it is omitted here.

Causal behaviour in the level is introduced by means of TL formulas (Sanchez, 1996b) in order to consider only physically possible behaviour and to reduce the number of transitions from each state. For instance, if FV is closed or being opened, the level cannot increase. This is stated by the following TL formula:

$$(\infty_1, \infty_2^{2,3,4,5,6}, \infty_3, \infty_4, \infty_5) \rightarrow \bigcirc [(\tau \neq 11) \wedge (\tau \neq 12) \wedge (\tau \neq 13)] \qquad (4.5)$$

These formulas are then translated to FSMs and incorporated into the model using appropriate operators (Sanchez, 1996b). For other constraints introduced into the model, see Sanchez (1996a).

Procedural controller superstructure synthesis. The procedural controllers superstructure is obtained according to the procedure described in Rotstein *et al.* (1997). First, all forbidden states are eliminated from the process model. Then, the maximal superstructure realising controllable behaviour is obtained.

Procedural controller synthesis. Applying the synthesis methods given elsewhere (Rotstein *et al.*, 1997) the procedural controller fulfilling the dynamics specifications is synthesised.

4.5 Specification in B

4.5.1 Process Modelling Specification

The individual components of the system are specified as B modules (*machines*) expressing the state and transitions of the component.

For example, the feed valve is specified as:

```
MACHINE FeedValve
SEES Tank_data
VARIABLES fvstate
INVARIANT
  fvstate: FVState
INITIALISATION
  fvstate := fv_closed
OPERATIONS

  start_open_fv =
     PRE fvstate = fv_closed
     THEN
        fvstate := fv_opening
     END;

  start_close_fv =
     PRE fvstate = fv_open
     THEN
        fvstate := fv_closing
     END;

  repair_fv =
    PRE fvstate = fv_stuck_open or
        fvstate = fv_stuck_closed
    THEN
        fvstate := fv_repair
    END;

  ....

  complete_close_fv =
     PRE fvstate = fv_closing
     THEN
        fvstate := fv_closed
     END

END
```

An operation definition *op = PRE E THEN S END* asserts that *E* is a precondition of *op – E* must be true at commencement of execution of *op* in order for its execution to be valid. In the above example, *start_open_fv* is only expected to execute if the feed valve is already closed.

A similar specification can be given for the relief and exit valves. Each of these machines represents the controllers record or knowledge of the state of the corresponding physical components, which may not match completely the actual state of these components – deduced from the events received by the controller. The record of the *level* state will be represented by a local variable in the controller specification in B.

The *Tank_data* machine declares shared types:

```
MACHINE Tank_data
SETS
  LState = {minimum, normal, high, maximum};
  FVState = {fv_closed, fv_opening, fv_open, fv_closing,
             fv_stuck_closed, fv_stuck_open, fv_repair};
  EVState = {ev_closed, ev_opening, ev_open, ev_closing,
             ev_stuck_closed, ev_stuck_open, ev_repair};
  RVState = {rv_closed, rv_open};
  CState = {c_idle, filling, overfull, levelling, emptying};
  SState = {on, off}
END
```

Actuator Specification. The aggregate of all the actuators, constrained by the forbidden states (e.g., that the exit valve must be closed if either of the other valves are not closed, etc.) is:

```
MACHINE
  Tank_Actuators
SEES Tank_data
INCLUDES FeedValve, ExitValve, ReliefValve
INVARIANT
  (evstate = ev_open   =>   rvstate = rv_closed &
                            fvstate = fv_closed) &
                                 /* Static constraint 1.1 */
  (evstate = ev_repair => rvstate = rv_closed &
                          fvstate = fv_closed) &
  (evstate = ev_opening => rvstate = rv_closed &
                          fvstate = fv_closed) &
  (evstate = ev_closing => rvstate = rv_closed &
                          fvstate = fv_closed) &
  (evstate = ev_stuck_open =>
          rvstate = rv_closed & fvstate = fv_closed) &
  (evstate = ev_stuck_closed =>
          rvstate = rv_closed & fvstate = fv_closed) &

  (fvstate = fv_open   =>   evstate = ev_closed) &
                                 /* Static constraint 1.2 */
  (fvstate = fv_opening => evstate = ev_closed) &
  (fvstate = fv_closing => evstate = ev_closed) &
  (fvstate = fv_repair  => evstate = ev_closed) &
  (fvstate = fv_stuck_open  =>  evstate = ev_closed) &
  (fvstate = fv_stuck_closed  =>  evstate = ev_closed)
ASSERTIONS
  (rvstate = rv_open => evstate = ev_closed) &
  (not(fvstate = fv_closed) => evstate = ev_closed) &
  (not(evstate = ev_closed) =>
               fvstate = fv_closed & rvstate = rv_closed)
```

Some formulae are written in the ASSERTIONS as general cases of a collection of invariant formulae (e.g., the fact that *evstate* is closed if *fvstate* is not closed), as this makes their proof more tractable.

```
PROMOTES close_rv, end_repair_fv, end_repair_ev, fv_stuck,
         ev_stuck, complete_close_ev, complete_close_fv,
         complete_open_ev, complete_open_fv,
         get_fvstate, get_evstate, get_rvstate
```

The PROMOTED operations are those of *FeedValve* etc which already maintain the above invariants – they do not need further constraints on their execution. These operations become operations of the *Tank_Actuators* machine without modification.

```
OPERATIONS

  c_open_rv =
    PRE rvstate = rv_closed &
        evstate = ev_closed
    THEN
      open_rv
    END;

  c_start_open_fv =
    PRE fvstate = fv_closed &
        evstate = ev_closed
    THEN
      start_open_fv
    END;

    . . . .

END
```

The preconditions of operations such as *c_open_rv* strengthen those of the unconstrained operations (here, *open_rv*) that they replace, in order to ensure that they are only validly called in situations where their execution maintains the invariant. In this case, we can only validly open the relief valve if the exit valve is closed, in order to maintain the invariant *rvstate = rv_open* $\Rightarrow$ *evstate = ev_closed*.

There are 153 proof obligations for the correctness of this machine (i.e., that are required to be proven in order to show that the constrained operations together with the promoted operations each maintain the safety invariants). All of these can be proven either automatically or with a small amount of manual involvement. The preservation of invariants by operations is the main source of proof obligations: each operation *op = PRE E THEN S END* gives rise to an obligation:

$$E \wedge Inv \Rightarrow [S]Inv$$

where *Inv* is the invariant. This means that every possible execution of *S* initiated in a state satisfying *E* and *Inv* terminates in a state satisfying *Inv*.

4.5.2 Procedural Controller Specification

High-level controller specification. The specification of the high-level controller can be derived by abstraction from the procedural controller obtained in Section 4.4.1. Sequences of low-level states joined only with uncontrollable transitions are replaced by high-level controller states, although we may further abstract collections of states into superstates which express some phase (Manna and Pnueli, 1992) in the process. For example, the *filling* state represents the processing phase that has as its goal that the feed valve is closed, the level is normal and the relief valve is closed — so that an *emptying* process may commence. The *emptying* state or phase has as its goal that the level is minimum and all valves are closed. Similarly for *levelling* (discharging excess fluid) and *overfull* (reacting to uncontrolled filling). Orthogonal to these states is the *shutdown* flag, which indicates whether the system should be attempting to shut down because the switch has been turned off in the current cycle. The high-level controller is shown in Figure 4.4. The dashed line separat-

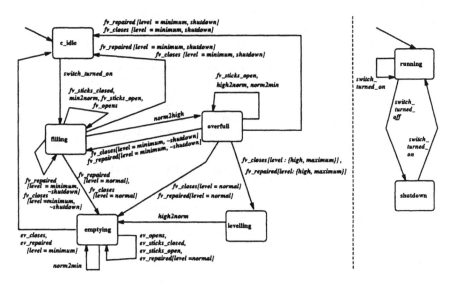

Figure 4.4. High level controller statechart

ing the two graphs indicates concurrent composition. Membership of the *shutdown* (ie, *shutdown = TRUE*) state affects the destination of the *fv_closes* and *fv_repaired* transitions only — in other cases the system behaviour is the same as in the *running* (*shutdown = FALSE*) state.

The B machine capturing the high-level controller follows:

```
MACHINE HL_Controller
SEES Tank_data, Bool_TYPE
INCLUDES FeedValve, ReliefValve, ExitValve
PROMOTES get_fvstate, get_evstate, get_rvstate
VARIABLES
   cstate, level, shutdown
INVARIANT
   cstate: CState &
   level: LState &
   shutdown: BOOL &
```

```
/* Safety constraints from Tank_Actuators */  &

/* Characterisation of high level states: */

(cstate = c_idle => fvstate = fv_closed &
                    rvstate = rv_closed &
                    evstate = ev_closed &
                    level = minimum) &

(cstate = filling  =>  rvstate = rv_closed &
                       evstate = ev_closed &
                       level: {minimum, normal}) &

(cstate = emptying =>  rvstate = rv_closed &
                       fvstate = fv_closed &
                       level: {minimum, normal}) &

(cstate = overfull  =>  rvstate = rv_open &
                        fvstate /= fv_closed) &

(cstate = levelling  =>  rvstate = rv_open &
                         fvstate = fv_closed &
                         evstate = ev_closed &
                         level: { high, maximum }) &

/* Some additional properties of the minimal super-
   structure, identified via the proof process: */

(level = maximum => fvstate /= fv_open) &
(level = high   =>  fvstate /= fv_open) &
(level = normal  =>  fvstate /= fv_open) &

(cstate = overfull => fvstate /= fv_open) &

(cstate = emptying & evstate = ev_closing
                          =>  level = minimum) &
(cstate = filling & shutdown = FALSE &
 fvstate = fv_closing => level = normal) &

(level = high   =>  rvstate = rv_open) &
(level = maximum  =>  rvstate = rv_open)
ASSERTIONS
 (rvstate = rv_open => evstate = ev_closed) &
 (fvstate /= fv_closed => evstate = ev_closed) &
 (fvstate = fv_open => rvstate = rv_closed)
```

The invariants of this machine express the safety invariants from *Tank_Actuators*, and then the meanings of the high level states (for example, that when the controller is in the *filling* state, this means that both the exit and relief valves are closed, and that the level is not higher than the *normal* point).

Notice that the invariants are true only *between* operation executions – thus it is valid to assert that *fvstate* $\neq$ *fv_open* whenever the level is *normal* because the *min2norm* operation sets FV to close.

The assertions are separated out as in the *Tank_Actuators* component.

```
INITIALISATION
  cstate := c_idle || level := minimum
OPERATIONS

  ll <-- get_level =
         ll := level;

  switch_turned_on =  /* Reaction to switch going on */
    PRE cstate = c_idle
    THEN
      cstate := filling ||
      start_open_fv ||
      shutdown := FALSE
    END;
```

An operation *e* describes how the controller responds to the event *e*. The complete response is given, as a change in the states of one or more components of the system. The sequence of atomic operation steps is not described, instead the $S_1 \mathbin{||} S_2$ statement is used to assert that both changes S_1 and S_2 happen (independently).

```
  fv_opens =  /* Reaction to FV opening */
    PRE cstate = filling &
        fvstate = fv_opening
    THEN
      IF level = minimum & shutdown = FALSE
      THEN
        complete_open_fv
      ELSE /* level > minimum  or  shutdown = TRUE */
        set_fv(fv_closing)
      END
    END;
    ....

  min2norm = /* Reaction to level increasing to normal */
    PRE cstate = filling &
        level = minimum  &

        rvstate = rv_closed
        fvstate /= fv_closed &
        fvstate /= fv_opening
    THEN
      level := normal ||
      IF fvstate = fv_open
      THEN start_close_fv
      END
    END;

  norm2high =  /* Reaction to level increasing to high */
    PRE cstate = filling &
        level = normal &

        rvstate = rv_closed &
        fvstate /= fv_closed &
        fvstate /= fv_opening
    THEN
      open_rv ||
```

```
          cstate := overfull ||
          level := high
      END;
    ....

  switch_turned_off = /* Reaction to switch going off */
      PRE cstate /= c_idle
      THEN
        shutdown := TRUE ||
        IF fvstate = fv_open & cstate = filling
                              & level = minimum
        THEN
          start_close_fv
        END
      END

  END
```

The operations of *HL_Controller* correspond to the events that are inputs to the controller on Figure 4.2, together with an enquiry operation for *level*.

The invariant captures most of the specifiers understanding of the system, and ensures that, for example, it is valid to open RV in the case that *norm2high* happens: the precondition of the operation, together with the invariant, shows that EV must be closed (as FV is not closed). Also, FV cannot be open if *level = normal* (it is signalled to close as soon as the level reaches *normal*).

There are 370 proof obligations for this machine, over 250 of which are automatically proved, and the remainder can be interactively proved with a minimal (under 2 hours) effort.

We can animate this specification in order to test that it correctly expresses the system requirements, before developing executable code. This involves symbolic execution of the operations of *HL_Controller*: the tools supporting B show for each operation execution how the state changes and whether the preconditions hold. An extract from such an animation is:

```
Animating HL_Controller.mch
============================          =========================
1: Initialisation                     2: switch_turned_on

   Current State                          Current State
     evstate  ev_closed                     evstate  ev_closed
     rvstate  rv_closed                      rvstate  rv_closed
     fvstate  fv_closed                      fvstate  fv_opening
     level  minimum                          level  minimum
     shutdown  FALSE                          shutdown  FALSE
     cstate  c_idle                           cstate  filling
============================          =========================
3: fv_sticks_closed                   4: fv_repaired

   Current State                          Current State
     evstate  ev_closed                     evstate  ev_closed
     rvstate  rv_closed                      rvstate  rv_closed
     fvstate  fv_repair                      fvstate  fv_opening
     level  minimum                          level  minimum
```

```
    shutdown  FALSE                        shutdown  FALSE
    cstate  filling                        cstate  filling
============================
5: min2norm  /* The precondition  fvstate /= fv_opening
                                             is false here */

   Current State
     evstate   ev_closed
     rvstate   rv_closed
     fvstate   fv_opening
     level   normal
     shutdown  FALSE
     cstate  filling
============================
```

The controller behaviour therefore meets our expectations in this scenario.

4.5.3 Tracing of Temporal Logic Requirements

Each of the temporal logic requirements for the system can be related to the specification *HL_Controller* and its implementation *HL_ControllerI* that will be presented in Section 4.6. They need to be translated into B notation from the original FSM constraint formulae: this is a trivial syntactic mapping.

– *fvstate = fv_open ∧ evstate = ev_open* cannot occur: this is expressed in the third conjunct of the invariant of *HL_Controller* (the first conjunct of *Tank_Actuators*).
– *fvstate = fv_open ∧ rvstate = rv_open* cannot occur. We can prove this as follows. From the invariants:

```
(level = high   =>  fvstate /= fv_open) &
(level = normal  =>  fvstate /= fv_open) &
(cstate = overfull => fvstate /= fv_open)
```

and the other invariants for *cstate* we can infer that *fvstate = fv_open* implies that *cstate = filling*. But in this case *rvstate = rv_closed*, so the result follows.
The formula:

$$fvstate = fv\_open \Rightarrow rvstate = rv\_closed$$

can thus be added as an assertion.
– The permission constraint:

$$fvstate = fv\_closed \lor fvstate = fv\_opening \Rightarrow$$
$$\neg (min2norm \lor norm2high \lor high2max)$$

is expressed by the preconditions of the operations *min2norm* etc including assertions that *fvstate ≠ fv_closed* and *fvstate ≠ fv_opening* when the event happens.
– The procedural obligation:

$$level = minimum \land fvstate = fv\_closed \land$$
$$evstate = ev\_closed \land rvstate = rv\_closed \land$$
$$switch\_turned\_on \Rightarrow \bigcirc start\_open\_fv$$

is expressed by the action *start_open_fv* of the *switch_turned_on* definition in *HL_Controller1*.

- The eventuality constraint:

$$level = normal \land evstate = ev\_opening \Rightarrow$$
$$(evstate \neq ev\_closed) \, \mathcal{U} \, (level = minimum)$$

can be verified by adding a new variable *until_flag* : *BOOL* to the controller, which is set to *FALSE* initially, and set to *TRUE* whenever the condition *level = normal* $\land$ *evstate = ev_opening* becomes true. For example:

```
fv_closes =
  PRE (cstate = filling or cstate = overfull) &
      fvstate = fv_closing
  THEN
    IF cstate = filling
    THEN
      IF level = normal
      THEN
        start_open_ev || until_flag := TRUE ||
        complete_close_fv ||
        cstate := emptying
      ELSE /* shutdown = TRUE, level = minimum */
        complete_close_fv ||
        cstate := c_idle
      END
    ELSE ...
```

It is set to *FALSE* once the *minimum* level is reached.
The $\mathcal{U}$ constraint is then formalised by the invariant:

$$until\_flag = TRUE \Rightarrow evstate \neq ev\_closed$$

This is automatically proved to hold.
In fact, here, the condition *cstate = emptying* covers all the states where *until_flag = TRUE*, so we do not need to add a new variable to *HL_Controller* in order to express the constraint.

- The liveness constraint:

$$cstate = filling \Rightarrow \diamond (cstate \neq filling)$$

is ensured by defining a *variant* function *var* of the controller state such that, whenever the system is in the *filling* state, each action of the controller decreases *var* by at least 1. *var* = 0 will occur once the target state *cstate* $\neq$ *filling* has been achieved.

4.6 Refinement and Design

The implementation of the high-level controller adopts a very similar structure to the specification, but calls *Tank_Actuator* operations in particular orders:

```
IMPLEMENTATION HL_ControllerI
REFINES HL_Controller
SEES
  Tank_data, FV_Sensor, Bool_TYPE
IMPORTS
  Tank_Actuators, cstate_Vvar(CState),
  level_Vvar(LState), shutdown_Vvar(BOOL)
PROMOTES
  get_fvstate, get_evstate, get_rvstate
INVARIANT
  cstate_Vvar = cstate &
  level = level_Vvar &
  shutdown = shutdown_Vvar
INITIALISATION
  cstate_STO_VAR(c_idle);
  level_STO_VAR(minimum);
  shutdown_STO_VAR(FALSE)
OPERATIONS

  ll <-- get_level =
    ll <-- level_VAL_VAR;              /* ll := level */

  switch_turned_on =
    VAR currstate
    IN
      currstate <-- cstate_VAL_VAR;/* currstate:=cstate */
      IF currstate = c_idle
      THEN
        c_start_open_fv;
        cstate_STO_VAR(filling);     /* cstate := filling */
        shutdown_STO_VAR(FALSE)
      END
    END;

  fv_opens =
    VAR lev, sht
    IN
      lev <-- level_VAL_VAR;
      sht <-- shutdown_VAL_VAR;
      IF lev = minimum & sht = FALSE
      THEN
        complete_open_fv
      ELSE
        complete_open_fv;
        c_start_close_fv
      END
    END;  ...

  switch_turned_off =
    VAR currstate, lev, fv
    IN
      currstate <-- cstate_VAL_VAR;
      lev <-- level_VAL_VAR;
      fv <-- get_fvstate;
      shutdown_STO_VAR(TRUE);
```

```
        IF lev = minimum & fv = fv_open
                          & currstate = filling
        THEN
          c_start_close_fv
        END
      END

  END
```

A *SEES* module inclusion represents a *monitoring* relationship between the including and included module, whilst an *IMPORTS* mechanism represents a *controlling* relationship. In the former case only enquiry operations of the seen module can be invoked in the seeing, whilst in the latter case update operations of the imported module can be invoked.

The similarity between this implementation and the specification leads to relatively few proof obligations (119) all of which can be automatically or interactively proved.

Tank_Actuators itself is implemented simply by "stubs" which tell the user when particular actions are executed. In an actual system, it would be an interface to device drivers for the valves.

There remains the question of how the controller actions are invoked, i.e., how the real-world events of the switch being pressed, the level changing, etc., are sent to the controller. In B, the most natural approach is a form of polling, where each polling cycle:

1. obtains the most recent values of the controllers record of the states of each component, then
2. obtains the actual sensed current values of the states,
3. compares the current and previous values and then
4. calls appropriate controller actions to handle any events which are deduced to have occurred on the basis of discrepancies between these values.

At the most abstract level we just have a single abstract *cycle* operation:

```
MACHINE
   Tank_Outer
SEES Tank_data
EXTENDS Tank_SubOuter
OPERATIONS

   cycle = skip

END
```

This will be decomposed into the steps described above:

```
MACHINE
   Tank_SubOuter
SEES
   Tank_data
OPERATIONS

   ofv,oev,olev,osw <-- get_old_states =
```

```
            BEGIN
              ofv :: FVState ||
              oev :: EVState ||
              olev :: LState ||
              osw :: SState
            END;

     ev,fv,lev,ss <-- get_new_states(oldevstate,
                                    oldfvstate,oldlevel) =
            PRE oldevstate: EVState & oldfvstate: FVState &
                oldlevel: LState
            THEN
              fv :: FVState ||
              ev :: EVState ||
              lev :: LState ||
              ss :: SState
            END;

    test_level(old_lev,lev) =
      PRE lev: LState &
          old_lev: LState
      THEN
        skip
      END;

    test_switch(old_sw,sw) =
      PRE sw: SState &
          old_sw: SState
      THEN
        skip
      END;

    test_fvstate(old_fv,fv) =
      PRE fv: FVState &
          old_fv: FVState
      THEN
        skip
      END;

    test_evstate(old_ev,ev) =
      PRE ev: EVState &
          old_ev: EVState
      THEN
        skip
      END

END
```

The implementation of *Tank_Outer* is:

```
IMPLEMENTATION
  Tank_OuterI
REFINES
  Tank_Outer
SEES Tank_data
IMPORTS
  Tank_SubOuter
```

```
PROMOTES test_fvstate, test_evstate, test_switch,
         test_level, get_new_states, get_old_states
OPERATIONS

  cycle =
    VAR oldfvstate, oldevstate, oldlevel, oldswitch, fv,
        ev, lev, ss
    IN
      oldfvstate,oldevstate,oldlevel,oldswitch
                                  <-- get_old_states;
        ev,fv,lev,ss <-- get_new_states(oldevstate,
                                         oldfvstate,oldlevel);

      test_level(oldlevel,lev);

      test_switch(oldswitch,ss);

      test_fvstate(oldfvstate,fv);

      test_evstate(oldevstate,ev)
    END

END
```

whilst the implementation of *Tank_SubOuter* carries out the actual sampling and signalling.

```
IMPLEMENTATION
  Tank_SubOuterI
REFINES
  Tank_SubOuter
SEES
  Tank_data, FV_Sensor, EV_Sensor, Level_Sensor,
  Switch_Sensor
IMPORTS
  HL_Controller, Switch
OPERATIONS

  ofv,oev,olev,osw <-- get_old_states =
    BEGIN
      ofv <-- get_fvstate;
      oev <-- get_evstate;
      olev <-- get_level;
      osw <-- get_sstate
    END;

  ev,fv,lev,ss <-- get_new_states(oldevstate,oldfvstate,
                                  oldlevel) =
    BEGIN
      ev <-- sample_ev(oldevstate);
      fv <-- sample_fv(oldfvstate);
      lev <-- sample_level(oldlevel);
      ss <-- sample_switch
    END;

  test_level(old_lev,lev) =
```

```
IF old_lev = lev
THEN skip
ELSE
  IF old_lev = minimum & lev = normal
  THEN min2norm
  ELSE
  IF old_lev = normal & lev = high
  THEN norm2high
  ELSE
  IF old_lev = high & lev = normal
  THEN high2norm
  ELSE norm2min   /* Other combinations of states
                        are erroneous */
  END END END
END;
```

. . . .

END

Notice that the valve states and tank level, etc are sampled in a fixed order, and changes in these states are notified to the controller in a fixed order, neither of which may correspond to the order in which the corresponding events occur in the real world. This is in contrast to the abstract procedural controller for the system or the gPROMS simulation (Sanchez, 1996a) which assume an immediate communication of events to the controller. Additional reasoning will be needed to obtain assurance that this jumbling of event orders does not affect the required functionality of the system. For example, if at the previous sample point *fvstate = fv_opening* and *level = minimum*, but *fvstate* changes to *fv_open* before *level := normal*, then both events will be detected in the current cycle. However it would be invalid for the *min2norm* event to be sent to the controller before *fv_opens* in this cycle, as *min2norm* has a precondition *fvstate ≠ fv_opening*.

Thus, some intelligence must be placed in the component which detects events from samplings of component states, and forwards them to the controller.

The *Sensor* machines are models of the sensor sides of the components. For example:

```
MACHINE
  Level_Sensor
SEES Tank_data
OPERATIONS

  ll <-- sample_level(oldlev) =
          PRE oldlev: LState
          THEN
            IF oldlev = minimum
            THEN
              ll :: { minimum, normal }
            ELSE
            IF oldlev = normal
            THEN
              ll :: { normal, minimum, high }
            ELSE
```

```
IF oldlev = high
THEN
    11 :: { normal, high }
ELSE
    11 := oldlev
END END END
    END

END
```

This specification expresses that, given a previous state value *oldlev*, the "next" state value can only be one of a certain set of values (i.e., adjacent or unchanged levels). This is a physical assumption which requires reasoning that the sampling period is fast enough that no other changes in the level can take place between two successive periods. No such timing specifications can be given in B, however.

The implementations of these components query the user for the appropriate values. Again, in the final embedded system they would be interfaces to device drivers.

The system is now complete, and code can be generated in order to run tests of its behaviour. 2607 lines of C code were generated from the above specifications. Figure 4.5 shows the global structure of the system (*E* denotes EXTENDS, *I* denotes INCLUDES or IMPORTS, and *R* denotes REFINES).

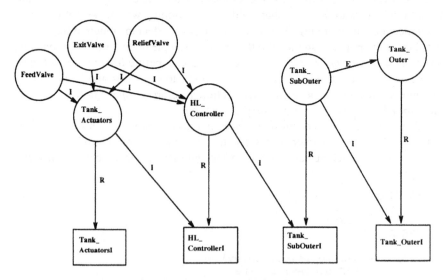

Figure 4.5. Global structure of tank system

4.7 Testing

We can execute the same scenarios which were run on the specification, on the executable C implementation. For example:

```
0 Tank_Outer Menu
1 cycle
2 Quit

Tank_Outer operation number? >1

Old exit valve state is:
ev_closed
Enter new state: ev_closed, ev_opening, ev_stuck_open, etc.
>ev_closed

Old feed valve state is:
fv_closed
Enter new state: fv_closed, fv_opening, fv_stuck_open, etc.
>fv_closed

Old level is:
minimum
Enter new level: minimum, normal, high, etc.
>minimum

Enter switch state: on, off:
>on

Starting to open Feed Valve

Tank_Outer operation number? >1
Old exit valve state is:
ev_closed
Enter new state: ev_closed, ev_opening, ev_stuck_open, etc.
>ev_closed

Old feed valve state is:
fv_opening
Enter new state: fv_closed, fv_opening, fv_stuck_open, etc.
>fv_stuck_closed

Old level is:
minimum
Enter new level: minimum, normal, high, etc.
>minimum

Enter switch state: on, off:
>on

Feed valve sticking closed
Starting to repair Feed Valve

Tank_Outer operation number? >1
Old exit valve state is:
ev_closed
```

```
Enter new state: ev_closed, ev_opening, ev_stuck_open, etc.
> ev_closed

Old feed valve state is:
fv_repair
Enter new state: fv_closed, fv_opening, fv_stuck_open, etc.
> fv_closed

Old level is:
minimum
Enter new level: minimum, normal, high, etc.
> minimum

Enter switch state: on, off:
> on

Completing repair of Feed Valve
Starting to open Feed Valve
```

and so forth.

4.8 Conclusions

We have shown how the B specification language and tool facilities can be used in combination with procedural controller synthesis to:

- define and verify high-level controller states which are suitable for operator inter-action with the system;
- validate and verify controllers synthesised via the process of Sanchez and Mac-chietto (1995);
- provide an alternative and diverse means of implementation of the controller.

The modularity mechanisms of B support a decomposition of verification into a number of steps: showing that the low-level controller operations maintain the safety invariants (that undesired states are avoided), provided they are called within their preconditions, and that higher-level controllers invoke these low-level operations within their preconditions.

Extension of B to cover temporal logic specification of dynamic behaviour, timing and deadlines of periodic actions, and the verification of implementations against temporal specifications would be of assistance in developing reactive systems in the chemical process domain. Additionally, more effective ways of expressing and verifying variants should be added to the language and tools.

CHAPTER 5

Formal Analysis of the Motorola CAP DSP

Bishop C. Brock and Warren A. Hunt, Jr.

5.1 Introduction

We describe our formal specification of Motorola's Complex Arithmetic Processor
(CAP) Digital Signal Processor (DSP) and our subsequent use of this specification in
formal analyses of the CAP hardware and software. The CAP was designed by Motorola Government Systems and Technology Group (Scottsdale, Arizona), which,
as a part of their business, builds and sells purpose-built products. The CAP is an
ASIC that was designed to efficiently implement a number of signal processing
algorithms required in digital communications. Motorola's CAP is a super-scalar,
pipelined DSP with seven memories and more than 20 functional units. Motorola's
specification for the CAP was captured using the Cadence Signal Processing (SPW)
(Cadence, 1994) toolsuite; the design is represented as a series of drawings that
specify register files, data manipulation units, and interconnecting busses. We have
completely specified the CAP (Gilfeather *et al.*, 1994) using the formal logic ACL2
(Kaufmann and Moore, 1996). Our specification is executable and can be used as a
simulator as well as a basis for proving the correctness of the CAP hardware design
and CAP programs. We believe our specification is bit-for-bit exact with respect to
the SPW specification produced by Motorola, and was created by hand translating
Motorola's SPW drawings for the CAP. We have used our CAP specification to analyse the CAP instruction pipeline and various CAP algorithms. We believe that the
specification developed is the largest of its kind, as this is the only formal specification of which we are aware for a complete commercial design. We believe that the
use of mathematical logic for modelling and reasoning about hardware designs such
as we have demonstrated here can provide assurance of circuit design correctness
well beyond what is available from current CAD techniques.

Due to the complexity of modern hardware designs, testing has been been ren-
dered ineffective as a means to ensure correctness. To more thoroughly explore

the state spaces reachable by modern designs we have been applying mathematical modelling to the specification and validation of digital hardware. The use of mathematical techniques for hardware design has been spreading (Bryant, 1989; Gordon, 1985; Johnson, 1989; McMillan, 1993; Seger and Bryant, 1993; Srivas and Miller 1995; Windley, 1995) for some years. This kind of approach to circuit validation is generally known as *hardware verification*. Circuits with the complexity of simple microprocessors (Birtwistle *et al.*, 1989; Hunt, 1994; Hunt and Brock, 1994; Sawada and Hunt, 1997; Srivas and Bickford, 1990; Srivas and Miller, 1995; Windley, 1995) have been given mathematical specifications, and their designs have been proved to implement their specifications. In addition, various hardware description languages have been formalised using a variety of formal methods (Brock and Hunt, 1997a; Gordon, 1995; Koos and Breuer, 1995). Yet, the transfer of hardware verification techniques to commercial engineering practice has been hampered by such factors as the use of non-standard notations, inaccessibility of the tools, and the significant mathematical sophistication required to use these approaches. In addition, formal techniques have been directed at only selected aspects of the design process. Important hardware characteristics such as testability and I/O behaviour have been largely neglected by the formal hardware modelling and verification community.

One of our goals is to work toward the point where documentation for a hardware system is a *formula manual*, a collection of fully formal specifications that provide a precise and complete basis for using a specified device. To assure that the formula manual is correct, it will be necessary to *prove* that a design meets *all* of its specifications. In fact, a test of the utility of a formula manual also includes the possibility of using it as the basis for constructing a hierarchy of formally verified systems, including larger hardware structures, operating systems, and user applications.

Industry-standard techniques for assuring the quality of hardware are simulation and test. These are crucial tools, but in addition we hope to model hardware mathematically and analytically prove its correctness. We attempted to address some of these issues by undertaking the formal specification of the CAP. In the following we present an informal description of the CAP, followed by our approach for capturing the CAP specification and the results obtained from the formal analysis of the CAP instruction pipeline design. We also summarise our verification of two DSP applications coded in the CAP assembly language. We end by reporting on the effort expended and give our conclusions.

5.2 History of the Project

Our formal analysis project was a 31-month effort aimed at determining whether mathematical specification techniques could be used on something as complicated as a commercial DSP. This effort was carried out at Computational Logic, Inc. (CLI). We believe that the remainder of this note will demonstrate that it is possible to formally model something of commercial complexity, and we view this project as a successful application of mathematical modeling of an evolving hardware design.

Note, we also have applied formal modelling techniques to the verification of the divide algorithm in the AMD5$_K$86 (Brock *et al.*, 1996) as well as other examples.

The project started in November of 1993 and ended in April of 1996. The work involved four people at various points throughout the project. Bishop Brock was the principal technical lead for the duration of the project. Brock was assisted by Ken Albin of CLI. Calvin Harrison, a Motorola employee, also worked on this project for two years. Warren Hunt helped with the management of the effort and participated in various technical aspects of this project. At the start of this project, Motorola had already completed an initial SPW version of the CAP design. Brock moved to Scottsdale, Arizona, to be close to the CAP development team for the first seven months of the project, and in Scottsdale he began the task of capturing the CAP specification in ACL2. Coincident with this effort was the development of the ACL2 system; thus we were attempting to use a newly developed tool. The sheer size of the CAP specification stressed the ACL2 system and many improvements in the ACL2 systems were a direct result of its use in this effort. Soon after Brock returned to CLI, Calvin Harrison, one of Motorola's CAP designers, moved to Austin and spent 18 months at CLI learning about formal methods and participating in the specification and verification effort. Except for Brock's visit to Scottsdale, all of the work on this project was done at CLI's Austin office.

This project was managed as eight separate but related tasks: the specification of the CAP, validating the accuracy of the CAP specification, analysis of the instruction pipeline, verifying CAP application programs, specifying the CAP pin-level I/O interface, constructing a mechanical testing interface between SPW and ACL2, and providing a technology transfer path. There were a number of intermediate results produced during this effort, but here we just report on the technical effort to create the formal specification and carry out various types of analyses. We do not describe other important enabling work, such as interfaces between the various tools used.

5.3 A Brief Description of the CAP

The CAP is a high performance, single-chip DSP co-processor optimised for communications signal processing. The CAP has been implemented as a stand-alone integrated circuit using 0.5 micron CMOS resulting in a 427 by 427 micron die. The actual mask-level design was produced by using Synopsis synthesis tools after the SPW system created a VHDL description of the SPW-based specification. Operating at 3.3 volts, the CAP requires about one watt of power. The CAP has a re-programmable 64-bit instruction word whose op-codes are assigned by a special assembler each time a CAP program is assembled. These 64-bit instructions are expanded internally by a set of decoding RAMs into 317-bit VLIW instructions for controlling the CAP internal resources. The CAP is both pipelined and super-scalar in its design and can execute a 1024-point, radix-8 complex FFT in 130 microseconds running at 33 MHz.

Figure 5.1 is a block diagram of the data paths of the CAP. The CAP architecture consists of a set of interconnected memory and arithmetic units operating in paral-

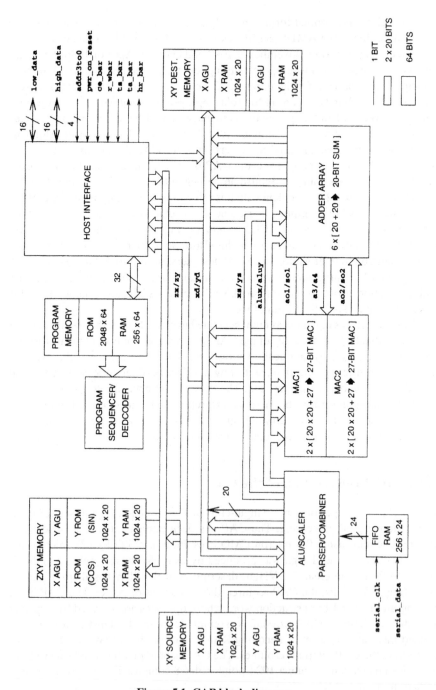

Figure 5.1. CAP block diagram

lel, controlled by a central sequencing/decoding unit. The CAP follows the Harvard architecture, with separate instruction and data memories, and is further optimised for vector processing with separate source and destination data memories, and dedicated parameter memories. All of the instruction, data, and parameter memories are on-chip and are accessed in a single clock cycle. The programming model of the CAP includes 252 programmer-visible registers. With very few exceptions, every data register is dedicated to a particular memory, arithmetic, or I/O unit; the architecture does not include any general-purpose registers. The program ROM includes monitor programs that control communications with the host processor and a library of DSP application subroutines.

5.4 The ACL2 System

This section[1] describes the ACL2 logic and its associated theorem-proving system. We have included this section for completeness, even though a thorough understanding of the ACL2 logic is not a prerequisite for our presentation of the formal analysis of the CAP. Thus, this section may be skipped by the casual reader.

ACL2 is an extended, completely reimplemented version of Nqthm (Boyer and Moore, 1998) that supports an applicative subset of Common Lisp as its logic (Kaufmann and Moore, 1996). The development of the ACL2 system was begun in 1989 by Bob Boyer and J Moore, and subsequently has been continued by Matt Kaufmann and J Moore. The ACL2 system has been publicly available since 1995. By formalising a logic around applicative Common Lisp we can take advantage of the exceptionally good optimising compilers for Common Lisp to get, in many cases, execution speeds comparable to C. Three guiding tenets of the ACL2 project have been to (1) conform to all compliant Common Lisp implementations, (2) add nothing to the logic that violates the understanding that the user's input can be submitted directly to a Common Lisp compiler and then executed (in an environment where suitable ACL2-specific macros and functions — the *ACL2 kernel* — are defined), and (3) use ACL2 as the implementation language for the ACL2 system.

The ACL2 logic is a first-order, quantifier-free logic of total recursive functions providing mathematical induction on the ordinals up to ε_0 and two extension principles: one for recursive definition and one for constrained introduction of new function symbols, here called encapsulation. The axioms of the logic are given in a file that is part of the ACL2 system. We briefly summarise them here.

The following primitive data types are axiomatised.

– **ACL2 Numbers**. The numbers consist of the rationals and complex numbers with rational components. Examples are -8, $22/7$, and #c(7 12) (the Common Lisp notation for $7 + 12i$);

---

[1] This section was written by J Moore and Bill Young of Computational Logic, Inc., and then edited for the purposes of this presentation.

– **Character Objects**. ACL2 supports 256 distinct characters, including Common
  Lisp's "standard characters" such as the character constants #\A, #\a, #\?,
  #\Newline, and #\Space;
– **Strings**. ACL2 supports strings of characters, e.g., "Out of range.";
– **Symbols**. ACL2 supports Common Lisp's symbols. Symbols are objects con-
  sisting of two parts, a package and a name. The symbol STEP in the package
  "FM9001" is written FM9001::STEP. The "current" package is used if no
  package name is written;
– **Lists**. ACL2 supports arbitrary ordered pairs of ACL2 objects, e.g.,
  (X FM9001::ADD ("Good Morning." (3 . 22/7))).

Essentially all of the Common Lisp functions on the above data types are axiomatised or defined as functions or macros in ACL2. Approximately 170 such
symbols are axiomatised.

In addition, we axiomatise several extensions to applicative Common Lisp and
implement them efficiently via Common Lisp macros and functions. Among the
extensions are a notion of state containing the file system and I/O streams, a single-
threaded notion of the "current state," and fast applicative arrays and property lists.

ACL2 has two extension principles: definition and encapsulation. Both preserve
the consistency of the extended logic. Indeed, the standard model of numbers and
lists can always be extended to include the newly introduced function symbols. The
definitional principle achieves this goal by showing that each defined function terminates. This is done by the identification of a decreasing measure into the ordinals.
The encapsulation principle achieves the goal by requiring the exhibition of witness
functions that have the alleged properties.

In one sense, ACL2 is an untyped language; in another sense it is a typed language in which arbitrary predicates may be treated as types and type checking is
arbitrarily hard. The system supports both views in a natural way with its notion of
"guards."

The guard on a function symbol is a formula about the formals of the function.
Guards can be seen as having either of two roles:

– they are a specification device allowing you to characterise the kinds of inputs a
  function "should" have, or
– they are an efficiency device allowing logically defined functions to be executed
  directly in Common Lisp.

Briefly, if the guards of a function definition are "verified," then the evaluation of
a call of that function on arguments satisfying its guard will have the following
property: *all subsequent function calls during that evaluation will be on arguments
satisfying the guard of the called function.*

This has two consequences corresponding to the two uses of guards, mentioned
above:

– your specification function is well-formed, in the sense that the values returned
  by this function on appropriate arguments only depend on the restrictions of the
  called functions to their intended domains;

– when a function whose guards have been verified is called on arguments that satisfy its guard, then the raw Lisp function defined by this function's definition event is used to evaluate the call.

Even when the user-supplied definition is not used, ACL2 uses a corresponding "executable counterpart" that generally performs, we expect, nearly as well as the raw Lisp function. Compilation can increase the speed of execution significantly. This means, in general, that ACL2 code can execute extremely efficiently.

"Guard verification" is the process of establishing that the guards of the functions called in the body of a definition are satisfied when the guard on the function itself is satisfied. Because guards are arbitrary terms, guard verification is, in general, undecidable. But if guards are primitive type expressions on the formals, guard verification is usually a trivial theorem proving problem and can be done by special syntactic means.

Encapsulation allows the introduction of new function symbols satisfying arbitrary constraints provided one can exhibit definitions of those symbols that make those constraints theorems. This allows for abstractions to be introduced conservatively. An encapsulation command takes the form of an arbitrary sequence of commands, e.g., definitions and theorems, some of which are labeled "local." When an encapsulation command is verified for admissibility, all of the subcommands are executed and each must be successful. But the effects of the command are obtained by executing only the non-local subcommands. To introduce a function symbol f of one argument that returns a rational result without specifying what rational is returned, it suffices to define (f x) locally to be 0 and then to prove and "export" the theorem (rationalp (f x)). The local definition of f is merely a witness to the consistency of the constraint. "Outside" the encapsulation, (f x) is known only to be rational.

A derived rule of inference, called "functional instantiation," gives ACL2 some of the features of a higher order logic by allowing one to instantiate the function symbols of a previously proved theorem, replacing them with other function symbols, provided one can prove that the new symbols satisfy the constraints on the old. For example, any theorem proved about the rational f above could later be used to obtain the analogous theorem about any rational function or expression.

The ACL2 theorem prover is a reimplementation of the Nqthm theorem prover for the ACL2 logic. Every proof technique of Nqthm has been implemented in ACL2. Many have been extended significantly.

One of the driving forces behind our design of ACL2 is that its architecture should be open so users can configure it in different ways. Nqthm was frequently used this way, so that to one user it was a theorem prover for MC68020 programs and for another it dealt with Unity programs. But Nqthm was not designed to be so flexible and its many built-in heuristics often had to be "tricked" making it sometimes awkward to "program." These lessons were not forgotten when ACL2 was designed and many more heuristics are now under the direct control of the user.

All of ACL2's proof techniques are sensitive to a hierarchically structured database of rules derived initially from previously certified "books." Furthermore, an evolving "theory," which is computationally determined by the user as a function of the current database and goal, specifies "views" of the database. Books and theories are discussed later.

The ACL2 proof techniques, in order of application are:

- **preprocessing**: This process expands some propositional functions and uses IF-normalisation, tautology checking (using OBDDs when so directed by the user), recognition of common cases, and equivalence closure;
- **simplification**: By far the most complicated proof technique, simplification combines primitive type checking, forward chaining, backward chaining, congruence based rewriting under arbitrary equivalence relations and their refinements, generalised alternative recursive definitions, verified conditional metatheoretic simplifiers, tautology checking, congruence closure, and generalised linear arithmetic;
- **destructor elimination**: This process trades "bad" terms for "good" ones by a "change of variables" technique driven from the database. For example, under suitable conditions, (- i j) might be reduced to k by replacing i everywhere by (+ k j);
- **cross-fertilisation**: Here hypotheses of the form (equiv lhs rhs), where equiv is an arbitrary equivalence relation, are used and possibly discarded. Such hypotheses are used by replacing certain occurrences (depending on available congruence rules) of one side of the equivalence by the other;
- **generalisation**: This process replaces (by new variables) certain terms involved on both sides of equivalence relations or in the hypothesis and conclusion of the goal. Restrictive hypotheses about the new variables may be added;
- **elimination of irrelevance**: Irrelevant hypotheses are thrown out, based on variable isolation and deduced type information;
- **mathematical induction**: This process attempts to find an induction scheme appropriate for the conjecture, based on the terms in the conjecture. The analysis involves the arbitrary well-founded relations used to justify recursive functions, user supplied rules linking function symbols to additional schemes, various techniques for merging and otherwise combining schemes, and selection heuristics.

ACL2's database is a hierarchical collection of "books." Each *book* is realised as a file but books can be included by reference into other books and multiple books can be read to construct the active database. Books allow multiple users to share one another's work. The book mechanism is related to the encapsulation mechanism; a book can hide the details of its proofs (locally) while exporting powerful collections of rules. Books can also define packages and declare a given package current for the purposes of the book, thus providing the namespace protection of packages. Books can also define "theories" and theory manipulation functions, as discussed below. When two books are loaded together, checks are done to insure their logical compatibility. Perhaps more than any other feature of ACL2, books will allow ACL2 to construct proofs of systems much larger than those created with Nqthm, simply because the database can be built incrementally by many different users and its complexity controlled by modularisation.

Books can be *certified*, which involves processing them and their subbooks in a way so as to determine that every definition and encapsulation is admissible and every alleged theorem is provable. Certificates containing details of the certification, including the checksums of the relevant books, are generated by the certification process. When a book is later included in a session, its proofs are not reconstructed but just assumed, provided the certification data is consistent. The certification process provides a means of version control that is integrated into the proof system. This is particularly important if multiple users are developing a system.

Each rule in ACL2 has a unique name. A rule can be used only if it is "enabled." Whenever ACL2 goes to the database to obtain information an appropriate rule name is found, checked for being enabled, and tracked in a "tag tree," a structure that follows the evolving proof construction and records relevant information. Pervasive tracking and use of enabled rule names provides the ACL2 user with much finer-grained control of ACL2 as well as more information, if desired, about the evolving proof.

To be "enabled" a name must be in the current theory, where a *theory* is a list of rule names. A theory thus gives a view of the database in the sense that a rule is seen only if its name is in the current theory. Theories are just objects in the logic, namely lists, and hence may be computed by ACL2 functions.

The ACL2 theorem prover prints a running commentary on its evolving proof attempt, explaining each transformation, the derivation of forced hypotheses, the use of hints, etc. In addition, if Emacs is available, ACL2 sketches the evolving proof tree as it goes, pruning branches that are proved. The proof tree facility is linked to the evolving proof output so that the commentary associated with any point in the tree can be obtained. This allows the user to ignore ACL2's scrolling commentary (indeed, many users simply do not display that buffer) and simply jump directly to trouble spots.

ACL2 is documented via an online documentation facility that is part of the ACL2 system. The documentation is also available in Postscript, HTML, and Emacs Info formats. Roughly 1.4 megabytes of documentation is available, including tutorials. The documentation facilities are also available to users who wish to document books and the definitions and theorems within them.

5.5 The CAP Specification

We have completed a formal specification for the entire CAP processor, including the CAP host interface. We believe our ACL2 specification of the CAP to be a clock-cycle accurate model of every well-defined behaviour of the CAP including normal instruction execution, I/O events, breakpoints, traps, and interrupts. We did not specify the cycle-by-cycle set of events that occur during hardware and software reset as these sequences were not germane to our studies.

Our specifications are written in a state-machine style. The formal CAP state includes all programmer-visible registers and memories, and a few special modelling components. Given an internal CAP state and the current values of the CAP input pins, our specifications compute two things: the next CAP state and the value of the CAP output pins. Formally, the next state of the CAP is specified by the ACL2 function[2]:

cap$state(*cap-state*, *cap-inputs*, *stall-p*).

This specification forms the basis of our formal reasoning about the CAP. The specification cap$state is an interpreter for CAP object code images resident in the CAP program memory, as further specified by the opcode memories for the arithmetic units. cap$state specifies the next state of the CAP for a single clock cycle. We have also defined multiple-cycle formal simulators for the CAP based on cap$state. The formal specification of the CAP output values on each clock cycle is given by:

cap$value(*cap-state*, *cap-inputs*).

Although we use cap$value during testing of the specification, we have not yet used this specification as the basis of any proofs about the output behaviour of the CAP model.

5.5.1 Method and Approach

Our approach to the formal specification of the CAP and verification of CAP programs was inspired to a very large extent by Yu's work on automated proofs of object code for the Motorola MC68020 processor using the Nqthm theorem prover (Yu, 1992). Like Yu, we elected to develop our specification as an interpreter for CAP object code programs. Modulo a simple reformatting procedure, this specification method provides a direct link between Motorola's programming environment for the CAP and our specification in that our specification directly executes object code produced by the CAP assembler CASM. Unlike the MC68020, the instruction set of the CAP is essentially microcode that directly controls the internal CAP functional units and memories, and one CAP instruction completes execution each clock cycle.

Thanks to the excellent foundation provided by Yu's work, and the improvement that ACL2 represents over Nqthm (Boyer and Moore, 1997), we were able to extend Yu's methods in several important ways. Like Yu we used fixed-precision integers as the basic data model for hardware registers and busses. Very briefly, this approach uses modular arithmetic as a model for hardware operations, e.g., a 20-bit unsigned adder is specified as $(a + b)$ mod 2^{20}. This model is more appropriate for the high-level reasoning tasks that we planned than a "bit-vector" model such as we used during the specification and verification of the FM9001 (Brock *et al.*, 1994; Hunt and Brock, 1992). Because of the richer set of built-in data types provided by ACL2, we used signed integers in our CAP instruction-set model as this is how data values are represented in Motorola's engineering model of the CAP. Our libraries

---

[2] The *stall-p* argument is present for the benefit of our pipeline equivalence work.

for hardware specification are essentially the ACL2 translations of Yu's Nqthm libraries extended to signed integers, and supplemented by a library supporting formalisation of common data structures. These basic, non-proprietary ACL2 libraries have already found use in other projects.

In a high-level behavioural model such as ours it is very easy to write specifications that violate the physical limitations of the hardware being modelled, for example by specifying that 11-bit values are written into a register whose physical implementation is only 10 bits. Our specification of the CAP utilises the ACL2 guard mechanism throughout, and every state component is strongly guarded according to an appropriate abstraction of its physical implementation. The ACL2 guard mechanism provides us with a mechanically checked proof that our specification for the CAP is well-typed.

The CAP hardware consists of several cooperating finite state machines controlled by a central instruction sequencer/decoder. The CAP host interface module and ALU also contain embedded state machines. The top-level specification is partitioned roughly as illustrated in Figure 5.1. Our CAP specification is somewhat more abstract than the CAP hardware in the sense that the instruction pipeline specification has been consolidated in our specification, providing a clear presentation of how the various stages of the pipeline actually interact. Our formalisation of the CAP follows a specific style. For every top-level module we create functions that describe their operation. We characterise modules in terms of their combinational outputs as a function of their inputs and current internal state, and we similarly characterise a module's next state. The top-level model represents a composition of the state machine specifications of the top-level modules. We elected to use this technique because the CAP architecture contains multiple parallel execution units, and this technique permitted a clean specification of each execution unit. We also believe that the hierarchical decomposition of the specification was critical to the success of our automated proof efforts. For example, the instruction sequencing unit is specified as an independent state machine. When necessary, we were able to reason about the next state of the instruction sequencer under various conditions without regard to what happens in the memory and arithmetic units. This was especially important in the pipeline equivalence proof.

5.5.2 Undefined Conditions

The CAP is a complex application specific processor, and many internal conditions can lead to arbitrary or undefined behaviour. During the course of this work we considered several approaches to modelling this behaviour. One possible approach is to not model undefined conditions at all and simply have the specification generate errors when they occur. This is much too restrictive for the CAP because arbitrary behaviour may be limited to an execution unit whose computation is not relevant to an application. We also considered using *constrained functions* to model undefined conditions. Constrained functions are an ACL2 construct for defining functions with sets of axioms they satisfy, instead of with an explicit function body. Unfortunately, constrained functions are not executable (they have no definitions), and we consider the executability of formal specifications to be critical to the widespread acceptance of formal methods in industry.

In the end we introduced an extension to the integer hardware model that allows us to directly represent undefined states down to the bit level. This extension gives us the ability to create an executable model of the CAP without over-specifying undefined conditions, yet easily reduces to the standard integer model during code proofs. In general, registers and buses in the CAP are modelled by pairs of signed integers. These two integers are known as the *determinate* and *indeterminate* words. Each bit of a register or bus is represented by one bit in the determinate word and one bit in the indeterminate word, allowing the encoding of a 4-valued logic. Thus we can represent unknown (X) values as well as high-impedance (Z) values. Note that the high-impedance value has an indeterminate effect on all circuits except certain specialised bus models. The truth table for this encoding is given below.

Determinate Bit	Indeterminate Bit	Decoding
0	0	0
1	0	1
0	1	X
1	1	Z

One of the most important aspects of our formalisation is that it is specified to reduce to the standard integer model in the absence of indeterminate values. That is, we never create a pair whose indeterminate word is 0. Instead, completely determined values are always represented by a single integer, the determinate word. When we do code proofs about the CAP we hypothesise that all of the data of interest is integer (hence determinate) data, thus we can reason about the behaviour of programs using standard integer functions (+, *, mod, etc.) rather than their 4-valued counterparts.

The indeterminate integer model was introduced solely for modelling purposes, and there is no loss of generality in our application code proofs when we hypothesise that all of the data of interest are integer data. This model also has many benefits during program development. Motorola's SPW-based (Cadence, 1994) specification provides only two values: Boolean True and Boolean False. Our four-valued data model allows us to represent unspecified behaviours and tri-state buses. The use of unknown values also permits a user to see if unknown values effect the computation in any way. This type of analysis is not possible with the Boolean model provided by SPW.

5.5.3 Executability

The CLI CAP specification provides complete breakpoint facilities. Any kind of condition can be specified, meaning that any pattern of data values or program steps can be identified by writing Common Lisp (ACL2) code which recognises conditions of interest. The breakpoint and record keeping facilities offered by the CLI

CAP specification are much more general than those provided by the SPW system. We believe that our specification offers the best currently-available means for simulating and debugging CAP programs.

The ACL2-based CAP specification executes several times faster than Motorola's SPW-based CAP specification. This is especially noteworthy considering that our specification is four-valued. The ACL2 CAP specification provides both greater modelling precision and better performance than the SPW specification. This suggests that formal modelling (at least in this instance) need not provide poorer performance than conventional modelling and simulation approaches. In addition, we believe this points to the importance of having executable specifications where possible. Engineers are very reticent to give up their existing tools. Currently, simulation is the principal tool used for design validation and verification. If, when using mathematical methods, an engineer has to give up the ability to simulate, then we have found it very difficult to convince an engineer to try mathematical methods. However, if an engineer can use the mathematical models in the same manner as he/she is used to, then the acceptance of a less familiar specification format is more likely to be tolerated, especially if some additional (other than simulation) benefits accrue from using a mathematical model.

5.5.4 Logistical Challenges

At the time we began our work on the CAP, Motorola already had a working prototype design. Thus there was very little possibility to explore whether the *design* of the CAP might benefit from a formal specification. Instead, we *specified* a pre-existing design. We captured the specification by studying the documentation, interviewing the designers, and by 'reverse engineering' the SPW schematics. The latter process was extremely difficult and time consuming, but we believe that this was the only way that we could guarantee that our specification was an accurate model of the processor.

A serious problem in capturing a specification for the CAP was the moving-target nature of the CAP design. Motorola's specification for the CAP was a set of very high-level requirements documents in which many aspects of the behaviour were left open. Because of the application-specific nature of the processor, the designers had tremendous leeway to add or delete features and modify functionality as appropriate, for example, to improve the performance of a particular application or in response to implementation constraints. Because our specification was 'outside the design loop', we were often forced to go through the exercise of studying the latest version of the design schematics to determine what changes had been made, and how they affected our specification.

We see no technical reason preventing the CAP specification from originally having been specified in ACL2 and then translated into a form suitable for the SPW system. The primary drawback to such an approach is that the graphical interface offered by the SPW tool suite would not be the primary interface for specifying the design. This actually points to the larger problem of attempting to integrate mathematical methods with commercial tools. In our experience with Motorola, it seems that available tools often drive the design process. In essence the process is considered more important than the efficiency or quality of a specific product. In the case of the CAP, and more generally SPW, we believe that we could build translators between our ACL2 tool suite and the SPW system. Such translators would provide a very rapid and believable means for converting designs and it would link our specification approach much more closely to an available commercial CAD tool.

5.5.5 Remarks

We have avoided presenting many details of the CAP specification in this high-level summary since hardware specification techniques using formal logics are by now well known, and to avoid disclosing any proprietary information. If the CAP specification is remarkable for any reasons, it is probably for its raw size, and the large and complicated model of the state of the CAP. The CAP specification consists of 250 definitions captured as approximately 16,000 lines of documented ACL2, compared for example to the approximately 6,000 lines of documented Nqthm for Yu's specification of the MC68020.[3] In spite of the size we were able to use the specification very effectively for formal reasoning.

5.6 Validation the CAP Specification

The purpose of validating our ACL2-based CAP specification was to make sure that our CAP specification, discussed above, is accurate with respect to the actual CAP design. Our ACL2 CAP specification was constructed by reading the SPW models of the CAP and then producing an ACL2 version. This translation was done by hand and is obviously subject to error. We have validated the accuracy of our specification by traditional testing methods. Our testing was performed by running computations on both the SPW model and the ACL2 model and comparing their results. Not all formal specification approaches provide executable models. The ACL2 execution facility provides a means of greatly increasing our confidence in the accuracy of our CAP specification.

Simply running application programs and comparing the final results can reveal discrepancies between models, but this approach does not catch cycle-by-cycle differences. Nor does this approach ensure that the internal state machines are in the same state after some computation. We instead chose to compare the total state of each model after each clock cycle of simulator execution. To make this possible, it was necessary to instrument our simulators so as to make this information available.

Accessing the state of our ACL2 CAP specification was trivial since our next-state function just returns the next internal state. To get access to every variable

---

[3] It is valid to compare the sizes of ACL2 and Nqthm specifications, bearing in mind that ACL2 may be a little more verbose due to the presence of guards in the function definitions.

during the SPW simulation was much more difficult. To provide a simulation capability, the SPW system translates a design into VHDL or C code, and then a VHDL interpreter or C compiler is used to provide a means to simulate the design. We extracted the internal state of the SPW simulation by using a symbol table to extract the values of the state directly from an executing program. Once we extracted the value of every state-holding device after every clock cycle, we could then compare the value of every state-holding device present in both models.

The comparison of state-holding values is more subtle than one might imagine. This is due to the four-valued nature of the ACL2 CAP specification. Many of the tests we used to validate the accuracy of the ACL2 model were tests for specific parts of the CAP design, and their behaviour on the rest of the CAP was not considered. On the SPW model, some Boolean value is always produced for every possible simulation, but such simulations may produce unknown values on the ACL2 CAP specification. This is because even though a simulation sequence is well-formed for a particular part of the chip, it may produce undefined results in other parts of the chip. Therefore, the two simulation models may not agree, but depending on the nature of the test such an unknown value may be fine. This led us to produce a mechanical filtering system that attempts to filter out simulation differences introduced as artifacts of the testing process before returning the final results for inspection.

We have compared the ACL2 and SPW models of the CAP with a number of different test programs. The tests supplied to us by Motorola took two forms: block-level tests that Motorola uses to validate the CAP architecture at a low level, and a QPSK modem application. Using a pin-level interface language we created, we performed tests that validated both that the correct answers were computed by our CAP specification and that the I/O was correctly specified.

Our testing uncovered a number of errors in the ACL2 specification of the CAP, but also uncovered errors in the CAP design as well as an error in the underlying Common Lisp system upon which we run ACL2. Most of the errors uncovered were in our ACL2 specification; this was expected as that was what this testing was designed to do. However, we find it interesting that this testing even uncovered problems with the CAP design itself.

So far, 20 test sets supplied by Motorola have been run for about 40 thousand execution cycles. These tests were primarily functional block tests created during the VLSI implementation phase of the design. A number of differences between the ACL2 specification and the SPW implementation were uncovered as well as problems in the support software. All of these differences were fixed. In addition, as a result of our specification testing, two implementation errors were discovered and reported to Motorola.

5.7 Analysis of the CAP Instruction Pipeline

The classical model of the operation of a programmable processor might be called a sequential execution model. In this model each instruction is fetched from memory, the processor state is updated by the effects of that instruction, and then execution continues with the next instruction. Pipelining an instruction set may produce an implementation that violates the sequential execution model, due to the fact that several instructions are executing in parallel. These violations are often referred to as *hazards*, and are further divided into control hazards and data hazards. Control hazards are conditions in which the sequence of instructions executed on the pipelined machine does not match that of the sequential execution model. Data hazards occur when the data path effects (i.e., register updates) of an instruction on the pipelined implementation do not match those of the sequential execution model.

Many pipelined implementations include special hardware support to detect and compensate for control and data hazards. The verification of these hardware schemes is currently a topic of great interest in the formal verification community (Aagaard and Leeser, 1994; Burch and Dill, 1994; Coe, 1994; Srivas and Bickford, 1990; Srivas and Miller, 1995; Tahar and Kumar, 1994). Other processor specifications simply advertise the 'hazards' as part of the specification, and require the programmer or compiler to be aware of the hazards and to program the machine accordingly. This allows a simpler implementation, and in certain cases leads to higher performance as well. The CAP implementation, along with other Motorola DSP designs (e.g., the DSP56000 family), clearly falls into the the category of processors that simply advertise the pipeline hazards as part of their specifications. Many pipeline hazards exist in the CAP implementation, and there is no hardware support for the detection and resolution of these hazards. Therefore, it is incumbent upon every CAP programmer to completely understand the instruction set specification, to understand where the hazards exist, and to know how to compensate for or even to exploit these hazards.

The task is not as daunting as it may sound at first, however. The CAP instruction set and instruction pipeline have been designed in such a way that for most purposes the programmer may ignore pipeline hazards, and consider CAP programs as if they were executing under the sequential execution model. In particular, the "core" of a DSP algorithm on the CAP typically consists of arithmetic instructions sequenced by DO and REPEAT instructions. These types of instruction sequences will always be hazard-free, although visible pipeline effects are a distinct possibility outside of these core algorithms. Our study of many DSP application codes for the CAP found that CAP programmers studiously avoid the potential hazards, however, and we have never seen a case where a CAP DSP application exploits a hazard to increase performance. In other words, although CAP programs execute on a machine with many potential visible hazards, CAP applications are programmed in such a way that their executions can be understood by the sequential execution model.

These facts suggested the following approach to applications verification. Simply put, we first created an abstract, pipeline-free model of the CAP, proved that this model was equivalent to the pipelined model under conditions typically present in real DSP applications, and then used the simpler non-pipelined model for applications verification. It is important to note that unlike other work on formal verification of pipelines, we did not prove that the CAP implementation resolves pipeline hazards. Instead, we characterisd sequences of instructions that will execute with-

out displaying certain classes of hazards, and then prove that these executions are
consistent with a suitable sequential execution model.

This work was beneficial to both the CAP architects and CAP programmers for
several reasons:

- **validation:** This work validates the implementation of the CAP instruction
  pipeline. One of the architectural goals for the CAP was to render the cores of
  DSP algorithms hazard-free. Given the assumption that our model of the CAP is
  valid, then our results show that this goal has been met;
- **documentation:** As a natural part of this work we created a formal specification
  of every pipeline hazard in the CAP implementation. This formal specification
  can be easily recast into a form more accessible to engineers and programmers,
  and, in fact, we have also created a simple prototype tool based on this specification that detects pipeline hazards in CAP programs. This tool is simple to use,
  completely automatic, and was used to uncover some potential problems in early
  versions of the CAP program ROM;
- **analysis:** We believe that it is possible to reason about the behaviour of DSP
  applications directly on the pipelined model of the CAP. However, we also believe
  that the statement and proofs of program invariants in this model would be quite
  difficult, especially in the context of the complexity of instruction sequencing
  in the CAP. We are now able to verify applications on the much simpler non-
  pipelined model, and our equivalence proofs provide a high degree of assurance
  that this is an accurate model of their behaviour on the pipelined model of the
  CAP.

5.7.1 Pipeline Equivalence Hypothesis

As mentioned above, we began our pipeline analysis work by attempting to characterise sequences of instructions that will execute without displaying certain classes
of pipeline hazards. Since hazard-free sequences will execute equivalently on both
our pipelined and non-pipelined models of the CAP, we normally refer to this specification as the *equivalence hypothesis*. There are many possible instruction sequences that lead to undefined or erroneous states in our CAP model, some of which
could be detected at assembly time, and others which can only be detected at run
time. Not all of these conditions are recognised by the equivalence hypothesis, thus
there is no guarantee that a program that satisfies the equivalence hypothesis will
execute without error. Instead, the equivalence hypothesis only guarantees that the
final states of a pipelined and non-pipelined execution are equivalent. There are also
many instruction sequences that expose the pipeline that might be used by a knowl-
edgeable programmer to increase performance. Thus the fact that a program does
not satisfy the equivalence hypothesis does not necessarily mean that the program
is erroneous, simply that it has the potential to expose the instruction pipeline.

The real "discovery" in this work was the discovery of the necessary conditions
on the three instructions in the pipeline and their formalisation in a way that was
sufficiently strong to prove the desired results, yet weak enough to allow a large

number of actual CAP application programs to satisfy this condition. After all, our ultimate goal was to verify real applications on the simpler non-pipelined model, so it would have done no good to produce a predicate that was too restrictive. Indeed, we believe that our equivalence hypothesis is weak enough to accept every ROM-resident DSP application currently available for the CAP.

Another goal of this work was to state the equivalence condition in such a way that it could in principle be applied at assembly time. For the most part the equivalence hypothesis is simply a statement about the three instructions currently in the instruction pipeline as the pipeline advances. The instruction pipeline is a straightforward FIFO queue that adds a new fetch-phase instruction and deletes the old execute-phase instruction every cycle. In principle it should be possible to compute every possible path that a program might take under normal conditions, (e.g., no traps or interrupts, suitably initialised sequencer state, assumption that every conditional branch might be taken, no self modifying code) and determine *a priori* if a subroutine or program will satisfy this hypothesis. Although we did not have time to explore this possibility in detail, the predicate has been structured in such a way that this should be possible.

We developed a preliminary form of the equivalence hypothesis based on our knowledge of the CAP architecture gained during the capture of the formal specification, and from Motorola internal documentation. Several obscure, undocumented conditions were also discovered as we attempted the equivalence proofs. The hypothesis was also weakened from time to time in response to the analysis of application programs for which it failed. The equivalence hypothesis is by no means the logically weakest hypothesis, in part because of our decision to structure it as an assembly-time check. Certain conditions only admit the *possibility* of exposing the instruction pipeline, and the actual determination of whether the pipeline is in fact exposed can only be made at run time. We should also point out that from the point of view of automated proofs using the equivalence hypothesis, it is much easier to eliminate all instructions that have the *potential* to expose the pipeline, rather then trying to characterise and prove exactly under which conditions they actually *do* expose the pipeline. It is probably correct to say that the equivalence hypothesis is only as weak as necessary to admit all of the ROM-resident DSP applications.[4]

The precise characterisation of instruction sequences that expose the pipeline is very technical. In the following our aim is simply to give the reader the general idea of the types of instruction sequences of interest. The definition of the pipeline equivalence hypothesis, pipe-step-ok-p, and an *n*-step version, pipe-step-n-ok-p, appear below.

DEFINITION:
pipe-step-ok-p(*cap-state*)

=

let *i-fetch* **be** i-fetch(*cap-state*),

---

[4] There are a few routines in the CAP monitor that 'fail' our predicate. Again, these programs are not erroneous, but in the worst case their behaviour can only be understood by considering the exact implementation of the three-phase instruction pipeline.

i-decode **be** i-decode(v-pipe(*cap-state*)),
i-execute **be** i-execute(v-pipe(*cap-state*))
in
non-interfering-hi-state-p(hi(*cap-state*))
∧ ¬ excluded-instruction-p(*i-fetch*)
∧ ¬ excluded-instruction-p(*i-decode*)
∧ ¬ excluded-instruction-p(*i-execute*)
∧ ¬ np-hard-agu-interference-p(*i-fetch*, *i-decode*)
∧ ¬ p_addr_start-interference-p(*i-fetch*, *i-decode*)
∧ ¬ np-soft-agu-interference-p(*i-fetch*, *i-decode*)
∧ ¬ lc-interference-p(*i-fetch*, *i-decode*)
∧ ¬ lc-interference-p(*i-fetch*, *i-execute*)

DEFINITION:
pipe-step-n-ok-p(*cap-state*, *input-list*, *n*)
=

if zp(*n*) **then** t
else   pipe-step-ok-p(*cap-state*)
    ∧ pipe-step-n-ok-p(cap$state(*cap-state*,
                                        car(*input-list*),
                                        nil),
                            cdr(*input-list*),
                            n − 1)
fi

One part of the equivalence predicate is not a function of the instruction stream. The CAP is a co-processor to a controlling *host processor*, and the interaction with the host is specified in the CAP *host interface* module, Our equivalence predicate also requires a few special conditions on the state of the CAP host interface module, and an input stream (produced by the host processor) that maintains the host interface in a conforming state. We have tried to capture a weak specification of a *non-interfering* host processor, where a non-interfering host processor is one which does not issue commands that may cause errors or expose the instruction pipeline. In particular, we were careful to allow all normal I/O operations. Note that in general the CAP can not recover or resume from interrupts signalled by the host, thus our non-interfering host interface specification also disallows interrupts.

The predicate excluded-instruction-p excludes illegal instructions, and five classes of CAP instructions that have the potential to expose the instruction pipeline. The excluded instructions are not allowed at any point in the instruction pipeline. An illegal instruction is any 64-bit word that does not encode a valid CAP instruction. The other excluded instructions include the LOAD_PROG and READ_PROG instructions, all DEBUG instructions, and immediate move instructions that modify the registers that control traps and breakpoints. Note that these instructions do not appear in typical DSP applications.

The predicate np-hard-agu-interference-p recognises illegal instruction sequences in which an immediate move to an address generation unit (AGU) register is
followed by an inappropriate AGU addressing mode.

The specification p_addr_start_interference_p disallows illegal instruction sequences that specify multiple updates to an internal register.

The predicate np-soft-agu-interference-p recognises certain sequences that expose the instruction pipeline caused by immediate moves to AGU registers.

The predicate lc-interference-p recognises the pipeline visibility conditions that
may arise from immediate moves to loop-counter registers followed by DO or
REPEAT instructions.

5.7.2 Pipeline Equivalence Statement

In general, the state of a pipelined implementation of an architecture is *never* equal
or equivalent to the state of a non-pipelined implementation of that architecture, due
to partially executed instructions in the pipeline. Several approaches to formally stating the equivalence between these two views of an architecture have been proposed
(Burch and Dill, 1994; Sawada and Hunt, 1997; Srivas and Bickford, 1990; Tahar
and Kumar, 1994; Srivas and Miller, 1995; Windley and Coe, 1994). Most previous work involved the definitions of complex abstraction functions from pipelined
states to the more abstract, non-pipelined states. These abstraction functions are
complicated by time abstractions where it may be necessary to reason about future
states whose delay is instruction or environment dependent. We felt that this type of
state abstraction would be difficult to produce correctly, difficult to understand, and
potentially very difficult to verify. Instead, we followed an approach suggested by
Burch and Dill (1994). We found their method for stating equivalence to be easy to
specify and intuitive. This formulation was also very straightforward for the proofs
about the CAP models as it does not include any cases on the instruction classes at
the top level.

Burch and Dill suggested that the problem of equivalent states can be stated by
including the idea of "flushing" the pipeline in the equivalence statement. Intuitively,
every instruction currently in the pipeline is allowed to complete. The resulting state
is then subjected to a simple data abstraction to produce the equivalent non-pipelined
state. Our formulation of this method appears in Figure 5.2. An execution of the
pipelined model appears on the left side of the diagram, and an equivalent execution
of the non-pipelined model appears on the right side of the diagram. The top of
the diagram is the equivalence statement for the execution of a single instruction.
The diagram as a whole indicates the equivalence for the execution of a series of
instructions.

Mapping from a pipelined state to a non-pipelined state involves two operations:

- **stalling:** The pipelined CAP model is stalled for two cycles, which flushes the
  instruction pipeline. Stalling is an abstract operation that we introduced into the
  pipelined specification for the purpose of these equivalence proofs. To stall, the
  decode- and execute-phase instructions are executed and moved forward in the

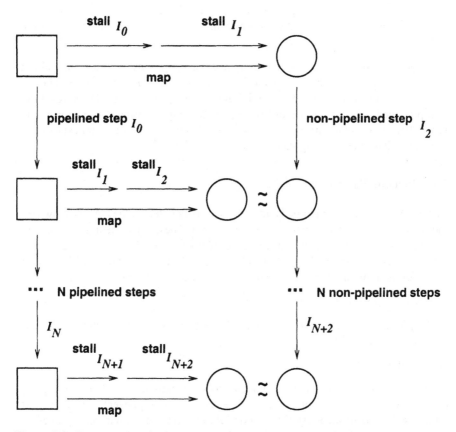

Figure 5.2. Commutative diagram showing the equivalence of the pipelined and non-pipelined models. The boxes represent the state of the pipelined machine, and the circles represent states of the non-pipelined machine.

instruction pipeline, without any change to the state of the instruction sequencing unit, and a NOP instruction is inserted into the pipeline as the next decode-phase instruction. Because of the regularity of the CAP instruction pipeline, stalling the processor twice is always guaranteed to flush the pipe;

- **mapping:** The mapping operation simply copies a portion of the machine state (*before* stalling) to the non-pipelined state. This is necessary in order for the non-pipelined model to check the pipeline equivalence hypothesis in support of application verification. The portion of the machine state that is copied is simply a modelling abstraction, and does not include any of the architected state of the CAP.

Note that both the pipelined and non-pipelined step operations, as well as the stalling operations, consume values from the input stream, one value per cycle. The input values consumed are indicated in Figure 5.2 by I_n. Also note that the resulting non-pipelined states are not necessarily equal, but only equivalent in an appropriate sense. For the present purposes the reader should consider this a technical distinction, and regard the resulting states as equal.

5.7.3 Pipeline Equivalence Proofs

The equivalence of the pipelined and non-pipelined models of the CAP is shown by the three major theorems appearing in Figure 5.3. These three theorems concisely summarise our formal analysis of the CAP instruction pipeline. All of these theorems share some common hypotheses which we will explain before going into more detail for the individual theorems. The first hypothesis is always:

cap-state-p(*cap-state*).

This hypothesis states that the formal model of the CAP state is well-formed, and all of the state components have the correct type. The hypothesis:

non-interfering-inputs-listp(*input-list*)

states that the *input-list* is a list of input vectors that satisfy non-interfering-inputs-p. These are input vectors that do not cause reset or interrupt events, or that would otherwise lead to erroneous states. All normal I/O operations with the host processor are allowed, however. The inequalities on the lengths of the input streams are formal requirements that ensure that the input streams provide enough valid input data to traverse the commuting diagrams for the number of cycles of interest, one input per cycle.

The theorem pipe-equiv-step-correct is the equivalence theorem corresponding to a single step in the commuting diagram, Figure 5.2. If the initial *cap-state* satisfies pipe-step-ok-p, then the diagram commutes for a single step. In addition to the non-interference condition on the host interface module state, the predicate pipe-step-ok-p simply checks that the execution of the three instructions in the virtual pipeline do not admit the possibility of pipeline-related errors or visible pipeline effects not compensated for by the non-pipelined model. Note that there are no other

THEOREM: pipe-equiv-step-correct
     cap-state-p(*cap-state*)
  $\wedge$ non-interfering-inputs-listp(*input-list*)
  $\wedge$ $3 \leq$ len(*input-list*)
  $\wedge$ pipe-step-ok-p(*cap-state*)
$\rightarrow$ cap-state-equiv(p-step(*cap-state*, *input-list*),
                np-step(*cap-state*, *input-list*))

THEOREM: pipe-equiv-step-n-correct
     cap-state-p(*cap-state*)
  $\wedge$ non-interfering-inputs-listp(*input-list*)
  $\wedge$ $n + 2 \leq$ len(*input-list*)
  $\wedge$ pipe-step-n-ok-p(*cap-state*, *input-list*, n)
$\rightarrow$ cap-state-equiv(p-step-n(*cap-state*, *input-list*, n),
                np-step-n(*cap-state*, *input-list*, n))

THEOREM: cap-pipeline-equivalence
     cap-state-p(*cap-state*)
  $\wedge$ pipe-step-ok-p(*cap-state*)
  $\wedge$ non-interfering-inputs-listp(*input-list*)
  $\wedge$ $2 + n \leq$ len(*input-list*)
  $\wedge$ $\neg$ np-err(np(np-step-n(*cap-state*, *input-list*, n)))
$\rightarrow$ cap-state-equiv(p-step-n(*cap-state*, *input-list*, n),
                np-step-n(*cap-state*, *input-list*, n))

Figure 5.3. Pipeline equivalence theorems

restrictions on the instructions in the pipeline other than that they satisfy pipe-step-ok-p. Our analysis covers every instruction sequence on the CAP, including many that lead to "undefined", erroneous states. The lemma pipe-equiv-step-n-correct extends this result for any number of cycles.

The final theorem, cap-pipeline-equivalence, states the equivalence in a way that is most useful for justifying applications verification on the non-pipelined machine. This theorem demonstrates that if no pipeline interaction was discovered during a non-pipelined execution (as indicated by the NP-ERR flag as accessed by the np-err function), then the execution was equivalent to an execution on the pipelined model. In other words, we have shown that the NP-ERR flag maintained by the non-pipelined model is equivalent in the proper sense to the predicate pipe-step-n-ok-p. Whenever we do an application proof we always include a proof that the NP-ERR flag is false at the end of execution of the application.

5.7.4 Proof Techniques

The proofs of the theorems presented in the last section are an excellent example of the power of ACL2 to deal with interesting, "industrial-strength" examples of hardware verification problems. It is interesting to note that these equivalence proofs represent only a modest part of our entire specification and analysis work on the CAP. Over the course of the project much more time was spent capturing the pipelined specification of the CAP than in creating the non-pipelined specification and completing the proofs of equivalence.

Some of the equivalence proofs were actually performed twice. The CAP design (and hence the formal specification) was under development by Motorola up until this work was completed. We initially performed a pipeline equivalence proof on a subset of the CAP architecture that included the XY and Z memories, the instruction sequencing unit, and the MAC models. This proof also used an equivalence hypothesis that was somewhat weaker then the final hypothesis. We had the very good fortune to be paid a visit by David Dill just when we were contemplating how to state the equivalence between the pipelined and non-pipelined machines. After Dill explained Burch and Dill's equivalence statement, we obtained the proofs for the CAP subset very quickly. The single step proof took only two weeks of effort, and the *n*-step extension only required another week.

The final theorems presented before were developed several months after the initial experiment. The final CAP models are much more complicated than the earlier subsets, particularly because of the presence of the host interface module with the added complications of I/O. We had initially expected that we would have to eliminate I/O events from the equivalence proof for simplicity, and were quite surprised that we could actually perform the proof even in the presence of I/O, albeit with a slight "fix." We also had to weaken the equivalence predicate substantially to allow it to accept all of the ROM-resident CAP applications, especially in the area of the pipeline visibility conditions associated with immediate moves to AGU registers. Weakening the predicate significantly complicated the proofs. The final results described here represent about five additional weeks of work.

By far the most difficult proof is the proof of the single-step equivalence lemma, pipe-equiv-step-correct. This proof requires the symbolic expansion of the two, three-clock-cycle paths around the commuting diagram, and then the comparison of the resulting states. Because of the control complexity of the CAP specification (even at the behavioural level of our models), this was clearly a problem that we did not want to address directly by a naïve expansion of the entire specification. Therefore the proof was accomplished by reasoning about the modules roughly at the level shown in Figure 5.1. Our goal was to capture the important properties of the modules with respect to the pipeline as a library of key lemmas, and carry out the proof at a high level. Once the requisite lemma library is in place the proof is direct from the top-level definitions. The only real "case split" in the final proof is based on whether the fetch-phase instruction is an instruction that swaps the XY memories or not.

The development of the proofs, and in particular the equivalence hypothesis, was an iterative process. We first directed the theorem prover to expand the pipelined and non-pipelined specifications for three clock cycles. Since the specifications were more or less stable, we stored away the precomputed expansions as lemmas to save time later on. We would then simply compare the resulting states. This comparison naturally split into a case for each top-level component of the resulting states that were not obviously equal after simplification. Analysis of the resulting terms suggested restrictions we needed to place on the pipeline, or suggested how we needed to state the properties that the high-level modules maintained when the pipeline equivalence hypothesis was satisfied. We then modified the predicate or proved the required properties. Often this process led to minor changes in the text of the specifications themselves that simplified the proofs.

5.7.5 A Prototype Hazard Analysis Tool

The pipeline equivalence hypothesis pipe-step-n-ok-p is a run-time check on an executing CAP program. We formulated the predicate this way because it seemed to be the easiest way to accomplish the proofs about the equivalence of the two models of the CAP. Except for the constraints on the host interface module, however, there is no reason in principle why the predicate could not be formulated as a static check on CAP object code. As a part of this work we implemented a "quick-and-dirty", static hazard checker for CAP programs. This hazard checker is an ACL2 program that reads a listing file created by the CAP assembler, creates a program memory image consistent with the listing file, and then explores all of the possible execution paths in the program memory checking for pipeline hazards. More precisely, the program generates every possible triple of instructions that might appear in the instruction pipeline under a reasonable set of assumptions, and then notes when any of these triples violates pipe-step-ok-p. One of the assumptions made is that every statement in the program is reachable. This means that the tool can be run on any assembler listing, regardless of the control structure (if any) of the assembled code.

We ran the tool on a preliminary version of the CAP program ROM supplied by Motorola. Naturally, the tool reported every occurrence of the "excluded" instructions such as LOAD_PROG. These kinds of instructions occur infrequently, and in fact only occur in special monitor routines, never in DSP applications programs. However, the analysis identified two serious hazards:

- in two cases an instruction sequence specified the simultaneous update of two registers in a register file with a single write port;
- in another case a register was being accessed before its intended value was available. Although this was a well defined instruction sequence, this also turned out to be a programming error.

It is gratifying that the application of the tool to the CAP program ROM resulted in few diagnostics. This result bolsters our assertion that CAP programmers do not exploit visible pipeline effects in DSP applications. Note that although the tool was coded in ACL2, it is by no means 'verified'. No formal *proofs* that every ROM-resident application satisfies the equivalence hypotheses have been done, but we are confident that they could be done in principle, and in fact these proofs have been done for the applications we verified.

5.7.6 Remarks

The non-pipelined model developed during the course of this work greatly simplifies the problem of formal verification of CAP applications. In attacking the applications verification problem this way we essentially traded one set of problems for another. In principle we should have been able to verify any CAP application directly from the original specification of the CAP. Instead, we first solved the more general problem of determining when CAP programs could be understood in terms of a sequential execution model. We believe that this effort was very well invested as the correctness of pipelined implementations relative to another abstract behavioural model is one of the most important questions in processor design today.

From a formal methods point of view, we believe that this work is valuable as a timely example of the application of formal verification techniques to an industrial processor design, and this example demonstrates that the ACL2 theorem prover is powerful enough to produce important results for real commercial designs. The CAP instruction pipeline is certainly not the most complex instruction pipeline that has been formally specified and analysed. Although others have considered a few instructions on a pipelined commercial processor design, or all instructions on academic examples, our results cover *every* instruction sequence on a commercially designed processor. This work is also the only case that we are aware of where the problem of the equivalence of pipelined and non-pipelined models is completely contingent on the program being executed, rather than predominately an intrinsic property of the hardware implementation.

From an engineering point of view, we believe that a specification like an "ill-formed" instruction sequence specification has value by itself, but is even more valuable when the quality and completeness of the specification has been checked by proofs of its important properties. The introduction of the sequential execution model and the proof of equivalence adds tremendous value above that of the specification itself. We added further value to the specification by including it in the prototype hazard analysis tool. This tool gives a CAP programmer the benefits of the mechanically-checked pipeline hazard specification without requiring any knowledge of formal methods. Within the limitations of our models, our equivalence hypothesis has been shown to be a complete specification of instruction sequences that do not cause the behaviour of the pipelined CAP to diverge from the sequential execution model. This is obviously an important piece of information that should be useful to Motorola as the CAP documentation is refined, and new CAP programmers are trained.

5.8 Verified Applications

Having completed our analysis of the CAP instruction pipeline discussed in the preceding section, we turned to the problem of program verification. We successfully demonstrated the utility of our specification of the CAP for formal reasoning by verifying DSP applications programs written in the CAP assembly language (CASM). These code verifications represent the mechanical verification of code for a superscalar architecture. We know of no other formal specification involving such a machine being used as the basis for a mechanical verification.

Our approach to the formal specification of the CAP and verification of CAP programs was inspired to a very large extent by Yu's work on automated proofs of object code for the Motorola MC68020 processor using the Nqthm theorem prover (Yu, 1992). Yu offered several philosophical reasons for verifying object code rather than high-level programs, but our motivation here is more pragmatic: there is no compiler targeting the CAP. The CAP architecture is highly specialised, and it requires a tremendous amount of knowledge and skill to program the CAP efficiently and effectively. For at least the time being all CAP programs will be coded by hand in assembly language.

Thanks to the excellent foundation provided by Yu's work, and the improvement that ACL2 represents over Nqthm, we were able to extend Yu's methods in several important ways. By many measures the programming model of the CAP is much more complicated than the MC68020. The CAP architecture includes 252 programmer-visible data and control registers, which in our formal model are represented as a deeply nested, hierarchical state structure. Regarding control complexity, the determination of the next program counter on the CAP is a function of as many as 10 different registers in the instruction sequencing unit. All of the program verifications we reported have invariants that mention more registers than even *exist* in the programmer's view of the MC68020. Our results demonstrate that it is possible to couple Yu's general approach with the power of the ACL2 theorem prover to automate object code proofs for large, complex, real-world processor models.

We have verified two CAP assembly language programs: a finite-impulse response (FIR) filter and a 5-peak search algorithm. The FIR filter is an archetypical DSP application, a discrete-time convolution of an input signal with a set of filter

coefficients. This FIR code is one that we developed specifically as an example, although it is based on a FIR algorithm for the CAP originally coded by a Motorola
engineer. We proved that the code computes an appropriate fixed-precision result,
but did not address any of the numerical analysis or DSP content of the algorithm.
The second program is a high-speed searching application. This application uses
specialised data paths in the CAP adder array to locate the 5 maxima of an input data
vector in just over one clock cycle per input data vector element. The 5-peak search
is a fascinating example of an application with a straightforward specification, implemented by a clever combination of hardware and software, whose correctness is
far from obvious. In this case the code we verified was obtained directly from the
CAP program ROM, exactly as written by a Motorola engineer.

5.8.1 Method

We reason about the behaviour of CAP object code using our so-called *non-
pipelined* model of the CAP. Although the CAP is implemented with a three-stage
instruction pipeline, it turns out that for most applications, most of the effects due to
the pipelined implementation are transparent to the programmer. Our non-pipelined
model does include those parts of the pipelined execution that are always visible, but
generally speaking one can view the CAP as executing each instruction sequentially
and atomically. Briefly, the use of the non-pipelined model of the CAP to reason
about the behaviour of an application is contingent on two factors:

- non-interfering host: The CAP is a co-processor to another processor referred to
  as the *host processor*. Our code proofs assume that the host processor is not interrupting the CAP or issuing illegal commands to the CAP while an application
  is running. In general, interrupting the CAP during the execution of an application is not something that can be recovered from. Therefore interrupts and other
  similar host commands are disallowed;
- pipeline equivalence hypothesis: Certain instruction sequences have the potential to expose the instruction pipeline in ways not compensated for by our non-
  pipelined model of the CAP. The behaviour of the pipelined and non-pipelined
  models are only equivalent if the instruction stream being executed can be proved
  to satisfy a rigorously defined set of conditions. We perform this proof as an integral part of the verification of every CAP application.

The justification for using the non-pipelined model of the CAP was based on the
formal simulator for the non-pipelined machine:

np-cap\$state-n(cap-$state$, $input$-$list$, n),

which models the effects of inputs provided by the host processor. None of the
applications we verified depend on I/O with the host processor. For code proofs we
use a simplified formal simulator in which the host is assumed to be completely
inert, i.e., one in which the input stream is constant and benign:

cap-step-n(cap-$state$, n).

We do not see this simplifying assumption as a significant loss of generality. For these experiments we chose to focus our efforts on demonstrating that the CAP specification can be used to reason about the behaviour of CAP applications, with a reasonable but not excessive concern for the generality of the results.

The specification and proof method is straightforward. We verify a CAP program by proving a theorem of the following general form:

precondition(*cap-state, arg1, . . . , argn*)
$\land$ cap-state-p(*cap-state*)
$\rightarrow$ postcondition(cap-step-n(*cap-state*,
                    t_prog(*cap-state, arg1, . . . , argn*)),
                    arg1, . . . , argn)

The precondition is an assertion about the initial machine state at the entry point to the program, and may mention zero or more arguments of the program or its specification. Informally, the precondition includes the requirements that the program counter be set to the entry point address, that the program memory and opcode memories are initialised properly, that the parameters are properly set up either in registers or memory, and that there is enough sequencer stack space to execute the program without overflowing the stacks. The hypothesis of the correctness theorem also includes a separate condition that the formal state argument is well-formed.

The postcondition is an assertion about the final machine state after execution of the program, including the return to the caller for subprogram verification. The postcondition may also mention zero or more arguments of the program or its specification. We require that the postcondition hold after some number of execution cycles of the non-pipelined machine, where the number of cycles may be dependent on the initial state and/or the program parameters. Thus an important part of every program proof is the construction of a function that computes the exact number of machine cycles[5] required to execute the program for the given parameters. Informally, the postcondition includes the requirement that the program counter be set to the correct return address, that the sequencer stacks are in an appropriate state, and that appropriate elements of the state have not been modified. Most importantly, the postcondition asserts that the final state is consistent with the program specification, which is stated as part of the postcondition predicate.

5.8.2 Techniques: The FIR Proof

The theorems that we prove about CAP application programs are completely based on the semantics of our non-pipelined model of the CAP, which is legitimised from the pipeline equivalence proof. This model is a formal, executable, behavioural-level ACL2 simulator for the CAP. Our methodology involves stating and proving assertions about the formal model of the state of the CAP before, during, and after the

---

[5] The CAP never delays, cancels, or stalls instruction, thus a new instruction always begins execution every machine cycle.

execution of a CAP program. The proof procedure is conceptually very straightforward. We first identify logical 'cut points' in the programs, i.e., convenient places to break the proof of correctness into manageable pieces. We then define an assertion predicate for each of the program cut points. We next prove that the symbolic expansion of the non-pipelined CAP specification from one cut point to the next, for the proper number of machine cycles, yields a state satisfying the assertion for the next cut point. Finally, all of the point-to-point proofs are linked together by simple backchaining.

In the following we give a brief account of these steps for the FIR filter application. For the present purposes the details of the program assertions are irrelevant.

In the FIR filter proof we identified 12 cut points in the 31-line program. For example, the lemma below characterises the execution of the first three instructions of the FIR filter prologue.

THEOREM: precondition-cut0
   precondition (*entry-state*) ∧ cap-state-p (*entry-state*)
→ cut0 (cap-step-n (*entry-state*, *cut0* − *entry-point*),
      entry-state)

This theorem states that if we start in a state that satisfies our precondition, then executing up to the first cut point yields a state that satisfies cut0. Note that the *entry state* is carried along by the intermediate assertions since the eventual postcondition describes a computation with respect to the *entry state*.

It is interesting to note that we found it necessary to partition straight-line code, like the 24-line prologue of the FIR filter, to make the verification problem tractable. Symbolic expansion of the CAP state produces large symbolic terms. When the CAP specification is expanded for multiple cycles the sizes of the terms grow exponentially. This is due to the fact that many behaviours of the CAP state are simply left as symbolic expressions, e.g., the evolving state of the host interface unit. In the FIR example we found that groups of 6 or 7 simple instructions represented the upper limit of our patience of waiting for the ACL2 prover to complete a proof. For longer instruction sequences it was more time-effective to partition the problem by inserting cut points and creating intermediate assertions.

The heart of the FIR filter routine is a REPEAT loop nested inside a DO loop. To prove the DO and REPEAT loops correct required inductive proofs. We simplified the problem by separating out the problems of the proof of the inductive step, which could be quite involved, from the overall inductive structure of the proof. For example, the proof of correctness of the inner loop of the FIR filter, which is a REPEAT loop, is done in two steps:

THEOREM: inner-loop-step
      inner-loop (*cap-state*, *outer-loop-state*,
                entry-state, *!points*, *!taps*)
  ∧ cap-state-p (*cap-state*)
  ∧ cap-state-p (*outer-loop-state*)

$\wedge$ cap-state-p(*entry-state*)
$\wedge$ $0 < $ *!taps*
$\rightarrow$ inner-loop(cap-step(*cap-state*), *outer-loop-state*,
          entry-state, *!points*, *!taps* $- 1$)

THEOREM: run-inner-loop
       inner-loop(*s*, *outer-loop-state*,
                   entry-state, *!points*, *!taps*)
   $\wedge$ cap-state-p(*s*)
   $\wedge$ cap-state-p(*outer-loop-state*)
   $\wedge$ cap-state-p(*entry-state*)
   $\wedge$ naturalp(*!taps*)
$\rightarrow$ inner-loop(cap-step-n(*s*, *!taps*), *outer-loop-state*,
          entry-state, *!points*, 0)

The first lemma, inner-loop-step, shows that one execution of the repeated instruction re-establishes the invariant inner-loop, as long as the number of taps remaining (*!taps*) is non-zero. The proof of inner-loop-step is accomplished by automated symbolic rewriting. Once we have the lemma inner-loop-step, the inductive proof of run-inner-loop is trivial.

When we said above that the point-to-point proofs are accomplished by symbolic rewriting, we are obviously glossing over much detail. The program correctness assertions for the CAP are very complex, containing dozens of individual conjuncts, many of which state the equality of the contents of formal registers with abstract expressions. Dealing with these equalities was a major challenge in program proof efforts. Briefly, we found that the best way to deal with hypotheses containing a large number of equalities was not to allow the hypotheses to expand, but rather to store these types of hypotheses as directed rewrite rules. For example, the specification initialization-invariant describes some of the register contents after an initialisation sequence in the FIR filter program.

DEFINITION:
initialization-invariant(*cap-state*, *entry-state*)
=
let *prec1* **be** get-cap('prec1, *cap-state*),
   xsn1 **be** get-cap('xsn1, *cap-state*),
   ysn1 **be** get-cap('ysn1, *cap-state*),
   zxsp1 **be** get-cap('zxsp1, *cap-state*),
   lc1 **be** get-cap('lc1, *cap-state*),
   lc2 **be** get-cap('lc2, *cap-state*)
   in
   linear-addressing-p(*cap-state*)
$\wedge$ *prec1* $= 2$
$\wedge$ *xsn1* $= 1$

$\wedge$ $ysn1 = 1$
$\wedge$ $zxsp1 = $ coeff-base $(entry\text{-}state)$
$\wedge$ $lc1 = $ points $(entry\text{-}state)$
$\wedge$ $lc2 = $ taps $(entry\text{-}state)$

In the proofs involving this assertion, we arrange it such that the definition of initialization-invariant is not allowed to expand, and instead use the following equivalent form of the assertion as a rewrite rule:

THEOREM: defp-backchain-initialization-invariant
    initialization-invariant $(cap\text{-}state, entry\text{-}state)$
$\rightarrow$ **let** *prec1* **be** get-cap $('\texttt{prec1}, cap\text{-}state)$,
    xsn1 **be** get-cap $('\texttt{xsn1}, cap\text{-}state)$,
    ysn1 **be** get-cap $('\texttt{ysn1}, cap\text{-}state)$,
    zxsp1 **be** get-cap $('\texttt{zxsp1}, cap\text{-}state)$,
    lc1 **be** get-cap $('\texttt{lc1}, cap\text{-}state)$,
    lc2 **be** get-cap $('\texttt{lc2}, cap\text{-}state)$
    in
    linear-addressing-p $(cap\text{-}state)$
$\wedge$ $prec1 = 2$
$\wedge$ $xsn1 = 1$
$\wedge$ $ysn1 = 1$
$\wedge$ $zxsp1 = $ coeff-base $(entry\text{-}state)$
$\wedge$ $lc1 = $ points $(entry\text{-}state)$
$\wedge$ $lc2 = $ taps $(entry\text{-}state)$

Storing assertions as directed rewrite rules is perhaps the biggest single factor that allowed us to successfully complete these proofs.

    Once lemmas linking the various program cut points are in place, program correctness has been reduced to trivial rewriting and backchaining. The total correctness of the FIR filter is stated by the following lemma:

THEOREM: correctness
    precondition $(s) \wedge$ cap-state-p (s)
$\rightarrow$ postcondition (cap-step-n $(s, \text{t\_fir}(s)), s)$

The function t_fir gives the run time of the application, in CAP clock cycles, as a function of the initial state (which contains the program parameters.) The function t_fir has a special structure to aid program verification, but can easily be shown to have the following value:

THEOREM: characterize-t_fir
let *points* **be** points $(cap\text{-}state)$,
    taps **be** taps $(cap\text{-}state)$
    in

parameter-invariant(*cap-state*)
$\rightarrow$ t_fir(*cap-state*) = *points* * (*taps* + 4) + 26

5.8.3 Remarks

We approached the problem of verifying assembly language programs using a general-purpose theorem prover, ACL2. These program proofs would not have been possible without the features of a general-purpose theorem prover such as induction, rewriting, and linear arithmetic. ACL2 is particularly well suited to this type of problem because of its straightforward logic, powerful heuristics and decision procedures, and high degree of automation. We have demonstrated that it is possible to use a formal specification of a complex commercial processor as the basis for interesting proofs about the behaviour of programs on that processor. There was very little about this work that was simple or straightforward, and our successes were achieved after numerous false starts. Our ability to complete these examples was due in large part to the fact that Computational Logic, Inc. has a great deal of experience in solving problems of this kind.

In this work we used ACL2 as an unadorned "proof-engine", and the power of this proof engine was usually not a limiting factor. Once we had discovered the secret to automating these proofs, the most time-consuming operation was the frankly tedious construction of the verbose program invariants. This mass of detail was unavoidable in this case due to the complexity of the underlying machine, the large number of parallel operations, and the low level of abstraction at which we were working. This problem highlights the need for application-specific interfaces to general-purpose proof systems. For example, we can imagine an interface to ACL2 that is geared to developing proofs about generic, programmable state machines. Such a system would have been an immense help in taking care of the large amount of 'bookkeeping' necessary for these proofs to hang together.

5.9 Effort Summary and Conclusion

We used our ACL2 specification for Motorola's CAP to verify the FIR and 5-peak search algorithms for the CAP, demonstrating that it is possible to mechanically verify complex algorithms on a complicated architecture. We showed that our non-pipelined model of the CAP was equivalent to the pipelined model when CAP programs obey certain constraints. All definitions and proofs were carried out using the ACL2 theorem-proving system.

5.9.1 Effort Summary

The CAP project was 31 months in duration. There was a great deal of work performed on this project which has not been discussed here, as this presentation concentrates on the mathematical modelling and proofs that were performed. Without the enabling efforts given by other team members, this project would not have been possible. Brock was the only formal methods expert to work on this project continuously. Brock was responsible for most of the CAP ACL2 model. In addition, he produced the non-pipelined abstraction of the CAP, invented the pipeline equivalence condition, mechanically proved the conditional equivalence of the two models, and used ACL2 to prove the two microcode programs reported here. Several other researchers and engineers contributed to the formal methods part of the project (e.g., the validation testing of the ACL2 against the SPW, a mechanically checked correctness proof for the address generation unit, an ACL2 macro to help formulate lemmas for expanding function definitions, a CAP assembler, a pin-level specification of the CAP I/O interface) but their work has not been the focus of this presentation and is not further discussed here. The mathematical modelling effort can be broken down as follows:

- **The ACL2 CAP Specification**: 15 months. Brock produced the first executable version of the specification in about 6 months, while resident at Motorola and interacting with the CAP design team. During that time he was also learning ACL2[6]. The first model was simple and incomplete. As the project progressed, a 4-valued logic was introduced, and the pipeline, full ALU and I/O modules were included. In addition, the CAP design evolved more or less continuously during this interval and the formal model tracked the design. Finally, ACL2 evolved also and the specification had to converted from ACL2 Version 1.7 to Version 1.8, which dramatically changed the treatment of guards, making proofs much easier;
- **Reusable Books**: 6 months. To perform proofs about the CAP specification many ACL2 books about modular arithmetic, logical operations on integers, hardware arithmetic and bit vectors, arrays, record structures, and list processing were created. These books are not CAP-specific and are hence reusable;
- **Equivalence of Non-Pipelined Model to the Pipelined Model**: 5 months. The non-pipelined model of the CAP shares perhaps 90% of its definition with the (pipelined) CAP specification. It was relatively easy to produce; however it required the reorganisation of the CAP specification so that such sharing was possible. The first conditional equivalence proof was carried out on a simplified model of the CAP and then repeated when the host interface module was added. A serendipitous visit by David Dill occurred just as Brock was beginning the first proof; Dill explained the methods in (Burch and Dill, 1994), which proved very useful. The details of the equivalence condition were derived from failed proofs. The condition was later weakened to so that it would accept the ROM-resident DSP application codes and the (now largely automatic) proof was repeated a third time to confirm the new condition. Brock then incorporated the predicate into an (unverified) automated tool that analyses CAP programs for pipeline visibility conditions. The tool requires no formal methods expertise to use or to interpret its output;
- **The FIR proof**: 1 month. Some of the work on reusable books was done in response to difficulties encountered during this task. In addition, CAP-specific

---

[6] He was already an accomplished Nqthm user.

books were developed for controlling the unwinding of the CAP model during such proofs. Both the FIR and 5PEAK work benefit from the fact that the non-pipelined model is simpler to reason about;

– **The 5-PEAK Search Proof**: 1 month. About half of the time here was devoted to the development of the specification of the 5PEAK code. After several false starts, it eventually involved the idea of sorting an arbitrary amount of data with a generalisation of the 5PEAK algorithm and then collecting the first 5 values. J Moore spent one week proving the fundamental properties of the generalised sort algorithm.

The times reported above are a rough estimate of the effort required to create the graduated sequence of ACL2 events that lead the ACL2 theorem prover to the proofs for the first time. This sequence of ACL2 theorem-prover definition and proof requests can be replayed in 2:30 (2 hours and 30 minutes) on a Sun Microsystems Sparcstation-20/712 with dual 75 MHz SuperSparc-II CPU's (each with 1 megabyte of cache) and 256 megabytes of main memory. Many of the lemmas are shared between the three main proofs (equivalence, FIR, and 5PEAK). A book need be certified only once and thereafter can simply be referenced without proof. The pipeline equivalence proof takes 1:45 (1:29 of which is spent certifying books that are reused in the two applications proofs). The analysis of the FIR algorithm can then be done in 33 minutes (17 minutes of which is spent certifying books used also in 5PEAK). The 5PEAK proof then takes 13 minutes.

5.9.2 Conclusions

It is possible to formally specify devices of commercial complexity. All aspects of the CAP user-level specification were captured including the CAP's I/O behaviour. The CAP specification is the largest formal specification of which we are aware, and its simulation performance is several times better than the compiled C-based simulator produced by the SPW toolsuite even though the formal specification is four-valued and the SPW specification is only two-valued.

We believe that the CLI specification of the CAP represents a truly commercial-sized example of using mathematical models to represent a hardware architecture specification. We know of no other effort where a super-scalar machine with a pipeline has been proved equivalent to an equivalent non-pipelined super-scalar machine. We believe that the challenge of using mathematical modelling techniques commercially will be the integration of such techniques with commercial tools.

Acknowledgements

This work was carried out entirely while the authors worked for Computational Logic, Inc.

The paper entitled *Formally Specifying and Mechanically Verifying Programs for the Motorola Complex Arithmetic Processor DSP* (Brock and Hunt, 1997b), and which appeared in the proceedings of the 1997 ICCD conference, is a shorter summary of this chapter.

CHAPTER 6

Bridging the E-Business Gap Through Formal Verification

Yonit Kesten, Amit Klein, Amir Pnueli and Gil Raanan

6.1 Introduction

Since its public emergence in the beginning of the 1990s, the Internet's role as a carrier of electronic business has increased at an ever growing rate. Many commercial organisations have realised the huge potential for revenue from e-business and are already conducting significant portions of their business online. Accessing the Internet for doing business has become an everyday experience, whether it is for buying books, managing financial accounts or submitting yearly tax reports.

But this race towards e-business is slowed down by people's lack of trust in the electronic medium, and the fear of exposing their most valuable personal and business information to an unsafe environment. Indeed the fact the Internet is readily accessible to everyone (honest users as well as sophisticated thieves) combined with the complexity of today's e-business applications, makes it very hard to provide adequate privacy protection to the online trader. A clear indication of this difficulty can be found in the increasing number of news reports describing successful attacks on companies conducting business online. Every such incident takes the trust in e-business a big step backwards.

Solving this trust problem requires, as a key component, a security solution. This solution must be robust enough to provide an extreme level of assurance that sensitive data is kept protected, even against the more sophisticated and persistent of the "online thieves". For this reason, Perfecto Technologies, a US/Israeli based software company, has chosen to incorporate formal methods in the development of its e-business security product. It is our belief that the open, commercial use of formal verification will contribute to a move on the part of the public towards

©1999 Perfecto Technologies Ltd. Reproduced with permission

trusting e-business. Furthermore it is our understanding that formal verification is a key technology for assuring the high level of protection required.

This chapter describes the application of formal methods for the verification of a software product, which delivers e-commerce security for the Internet. The work is an ongoing effort that involves both the company's staff, and academic researchers. Results of the research are used as feedback into the software development process, as well as improving our understanding of formal verification of a software project.

The rest of the chapter is organised as follows. In Section 6.2 we give a short description of both the hardware platform, and the software to be verified.

In Section 6.3 we present the verification framework, discussing our choice of verification tools, system description languages and property specification languages. We discuss problems encountered with these languages in today's existing verification tools, explaining our choice of performing deductive verification manually.

In Section 6.4 we present a compositional model-checking verification of the Top Level Design (TLD) of our system, using the SPIN tool. We present our methodology for using the well known assume-guarantee paradigm, tailored for the specific characteristics of our system and the SPIN tool.

In Section 6.5 we discuss the verification of the detailed design of our system, combining model-checking and deductive proof techniques.

We conclude in Section 6.6 with a summary of the presentation and some advice to developers of tools for deductive verification.

6.2 Description of Application

The software to be verified is an e-commerce Internet security server ("the product"). The software is usually placed between the e-commerce server (typically a web-server which provides web enabled interface to the e-commerce engine - database server, application server, etc.) and the Internet, usually on the seller's premises. The Internet connection of the e-commerce server must pass through the security server (the product). Clients of the e-commerce applications access the e-commerce server across the Internet, and through the seller's Internet gateway (routers, firewalls, etc.), and finally through the security server. The product, therefore, completely controls all the e-commerce transactions. Monitoring is performed at the application level, that is, the product "understands" the protocol used for the transactions.

The product consists only of software, running on top of an operating system. The hardware platform consists of two CPUs, connected through a dedicated bus. A typical configuration would be two PCs connected via an Ethernet cable, but many other configurations are possible. A patent pending technology, coupled with the above architecture, enables the separation of security functions and non-security functions, such that the non-security functions cannot compromise the security of the system. Hence, it is required to verify only the security functions. In the above

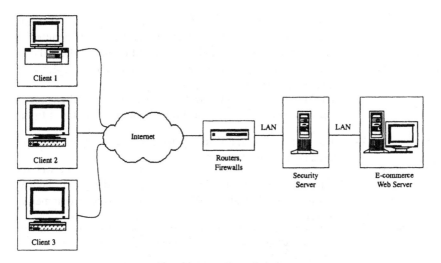

Figure 6.1. Product orientation

configuration, the security functions are performed in one CPU (the *secure CPU*), and the non-security functions are performed in another CPU (the *insecure CPU*).

As presented in Figure 6.2, the security functions comprise of the following modules:

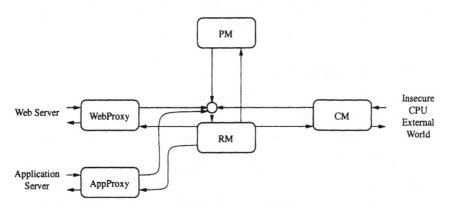

Figure 6.2. System structure

CM — This module interfaces with the physical device driver of the bus which connects the two CPUs. Data to be transmitted to the insecure CPU are handed to the CM (by the RM), and data that arrives from the insecure CPU is handled in the CM, which relays it to the RM.

RM — The "nerve center" of the system. It is a data dispatcher, receiving data from various other modules and dispatching it to the destination modules.

PM — The security engine of the system. Processes all the transactions to/from the e-commerce server.

WebProxy — This is a proxy module which communicates with the web (e-commerce) server. The WebProxy receives data from the RM and relays it (typically over TCP/IP) to the web (e-commerce) server.

AppProxy — A proxy module which provides a function similar to that of WebProxy, for a non web-enabled server.

Incoming data (from the insecure CPU connected to the external, potentially adversary, world) arrives at the CM, which relays it to the RM, which routes it to the PM. The PM processes the data, ensures that it is safe, and returns it to the RM, which moves it to the WebProxy, which delivers it to the final destination, the e-commerce server. The software is written mostly in C++ (with some GUI functions in Java), containing tens of thousands of lines of code. It is important to note that not all the code is relevant to the verification effort: there are some functions, notably the GUI (Graphic User Interface), which have nothing to do with the (security) properties to be demonstrated, and thus are irrelevant to the whole verification process. These functions are not included in the above description.

6.3 The Verification Framework

As claimed in (Manna and Pnueli, 1995), a framework for formal verification should consist of the following components:

- a *computational model*, providing a common semantic base for the system and the properties we wish to establish for it;
- a *specification language* in which we can express the properties that need to be verified;
- a *system description language* in which we can describe the system whose properties need to be verified;
- a family of *verification techniques* by which such a verification can be successfully carried out. These usually include model checking, methods for deductive verification, and combinations thereof.

For our verification effort, we use the computational model of *fair discrete system* (FDS) which is a slightly modified variant of the *fair transition system* (FTS), which is presented in (Manna and Pnueli, 1995) and underlies the *stanford temporal verifier* (STeP).

The official specification language we use is (*linear*) *temporal logic* (LTL) (Manna and Pnueli, 1995). However, in the context of verification by SPIN, we often express temporal properties by the corresponding automaton. In this chapter we report only about the verification of *safety properties*.

For the set of verification techniques, we use model checking by SPIN, and manual deductive verification, using the deductive verification methodology expounded in (Manna and Pnueli, 1995) and implemented in STeP(Bjørner *et al.*, 1995). Eventually, we intend to switch to computer-aided deductive verification by the STeP tool.

Currently, we use two system description languages according to the verification technique applied. For model checking with SPIN, we use the SPIN system description language PROMELA. For deductive verification, the natural candidate would have been SPL, the system description language of STeP (and the one recommended in (Manna and Pnueli, 1995)). However, in order to provide an adequate and faithful representation of the concurrency programmed in our product (which is programmed in C++), we found it necessary to reason in terms of an extended version of SPL, to which we refer as SPL^{++}.

The main feature missing from SPL in its current form is the ability to define a class of processes and instantiate them dynamically as the need arises. This feature is central to C++ and also exists in PROMELA.

The inability of SPL in its current form to express dynamic process creation was the main obstacle to the use of the STeP tool for deductive verification in our project. This led to the decision to revert to manual deductive verification, where we use SPL^{++} or sometimes even the actual C++ program as the system description language. As soon as the STeP tool is enhanced to support SPL^{++} or a similar extension of SPL, we intend to incorporate computer-aided deduction into our process.

6.3.1 Extending SPL into SPL^{++}

Wishing to minimise the number of extensions, we realised that we could use an existing mechanism in SPL for declaring a process class and needed a single new statement which created a new instant of a process class.

To define a process class named P we included in our SPL^{++} program the following statement:

$$\Big\|_{i=1} P[i] :: \left[\begin{array}{l} \textbf{loop forever do} \\ \quad \left[\begin{array}{ll} \ell_0 : & \textbf{dormant} \\ & \cdots \\ \ell_k : & \cdots \end{array}\right] \end{array}\right]$$

The schematic statement **dormant** represents the state of the process when asleep. According to this view, infinitely many (virtual) processes, all of which are initially dormant, are introduced when the program starts. The act of "creation" of a new instance is represented by (locating and then) waking a dormant process.

Borrowing from the syntax of PROMELA, we introduce the statement:

$$id := run(P),$$

which wakes a dormant process and places its identity (an index) in the variable *id*.

To illustrate the application of these two concepts, consider the C++ program SUM-SQUARES, presented in Figure 6.3.

```
class Number
{   // Number object, with the obvious interface
    public:
        Number(int v) // Constructor
        {   num=v; }
        // arithmetic operators, etc.
        int square()
        {   return num*num; }
    private:
        int num;
};
void main()
{   int n,sum=0;
    // Sum the first 10 squares
    for(n=1;n<=10;n++)
    {   Number x(n);      //construct a Number object named x,
                          //                    initialized to n.
        sum+=x.square();  // call the square member function
    }
}
```

Figure 6.3. A C++ program SUM-SQUARES

In Figure 6.4, we present the SPL^{++} representation of program SUM-SQUARES. Note that the class *Number* is represented by *Number[i]*, a parameterised process array, and the method entries to this C++ object have been translated to the (synchronous) channels *cNumber* and *csquare*, which are local to *Number[i]*. While being local, implying that there are individual instances of these channels for each *Number[i]*, they are also *public* in the sense that any external agent which knows the process-id *i* can send and recieve messages through them referring to *Number[i].cNumber* and *Number[i].csquare*.

The invocation Number x(n) of the principal method *Number* has been separated into a wake call for process *Number* followed by a synchronous output of the value of *n* to channel *Number[x].cNumber*, where *x* is the process-id obtained in the wake-up call. Similarly, the C++ invocation c.square() has been translated to a synchronous input from channel *Number[x].csquare*.

We conclude the discussion of the extension of SPL by providing an FDS semantics for the newly introduced statement *run*. Assume that *P[i]* is a parameterised process containing the statement **dormant** at location ℓ_0.

Then, for each occurrence of the statement:

$$m: x := run(P); \widehat{m},$$

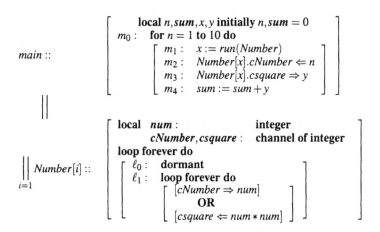

Figure 6.4. The SPL^{++} **representation of program SUM-SQUARES**

we add to the transition relation of the SPL^{++} system the disjunct:

$$\exists i : at\_P[i].\ell_0 \wedge at\_m \wedge x' = i \wedge at'\_P[i].\ell_1 \wedge at'\_\widehat{m} \wedge assigned(\pi, x, P[i].\pi).$$

This disjunct describes the situation where an invoking process is at location m and there exists a process instant $P[i]$ which is at location ℓ_0, and therefore dormant. The transition assigns to x the process-id i, and advances the invoking process and the waken process to locations $\widehat{m}$ and ℓ_1, respectively. The $assigned(\pi, x, P.\pi[i])$ clause states that the values of all other variables, i.e. all variables excluding π (the control variable of the invoking process), x, and $P[i].\pi$ (the control variable of the awakened process) are preserved.

6.4 Model Checking the TLD

Our first formal verification effort concentrated on the verification of the top level design (TLD) of the system. Through this experiment, we hoped to identify a method powerful enough to handle the verification of the complete system. In this experiment, we chose to use the model checker SPIN (Holzmann, 1991) which was advertised as being specially designed for the verification of software and communication protocols, in particular.

Unfortunately, in spite of the high abstraction we applied in deriving the TLD view of the system, it was still too big to be completely verified in one go. This forced us to revert to compositional model checking based on the assume-guarantee paradigm. This paradigm is very well known and many variants have been developed over the years, e.g., (Jones, 1983), (Barringer and Kuiper, 1985), (Pnueli, 1985), (de Roever, 1985), (Zwiers, 1989), (Pandya and Joseph, 1991), (Abadi and

Lamport, 1993), (Jonsson, 1994), (Kurshan and McMillan, 1995), (Abadi and Lamport, 1995), (Collette and Cau, 1995), (Clarke *et al.*, 1996), and (Wu *et al.*, 1997). Yet, in order to use this paradigm in our context we had to develop our own variant (heavily inspired by all this previous work).

In this section, we report on our approach to the verification of the top-level design of our system, using compositional model checking with the SPIN tool.

6.4.1 Systems and Their Safety Properties

We will illustrate our approach to compositional verification on the simple case of two processes communicating by synchronous channels, as depicted in Figure 6.5.

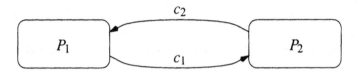

Figure 6.5. Two processes

We assume that processes in the system are presented as PROMELA programs, where communication is restricted to synchronous (rendezvous) channels. The computational model we use for representing the behaviour of systems and their specifications assumes V a finite set of typed *state variables*. In particular, for each channel c_i with range of messages R_i, the set V includes a corresponding variable C_i which ranges over $R_i \cup \perp$, where the special value $\perp$ denotes a state in which there was no communication over channel c_i.

A system *state* is any valuation of the state variables consistent with their types. For a state s and a state variable $x \in V$, we denote by $s[x]$ the value assumed by x in state s. A *run* of a system S is a finite non-empty sequence of states $r : s_0, s_1, \ldots$ such that s_0 satisfies the initial condition, and for every j, $0 < j < |r|$, the state s_j can be obtained from s_{j-1} by executing one of the statements in the program for the system S which is enabled on s_{j-1}. In particular, $C_i = m \neq \perp$ in state s_j iff the statement executed in passing from s_{j-1} to s_j sent the message m on channel c_i, e.g., by a sender executing $c_i!m$ jointly with a receiver executing $c_i?y$.

For a subset of the state variables $U \subseteq V$ and a state s, we denote by $s{\downarrow}_U$ the *projection* of the state s on the subset U. That is, $s{\downarrow}_U$ is the U-state obtained by removing from the state s the valuation of the variables which belong to $V - U$. In particular, $s{\downarrow}_{C_i}$ retains only the value assumed by the variable C_i, namely, the message sent on channel c_i in the step leading to this state (we write $s{\downarrow}_{C_i}$ as an abbreviation for $s{\downarrow}_{\{C_i\}}$). For a run $r : s_0, s_1, \ldots$, we denote by $r{\downarrow}_U$ the projected run $s_0{\downarrow}_U, s_1{\downarrow}_U, \ldots$. Finally, for a run r and a channel variable C_i, we denote by $r{\Downarrow}_{C_i}$ the *compressed projected run* obtained by removing from $r{\downarrow}_{C_i}$ all the bottom elements. For a run r, $r{\Downarrow}_{C_i}$ represents the list of messages emitted on channel c_i during the run in the order of their emission. In the CSP terminology, this is called the c_i-restricted trace of r (Hoare, 1985).

In this study, we were mainly interested in the study of *safety properties* (Lamport, 1977). This is why it is sufficient to consider the semantics of a system as given by the set of all of its runs, and consider as properties to be verified only *safety properties*. A safety property can be formally characterised as a property which is expressible by a temporal formula of the form $\varphi : p$, where p is a *past formula* (Manna and Pnueli, 1990). An equivalent characterisation is that a safety property is one which can be recognised by a finite-state automaton which has no transition from a non-accepting to an accepting control state.

The main feature of a safety property φ is that if it is violated by a run r then it cannot be satisfied by any run extending r. A typical example is the property specifiable by the formula $\varphi : (x > 0)$ stating that, at all states of all runs, the value of x is always positive. It is obvious that if a run r violates φ then one of the states in r must have a non-positive value of x and, therefore, no extension of r can satisfy the requirement "x is always positive".

We write $r \models \varphi$ to denote that the run r satisfies the property φ, and write $S \models \varphi$ if φ is *S-valid*, i.e., all runs of S satisfy r.

A safety formula φ is said to be a *channel property* of channel c if:

C1. $r \models \varphi$ for every r such that $r\Downarrow_c$ is the empty sequence. That is, φ holds over all runs which did not send even a single message on channel c.

C2. If r_1 and r_2 are runs such that $r_1\Downarrow_c = r_2\Downarrow_c$, then $r_1 \models \varphi$ iff $r_2 \models \varphi$. That is, the truth value of φ on a run r is fully determined by $r\Downarrow_c$, the sequence of messages transmitted by the run r on channel c.

6.4.2 A Compositional Proof Rule

Normally, there is no chance of being able to verify, using model checking techniques, any of the properties of the system by submitting the entire system to a model checker such as SPIN. A frequently used approach, which we refer to as the *compositional approach*, is to consider modules (processes) of the system separately and verify every property by considering only the processes which are responsible for the variables on which the property depends.

For example, in the system of Figure 6.5 we may wish to prove two safety properties: φ_1 and φ_2, where each φ_i depends only on the variables determined by process P_i, for $i = 1,2$. This suggests that property φ_1 should be model-checked on a model consisting of process P_1 alone. Unfortunately, while the property φ_1 may depend only on variables manipulated by process P_1 the range of behaviours of P_1 when run alone may differ radically from its behaviours when coupled with P_2. In particular, when run in isolation it may produce a behaviour which violates the property φ_1, while such a behaviour is impossible in the real system due to the interaction and constraints imposed by P_2. There is a danger that we may erroneously conclude that property φ_1 is not valid over the system while, in fact, it is.

To overcome this difficulty, we never study any of the processes in complete isolation. Instead, we typically identify channel properties, say I_1 and I_2 which are intended to capture the properties of the communication on channels c_1 and c_2 which (for our application) is the only way the two processes can interact with one another.

As a first step in the application of this idea, it is necessary to confirm that the proposed channel properties are indeed valid for all computations of the joint system $P_1 \| P_2$. This can be done using rule COMP presented in Figure 6.6.

$$
\begin{array}{lll}
\text{L1.} & P_1 & \models & (I_2 \to I_1) \\
\text{L2.} & P_2 & \models & (I_1 \to I_2) \\
\hline
& P_1 \| P_2 & \models & I_1 \wedge I_2
\end{array}
$$

Figure 6.6. Rule COMP

Such a rule is often described as an *assume-guarantee* paradigm. Premise L1 of the rule can be interpreted by saying that, under the *assumption* that the environment maintains the property I_2 on channel c_2, process P_1 *guarantees* to maintain the property I_1 on channel c_1. Premise L2 states the symmetric obligation for process P_2. The rule claims that if these two obligations hold then both I_1 and I_2 will be maintained in all runs of the combined system $P_1 \| P_2$.

This rule is not sound for arbitrary properties I_1 and I_2. In the general case, the most general conclusion that can be inferred from premises L1 and L2 is $(I_1 \to I_2) \wedge (I_2 \to I_1)$ which does not necessarily imply $I_1 \wedge I_2$. However, in our case we are guaranteed of the following assumptions:

A1. $s_0[C_1] = s_0[C_2] = \bot$, for every initial state s_0. That is, no message has been transmitted on entering the initial state.

A2. I_1 and I_2 are safety channel properties for channels c_1 and c_2, respectively.

A3. At most one message can be transmitted at any execution step. That is, either $s[C_1] = \bot$ or $s[C_2] = \bot$ for every state s appearing in a run of $P_1 \| P_2$.

As we will now show, these assumptions guarantee that rule COMP is sound.

Claim. Under the assumptions A1–A3, rule COMP is sound.

Proof:.

Assume, to the contrary, that rule COMP is unsound. Let $r : s_0, s_1, \ldots, s_n$ one of the shortest counter examples to the rule. That is, r satisfies premises L1 and L2 but does not satisfy the conclusion $I_1 \wedge I_2$.

For $k \leq n$, we denote by $r^{(k)}$ the k-prefix $r^{(k)} : s_0, \ldots, s_k$ of r.
Obviously, $n > 0$. This is because, due to assumption A1, $r^{(0)} \Downarrow_{C_1} = r^{(0)} \Downarrow_{C_2}$ is the empty sequence, and by clause C1 of the definition of a channel property, both I_1 and I_2 should hold over $r^{(0)}$.

Since r is one of the shortest counter-examples, we can assume that $r^{(n-1)} \models I_1 \wedge I_2$. By assumption A3, either $s_n[C_1] = \bot$ or $s_n[C_2] = \bot$, and we assume, with no loss of generality, that $s_n[C_2] = \bot$. Consequently, $r^{(n)}\Downarrow_{C_2} = r^{(n-1)}\Downarrow_{C_2}$ and, due to clause C2 of the definition of a channel property and the fact that $r^{(n-1)}$ satisfies I_2, it follows that also $r^{(n)} = r$ satisfies I_2. Applying premise L1 to r, we conclude that I_1 holds over r. Thus, both I_1 and I_2 are satisfied by r, contradicting our hypothesis that r does not satisfy $I_1 \wedge I_2$. $\square$

Once we establish I_1 and I_2 as valid channel properties for the system $P_1 \| P_2$ we can use them for model-checking any local property φ_1 which only refers to the variables manipulated by process P_1. To do so, we model check the validity of the implication $I_2 \rightarrow \varphi_1$ over process P_1. Note that both this verification task and the ones needed for establishing the premises of rule COMP apply model checking to a single process rather than to the complete system. This is the main advantage of the compositional approach.

Obviously, the method described here can be applied to a system consisting of an arbitrary number of processes, as long as every channel connects a unique sender to a unique receiver.

6.4.3 Implementing the Compositional Verification in SPIN

Since our application involves more than two communicating modules, we decompose the TLD into clusters of processes, each cluster small enough so that it can be locally verified by SPIN. Having defined such a cluster, we identify the incoming and outgoing channels, connecting the cluster to the rest of the design.

In Figure 6.7 we present the general setup of a typical cluster.

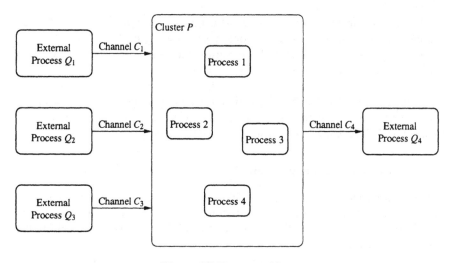

Figure 6.7. Decomposition

The general form of the local verification that has to be applied to each of the clusters is:

$$P \models (I_1 \wedge I_2 \wedge \ldots \wedge I_n \rightarrow J), \tag{6.1}$$

where $I_1, \ldots, I_n$ are the *assumptions* for the behaviour on the incoming channels, such as $C_1, \ldots, C_3$ in Figure 6.7, and J is the property that the cluster *guarantees* on its output channel, such as C_4 in Figure 6.7. It is assumed that $I_1, \ldots, I_n, J$ are channel safety properties. Note that the composition rule requires that we associate a unique invariant $I_{i,j}$ with every channel $C_{i,j}$ connecting cluster P_i to cluster P_j. The invariant $I_{i,j}$ will appear as an assumption (one of the I_k's) in the verification task for cluster P_j and as a guarantee (the J) in the verification task for cluster P_i.

Let us consider how to represent the verification task (6.1) for a representative cluster P to the SPIN tool. Obviously, we can represent the cluster of processes P as a set of concurrent PROMELA processes. The remaining question is how to represent the assumptions $I_1, \ldots, I_n$ and the guarantee J where, up to now, we considered these specifications as temporal formulas.

In theory, SPIN provides a special mechanism for representing non-trivial temporal properties. This is the *never* claim which identifies a single automaton (represented as a PROMELA process) which runs in synchronous parallelism to the application and monitors its behaviour. Unfortunately, this mechanism is too restricted for us since we need to attach to the cluster a set of automata corresponding to the assumptions and the guarantee.

Consequently, we decided to construct our own processes which represented automata and monitor for the satisfaction of their corresponding temporal properties. Unlike the single *never* automaton, these automata processes run in asynchronous parallelism (interleaving) to the rest of the system, but communicate with the cluster via synchronous channels.

For the guarantee property J, we construct an *acceptor process* A, which is an automaton *accepting* precisely the set of sequences satisfying J.

For each assumption property I_i we construct a *generator process* G_i, which is an automaton *generating* precisely the set of all sequences satisfying I_i.

We refer to the set of processes P, G_i and A as the PROMELA *model* for the verification task (6.1). The verification is performed by running the PROMELA model within SPIN. Each generator and acceptor is connected to the cluster by a single channel. In Figure 6.8, we present such a PROMELA model.

6.4.4 Construction of Acceptors and Generators

Since each channel $C_{i,j}$ is associated with a single channel safety property $I_{i,j}$, we have to construct for such a channel first an acceptor $A_{i,j}$ which accepts all the behaviours satisfying $I_{i,j}$, and then a generator $G_{i,j}$ which generates precisely the set of all sequences satisfying $I_{i,j}$.

Acceptors. Construction of acceptors is fairly easy. Assume the channel name is "c", and it should comply with a channel safety property J. We assume that we know how to construct for the property J a finite state deterministic automaton over the finite alphabet of c, with a single error state E (where all other states are accepting), which accepts precisely the sequences satisfying J. The translation of this

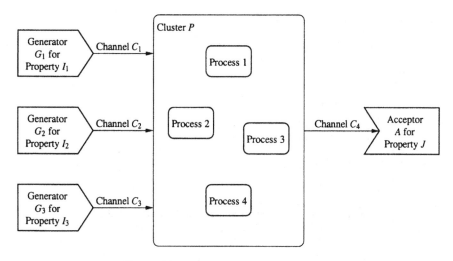

Figure 6.8. A PROMELA **model for a cluster**

automaton to PROMELA is straightforward. Every non-error node of the automaton is represented by the input statement $c?y$, followed by a case selection statement branching to different locations according to the value of the input y. The error state is represented by the statement `assert(0)` which aborts the computation, announcing an error.

For the simplest cases, this *explicit state* representation of the automaton for J and its PROMELA translation is adequate. However, in many cases, the alphabet is structured, such as the integers in the range 0..255 and the conditions are often expressed succinctly by predicates over the alphabet, such as $y < 128$. In these cases, the PROMELA acceptor is represented more compactly using auxiliary variables to represent part of the state.

For example, in Figure 6.9, we present a PROMELA acceptor that accepts all length 3 sequences of integers which form a permutation of $\{1,2,3\}$.

Note that this automaton may reject the input at three locations. It rejects after the first input iff this input is not in the range $[1..3]$. It rejects after the second input iff this input is not in the range $[1..3]$ or it is equal to the first input. Finally, the last input is rejected iff it is not in the range or it equals one of the previous input. Note that the explicit state automaton corresponding to this PROMELA process will have at least 9 states and 20 edges.

Generators. Construction of generators is less straightforward. An important element in the construction of generators is that we should have a systematic way of translating an acceptor to a generator, automatically if possible. This is important because, as we have already mentioned, for each channel $C_{i,j}$ we need an acceptor $A_{i,j}$ and a generator $G_{i,j}$. The soundness of the composition rule hinges on the assumption that the set of sequences generated by $G_{i,j}$ is equal to the set of sequences accepted by $A_{i,j}$, i.e. that they both refer to precisely the same property.

```
active proctype accept_c5()
{
   byte x,y,z;

   atomic
   {
   do
   :: c?x -> assert((1<=x) && (x<=3));
      c?y -> assert((1<=y) && (y<=3) && (y!=x));
      c?z -> assert((1<=z) && (z<=3) && (z!=x) && (z!=y));
   od;
   }
   unless end_ver;
}
```

Figure 6.9. An acceptor for all permutations over $\{1,2,3\}$

In a case where the acceptor is derived from an explicit-state automaton, the conversion from acceptor to generator is straightforward. Every edge connecting automaton state q_i to $q_j \neq E$ and labelled by the letter A, should be translated to the PROMELA statement $c!A$ connecting the locations corresponding to q_i to q_j. In a case where q_j equals E, the error state, we omit the corresponding output statement. Such a generator will never generate a wrong output.

The situation is more involved if the acceptor process uses auxiliary variables, such as the acceptor of Figure 6.9. Due to space limitations, in Figure 6.10 we will only present the generator obtained by applying our systematic conversion to this acceptor.

```
active proctype generate_c()
{
   byte x,y,z;

   atomic
   {
   do
   :: x = random(1,3); c!x;
      y = random(1,3); end_var = (y==x); c!y;
      z = random(1,3); end_var = ((z==x) || (z==y)); c!z;
   od;
   }
   unless end_ver;
}
```

Figure 6.10. A generator for all permutations over $\{1,2,3\}$

The way this generator operates is that it first draws a random number in the range 1..3 and outputs it. Next it draws a second random number y in the same range. After drawing it, the generator applies the same test to y relative to x. If y should be rejected, the automaton does not cause an error abortion of the complete system by asserting *false*. Instead, it raises a special Boolean flag end_var which causes the complete system to terminate immediately but in a non-error state. The reason for this different behaviour is that if the generator was planning to send a wrong value, then one of the assumptions would be about to be violated and we are not interested in the behaviour of the tested cluster if the assumptions do not hold. Technically, immediate termination is ensured by enclosing all processes in the system by the unless end_var clause which interrupts and terminates all processes as soon as the flag end_var is raised.

6.4.5 Results of the TLD Verification

The case study described below served to demonstrate the strength of the method together with its limitations. Eventually, it was decided to discontinue the application of this method, although the techniques developed may be of some use in further developments.

The case study included the 5 modules presented in Fig. 6.1 : WebProxy, PM, CM, RM and AppProxy, plus an additional trivial module that has been added for technical reasons. The data transmitted over the channels connecting these modules contains 3 or 4 fields (depending on the channel): a "destination" field, a "session" field, and a "data" field, sometimes a "from" field. In the table below, we summarise for each module the number of incoming and outgoing channels, and the number of overall processes (including acceptors and generators) which were involved in its modular verification:

Module Name	Incoming Channels	Outgoing Channels	Overall Processes
CM	2	2	7
RM	1	4	7
PM	1	1	4
WebProxy	2	2	7
AppProxy	2	2	7

The results from the verification, carried out by SPIN, were all positive. However, the execution (on a Pentium-II/333MHz, 100MHz bus, 512KB L2 cache, 256MB SDRAM, SPIN-3.2.3/Linux-2.0.29, -DSAFETY, -DMA=117 used) took too long (6 hours and 46 minutes for the most complex module - RM). The experiment is considered, therefore, to be unsuccessful in that it appears to reveal a scalability problem inherent to the implementation of the acceptors/generators scheme. While we gained a lot of expertise and insight by developing and applying this technique, and managed to verify a certain portion of the TLD, we decided not to use this method for the verification of the detailed design.

us, 512KB L2 cache, 256MB SDRAM, SPIN-3.2.3/Linux-2.0.29, -DSAFETY, -DMA=117 used) took too long (6 hours and 46 minutes for the most complex module - RM). The experiment is considered, therefore, to be unsuccessful in that it appears to reveal a scalability problem inherent to the implementation of the acceptors/generators scheme. While we gained a lot of expertise and insight by developing and applying this technique, and managed to verify a certain portion of the TLD, we decided not to use this method for the verification of the detailed design.

6.5 Detailed Design Verification

The results reported in the last section demonstrated that SPIN alone (or rather, model checking alone) cannot meet the requirements imposed by a complex software system. At the beginning we thought that the problem was inherent to an explicit-state model checker such as SPIN, and that switching to a symbolic model checker, such as SMV, may solve the scalability problem. Indeed, we tried SMV on a subset of the case studies and observed a speedup factor of about 1000:1. However we soon realised that no matter how fast they are, no model checking tool is able to handle the complete problem; in particular, model checkers cannot handle data intensive problems.

6.5.1 Why Combine the Methods?

It appears that the most versatile and powerful method of handling data-intensive problems is to use a deductive method. The main candidate tools for supporting deductive verification are STeP (Bjørner *et al.*, 1995) and PVS (Owre *et al.*, 1992). After some preliminary attempts we ran into the problem that none of these tools provided us with a system description language that fitted our needs, namely analysing multi-threaded programs written in C++.

The PVS tool requires translation of the program into formulas of high-order logic, and if we wish to perform verification of temporal properties, it is also necessary to include the theory of temporal logic.

At first glance it seems that STeP is more user friendly since it has its own system description language SPL. When we tried to use STeP, it became clear very quickly that, while SPL is quite adequate for dealing with distributed systems, its inability to represent dynamic process creation, as explained in Section 3, is a most serious obstacle to widespread use for verifying C++ programs.

Obviously, the problems we complain about are purely technical, and all that is needed to solve them is a translator from C++ to either high-order logic or to a fair transition system which is the low-end interface to STeP. Given enough time, we probably would have constructed such a translator and then continued to use these powerful tools. However, being under time pressure to advance the product as well as to make progress with the verification, our final decision was to use the temporal deductive methodology proposed in (Manna and Pnueli, 1995) but conduct the proofs *manually*.

The strategy we have formulated and applied so far consists of a combination of *model checking* with *deductive verification*, where:

– model checking is used for handling *control-related* issues, such as concurrency, deadlocks, mutual exclusion, and non-interference. It is applied to a simplified model of the system in which almost all data has been abstracted away;
– deductive verification is used for analysing the data-intensive parts of the system.

Besides separation of concerns, the main interaction between the two methods is that a thorough analysis of non-interference can lead to a significant simplification of the deductive verification task. In particular, when a certain segment in a given object's member function is known to be "isolated" from outside interference, we can verify its data transformations as though it were a sequential program.

6.5.2 Augmenting Deductive Verification by Model Checking

The chief purpose of employing model checking in our scheme is to resolve concurrency issues automatically. These issues include:

– safety: Mutual Exclusiveness (Non-Interference);
– liveness: Deadlocks.

Deadlocks are not safety properties, and the fact that SPIN can detect them is, of course, an advantage, but verification of their absence is an end in itself, without interaction with the deductive verification. Non-Interference, on the other hand, is crucial for the deductive phase: then, it is very helpful to know that some variables can only change by the thread being analysed (and not by other threads running concurrent to it). To some extent, non-interference can be thought of as "serialising" threads, and making them independent of each other (in limited code segments), with the obvious benefits for the deductive analysis.

The basic temporal formula that represents non-interference is:

$$(at\_\ell_i \wedge at'\_\ell_i \rightarrow x = x') \qquad (6.2)$$

It can be proven using SPIN in the following way: the system to be analysed is represented as PROMELA processes. Then for each variable x for which the above formula should hold (at label 1 of process P with process identity i) an analysis is carried out, and each transition that writes on x is marked by a label. The SPIN equivalent of the above formula then takes the following form (for each label a in process Q with process identity j):

```
[](P[i]@l -> !Q[j]@a)
```

This formula can be checked as a never claim by SPIN , for each (Q,j,a) tuple. Note that we abstract away all the data manipulations.

The analysis can be extended naturally to cases in which even *access* to a variable should not occur while a certain thread is in a certain state.

We give an example of the usage of model checking, adapted from real-life code. The example is a system of threads accessing a shared data object, using a locking mechanism to synchronise the access to that object. Threads can read, write or destroy the data object. An object can be read concurrently by several threads.

However, when a data object is written or destroyed by one thread, it must not be read by other threads. A "group" is a special object, containing validity information for the data object. Due to implementation restrictions, the data object's validity must first be ensured via a lookup in the group object, and only then may the data object be accessed. The group object itself is accessible directly, and can be both read and written.

There are K "user" threads in the system, which write the data object, and a "garbage collection" thread, which destroys the data object. These are, of course, simplified versions (for the sake of the example) of the actual threads, that may read and write nondeterministically to several objects, repeatedly.

Model checking provides the necessary non-interference assurance, stating that the data object cannot be written (or destroyed) while it is being read, nor can it be destroyed and written at the same time.

The PROMELA code is as following:
The "user" threads:

```
active [K] proctype user()
{
        ReadLock(group);
        /* pointer to object */
        if
        :: object_exists ->
           WriteLock(object);
           ReadUnlock(group);
           do
           :: skip ->
write:        skip;  /* perform writing */
              WriteUnlock(object);
              /* give up control */
              /* resume control */
              WriteLock(object);
           :: skip -> WriteUnlock(object); break;
           od;
        :: else ReadUnlock(group);
        fi;
}
```

The "garbage collection" thread:

```
active proctype remove()
{
        WriteLock(group);
        WriteLock(object);
        object_exists=false;
        WriteUnlock(group);
```

```
          WriteUnlock(object);
          /* perform removal */
destroy: skip;
}
```

Where the four macros used for semaphore simulations are:

```
#define ReadLock(var) atomic {!var.WRITE
                                  -> var.READ++ }
#define ReadUnlock(var) {var.READ--}
#define WriteLock(var) atomic {!var.WRITE &&
                  !var.READ -> var.WRITE=true}
#define WriteUnlock(var) {var.WRITE=false}
```

Note that the "user" threads release and re-acquire their lock on the object as necessary. This is an optimisation applied to the original locking design, wherein the threads held their lock on the object throughout the writing phase. The outcome of this optimisation is revealed once SPIN is used to re-assess the safety properties (assume K=2):

```
[]  !(user[1]@write && user[2]@write)
[]  !(user[1]@write && remove[0]@destroy)
[]  !(user[2]@write && remove[0]@destroy)
```

Contrary to the original design, SPIN reports a never claim violation for this system. Examining the error trail uncovers the following flaw: the basic assumption of the design is that a "user" thread accesses an object only after checking that its existence bit (in the group object) is up. This no longer holds for the modified system: the remove thread may engage in a deletion operation (once a "user thread" gives up his lock on the object), with a "user" thread re-acquiring the lock and writing data on the object, a scenario which violates the second or the third LTL formula of the above.

This resulted in a complete redesign of the whole locking scheme.

6.5.3 Deductive Verification of Data Transformations

Having verified non interference between threads (6.2), we can now verify heavy data transformations in single threads (as though they are sequential programs). We give two examples using the deductive verification rules presented in (Manna and Pnueli, 1995).

Example 1: Using the WAIT rule to ensure a proper implementation of a procedure. Assume a procedure of the following structure:

$$\begin{bmatrix} E: & (entry \quad point) \\ B: & \cdots \\ X: & \end{bmatrix}$$

We write $((at\_E \wedge precondition) \rightarrow (at\_E \vee at\_B) \, \mathcal{W} \, (at\_X \wedge postcondition))$
to state the fact that once control is in the routine then control remains within the procedure body B until it gets to the exit point, X, with the postconditions fulfilled, thus guaranteeing the proper $(precondition \rightarrow postcondition)$ action of the procedure.

For instance, this rule can be used to verify a sort algorithm, provided the array it sorts does not change (while the program counter is inside the sort code) by other threads. The *precondition* may also be T in this case, and the *postcondition* would require a sorted array (a conjunction of inequalities, one per each unordered pair of array indices).

Example 2: Using the BACK-TO rule to ensure that if a procedure terminates successfully, then some expected action was previously taken by it. Assume a procedure of the following structure:

$$
\left[
\begin{array}{l}
\cdots \\
\textbf{if } (\cdots) \textbf{ then} \\
\quad \left[
\begin{array}{ll}
G_1 : & \text{an action, in case of } \textit{true} \\
G_2 : & \cdots \\
G_3 : & return\_code := GOOD; \\
G_4 : & \textbf{go to } X;
\end{array}
\right] \\
\textbf{else} \\
\quad \left[
\begin{array}{ll}
B_1 : & \cdots \\
B_2 : & return\_code := BAD; \\
B_3 : & \textbf{go to } X;
\end{array}
\right] \\
X :
\end{array}
\right]
$$

We write:

$$((at\_X \wedge return\_code = GOOD) \rightarrow ((at\_G_3 \vee at\_G_4) \, \mathcal{B} \, at\_G_2))),$$

Then we write:

$$(at\_G_2 \rightarrow postcondition)$$

$$(at\_G_2 \wedge postcondition) \rightarrow (postcondition \, \mathcal{W} \, at\_X \wedge postcondition)$$

Combining them into the desired formula:

$$((at\_X \wedge return\_code = GOOD) \rightarrow postcondition)$$

If *postcondition* involves global (shared) variables, then for the third property to hold, it must be ensured that these variables are protected from interference by other threads.

We used the above rules, in the manner described in the examples, to verify non-trivial data transformations, some as complex to analyse as the sort algorithm. The verification leaned heavily on the non-interference LTL formulae verified by SPIN . The combination of the two methods resulted in a core module of the product being successfully verified.

6.6 Conclusions and Further Research

In this chapter, we have reported the experience of Perfecto Technologies in the application of formal verification to a software security product, and the lessons we learned from this experience.

Starting with model checking by SPIN, we succeeded in verifying a certain portion of the TLD of the system. To do so, we developed a compositional approach, specially geared to verification by SPIN. One of the conclusions we reached was that model checking alone cannot scale up to verify the detailed design, but may suffice for the verification of the top-level design, provided one uses compositionality.

For verification of the detailed design, we finally settled on a combination of model checking for the control-intensive part and manual deductive verification for the data-intensive part. The two methods interact by the deductive verification benefiting from proofs of non-interference established by model checking.

The preference for manual verification was forced on us because none of the existing support tools for deductive verification provided a system description language adequate for modelling multi-threaded C++ programs. We indicated in Section 3, how such a system description language may be developed with minimal extensions. We call upon developers of tools for deductive verification to pay more attention to providing a convenient interface language if they wish to attract users from the C++ community.

As for the interaction between formal methods and the industry, it is our belief that the incorporation of formal methods into commercial software will be beneficial to both of these domains. In particular, we think that expanding the presence of formal methods in the industry will bring a very positive contribution to the evolution of this field.

Acknowledgements

The authors would like to thank Eran Reshef (Perfecto Technologies Ltd.) and Eilon Solan (Northwestern University, IL., USA) for their continuous help and advice, Elad Shahar (The Weizmann Institute of Science) for his help with the SMV system, and Yaron Galant (Perfecto Technologies Ltd.) for his help with the introduction.

This work was supported in part by the Minerva Centre for the Verification of Reactive Systems.

CHAPTER 7

A CAD Environment for Safety-Critical Software

Nancy Leveson, Mats Heimdahl and Jon D. Reese

7.1 Background

The goal of the University of Washington, University of Minnesota, and Safeware Engineering Corporation Safety-Critical Systems Projects is to develop a theoretical foundation for software safety and to build a methodology upon that foundation. This paper describes the methodology and a set of safety analysis techniques (and prototype tools) to support it. The prototype tools are being developed in order to evaluate the techniques. To ensure that the procedures scale up to realistic systems, the tools and techniques are being evaluated on real systems, including TCAS II (Traffic Alert and Collision Avoidance System), an airborne collision avoidance system required on most aircraft that fly in U.S. airspace, a NASA experimental flight management system, a NASA robot used to service tiles on the Space Shuttle, and proposed upgrades to the U.S. Air Traffic Control System.

7.2 Introduction

An *accident* or *mishap* is traditionally defined by engineers as an unplanned event or a series of events that leads to an unacceptable loss, such as death, injury, illness, damage to or loss of equipment or property, or environmental harm. Although computers themselves are relatively safe devices — they rarely explode, catch on fire, or cause physical harm — they can contribute substantially to accidents when they operate as a subsystem within a potentially dangerous system. Examples include computers that monitor and control nuclear power plants, aircraft and other means of transportation, medical devices, manufacturing processes, and aerospace and defense systems. Because computers are relatively safe when considered in isolation and only indirectly contribute to accidents, any solution to computer or software safety problems needs to stem from, and to be evaluated and applied within, the context of system safety.

System-safety engineers define safety in terms of *hazards* and *risk*. A *hazard* is a set of conditions (a state) that can lead to an accident given certain environmental conditions. Examples of hazards are pressure above some threshold in a boiler or failed brakes in a motor vehicle. *Risk* is a function of (1) the likelihood a hazard will occur, (2) the likelihood that the hazard will lead to an accident, and (3) the worst possible potential loss associated with such an accident. Risk can be reduced by decreasing any or all three of these risk factors.

System-safety engineering, a subdiscipline of system engineering, applies scientific, management, and engineering approaches to reduce these risk factors in the system as a whole. System-safety engineering involves: (1) identifying hazards, (2) assessing these hazards as to criticality and likelihood, and (3) designing devices to eliminate or control hazards.

When a computer is used to control a hazardous system, the software can potentially contribute to (or reduce) risk through its effect on system hazards. Although system-safety engineers have techniques to deal with hazards in physical systems, the introduction of computer control has created new and unsolved problems both for system engineers and computer scientists.

Software safety is a system problem, not just a software problem: any effort to make software safe that is not integrated with the corresponding procedures to handle hazards at the system level will be limited in effectiveness. For the past 15 years, Leveson and students have been studying ways to extend and adapt to software the methods used to control risk in the larger system within which the software is embedded. This work has resulted in methods for software hazard analysis (identifying software hazards using models of the system) (Leveson and Stolzy, 1987), analysis and review criteria for real-time software requirements specifications (Jaffe and Leveson, 1989; Jaffe et al., 1991), evaluation of current fault-tolerance methods (Brilliant et al., 1989, 1990; Knight and Leveson, 1986; Leveson et al., 1990; Shimeall and Leveson, 1991) along with proposals for software design to enhance safety (Leveson, 1983, 1986; Leveson and Shimeall, 1983; Leveson et al., 1983), and safety verification techniques (Leveson et al., 1991; Leveson, 1983; Leveson and Harvey, 1983; Leveson et al., 1997; Leveson and Palmer, 1997; Reese and Leveson, 1997a, b).

Some of the techniques that have evolved from this research are being used on industrial projects around the world. However, the set of techniques have developed in isolation so they are difficult to use together, do not cover some important problem areas, and cannot be used in an integrated methodology: our first efforts concentrated on clarifying the problem and investigating the solution space so that we understood what we needed before we started to construct a methodology and associated tools. However, we have refined the early models and approaches as we have come to understand the problems better. We are ready to take what has been learned and design a consistent, integrated approach to ensuring software safety.

Such an approach, called Safeware, has been outlined by (Leveson, 1995). The basic methodology involves applying software hazard analysis and hazard control procedures throughout software development, based on the identified system hazards. These efforts are closely tied to the system level hazard analysis and control. Early and continuing analysis procedures guide and direct the software as it is developed instead of simply attempting to verify safety after the software is completed.

One of the complications in building complex systems is that they cannot be built successfully without the interaction of multiple disciplines — the most challenging systems include electromechanical components, computers, and humans all working together to achieve system goals while, at the same time, having to satisfy constraints related to safety, pollution, physical limitations of the equipment, maintenance requirements, and so on. The Safeware methodology stresses the necessity to take a *system* viewpoint by building bridges between system engineering, software engineering, human–machine interaction, cognitive engineering, and organizational sociology.

Our current problems in building such systems lie not only in communication among the engineering subdisciplines, but also in a lack of system-level viewpoints and approaches. Many of the most important properties of these complex systems are not tied to the individual components but arise in the interfaces between and interactions among the components — that is, they are system properties rather than component properties. For example, most accidents arise in the interfaces between the components — they are not caused by individual component failures. Dealing with these system-level properties requires modelling languages and analysis techniques that consider the system as a whole, including the electromechanical components and not simply the computer. In general, we cannot build complex systems by optimising the individual components and assuming that the result will achieve *system* goals and satisfy *system* constraints.

In addition, effective safety programs need to consider not only the physical components of systems, but also the properties of the organisation(s) within which the system is being designed, built, and operated. The root causes of accidents are often organisational rather than purely technical. In fact, organisational deficiencies are often found to cause accidents despite good technical safety programs. Thus, we believe that our problems in building high-quality complex systems cannot be solved piecemeal. People, organisations (both formal and informal), and technology need to be viewed as interconnected parts within a larger and more useful system boundary.

The Safety-Critical Systems Project at the University of Washington, the University of Minnesota, and Safeware Engineering Corporation is attempting to provide a theoretical foundation for the safety of complex systems composed of hardware, software, and human elements as well as provide techniques and tools to support the Safeware methodology.

7.3 The Safeware Approach to Building Safety-Critical Computer-Based Systems

The Safeware approach to building safety-critical computer-based systems includes special management structures and procedures, system hazard analysis, software hazard analysis, software requirements modeling and analysis for completeness and safety, special software design techniques including the design of human–computer interaction, verification (both testing and code analysis), operational feedback, and change analysis. The software safety activities are all a subset of the overall system safety activities: any efforts to treat the safety aspects of computers or the HMI support must be intimately tied to the overall system engineering and system safety engineering activities. Thus, an important part of the methodology involves coordination among the various activities and establishing communication and feedback channels.

The Safety-Critical Systems Project is defining and evaluating specific techniques for implementing this methodology and building prototype tools. The techniques and tools are being evaluated by applying them to real (or realistic) systems. Because we believe that the initial development activities are the most crucial with respect to building complex systems (in terms of achieving and being able to ensure certain required properties), and because the fewest tools exist for this stage of development, we are focusing first on building a CAD environment for computer-based systems to aid in modelling and analysis during overall system design and software requirements specification. The environment will act as a workbench for system engineers, software engineers, and human factors experts and will enhance communication by using common models and analysis tools that execute on the models.

Note the difference between our software CAD environment and traditional software development environments. The latter usually focus on software design and coding while our system development environment draws a much wider boundary on what parts of the life cycle are supported.

Figure 7.1 shows the various components of the environment. At the heart is an executable model of the software and, ideally, other components of the system including humans. This overall model is composed of blackbox models of the behaviour of the individual system components and their interface. In the modelling language, we emphasise readability by application experts, operators, and those who specialise in various engineering disciplines (system engineers, human factors experts, subsystem engineers, etc.) so that they can provide input to the design of the system and can review the design and the analysis results. Although analysis tools help to increase confidence in our designs, the majority of the errors will be found by experts reading the requirements and system design documents. In addition, input into the early system design process by application experts and operators will lead to more useful and usable systems.

In order to make the models mathematically and machine analysable, the modelling language must have a formal foundation. We have defined a general underlying state-machine model for the modelling language. This mathematical model

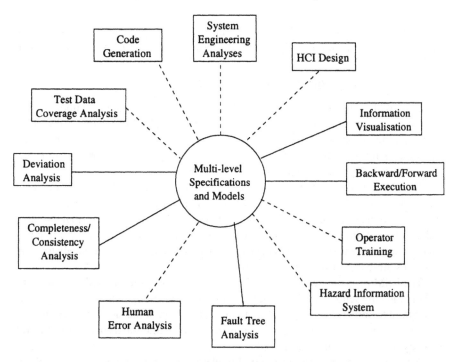

Figure 7.1. Components and interactions in a CAD environment for safety-critical systems

need not be read by anyone — it is purely to define the semantics of the modelling language and aid in the development of analysis tools.

The model can be used to generate various types of analyses such as fault trees, reliability models, hazard analysis, timing analysis, human–computer interface analysis, consistency and completeness analysis, human-error analyses, and so on. In addition, the information from the model can be used in simulator construction and in operator training. Many of the mistakes made by airline pilots, for example, can be traced to incomplete or inaccurate understanding of the operation of the flight management computer, especially those operations used less often (Palmer *et al.*, 1993; Sarter and Woods, 1993). We found that our TCAS specification could be read by pilots, who provided much useful input during its development. If the model is readable and understandable by operators, then it could have further uses in training and operations.

The model can also be used as a requirements specification for the software designers (and perhaps other component designers, depending on the information included about the non-computer parts of the system). In addition, preliminary work indicates there is good reason to believe that at least part of the production code can be generated automatically from the model (Keenan and Heimdahl, 1997). With respect to verification, the model itself will be validated during the systems engineering process, partly by using the tools we are developing. Later it can be used to generate test data (or to provide requirements coverage analysis) when the software is eventually verified.

The rest of this chapter describes the underlying formal model, our modelling language, and some of the analysis tools that are working or are under development.

7.3.1 Underlying Formal Model

We start with a model of the blackbox behaviour of the system components. A blackbox statement of behaviour permits statements and observations to be made only in terms of outputs and the inputs that stimulate or trigger those outputs. The model does not include any information about the design of the component itself, only its externally visible behaviour.

In order to make our language formal enough to be analysable (and yet readable and reviewable by non-mathematicians), we have defined a formal model that underlies the more readable specification language(s). The underlying formal model is independent of any specific, existing requirements language — we call it a requirements state machine (RSM). It is basically a Mealy machine and thus an abstraction of most state-based specification languages.

The RSM rests on the concept of a basic control loop (see Figure 7.2). The controller reads the sensor data and using this information, along with perhaps other information, formulates and issues a command to an actuator that actually manipulates the process in some way to achieve the overall goals while satisfying constraints on the way those goals can be achieved.

All control software has an internal model of the process that it is controlling, ranging from a very simple model including only a few variables to a much more complex model. The RSM simply represents this model using a state machine and defines the required behaviour of the software in terms of transitions in this machine. Hazards and accidents often result from mismatches between the software view of the process and the actual state of the process — that is, the model of the process used by the software gets out of synch with the real process. For example, the software does not know that the plane is on the ground and raises the landing gear or it does not identify the object as friendly and shoots a missile at it. The goal of requirements completeness analysis basically is to ensure that the model of the process used by the software is sufficiently complete so that no hazardous process states are included.

We use a simple Mealy machine for the RSM because we believe that finite-state machine models are understood by engineers more easily than other types of formal languages suggested for requirements (such as process algebras or higher order logics). Transitions are labelled with logical expressions of the form *Input predicate / Output predicate*, and a transition is taken if the *Input predicate* on that transition evaluates to **true**. If an output is to be produced, the constraints on that output are expressed in the *Output predicate* associated with the transition.

Because incompleteness of requirements plays such an important role in accidents, we first identified a set of criteria for evaluating requirements completeness using our model by associating each part of a basic control loop with the RSM and then defining semantic completeness criteria and heuristics in terms of the parts of the state-machine model (Jaffe and Leveson, 1989).

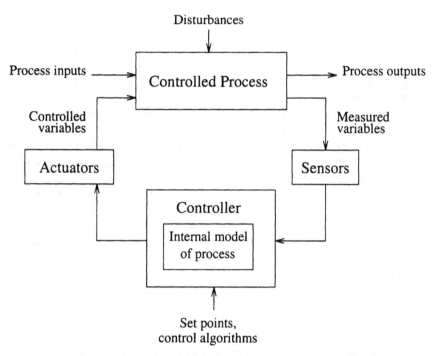

Figure 7.2. A basic control loop. A black-box requirements specification captures the controller's internal model of the process. Accidents occur when the internal model does not accurately reflect the state of the controlled process.

The RSM is defined as a seven-tuple $(\Sigma, Q, q_0, P_t, P_o, \gamma, \delta)$ where:

- Σ is the set of input and output variables used by the controller software. Criteria here ensure that all sensor input is used by the controller. Additional criteria require that legal output values that are never produced by the computer are identified and investigated for potential incompleteness.
- Q is the finite set of states of the controller and q_0 is the initial state. Correctness criteria defined on Q and q_0 primarily ensure that startup and shutdown behaviour is completely and correctly specified. Most accidents occur during startup or shutdown or during transitions from normal to non-normal operation.
- P_t is the set of Boolean functions over Σ; they represent predicates on the values and timing of the inputs from the sensors. These predicates are called *trigger* predicates since they trigger a state change in the RSM. Criteria here ensure the complete description and handling of inputs including essential value and timing assumptions and robustness in the system implementation. A *robust* system will detect and respond appropriately to violations of assumptions about the system environment (such as unexpected inputs). Robustness with respect to a state-machine description implies the following:
  1. every state must have a behaviour (transition) defined for every possible input;
  2. the logical OR of the conditions on every transition out of any state must form a tautology;
  3. every state must have a software behavior (transition) defined in case there is no input for a given period of time (a timeout).
  Thus, the software must be prepared to respond in real time to all possible inputs and input sequences — there must be no observable events that leave the program's behaviour indeterminate.
  Although this type of completeness criterion ensures that there is always one transition that can be taken out of every state, it does not guarantee that all assumptions about the environment have been specified or that there is a defined response for all possible input conditions the environment can produce. Many of these assumptions and conditions are application dependent, but some are essential for all systems; additional criteria check this essential information. Timing assumptions are especially critical here, and they are often left out of or left incomplete in requirements specifications.
- P_o is the set of Boolean functions over Σ; they represent predicates on the outputs of the controller software. Criteria ensure the complete specification of value and timing requirements for outputs including some special requirements for the specification of environmental capacity, data age, and latency.
- γ is the trigger-to-output relationship. Criteria here relate not to input or output predicates alone but to their relationship. These include requirements in most process-control systems for graceful degradation and for using feedback information.
- δ is the state transition function. Correctness with respect to the state transition function involves properties of the paths between states and the predicate sequences describing these paths. Few absolute criteria can be identified as with the

other parts of the RSM; most of the criteria are application-dependent. However, general properties or heuristics can be identified that, together with application-specific information, can be used to guide the analysis process. These include properties associated with basic reachability, recurrent or cyclic behavior, reversible behavior, reachability of safe states, preemption of transactions, path robustness, and general analysis of consistency with required system-level constraints.

Lutz, at JPL, experimentally validated these completeness criteria by determining whether they would have detected the 192 safety-critical errors found during system integration testing of the Galileo and Voyager spacecraft (Lutz, 1993). The criteria identified 150 of these errors; the others were design errors and could not have been found by our blackbox requirements criteria. Companies and government agencies are using our completeness criteria in their standard requirements review processes. We have extended the original criteria to include many more, primarily related to human-computer interaction. In addition, we are trying to provide assistance with the requirements development and review process by incorporating many of the criteria into the syntax of our new specification language design and by automating the checking of those criteria that cannot be enforced by the language design.

7.3.2 Modelling Language

The RSM is only a theoretical model — it is not appropriate for use as a specification language. Our original modelling and specification language, RSML, was devised for the FAA during an experimental application of formal methods in a form that was readable by application experts (such as pilots) and those not trained in formal methods. To make sure that the results were realistic, we developed the language using TCAS II (a collision-avoidance system now required on all commercial aircraft with more than 30 seats that fly in U.S. airspace). This project was such a success that the FAA adopted our specification as the official system requirements specification for TCAS II (Leveson *et al.*, 1994).

A complete description of RSML can be found in (Leveson *et al.*, 1994). In this chapter, we only provide a short overview. RSML uses some of the features introduced in the Statecharts formalism (Harel, 1987). RSML and Statecharts extend finite state machines with hierarchies of states, parallelism, and conventions that reduce the number of states and transitions needed to define a state machine. Figure 7.3 shows a part of the RSML model for TCAS II. This state machine models Intruder-Status, which denotes how close an intruder is to our own aircraft. For instance, the state Other-Traffic indicates that the intruder is far away while Threat indicates that the intruder is very close. If an intruder is declared a threat, that is, if the state machine is in state Threat, seven parallel state variables become important. The state machine labelled Sense, for example, is a state variable contained inside Threat that models the advisory that should be displayed to the pilot. The details of the Sense (as well as the other six state variables within Threat) are shown separately.

Transitions are visualised as arrows in the state machine (the "bar" to the left in the model is a transition bus indicating that the states connected to the bus are fully interconnected, that is, there is a transition from every state to every other state). To keep the graphical notation clean and readable, the detailed description of the transitions are defined separately.

The transitions in the state machine are described by using a trigger event to specify when the transition can be taken, a guarding condition specifying the conditions under which the transition can be taken, and an output event (or action) generated when the transition is taken. Figure 7.4 shows a transition definition from the TCAS II requirements. For readability, the guarding condition is presented using a tabular representation of disjunctive normal form (DNF) that we call AND/OR tables. The subscripts on the names indicate the type (e for event, s for state, v for variable, and m for macro) and the page numbers where the names are defined. Page numbers are automatically updated when changes are made to the specification.

The far-left column of the AND/OR table lists the logical phrases. Each of the other columns is a conjunction of those phrases and contains the logical values of the expressions. If one of the columns is **true**, then the table evaluates to **true**. A column evaluates to **true** if all of its elements are **true**. A dot denotes "don't care." Thus a transition is made from Threat to Other-Traffic when altitude reporting from the other aircraft has been lost (we have not received a recent message reporting its altitude), and we do not have a valid bearing on the aircraft. Alternatively, a transition is made when altitude reporting has been lost and we do not have a valid range, etc.

One goal of RSML is to minimise the "semantic distance" between the development model and the mental models users and engineers have of the desired operation of the system to be built. If this semantic distance is small, then presumably designers and reviewers will find it easier to build the model and review it for errors. In addition, many formal requirements specification languages use mathematical languages that are easily manipulated but are very difficult to read and are far from the way that experts think about their systems. Finally, including functional decomposition and software design in the requirements specification also increases the distance between the specification and the user's mental models. In our methodology, we model (using RSML) only blackbox descriptions of the external behaviour of the system component in terms of properties of external variables — we do not use internal variables nor do we include internal component design features.

The requirements review process involves validating the relationship between changes in the real-world process and the specified changes and response in the requirements model. Therefore, reviewability will be enhanced if the requirements model explicitly shows this relationship. Moreover, when the description of the required component behaviour includes more than just its blackbox behaviour, the semantic distance between the desired system behaviour and the specified component behaviour increases, and the relationship between them becomes more difficult to validate. TCAS application experts who know very little or nothing about com-

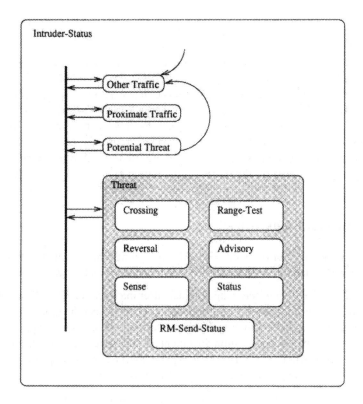

Figure 7.3. Fragment of TCAS II specification in RSML

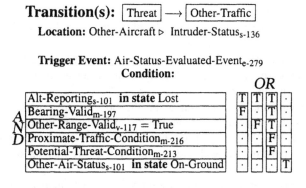

Transition(s): | Threat | $\longrightarrow$ | Other-Traffic |

Location: Other-Aircraft ▷ Intruder-Status$_{s-136}$

Trigger Event: Air-Status-Evaluated-Event$_{e-279}$

Condition:

OR

Alt-Reporting$_{s-101}$ **in state** Lost	T	T	T	·
Bearing-Valid$_{m-197}$	F	·	T	·
Other-Range-Valid$_{v-117}$ = True	·	F	T	·
Proximate-Traffic-Condition$_{m-216}$	·	·	F	·
Potential-Threat-Condition$_{m-213}$	·	·	F	·
Other-Air-Status$_{s-101}$ **in state** On-Ground	·	·	·	T

(AND — rows grouped on left)

Output Action: Intruder-Status-Evaluated-Event$_{e-279}$

Figure 7.4. The definition of the transition between *Threat* and *Potential-Threat*

puters or software have been able to read our system requirements model of TCAS and find and help correct errors in it.

We are currently taking what we learned from using RSML on real projects and systems and from watching how others use RSML and we are creating a new language called SpecTRM-RL (the Requirements Language for our Specification Tools and Requirements Methodology). Our goals in the design of SpecTRM-RL include enhancing readability, eliminating or changing features (such as internal broadcast events) we have found to be especially error prone in use, providing more support for building blackbox models (specifiers who are used to including internal design in their specifications seem to have difficulty building pure blackbox models), and enforcing some of our identified completeness criteria in the language syntax.

7.3.3 Analysis and Support Tools

Some prototype tools for our software CAD environment have been developed and others are in the planning stages. All will be evaluated on realistic systems.

Parser and graphical interface. The graphical user interface (GUI) will support entry, review, change management, and formatting of RSML specifications. We plan to tie our other analysis tools into this graphical interface. We also support pretty printing of the requirements specification document (RSML specification). Although we have a minimal working version of the graphical interface, many improvements are planned and are being implemented to make the interface more usable.

Visualisation. Complete specifications of complex systems can themselves become very large and complex. Although a specification language can help eliminate accidental complexity, the inherent complexity of many of today's systems inevitably leads to large and complex specifications. Because understanding the specification is crucial for human detection of errors, we are experimenting with various types of visualisation techniques to assist the reviewer and analyst in understanding the model and the analysis results. For example, Pinnel has built a tool for creating various animations and visualisations as the RSML formal model is executed (Pinnel, 1997).

In another project, Heimdahl has investigated mechanisms to simplify a formal specification and present information to analysts and reviewers in digestible chunks (Heimdhal and Whalen, 1997).

When reviewing and or inspecting a specification, we are primarily interested in answering questions about the behavior of the specification. For example, during our work with TCAS II, we asked questions such as "When do we downgrade a threat that has stopped reporting altitude?" and "How do we treat an intruder that is considered to be on the ground?".

Most questions regarding a specification involve an action, as in, downgrading an intruder that is considered to be a threat, and a specific scenario, such as, when the intruder has stopped reporting altitude. To help answer questions of this type we have evaluated a two tiered approach to specification reduction.

First, we allow the analyst to reduce an RSML specification based on the specific scenario of interest. Our tool accepts a *reduction scenario* that is used to reduce the specification to contain only the behaviours that are possible when the operating conditions defining the reduction scenario are satisfied. We call such a reduced specification the *interpretation* of the specification under this scenario.

Second, we allow the analyst to slice (Weiser, 1984) the interpretation based on different entities in the model, to highlight, for example, the portions of the specification affecting the value of an output variable or the information affecting whether a specific transition can be taken.

Initial results show that the slicing approach is very useful and would have helped us answer a set of questions we encountered in previous investigations. More experimentation with various reduction and visualisation techniques is needed, but these initial results are promising and show that slicing of state-based specifications provides many benefits for specification readability and understandability.

Simulator. The Simulator executes the specifications (models) so that designers can better visualise how the system will behave in practice. This tool interacts with the GUI tool so that the progress of the simulation and the current state can be seen on the screen. Details of the simulation can also be printed.

Forward simulation can be started from a prespecified set of input messages. Simulation "steps" are divided into microsteps. A microstep is taken by choosing a set of transitions that are each triggered by an event generated during the previous microstep. This event may be generated by a transition, a message receipt, or a timeout. A full step is completed when no more microsteps can be taken. After completing a step, a system-wide queue is checked to determine when the next timeout or message is scheduled to occur. The global clock is advanced to this time, and the component that received the timeout or message begins a new step. The simulator can be executed from start to completion or it can be single-stepped (either a microstep or a step at a time) with the currently active states highlighted on the screen. Although the simulator currently executes models of single components, we are extending it to handle multiple components and a rich set of interface options.

The simulator also works backward. Backward simulation is used by our safety analysis tools. It requires finding configurations such that there exist a set of transitions that can lead from each of these configurations to the current configuration in a microstep. Because of the richness of the guarding condition language, guarding conditions are for the most part ignored during backward simulation and therefore, infeasible backward execution paths may be generated. These infeasible paths can be eliminated either by manual inspection or by some limited forms of automatic pruning. We are working on more effective ways to reduce the number of previous states considered.

Consistency and completeness analysis. The robustness criteria described earlier require checking for consistency (no two transitions out of a state are satisfied simultaneously) and transition completeness (there is a transition defined for every possible input and input sequence). The Consistency and Completeness Analysis tool automatically identifies inconsistencies and incompleteness in an RSML specification (Heimdahl and Leveson, 1995). Consistency checking identifies transitions with overlapping guarding conditions and reports them to the analyst while completeness checking identifies all conditions for which no transition has been specified.

Compositional properties of the RSML semantics allow the specification to be analysed in small pieces and the analysis results to be combined into a statement about the complete specification (Heimdahl, 1995). This compositionality allows incremental analysis of the requirements, that is, the different pieces of the model can be analysed as they are completed and the results combined at a later time.

In addition to the results from the analysis algorithms (reporting inconsistency, incompleteness, and nondeterminism), the tools generate other useful information such as event propagation tables and use hierarchies for transitions, macros, and functions.

The initial prototype implementation of our tool represented AND/OR tables symbolically using Binary Decision Diagrams (BDDs) (Bryant, 1986). The approach provides excellent performance in terms of execution time and the analysis will find all potential errors. Unfortunately, the accuracy of the BDD approach is, in some cases, inadequate and the analysis may generate spurious error reports. When analysing complex models, the number of spurious (false) error reports can become a problem.

To overcome the problems with spurious error reports, we have extended our tool to generate proof obligations for a theorem prover (Heimdahl and Czerny, 1996). Integration with a theorem prover has helped us to achieve the level of accuracy required to easily interpret analysis results from the most complex parts of the TCAS II requirements. In the future, we want to extend the analysis tools to check for the entire set of completeness criteria we have defined and not just the robustness criteria.

Safety analysis. Safety analysis uses backward analysis techniques to start from a hazardous state and identify the predecessor states. Information from the analysis can be used to eliminate hazards from the design or to design controls for the hazards.

Backward search techniques start with a hazardous state and build trees showing the events that could lead to this state. The analysis starts from hazards identified during the preliminary hazard analysis and identifies their precursors. This information can be used to determine if and how a system can enter a hazardous state during normal system function. Such information usually leads to changes in the basic system design. Backward search can also reveal how the system can end up in a hazardous state if some failure (such as a missed event or transition or an incorrectly triggered transition) occurs. If failures are found to lead to a hazard, the designers must either ensure their absence or incorporate mechanisms to prevent hazards in their presence.

Deviation analysis. Deviation analysis is a new forward analysis technique developed by Reese (1995) that takes its inspiration from HAZOP (HAZards and OPerability analysis), a very successful analysis procedure in the chemical process industry. Both techniques are based on the underlying system theory that many accidents are the result of deviations in system variables. A deviation is the difference between the actual and correct values.

Figure 7.5 shows an overview of the procedure. The analyst provides a formal software requirements specification (e.g., an RSML or SpecTRM-RL specification), which the procedure automatically converts into a *causality diagram*. The causality diagram is an internal data structure that encodes causal information between system variables, based on the specification and the semantics of the specification language. The simplicity of causality diagrams makes the search algorithm more straightforward and easier to adapt to a new specification or programming language. Causality diagrams may also be helpful to the analyst in understanding how system variables are inter-related.

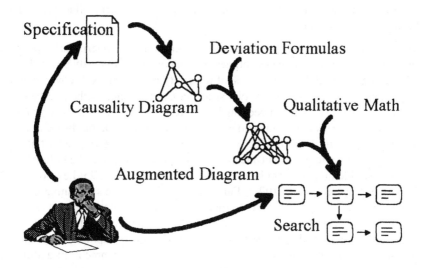

Figure 7.5. Overview of deviation analysis procedure

At this point, the causality diagram describes the relationship between the actual values of system variables, but not their deviations. The procedure next augments the causality diagram with *deviation formulas* so that variable deviations are represented.

After the analyst's specification is converted to a causality diagram, the procedure is ready for the analyst to identify the safety-critical software outputs and at least one deviation in the input environment.

The augmented causality diagram, safety-critical software outputs, and the initial deviations are passed to the search program, which constructs a tree of states. The initial deviations are at the root of the search tree. Leaves are either dead-end searches (in which the state does not contain any deviations) or states containing safety-critical deviations.

The search is based on applying *qualitative mathematics* to the causality diagram. Qualitative mathematics partitions infinite domains into a small set of intervals and provides mathematical operations on these intervals. The use of fixed intervals simplifies the analysis compared to iterations over the entire state space. Like HAZOP, it also lends itself naturally to the qualitative nature of deviations, such as "slightly too high."

The output of the procedure is a list of *scenarios*. A scenario is a set of deviations in the software inputs plus constraints on the execution states of the software that are sufficient to lead to a deviation in a safety-critical software output. The deviation analysis procedure can optionally add further deviations as it constrains the software state, allowing for the analysis of multiple independent failures (leading to the independent deviations.)

Inter-component communication analysis. We know that the interfaces between the software and the embedding environment is a major source of costly errors. For example, Lutz reported that 20% - 35% of the safety related errors discovered during integration and system testing of two spacecraft were related to the interfaces between the software and the embedding hardware (Lutz, 1992, 1993). The problems often involve, for example, misunderstandings about how the hardware operates, incompatibilities in the timing between the sending and receiving side, failure to detect and respond to inputs outside the normal operating regime, and failure to prevent undesirable outputs from being generated (Lutz, 1992, 1993; Leveson, 1986; Melhart, 1990; Jaffe *et al.*, 1991). Furthermore, the software's operating environment is likely to change over time, further complicating the issues related to system level inter-component communication. Thus, it is imperative that a requirements specification for an embedded software system rigorously captures the interfaces and the communication between the software and its environment. In addition, a specification language should support analysis techniques that can help assure, for example, that two components communicating over a channel have compatible communication definitions, that input and output value assumptions are compatible, and that compliance with communication relates safety and liveness assertions.

In our approach to inter-component communication analysis we introduce a formal approach to the specification of system-level communication and show how this formalism can be used to analyse the communication definition for a wide variety of properties (Heimdahl and Thompson, 1997). We encapsulate information about the physical properties of the communication (such as timing assumptions) in an interface specification and encapsulate the definition of how incoming and outgoing messages are treated in communication handlers associated with the interfaces, for instance, under which conditions we are allowed to generate a specific output. In addition to rigorous capture of the communication, the formality of the specification allows us to automatically verify certain types of communication-related constraints. The analysis procedures we have investigated allow us to check a specification for the following properties.

1. Compatibility of the physical connection, for example, are the timing assumptions between the sending and the receiving side compatible?
2. Compatibility of input and output variables, for example, are the value assumptions on the output from one component compatible with the input variables in another component?
3. Compliance with safety and liveness constraints, for example, can an output variable be generated under certain conditions and do we handle out of bounds inputs correctly?

Human error analysis. In avionics and other high-tech systems, computers are no longer simply reading sensors, integrating the information, and displaying it for operators to use. Many systems today provide either shared control between the computer and the operator, or total computer control with the operator controlling or monitoring the computer (rather than the process itself). Recent accidents in commercial aircraft and other complex systems have resulted from difficulties in integrating computer and human control.

Mode confusion is a good example of the problems. Mode confusion occurs in systems that allow the same operation to have different effects depending on the current system mode. Mode errors occur in simple systems when an operator acts in a way appropriate to one mode when the system actually is in another mode. Advanced automation systems, where computers implement control actions of their own, add new types of mode-related problems because the system status and mode (and thus behaviour) can change, independent of direct and immediate operator commands. Controllers in these systems, such as pilots, have the added cognitive task of keeping track of the computer-directed mode changes. Problems are also arising because the operators do not understand the logic of the automated systems.

The safe design of the human-computer interface and cockpit procedures is dependent on appropriate design of the software, and appropriate design of the software can only be assured in the context of the operator tasks and cognitive abilities. We are developing techniques and tools that assist in design and verification of the coordination, interaction, and interfaces between system components — human, hardware, and software (Leveson *et al.*, 1997; Leveson and Palmer, 1997).

Test data generation and coverage analysis. We are working on tools to aid in the testing of software implemented from RSML models to ensure that they conform to the specification. For example, coverage analysis tools will determine how much of the specification has been "covered" in the testing process based on various levels of coverage criteria. These tools are still in the development stage.

Code generation. To simplify and automate the design and implementation process, we have investigated the possibility of automatically generating code from RSML specifications. The semantics of RSML is relatively simple and is defined as a composition of simple mathematical functions defined by the state transitions in the model (Heimdahl and Leveson, 1996). We have developed a prototype tool that translates an RSML specification to executable code. The translation closely follows the formal semantics of RSML and, thus, makes verification of the correctness of the generated code simple (Keenan and Heimdahl, 1997). For the translations where this straightforward approach generates obviously inefficient code, we have defined easily verifiable automated correctness preserving optimisations.

Our goal is to generate production quality code directly from RSML specifications with as little human intervention as possible. To determine if this is a realistic goal and to get some early feedback on our approach, we have applied our translation technique to several small sample RSML specifications, including a part of the TCAS II requirements specification. Initial results show that the generated code is approximately 5–10 times slower and about twice as large as highly optimised hand generated code. These results indicate that automatic code generation is feasible, at least in the domain for which RSML was developed, and that our easily verifiable translation is a promising start.

Hazard information system. These tools include the facilities needed to build audit trails for identified hazards and support basic system safety activities.

7.4 Conclusions

This chapter has described a philosophy for building safety-critical systems and a set of techniques and prototype tools to implement that philosophy. The prototype tools are at varying stages of development. Evaluation by applying the tools to a variety of real systems is being performed in parallel with development (Leveson *et al.*, 1994; Modugno *et al.*, 1997; Ratan *et al.*, 1996). The information obtained is being used to improve our specification languages and analysis tools.

Acknowledgements

This work is partially funded by NASA/Langley, the California PATH Automated Highways Program, and the NSF.

CHAPTER 8

Scheduling and Rescheduling of Trains

Dines Bjørner, Chris George and Søren Prehn

8.1 Introduction: The PRaCoSy Project

The PRaCoSy (Peoples Republic of China Railway Computing System) project was a collaborative project between the Chinese Ministry of Railways and UNU/IIST, the United Nations University International Institute for Software Technology in Macau. The first phase ran from September 1993 to December 1994 and the second from August 1995 to March 1996.

The project aimed to develop skills in software engineering for automation in the Chinese Railways. A specific goal was the automation of the system for monitoring the movement of trains and rescheduling their arrivals and departures to satisfy operational constraints.

8.1.1 The Problem

Efficient use of railway resources involves good allocation of resources: railway track, rolling stock and staff. This project was concerned with the allocation of the track. There are two activities involved:

- scheduling: the creation of a timetable for all types of trains: passenger, freight, military, etc.
- rescheduling: the modification of the timetable to take account of disturbances such as lateness of trains and breakdowns.

A computerised system to support these activities is called a *dispatch* system; *dispatchers* are people responsible for monitoring and coordinating the movements of trains, ensuring that they run as far as possible according to the timetable. They do this by communicating with stations the timetables and adjustments to them. Technically, a *station* is anywhere that there are switches (points) enabling trains to move from one line to another, or where different lines meet. In particular it includes both passenger stations and marshalling yards for freight trains.

In China dispatching is done by dispatchers working in *dispatch units* and communicating with stations and other dispatch units. They make decisions about how to make changes to the arrivals and departures of trains in order to minimise the effects of disturbances. Currently the work is entirely manual (pencil and paper) and slow. The slowness is due to both the manual methods and poor communications.

When dispatchers make decisions to dispatch, delay or reroute trains they need to check a number of things. Is a new route feasible? Are there enough platforms or tracks in each station to hold the trains intended to occupy it at any one time? Are there clashes over the occupation of tracks or of lines between stations? Are the rules in China about minimum separations between departures and arrivals being adhered to? Can the trains make the journeys in the times allowed to them, according to the normal and any special speed restrictions? Knowing and conforming to these rules is part of the skill of the dispatcher, but also something the computer can check more rapidly and more accurately, allowing the dispatcher to concentrate on the tactical decisions of what changes to try.

It might seem that dispatching is a safety-critical activity in that it involves keeping trains a safe distance apart. This is in fact not the case: there are other safety systems to prevent accidents. But a timetable that predicts an impossible future is of little use; it will simply make more rescheduling necessary as the problems become manifest.

The area chosen for the initial stage of the project was the 600km line between Zhengzhou and Wuhan. This includes part of the main north-south line between Beijing and Guangzhou (Canton) and is one of the busiest railway areas in China. It is also a critical national infrastructural resource. The area includes 8 dispatch units and 90 stations (see Figure 8.1).

8.2 The Running Map Tool

Figure 8.2 shows the prototype *running map* tool that was produced in Phase 1 of the project.

This closely copies the large sheets of paper that are used currently by dispatchers. Stations are listed vertically, time passes horizontally, and the paths of trains are shown in the central area. Currently the display is showing part of a timetable for trains running between Nanjingxi and Shanghai (the southern portion of the line from Beijing to Shanghai). Consider train Y1, due to depart from Nanjing at 08:28. Note that it is due to overtake train K335 in Danyan. Now suppose Y1 leaves Nanjing a few minutes late. There are several possibilities:

- Y1 may be able to travel more quickly than timetabled and pass through Danyan on schedule;
- Y1 may pass through Danyan only a very short time before K335 is due to leave; K335 will then be delayed;

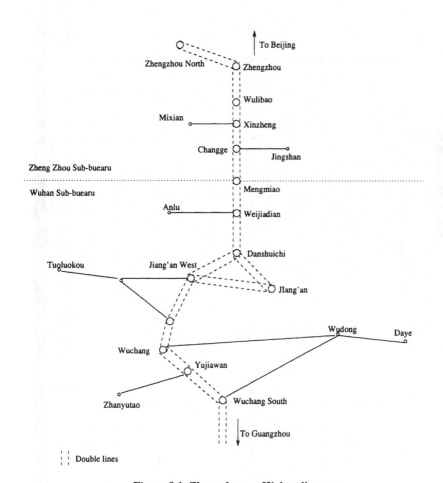

Figure 8.1. Zhengzhou — Wuhan line map

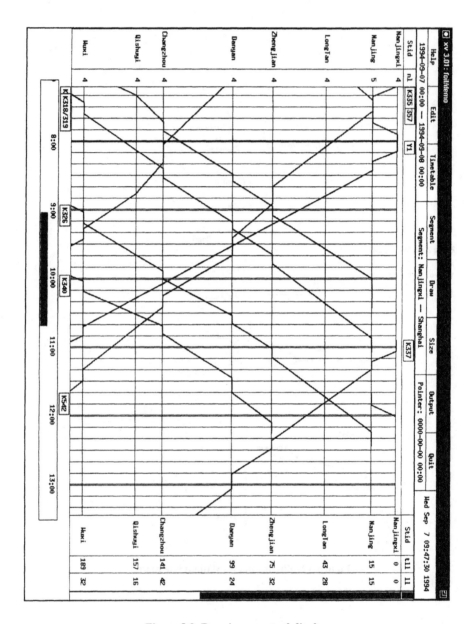

Figure 8.2. Running map tool display

- Y1 may pass through Danyan just after K335 has left and (unless they are or can be put on different lines) Y1 will be delayed. The extent to which Y1 is delayed will depend on the signalling, and hence the train capacity, of the line between Danyan and Changzhou.

The dispatcher has to decide which of these will occur and react accordingly. If K335 is not a passenger train it might be possible to dispatch it from Danyan early, or even cancel its stop there, so that Y1 can overtake it at Changzhou (which might also mean changing K335's track at Changzhou). Alternatively K335 can be told to wait at Danyan until Y1 has passed and, perhaps, be delayed at Changzhou but be back on time at Wuxi since it seems to travel comparatively slowly from Changzhou to Wuxi.

In this case the dispatcher has perhaps nearly an hour to make his decision, work out the detailed adjustments and transmit them, but this is unusually long. The display shown here is also unrealistically sparse; it only shows a typical timetable for passenger trains.

The dispatcher needs information about how fast trains are allowed to travel on different lines, on the tracks available at stations, on the lines available (including the possibility of switching a train to the "opposite" line), on the capacity of lines, on the relative priorities of trains, etc.

The mode of operation of the tool for rescheduling is that the dispatcher can make adjustments either graphically (by clicking and dragging on the display) or textually (by clicking on a train identifier icon to bring up a textual timetable for the train and editing it). If such an operation breaks one of the "rules" (see Section 8.4.5) then a pop-up window will appear describing the infraction. When the dispatcher is happy with the adjustments they can be "committed" and the new timetable is output.

The same tool can be used for scheduling — the creation of timetables. This is done by starting with the "basic" passenger timetable for 24 hours for the current period, such as Summer, and then adding all the freight and additional trains required for that day. This is then split into 12-hour *shift plans* and then again into 3-hour *stage plans*. A dispatcher is typically operating one stage plan and also reflecting "knock-on" effects into the next one.

The display shows one *segment*, which is a set of stations connected linearly by lines. The area covered by a dispatch unit will typically involve several segments. So, for example, train K340 terminates at Zhengjian but train K326 continues from Nanjing on a different segment. The textual display for the trains shows this. It is possible to switch the display to different segments.

This prototype tool is only intended to aid planners and dispatchers. It does not try to find solutions to problems. It was felt that such a "passive" tool would be much more likely to find acceptance initially than one that tried to take over the existing dispatching job. It was also felt that it would take some time to understand the tactics used by actual dispatchers, and to create a tool whose proposals would be respected by them.

8.2.1 Methodological Approach

PRaCoSy is one of UNU/IIST's *advanced development projects*. In these projects the work takes place at UNU/IIST in Macau and is done by "fellows" from one or more developing countries trained and supervised by UNU/IIST staff. In this project the fellows were (except for one) software engineers from the Chinese Railways.

The purpose of such projects is both to train the software engineers involved and also to improve the software capability of their institution. A main component in this capability is the development of *domain models* in their area of interest — railways in this case. So a major part of the project was devoted to domain analysis and the modelling of railways.

Work done by UNU/IIST involving public funds is automatically in the public domain. So software production within such projects is limited to prototype, demonstrator software.

Three stages were therefore followed in Phase 1 of the project:

- domain analysis: thorough understanding and documentation of the components of a railway;
- requirements capture: documentation of the various functions required to support scheduling and rescheduling;
- software development: production of a prototype tool.

In Sections 8.4, 8.5 and 8.6 we describe these three stages.

Phase 2, involving new Fellows had two main tasks:

1. following evaluation of the prototype running map, to consider and specify the changes needed to make a tool that could actually be used by dispatchers;
2. to consider the problems of a distributed running map, allowing for dispatchers and dispatch units to operate concurrently while maintaining a consistent view of the schedule and adjustments to it.

Phase 2 is described in Section 8.7. In Section 8.8 we draw some conclusions.

8.2.2 Levels of Formality

Throughout the project the approach was *formal* using the RAISE specification language and method (RAISE, 1992, 1995). There are a variety of ways in which formality may be applied to software development:

- the "lightest" approach is to write an initial specification and then use it to produce programming language code;
- a "heavier" approach is to write the initial specification and then to *refine* it in one or more steps into a more concrete specification before producing a program from it. This approach gives the opportunity to:
  - *prove* the refinement steps are correct, the "heaviest" and most expensive approach, or to
  - *justify* the refinements wholly or partly informally, the "rigorous" approach (Jones, 1980).

Other variations are also possible. A common tactic is to choose particularly critical properties of a system and prove only those for the initial specification and refinements. Safety-critical properties are often tackled in this way.

Common to all these approaches is the pivotal role of the initial specification. It is this that is meant to describe the domain and the system requirements, and it must be shown to be correct with respect to the client's or customer's notions of what they want. We call this *validation*. Validation is inevitably informal (assuming your client is not able to present you with a formal specification) because their requirements are written in natural language, which is inevitably ambiguous and typically incomplete in some respects and inconsistent in others.

In this project we adopted the "light" approach, which we saw as most appropriate for a system that was not safety-critical. It therefore differs from examples such as (Dehbonei and Mejia, 1995), (Hansen, 1994), (Ogino and Hirao, 1995) and (Simpson, 1994). (Although a description of a system to monitor rail freight (Dürr *et al.*, 1995) points out that systems whose failure is expensive may also be considered critical.) We also wanted to adopt a "rapid prototype" style of development. Such a style is particularly appropriate when you hope to provide computer support for an activity previously done manually, and where user acceptance may be part of the problem. "The tool must be acceptable to users" is hard to formalise! A brief introduction to the RAISE Specification Language and the style adopted is given in Section 8.3.

We believe that much of the advantage of formality lies in creating the initial specification. It serves to isolate and clarify the important concepts, to make them amenable to formal or informal, but still precise, analysis, and also to clarify those aspects which are not or cannot be formalised, the "non-functional" requirements like acceptability. A development plan can then make sure that these are dealt with in some way. (A general discussion on non-functional requirements and how to deal with them is beyond the scope of this chapter.) Getting more out of formality, proving critical properties or doing refinement, gives further confidence in correctness but at substantial cost: there is a law of diminishing returns.

8.3 The RAISE Specification Language

The RAISE Specification Language (RSL) (RAISE, 1992) is a "wide spectrum" language: it is possible to describe applicative or imperative, sequential or concurrent systems. The normal style proposed in the RAISE method (RAISE, 1995) is to start with an abstract, applicative sequential specification and to develop this into a concrete specification, initially still applicative and then, usually, imperative and perhaps concurrent. Phase 1 of this project adopted the "light" approach referred to previously. It only used the applicative sequential style and was rather more concrete than a style one would adopt using a "heavier" approach. Phase 2 used a more abstract approach to analysing the distribution of the running map tool and also developed a concurrent specification to describe an architecture for it.

RSL specifications are collections of modules, usually **schemes** which are named (and possibly parameterised) **class** expressions. We do not present the complete specification here; for Phase 1 this can be found in (Prehn, 1994) and for Phase 2 in (Dong, 1996). Both are available via the UNU/IIST home page `http://www.iist.unu.edu`. Neither do we show here the division into modules. Most modules have a particular "type of interest" and provide functions to create, modify and observe values of this type. There are modules describing the type *Track*, then one using *Track* to define *Station*, one defining *Line*, then one using *Station* and *Line* to define *Network*, and so on.

A typical applicative class expression contains one or more **type** declarations, one or more **value** declarations for defining constants and functions and perhaps some **axiom** declarations containing axioms used to constrain the values.

8.3.1 Types

Type declarations may be "abstract" or "concrete". An abstract type, also termed a "sort", is just given a name. If we declare:

type *Date*

then *Date* is a sort. We know nothing about its structure, about how dates will be represented. It might later be modelled as a natural number (the type **Nat**) interpreted as days since some base date, or a record of the day, month and year.

If *Date* is defined as a sort it is still possible to constrain it to say, for example, that *Date* values are totally ordered. We might do this by introducing an operator and some axioms:

value
    $\leq$: *Date* $\times$ *Date* $\rightarrow$ **Bool**
axiom
    [*reflexive*]
        $\forall\, d : Date \cdot d \leq d,$
    [*transitive*]
        $\forall\, d1,d2,d3 : Date \cdot d1 \leq d2 \land d2 \leq d3 \Rightarrow d1 \leq d3,$
    ...

In the Phase 1 specification only a few rather uninteresting types, like identifiers for tracks, stations, trains, etc., were defined as sorts, and no axioms were given. In this case all we have for values in the type are equality and inequality (with the standard congruence properties).

A "concrete" type is defined by being equal to some other type, or a type expression formed from other types. For example:

type
    Year = **Nat**,
    Month = $\{| \, n : \mathbf{Nat} \cdot n \geq 1 \land n \leq 12 \, |\},$

$Day = \{| \ n : \textbf{Nat} \cdot n \geq 1 \wedge n \leq 31 \ |\}$,
$Date = \{| \ d : Year \times Month \times Day \cdot is\_day(d) \ |\}$

defines *Date* concretely in terms of tuples of *Year*, *Month* and *Day*. **Nat** is built in, together with literals like *0* and *1*, plus standard operators like $+$ and $\leq$. *Month*, *Day* and *Date* are all subtypes: *is_day* will be a function defined elsewhere (to deal with months of less than 31 days and with leap years). *is_day* has result type **Bool**, and so might be termed a predicate: predicates are not distinguished from functions.

$\times$ is a type constructor. Others used here are **-set** (finite power set), * (finite sequence), $\overrightarrow{m}$ (finite map), $\rightarrow$ (total function) and $\overset{\sim}{\rightarrow}$ (partial function). Each has a number of corresponding operators, such as $\in$ (membership) and $\subseteq$ (subset) for sets, **dom** (domain) and **rng** (range) for maps. Function, map and list (index) applications are written by enclosing arguments in brackets, as in *is_day(d)*.

We also commonly use "variant" and "record" types. Alternatives to some of those above are:

type
$\quad Month == Jan \mid Feb \mid ... \mid Dec$,
$\quad Date' :: year : Year \ month : Month \ day : Day$,
$\quad Date = \{| \ d : Date' \cdot is\_date(d) \ |\}$

Here *Month* is a variant (in this case just like an enumerated type in other languages: more complicated variants, including recursive ones, are possible). The ellipsis ..., used here for convenience, is not valid RSL. *Date'* is a record. It is much like the tuple used earlier for *Date* but allows convenient extraction of components, by "destructors" like *year*. Destructors are functions, so if *d* is a *Date'*, *year(d)* is its year.

8.3.2 Constants and Functions

Constants and functions are values, and must be given at least "signatures" — names and types:

value
$\quad start : Date$,
$\quad next : Date \rightarrow Date$

In a concrete style we often give "explicit" definitions for values. So we might write:

value
$\quad start : Date = mk\_Date'(0, Jan, 1)$,
$\quad tomorrow : Date \rightarrow Date$
$\quad tomorrow(d) \equiv$
$\qquad$ **if** $end\_of\_month(d)$ **then** ...
$\qquad$ **else** $mk\_Date'(year(d), month(d), date(d) + 1)$
$\qquad$ **end**

mk_X is the "constructor" for a record type *X*.

More implicit styles are also possible. For example, one might define *yesterday* as the left inverse of *tomorrow* by a postcondition:

value
  yesterday : *Date* $\xrightarrow{\sim}$ *Date*
  yesterday(*d*) **as** *d'*
    post *tomorrow*(*d'*) = *d*
    pre *d* ≠ *start*

Or we might use an axiom:

value
  yesterday : *Date* $\xrightarrow{\sim}$ *Date*
axiom
  ∀ *d* : *Date* · *yesterday*(*tomorrow*(*d*)) = *d*

If we are doing more formal development we might start with the axiom or postcondition for *yesterday* and later devise the explicit algorithm and then prove it satisfies the earlier specification. This is a simple example of refinement.

8.3.3 Benefits

All this looks like rather like functional programming, and, apart from the axioms (which were rarely used in this "light" style), directly implementable. So why bother with a specification?

The built-in data structures are much more convenient to use than those available in a language like C. This allows very rapid modelling of the domains involved and convenient and terse expressions of the functions. These are easy to read, easy to discuss with others, and easy to modify. And it is also easy to express critical properties, either as theorems or as earlier specifications, and then prove them (which is not always so easy!). Some of this would also be true in a functional programming language, or in one having the built-in types as generic modules. But the ability to state and reason about critical properties (informally or with a proof tool) would still be lacking.

Second, there are functions even in this style which are not immediately executable but which are expressible as simple specifications. For example, suppose we want to state the property that in a timetable, if a train stops it does so for at least *min_stop* minutes. Assume that from a station visit *STV* we can extract or calculate an arrival time *arr* and a departure time *dep*. We can define a predicate on a timetable of type *TT*:

value
  min_arr_dep_separation : *TT* → **Bool**
  min_arr_dep_separation(*TT*) ≡
    (∀ *stv* : *STV* · *is_in*(*stv*, *tt*) ⇒

$$dep(stv) = arr(stv) \lor$$
$$dep(stv) - arr(stv) \geq min\_stop)$$

This specification is not executable because of the universal quantification. The specification does not say how we extract all the station visits from the timetable. Instead it is expressed at the level of the requirement. Hence it is easy to validate against the requirement. It is important that the initial specification has this property of being "at the appropriate level" for validation, for checking that it meets the requirements. If we are forced to write something executable, and give thought to the algorithm as well as the condition, this makes things much more difficult.

Neither does this specification say what we would do if the timetable did not meet the requirement. Presumably we would like the final program to say something rather more informative than "false".

We will see in Section 8.6 how the problems of algorithm and message generation were dealt with when we translated to C.

We shall also see in Section 8.7.3 how the specification in terms of such predicates over timetables led to a completely different style of implementation, using constraint propagation.

We are not advocating such a style for all projects. Critical applications will need more statements of even higher level properties and hence a greater degree of abstraction and of proof. We are trying to show how a "light" approach can be extremely valuable in obtaining a precise definition of the problem domain and in capturing the main requirements.

A more abstract approach is also useful in tackling issues that we want to separate from the details of the example being dealt with. The work done in Phase 2 on distributing maps, described in Section 8.7.2, is an example of this.

8.4 Domain Analysis

The purpose of domain analysis is to understand and document the components of the system and its environment. So in our case we ask immediately *What is (re)scheduling?* This leads immediately to descriptions in terms of *running maps*, *timetables* and railway *regulations*, which in turn involve terms like *network* of *lines* and *stations* and *time intervals*. To understand these terms in the fullest sense we need assurance that what we think they mean corresponds to what our customers think they mean, and when our customers speak a different language and come from a different cultural tradition it is particularly critical. Even if we were experts in railways there is a significant, perhaps even enhanced, danger that the differences in railway cultures will cause problems. In Phase 1 the Fellows were not experienced in dispatching.

This problem was tackled from two directions: informal and formal.

8.4.1 Informal Description

The informal domain descriptions involved several components. They were intended for domain experts, i.e. railway staff, especially dispatchers, rather than computing experts:

- synopsis: a summary of the domain;
- narrative: a more detailed explanation of the domain in terms of its *components* and *processes*;
- terminology: a list of technical terms and their definitions.

In fact the first document in this group was translated from Chinese; it was the first "statement of requirements". Then we produced a synopsis and narrative and effectively "replayed" our understanding of (currently relevant) parts of these requirements. At the same time the terminology document was written in English and then translated to Chinese so that it could be more effectively checked by people in China.

8.4.2 Formal Description

At the same time as trying to capture the domain in natural language, a formal model was constructed. This formal model was to be the basis for the requirements capture and software development, and hence the basis for its correctness (or otherwise). There were two components:

- domain specification: specifying the intrinsic domain notions in RSL (RAISE, 1992);
- data flow diagrams: recording basically the *organisation* of the activities involved in (re)scheduling. Figure 8.3 is an example.
  - the labelled arrows were accompanied by descriptions of the data, for example. E1 is "Station states; track states; time traces". Time traces are relevant events like train arrivals and departures, with times.
  - we did not claim any mathematical semantics for our data flow diagrams; they should perhaps be termed "semi-formal" in that they almost certainly could be formalised (Larsen *et al.*, 1994) but we did not want to use them in a formal way. That is, we had no intention of *reasoning* that our system would be correct with respect to them.

8.4.3 Aspects of Domains

In doing domain analysis we consider and document a number of aspects:

- intrinsics: The essential technical aspects of the domain — in our case such things as lines, stations, trains, timetables, etc.

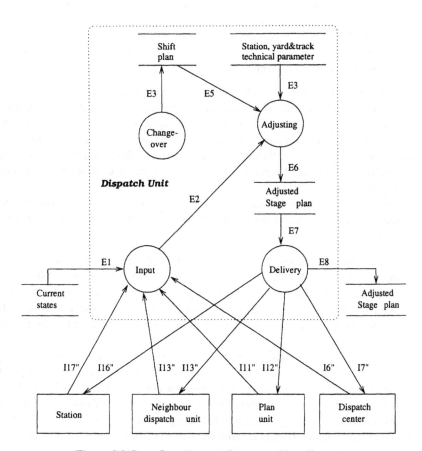

Figure 8.3. Data flow diagram for stage plan adjustment

- support technology: The technical aspects of the domain that depend on a particular technology and which may change with time. Thus particular signalling and interlocking mechanisms would be in this category;
- regulations: The regulations that affect the system, i.e. that it must conform to or for which breaches must be detected and handled in a special manner. This is obviously important for railways, and would be important in any safety-critical system;
- staff: The maintainers and (for safety-critical systems, for example) its inspectors or people who license it for use;
- clients: The users of the system;
- computing and communications platforms: Details of the hardware on which the system is to run or with which it is required to interact.

The intrinsics are documented by creating a formal description, a specification of the system. Support technology aspects may be captured by extensions of the intrinsics, but in general we try to avoid this, to make at least the initial specification independent of them. Regulations should be captured formally. Other aspects are typically mostly informal; they are (like support technology) likely to give direction later in the development but not be captured in the initial specification, which should be high level and abstract.

Why do we stress the idea of domain analysis prior to requirements capture? These notions are normally regarded as part of requirements capture. There are two reasons:

- domain analysis involves understanding the environment of the system as well as the system itself. That is, we look more widely than the boundaries of the system; we try to understand the world (including the human culture) within which it will operate. Only when we have thoroughly understood this do we attempt to define all the processes in this domain, the facilities our system will provide. Defining these facilities (again mostly formally) will be the requirements capture step;
- domain analysis is often wider than the immediate concerns of the current system: it can be the basis of other systems in the same domain. For example, the model of lines and stations we developed for the running map tool provided the basis for work developing tools for station management (Yulin, 1995). This has obvious reuse advantages for anyone hoping or planning to produce further software in the domain. Using the same underlying domain model also makes it much easier to ensure that systems will interoperate correctly. In fact the model used to describe station management needed more detail about switches and crossovers, about the detailed routes between lines and tracks. We defined a notion of a *unit* as a piece of track with *connectors*. Lines and tracks are constructed from linear (two-connector) units. Switches and crossovers have three or more connectors. Units have possible paths through them (so we can distinguish between switched and non-switched crossovers, for example) and also states (so that we can model the changing of a switch). The notions of line and track used in the model presented here can be easily extended with information about their constituent units.

8.4.4 Specification of the Railway Network

The *network* consists of *stations* connected by *lines*. A station consists essentially of a number of *tracks*. Figure 8.4 shows a station with five tracks.

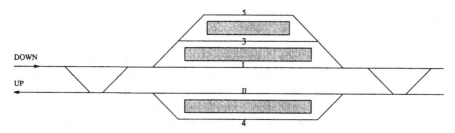

Figure 8.4. Example station layout

The Roman numbering of the "through" tracks used for non-stopping trains, and the even/odd numbering for up/down lines are Chinese conventions.

8.4.4.1 Tracks. For each track there are a number of lines from which the track can be reached, and a number of lines that can be reached from the track. Tracks also have lengths and types. Stations, lines and tracks all have identifiers. We define the type *TR* to model tracks:

type
    TR :: *flns* : *LNid*-**set** *tlns* : *LNid*-**set** *t* : *TRtype* *lng* : *LNG*,
    TRtype == *LINE* | *SIDING* | *PLATFORM* | *FREIGHT*,
    LNG = **Nat**,
    LNid

This and the rest of the specification were written in RSL, and the RAISE tools (Bruun, 1995) were used to type check them and "pretty print" them.

    TR is a record with four components: the possible incoming lines *flns*, outgoing lines *tlns*, type *t*, and length *lng*. *TRtype* is a variant type containing four constant values.

8.4.4.2 Stations. The station type *ST* is then a finite map (in general a many-one relation) of track identifiers to tracks:

type *ST* = *TRid* ⇒ *TR*

8.4.4.3 Lines. Lines go from one station to another, have a type, a length and a maximum speed:

type

   $LN' :: s1 : STid \ s2 : STid \ lt : Ltyp \ lng : LNG \ sp : SP,$
   $Ltyp == UP \mid DOWN \mid BOTH,$
   $SP = \mathbf{Nat},$
   $LN = \{\mid ln : LN' \cdot s1(ln) \neq s2(ln) \mid\}$

We expressed the requirement that lines link different stations by use of a subtype definition for the type *LN*.

8.4.4.4 The Network. The network consists of a collection of stations, modelled as a map, and a collection of lines, also modelled as a map. But there is a convention that for any two stations connected by one or more lines, one direction between them is *UP* and the other is *DOWN*. (The running map display also follows this convention in its orientation.) We want to observe this convention in the way we label lines by their end stations: going *DOWN* from *s1* to *s2*. So if there is a line from one station to another then any lines between these two stations will have the stations in the same order, i.e. none will have them in the opposite order:

type

   $ST\_m = STid \xrightarrow{m} ST,$
   $LN\_m' = LNid \xrightarrow{m} LN,$
   $LN\_m = \{\mid lnm : LN\_m' \cdot is\_wf\_LN\_m(lnm) \mid\}$
value
   $is\_wf\_LN\_m : LN\_m' \to \mathbf{Bool}$
   $is\_wf\_LN\_m(lnm) \equiv$
      $(\forall \ ln, ln' : LN \cdot$
         $\{ln,ln'\} \subseteq \mathbf{rng} \ lnm \Rightarrow (s1(ln),s2(ln)) \neq (s2(ln'),s1(ln')))$

The network is the combination of the line map and the station map, modelled as a cartesian product (tuple), but with a number of well-formedness conditions:

type

   $NW' = ST\_m \times LN\_m,$
   $NW = \{\mid nw : NW' \cdot is\_wf\_NW(nw) \mid\}$
value
   $is\_wf\_NW : NW' \to \mathbf{Bool}$
   $is\_wf\_NW(stm, lnm) \equiv$
      $(\forall \ ln : LN \cdot ln \in \mathbf{rng} \ lnm \Rightarrow \{s1(ln),s2(ln)\} \subseteq \mathbf{dom} \ stm) \land$
      $(\forall \ s : STid \cdot s \in \mathbf{dom} \ stm \Rightarrow$
         $InstoST(s,lnm) \cap InsfromST(s,lnm) = \{\} \land$
         $(\forall \ tr : TR \cdot$
            $tr \in \mathbf{rng} \ stm(s) \Rightarrow$
               $flns(tr) \subseteq InstoST(s,lnm) \land tlns(tr) \subseteq InsfromST(s,lnm)))$

The well-formedness conditions for the network are:

− the stations at the ends of lines are in the station map, and

- for each station in the station map:
  - the lines into the station are disjoint from the lines out of the station, and
  - for each track in the station, the lines into it are a subset of the lines into the station and the lines from it are a subset of the lines from the station.

The auxiliary function *InstoST* is defined as follows:

value
    InstoST : *STid* × *LN_m* → *LNid*-**set**
    InstoST(*s*,*lnm*) ≡
        { *lnid* | *lnid* : *LNid* • *lnid* ∈ **dom** *lnm* ∧ *is_Into*(*lnm*(*lnid*),*s*) },

    is_Into : *LN* × *Stid* → **Bool**
    is_Into(*ln*, *s*) ≡
        let *mk_LN'*(*s1*,*s2*,*lt*,_,_) = *ln* **in**
           (*lt* = *DOWN* ∧ *s2* = *s*) ∨ (*lt* = *UP* ∧ *s1* = *s*) ∨
           (*lt* = *BOTH* ∧ *s* ∈ {*s1*,*s2*})
        end

InstoST defines the lines into a station using a set comprehension: it returns those lines in the line map that go into the station. A line goes into a station *s* if it is a *DOWN* line and its second end station is *s* or if it is an *UP* line.
    InsfromST is defined similarly.

8.4.5 Specification of Timetables

The following concepts were defined:

Station visit: A record of station and track identifiers, arrival and departure times, optional departure line, arrival and departure lengths of trains. The well-formedness condition is that the arrival is not earlier than the departure (equality indicating passage through without stopping). Time is modelled by a type *T*, a subtype of **Nat** including those times in minutes that represent dates from the (arbitrarily chosen) beginning of 1993 to the end of 2399:

    type
        STV' :: *s* : *STid* *tr* : *TRid* *a* : *T* *d* : *T* *dln* : *OptLN* *al* : *LNG* *dl* : *LNG*,
        STV = {| *stv* : *STV'* • *d*(*stv*) ≥ *a*(*stv*) |},
        optLN == *nil* | *mk_LN*(*l* : *LNid*)

Journey: A sequence of station visits. The well-formedness condition is that the sequence is non empty, departure at one station precedes arrival at the next, and only the last visit may have no departure line.

    type
        J' = *STV**,
        J = {| *j* : *J'* • *j* ≠ ⟨⟩ ∧ *is_wf_J*(*j*) |}

value
    $is\_wf\_J : J' \to$ **Bool**
    $is\_wf\_J(j) \equiv$
        $(\forall\ i : $ **Nat** $\cdot$
            $\{i,i+1\} \subseteq$ **inds** $j \Rightarrow$
                $a(j(i+1)) > d(j(i)) \land (dln(j(i)) = nil \Rightarrow i = $ **len** $j))$

There is an additional function expressing the well-formedness of a journey with respect to a network. It requires that the stations exist, the track exists in the station, the departure and arrival lengths are not less than the track length, and (for visits apart from the last) the departure line is a line from the station to the next, goes from the track, leads to the next track, the departure length equals the next arrival length, and the travel time is consistent with the maximum speed and length of the line.

Segment: A non-empty sequence of stations. The well-formedness condition is that the adjacent stations are connected by at least one line, and the segment is listed in the *UP* order.

Timetable: A map from train identifiers to journeys. Train identifiers include a date as well as a (sort) identifier so that we can distinguish between the same train on different days.

type
    $TNid :: id : TNid\_\ dt : Date,$
    $TNid\_,$
    $TT = TNid \xrightarrow{m} J$

A "basic" 24-hour timetable, such as the Summer one, has all dates set to zero. We do not use a subtype for well-formedness of timetables since we expect that during adjustment they will temporarily be ill-formed. Instead we specify a function that can be used to check them.

There are three kinds of well-formedness conditions for timetables:

1. Consistency between the timetable and the network, i.e. all journeys are well formed.
2. The physical constraint that trains on the same line cannot overtake.
3. A number of regulatory rules. There are minimal time separations between:
    - trains occupying the same track
    - two station entries on the same line
    - two station exits on the same line
    - occupations of a line in opposite directions.

Projection: A restriction of a timetable to a particular segment and a particular time period. A projection of a timetable gives the display of the running map tool.

Before discussing, in Section 8.5, the stage of requirements capture it is worth reflecting on what the domain analysis achieved. We had a formal and hence very specific semantic definition of all the concepts that are commonly used in (Chinese) railway circles but were initially difficult for outsiders to grasp (apart from the translation problem from Chinese to English). The specifications we generated (accompanied by commentary much like that used in this chapter) were examined and discussed by the Chinese fellows at UNU/IIST, so that we gained assurance that these particular definitions are the correct ones.

We had also defined a number of well-formedness conditions. Many of these are consistency requirements — stations at ends of lines exist, trains visit existing stations on existing tracks by existing and reachable lines, etc. Many others express *regulations* about the way that Chinese railways are operated. Hence the specification provides a *theory* of railway networks and of the operation of trains: we can formulate expected properties as theorems and justify them, either formally by theorem proving or informally. Doing so is an essential part of *validating* the specification, i.e. checking that it meets its requirements. It is an important feature of the model that it allows the easy and transparent statement of regulations as well-formedness functions, so that validation is simple. We can validate that a well-formed timetable complies with a regulation by pointing to the predicate expressing it. A close correspondence between requirements and the structure of the specification also provides a good basis for requirements tracking.

8.5 Requirements Capture

Requirements capture extends the formal specification produced by the domain analysis with the definitions of the operational facilities that the system will provide to its users. In our case the domain analysis gave us in particular a definition of a timetable together with all the railway regulations that make a timetable well-formed. The task in requirements analysis is then to specify the running map tool. We already had the functions to project a timetable on to a particular period and a particular segment, hence defining the contents of the main window of the running map tool. We defined in addition:

– functions to input timetables to the tool — to support *scheduling*;
– functions to modify a timetable — to support *rescheduling*.

The first of these resulted eventually in a separate tool for timetable input, as the mainly graphical means of editing timetables in the running map tool turned out to be too clumsy for inputting large amounts of data. Then the normal mode of operating the running map tool was to start by loading a complete timetable. There are several kinds of timetable. The process starts with a *basic* timetable, which is not set to any particular day. From a basic timetable, 12-hour *shift plans* are generated by planning units, and from these typically 3-hour *stage plans* are generated and used for rescheduling by dispatch units. The ability to project over periods and segments allows all these activities to be supported.

Rescheduling is currently done manually, by drawing lines on large sheets of paper (prepared with the segment stations listed) indicating how the trains should move and stop. Rescheduling is done by erasing and redrawing. A computer tool to support this activity clearly needs to be mainly graphic, with the possibility to draw lines, move them, shift points on them, etc. But the display is also essentially an abstraction. It does not show which line between stations is being used by a train, or which track in a station. It is also hard to read precise times. (Hand drawn running maps do have more annotations to help with some of these problems.) The tool has, therefore, a number of tabular displays that can be shown by clicking on a train identifier, to show complete details of its journey, or on a station, to show complete details of all visits to that station. Changes can be made by editing either the tables or the graphic display.

We also attempted to formally specify the widgets generating the actual display of the running map tool, which is (X) window-based. This captured quite well the hierarchy of processes and the effects of events — button pushes, mouse clicks etc. — but says nothing about the appearance and is of little use in judging the usability of the tool. This specification was actually produced after the tool as part of its documentation. We started the development stage, therefore, with a formal specification of the kernel of the running map tool, the part that checks for well-formedness of timetables plus a specification of the projection of a timetable that would form the basis of the centre of the display, but not of the buttons, pop-up menus, etc. that would form the user interface. Instead we drew the graphic design and checked informally that the functions required from the data flow diagrams could be supported.

It would also be possible to start requirements capture by making an *abstraction* of the specification from the domain analysis. It has been found elsewhere (Dandanell *et al.*, 1993) that the first specifications one writes, with the aim of understanding the problem, are often more concrete than is appropriate for starting development. There are standard techniques in RAISE for producing a more abstract specification from a concrete one (RAISE, 1995).

8.6 Software Development

8.6.1 Design

It was decided to code the tool essentially from the initial specification rather than doing any formal development, at least in the sense of data structure development. Formalising the basic concepts by domain analysis and identifying and formalising all the functions needed to create and modify timetables had placed the project on a firm footing. There were two design tasks to be undertaken: the graphical user interface (which we had not specified formally) and the C data structures. The latter was part of translation.

The running map tool graphical interface was created using Athena widgets and a detailed design of the tool was done showing its intended appearance, the widget tree and, for each listing, the widgets, their classes and attributes. The final tool (which follows this design precisely) was illustrated in Figure 8.2.

The display separates stations (vertically) in proportion to their distances so that a train running at constant speed appears as a line of constant slope. The transformation to achieve this for any given segment was defined (in standard mathematical notation).

We wanted to be easily able to instantiate the tool for particular networks, and hence to be able to communicate these and to be able to inspect and edit them easily. Descriptors in, essentially, BNF were defined for them, therefore. Then corresponding C data structures were defined and the procedures to parse and unparse them written. Timetables were handled similarly.

There was a change between the specification and the final code in that the functions to check for well-formedness were developed into functions that generated messages about any breach of well-formedness. These messages then appear in pop-up windows.

8.6.2 Translation

We thought that a fairly simple strategy for encoding the data structures would suffice for a demonstrator tool. Of the data structures we had used, records, cartesian products and enumerated types either exist in C or could be coded immediately. For maps we used a simple strategy of encoding a map as a linked list, with the domain element added as an extra field to the range element. For example we have the following RSL type definitions and the corresponding C definitions:

type

$$LN\_m' = LNid \xrightarrow{m} LN,$$
$$LN\_m = \{| \ lnm : LN\_m' \cdot is\_wf\_LN\_m(lnm) \ |\}$$

```
typedef  struct LN_m_  * LN_m;
struct LN_m_ {
        LN       ln;          /* the line record */
        LN_m     next_p;      /* next_pointer */
};
```

type

$$LN' :: s1 : STid \ ...,$$
$$LN = \{| \ ln : LN' \cdot s1(ln) \neq s2(ln) \ |\}$$

```
typedef struct LN_  * LN
struct LN_ {
        LNid     lnid;
        STid     s1;
        ...
};
```

So what has happened to the subtypes? Functions were written for them in C (whether, as with *LN_m*, the RSL used a separate function, or, as with *LN*, it did not). For example, the C function is_wf_LN:

```
/* well_formed line check */
/* s1 must be different from s2.*/
bool is_wf_LN(LN ln)
{       if (Ident_eq(ln->s1, ln->s2))
          {error("Warning error:
                    expected a different station name
                    in line %s:\n", ln->lnid);
            return false;
          }
        return true;
};
```

As well as making the check, the C code also includes the generation of a suitable error message. Such functions are then used as part of the parsing of data used to instantiate the tool; see Section 8.6.1. The well-formedness conditions on timetables are checked both on initial loading of a timetable and also after rescheduling changes; they produce messages in pop-up boxes.

Functions that involved existential or universal quantification were coded as iterative functions over the linked lists. Comprehended expressions were translated similarly. For example, the function *InstoST*, for collecting the set of identifiers of lines into a station, was specified and then translated as follows:

value

 InstoST : *STid* × *LN_m* → *LNid*-**set**

 InstoST(s,lnm) ≡

  { *lnid* | *lnid* : *LNid* · *lnid* ∈ **dom** *lnm* ∧ *is_lnto(lnm(lnid),s)* }

```
/* apply a line map and a stid.
                    return a lnid_set to stid.*/
IDS lnstoST(LN_m lnm, STid stid)
{   LN_m plns = lnm;
    IDS  ls   = IDS_NULL;
    while (plns != LN_m_NULL){
      if (is_lnto(lnm_get_ln(plns), stid))
        ls = ids_add(ls,
                ln_get_lnid(lnm_get_ln(plns)));
      plns = lnm_next(plns);
    }
    return ls;
};
```

Hence the specification could be regarded as "translatable" to a large extent. At the time, mid-1994, the translator from RSL to C++ (Bruun, 1995) was still under development. If we used it now it could translate the map types since it has built in a standard translation for maps (not unlike the one we used). The universally and existentially quantified expressions would still need hand translation though. All the functions had been specified explicitly, i.e. not using post conditions or axioms, and many could be translated directly (and could have been translated by a tool).

It is readily apparent that the RSL specification is much easier to read than the C code and hence much easier to validate against the requirements (and easier to change if found to be incorrect). The separation of specification from coding supports a separation of concerns between conceptual correctness (is this the appropriate condition?) from algorithmic correctness and the appropriateness of the messages generated. In addition the separation of the two levels would make it possible to change the data structures used (to sorted linked lists or trees or hash tables rather than unsorted linked lists for some of the maps or sets, for example) if found necessary, without changing the specification.

The C function lnstoST uses a type IDS modelling sets of identifiers (again as linked lists) together with functions like ids_add (for adding an identifier to a set). There are functions for deletion, for set union, intersection etc. all collected into a separate module. This was typical of the general approach: each of the RSL modules defining tracks, stations, lines, network etc. were extended with functions to create such an object, add it, delete it, get each component of it, and check its well-formedness. This meant that the C code generated, as well as following the modularity of the specification, had a distinctly "object-oriented" flavour to it, with each kind of entity accessed and manipulated by its own particular collection of functions.

8.7 Phase 2

The first group of Fellows returned to China in December 1994. Two more fellows were supposed to come from Zhengzhou in January 1995 but there were problems and they did not come to Macau until August of that year.

8.7.1 Improving the Running Map Specification

The main comments they reported on the prototype running map was its inability to handle different kinds of train (passenger, freight, special and military) and locomotive (electric, diesel, and steam). It also lacked a number of special symbols used as annotations: to show new trains starting, terminating, coming from a neighbouring dispatch unit, going to a neighbouring dispatch unit, trains merging, trains splitting, temporary speed restrictions on lines, lines blocked by accidents or for repair, etc.

There were a number of standard intervals for two trains arriving at a station on the same line, departing on the same line, etc. In the original model these were assumed to be constant: in fact they depend on the station and the line. The times for travel on lines are also not in fact constant: they depend on the type of locomotive and whether the line is being used in the "opposite" mode (an *UP* train on a *DOWN* line, or vice versa). There are also additions for acceleration and/or deceleration if the train is starting from rest and/or stopping. These were documented from the official Chinese manuals, with formulae and diagrams and then included in a new specification, cross referenced by comments to the formulae in the documentation.

These changes were quite straightforward to make. They appeared only in the record types for stations, trains and lines (each in separate RSL modules) and in the predicates used to check the well-formedness of the timetables. The overall structure of the specification and the types for the network and timetables were unaffected.

8.7.2 Distributing the Specification

The prototype running map and its specification assumed a single timetable that could be projected into several segments. But in practice scheduling is done on an area basis by *planning units*, who pass schedules on to *dispatch centres* who partition them amongst *dispatch units*. These dispatch units do the actual rescheduling, communicating with stations, their dispatch centre and neighbouring dispatch units. We needed to work out how to distribute a timetable and the adjustments to it, and to analyse when adjustments to one component would affect others.

This was done by specifying a general theory of *distributing* a map according to a *partition* of its domain. This could be applied by representing a timetable as:

type $TT = STid \times TNid \xrightarrow{m} STV$

and then partitioning this according to which dispatch unit (DUid) each station belongs to. The distributed timetable would have a type:

type $DTT = DUid \xrightarrow{m} TT$

The theory of partitioning was developed generically and then instantiated in this way.

In the generic theory the notion of *delegability* was defined . A function f to change a map is *delegable* if the diagram in Figure 8.5 commutes:

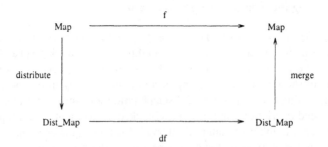

Figure 8.5. Correctness of distributed function

Here *df* is f applied to just one component of the distributed map (and only exists if f has a domain value of the map as a parameter, allowing the component to be identified). *merge* is the inverse of *distribute*. Intuitively, a function to adjust a timetable is delegable if the change can be made by one dispatcher and the resulting timetable, formed by merging the distributed ones, would be the same as if the adjustment had been made to an undistributed timetable. An algorithm for checking delegability was defined and proved correct using the RAISE justification editor (Bruun, 1995) (the only time formal proof was used in this project).

A similar notion was applied to the concept of *analysing* a map and generating messages (to be used for the messages reporting infractions of the timetabling rules). We need to know when, after an adjustment, we will not create any spurious messages or lose any messages because of the distribution, i.e. when we analyse each component separately. This can be defined in terms of a similar commuting diagram.

Another notion, not directly related to distribution but expected to be of use, was that of *partial analysis*. For a particular adjustment function, what analyses need to be redone and which are guaranteed to generate the same messages? Knowing this will enable us to only perform some of the checks after changes, and to reliably improve the speed of the running map tool.

These ideas were formally specified and instantiated for timetables (George, 1995). This would have enabled all the functions for adjusting timetables and for checking for well-formedness to be checked for delegability and distributability, and for communication procedures with neighbouring dispatch units to be defined where necessary.

This is an example of a general method for defining distributed systems that has been found to be effective on several systems. First the complete system is specified as one entity. Then the division into components is done and the notion of correctness of the distributed system defined in terms of some equivalence with the original. This gives a theory about the communications and high level protocols needed in the distributed system. Trying to work "bottom up" from specifications of the distributed components makes things much more difficult because it lacks the notion of correctness.

It is also worth noticing that the analysis can be done without any need to specify the distributed system as a concurrent system: the analysis is all done on an applicative model, and can even, as here, be defined initially in terms of a parameterised abstraction of the original model, later instantiated to the actual one.

A development of the applicative distributed running map to a concurrent system was done (Mei, 1995).

8.7.3 A Constraint-Based Approach

Jimmy Ho Man Lee and Ho-Fung Leung of the Intelligent Real-Time Systems Laboratory at the Chinese University of Hong Kong set up a joint project with UNU/IIST during the academic year 1995–6 involving two final-year undergraduates and a Ph.D. student. They wanted to take the running map tool further, into a tool that would apply constraint propagation techniques to the rescheduling problem, and generate proposed solutions.

They were given the RAISE specification from Phase 1, and given a brief tutorial on how to read it — they had no previous experience with formal specification. They also had all the other documentation and the existing prototype. They were able, with little interaction, to reproduce the existing tool (on a different platform as well as with a different implementation technique). This is a striking example of the use of a formal description to state requirements precisely, and even to transmit them to people previously unacquainted with the notation after minimal training. It also shows the benefit of specifying the conditions to be checked rather than the algorithms to do so. The conditions can be validated against those in the existing documentation, because they are expressed in a similar mathematical style at the same level of abstraction, and also fairly easily communicated to others.

They were also able to devise and implement some strategies for rescheduling (Chiu *et al.*, 1996).

8.8 Conclusions

8.8.1 Achievements

Phase 1 took just over a year, involving most of the time of five fellows from the Chinese railways (though one also worked much of the time on his MSc thesis on station management (Yulin, 1995), and also as a system administrator) and the part time help of, initially, the first and third of the authors of this chapter, then the first and second. The RSL specification for Phase 1 was some 850 lines and the C code 15 000 lines (of which 5 000 are the non-specified graphical user interface). The modular structure of the C code follows that of the specification closely. The documentation runs to 600 pages. Many of the **PRaCoSy** documents are available on the World Wide Web, via the UNU/IIST home page http://www.iist.unu.edu.

This is rather more than a normal industrial development of such a system, but a lot of time was spent on domain analysis and on training the fellows not only in RAISE (and C) but also in a number of software engineering disciplines. It also included work to set up configuration management and version control systems. Last but not least, the fellows were working in a foreign language.

The quality of the resulting tool is very high for a prototype. No records were kept of errors found but few were discovered. The performance was initially poor, but after some tuning in terms of extra code to determine what checks needed to be re-done after changes to the running map it became quite acceptable (running on a SUN sparc workstation).

Phase 2 lasted 8 months and involved 2 Fellows from the Chinese railways. This phase was unfortunately curtailed when the two fellows were called back to Zhengzhou, for reasons that were never fully explained to us, but seemed to involve their being needed for other projects. At the time they left we had incorporated the changes needed to the network and the timetables (while preserving the structure of the specification) and were close to translating to a new prototype.

8.8.2 Role of Formal Methods

Formal methods are often claimed to be expensive to introduce, difficult and expensive to use, to lack adequate tools, to be inapplicable to large examples, to be incomprehensible to customers, to be applicable if at all only to safety- or mission-critical systems (Hall, 1990; Bowen and Hinchey, 1995a). This project provides some evidence to counter these claims.

The Fellows from China were "up to speed" with RAISE in quite a short time. The "light" use of RAISE as a means of describing the domain and software requirements clearly and providing a basis for the code to be written was, we believe, very effective and provided a development route for a non-critical system that was both fast and reliable. The system is not extremely large, but is certainly considerably more than an academic example. The RAISE tools are robust, fast, capable of supporting projects involving several people, and produce good documentation. The success of the separate group from Hong Kong in re-implementing and further developing the running map tool using a different technology, using a formal specification as their main input, is striking. The use of a formal method in a "rapid prototyping" style is unusual, at least in the literature, but proved effective, and we believe that Phase 2 could have rapidly produced a second, distributed prototype involving all the extra details needed by dispatchers in a very short time. The substantial initial work analysing and describing the railway domain also proved effective in supporting one Fellow's separate work on station management.

At the same time, we must point out the need for experts in training and assisting such a project. Using formal methods involves a different approach, in which analysing, understanding and defining the problem is the major task, and writing the code is deferred until quite late. This involves skill and judgement, and industries are well advised to seek external help initially until they have developed their own experts. It also takes time to develop an appropriate culture, in which a project that has so far produced lots of specifications but no code is not automatically seen as in danger.

8.8.3 Further Work

The project stopped very abruptly which, whilst not an unknown event, was still very disappointing to those involved. Recently, however, interest has been expressed in India and in Russia in continuing the work.

For India, the running map tool was ported to Linux. This exposed several of the usual problems in the behaviour of the tool due to differences in the behaviour of C compilers (even though both were gcc) and in the behaviour of the widgets (again supposedly identical) but none (apparently, but without substantial testing) in the code for checking timetables.

Acknowledgements

The authors of this chapter trained, advised and assisted, but the actual work was done by others.

Most of the work was done by the Fellows from the Chinese railways: Dong Yulin, Jin Danhua, Liu Xin, Ma Chao and Sun Guoqin in Phase 1; Liu LianSuo and Yang Dong in Phase 2.

Srinivasan Parthasarathy from Hyderabad, India, worked on the project for 9 months in Phase 1 as a visiting researcher, and Hong Mei from Fudan University, Shanghai, China worked on it as a Fellow for 2 months between the two main phases.

CHAPTER 9

Lessons from the Formal Development of a Radiation Therapy Machine Control Program

Jonathan Jacky

9.1 Introduction

Formal methods work best where traditional programming methods do not work very well: problems that are too difficult to solve by intuition or too novel to solve by modifying some existing program or design. We are developing the control program for the therapy operator's console for a unique radiation therapy machine. This is not a pilot study or demonstration project; we will use this program to administer neutron therapy at our clinic. The program is safety-critical; it could contribute to delivering a treatment that differs from the prescribed one, irradiating the wrong volume within the patient or delivering the wrong dose (there are also hardware protection mechanisms that work independently of the control program). Errors in medical software can have serious consequences (Jacky, 1996; Leveson and Turner, 1993; Leveson, 1995), and our experience shows that development methods typically used in this field are only partially effective at eliminating errors (Jacky and White, 1990). We decided to try a more rigorous method.

Moreover, our machine is a unique resource that justifies an unusual development effort. It is not a conventional therapy linear accelerator that provides electron and X-ray beams; it uses a cyclotron to produce a neutron beam, which produces better clinical results than conventional machines for some cancers (Griffin *et al.*, 1998). The computer controls are an essential part of the system and have had dramatic clinical impact because complex shaped fields are necessary to avoid unacceptable complications in neutron therapy (Austin-Seymour *et al.*, 1994). This unique machine is maintained and upgraded by our department, not the manufacturer. The program we are developing is a replacement for a program that was developed by the therapy machine manufacturer and has been in use since the machine was installed in 1984 (Kalet *et al.*, 1997). There is no reuse of code, design or specifications from the earlier program.

9.2 What the Program Does

The purpose of the therapy console program is to help ensure that patients are treated correctly, as directed by their prescriptions. The treatment console computer stores a database of prescriptions for many patients. Each patient's prescription usually includes several different beam configurations called fields. Each field is defined by about fifty machine settings (positions, dose etc.) that must be set properly to deliver the prescribed treatment. The console program enables the therapist to choose fields from the prescription database. The program sets some settings automatically, but others (external motions that present collision hazards) must be set manually by the therapist. The program checks all settings against the prescription and ensures that the radiation beam can only turn on when the correct settings for the chosen field have been achieved (subject to override by the therapist for some settings in some circumstances). The therapist can turn on the therapy beam (by a separate nonprogrammable mechanism) after the program indicates that the machine is ready.

The program provides a user interface (so the therapist can select prescriptions and view machine status) and controls devices. Low-level device control (such as turning the beam on and off and guiding machine motions) is performed by other nonprogrammable mechanisms, programmable logic controllers (PLCs), and simple embedded computers. The therapy console program provides some of these low-level controllers with endpoints (such as positions and doses), and it enables (or disables) motions and activation of the beam. The delegation of functions among the software and hardware components was a prerequisite to the work discussed here and is described elsewhere (Jacky *et al.*, 1990, 1992).

9.3 What the Project Produced

We wrote about 250 pages of informal specification and design description, about 1200 lines of Z and about 6000 lines of code[1]. Table 9.1 reports the size of each product.

The informal specification (Jacky *et al.*, 1990, 1992, 1995b) describes the system in prose, diagrams, tables and a few formulas. Part I (Jacky *et al.*, 1990) is an overview of the entire facility, part II (Jacky *et al.*, 1992) specifies the user interface for every console (including accelerator operators' consoles) and part III (Jacky *et*

---

[1] Our estimates for the completed project. Table 9.1 reports the sizes at this writing.

Table 9.1. Development products (documents and code)

PRODUCT	SIZE	
Informal specification: overview, entire facility	106 pages	
Informal specification: user interface, entire facility	235 pages	
Informal specification: user interface, therapy only	45 pages	
Informal specification: hardware and files, therapy only	131 pages	
Formal description (Z texts)	77 pages	(1137 lines)
Implementation Guide	42 pages	
Program code	4786 lines	(41 files)
Test scripts	35 pages	

al., 1995b) describes hardware interfaces and external file formats for the therapy console program only.

The formal description (Jacky *et al.*, 1995a) is expressed in the Z notation (Spivey, 1992a); its contents are discussed in Sections 9.4 and 9.5 below. It comprises 1137 lines of Z (207 paragraphs, including 131 schema definitions), presented in a 77 page report (Jacky *et al.*, 1995a) (most of this report is prose)[2]. Concurrency is handled in Z by the interleaving model recommended by Evans (1994): the state is shared by all processes, but operations can be invoked by different processes. The real time clock (needed for timeouts) is modelled in Z as an ordinary state variable.

Most of our Z texts express a detailed design: a collection of state variables, operations on those variables, and a partition of the variables and operations into modules. We used Z to discover the design, not just to document an already existing design. There are few descriptions of other therapy control systems and these do not provide enough detail to serve as examples (Weinhous *et al.*, 1990). We had to create our own. We used no other design notation (except prose). We also wrote an implementation guide in prose (Jacky *et al.*, 1996) to explain our use of the platform's system software and other design information not expressed in the Z texts.

The program is coded in ANSI C; concurrency and device control is provided through EPICS (Dalesio *et al.*, 1991), a library originally developed for controlling research accelerators, which is built on a commercially available real-time embedded software development product. The user interface (display and keyboard) is handled by the X window system, programmed using Xlib only.

We derived most of the code directly from the Z texts by intuition and verified it by inspection, without any intermediate formal refinement steps. The Z design is so detailed that most of the translation is obvious. Z basic types and free types become enumerations. Z state variables become program variables and data structures. Z operation schemas become functions and procedures. A Z state schema and the operation schemas on that state become a module (in C, an .h file and a .c file that define a collection of constants, types and variables and the functions that use

---

[2] The line count is the number of nonblank lines output by running the Fuzz tool -v option (Spivey, 1992b) on the report. This output is similar to the LATEX source for the Z formulas.

them). Z schema inclusion becomes module inclusion (C `#include` directives). Some examples appear in (Jacky, 1997).

The code can be classified into categories defined in the implementation guide. Table 9.2 shows the lines of Z description, code[3], and any derivation or proof in each category. The table reveals that we modelled different parts of the program at very different levels of detail, according to our judgment about the novelty and difficulty of each portion. Some portions of the program have no formal description at all, while the formal description of some portions is as large as the code itself.

Table 9.2. Lines of formal description, proof, and code

CATEGORY	Z	PROOF	CODE
Process and event handling	40	40	433
Pervasive constants and types	73	—	200
File handling and persistent data	52	—	672
Operations and volatile data	764	20	747
Graphics utilities	—	—	589
Graphics displays	—	—	1233
Low-level device control	208	—	912
Total	1137	60	4786

To prepare for this project, Jacky wrote some smaller Z descriptions of portions of the accelerator controls (Jacky, 1990, 1993, 1995) (106, 166 and 178 lines of Z, respectively); these have not yet been implemented.

The program is not yet complete and we have not begun acceptance testing. Tables 9.1 and 9.2 report the work accomplished as of this writing. Additional information about project organisation, staff, assurance methods, and level of effort appears in (Jacky *et al.*, 1997).

9.4 Writing the Formal Description

We found it quite difficult to produce a formal description that faithfully expresses the informal requirements and also serves as a useful basis for developing code. There are problems of scale and organisation and not much guidance from the small examples in the literature. After many revisions we obtained a satisfactory solution by applying the following strategies.

9.4.1 Write Strong Invariants

The advantage of writing specifications in Z (or some similar notation) instead of code (or another operational notation) is that Z can describe states directly. Usually,

---

[3] Noncomment, nonblank lines of code.

fundamental requirements and the designer's intent are most naturally expressed as states (or sets of states): *assumptions* and *trigger conditions* can both be formalised as *preconditions*, *goals* become *postconditions*, and *safety requirements* become *invariants*. Code and other operational notations can only express these concepts indirectly (as the result of executing sequences of transitions).

It is possible to specify a system as nothing more than a collection of state transitions (Z operation schemas). Such specifications closely resemble code (in Z the "after" state would be given explicitly in equations that resemble assignment statements: $x' = \ldots$ etc.)[4]. In such transition-oriented specifications, transitions often seem arbitrary and unmotivated (because there is nothing else in the formal specification that they can be derived from or checked against). In fact no transition should be arbitrary; every transition should *make progress towards a goal* while *preserving the invariants*, but merely describing each transition (as assignments, or implicitly with pre- and postconditions) cannot express this. A specification in this style does not take advantage of Z; it conveys essentially the same information as the code itself. It may be more convenient or readable than the code, but it cannot support any deep analyses because it does not directly express the designers' intent.

Analysis of such transition-oriented specifications is limited to checking generic properties that are independent of any particular application, such as completeness, consistency, and determinism (Heimdahl and Leveson, 1995; Anderson *et al.*, 1996). (Anderson *et al.*, 1996) did check some application-specific properties, but these were conjectures posed by the analysis team. We believe that system designers should provide the properties to be checked.) These analyses can reveal some errors, but any generic analysis is necessarily weak because it cannot check the application-specific properties that are of greatest interest. A system that is complete, consistent and deterministic may nevertheless fail to satisfy its requirements.

In contrast to this transition-oriented style, Z encourages specifiers to write explicit invariants that can express the designers' intent more directly. Invariants convey additional information which is not present in the code and cannot be unambiguously derived from it (or "reverse engineered"). This additional information supports deep analyses that can reveal whether or not the specified transitions actually achieve the designers' intent. Each proposed transition can be checked to confirm that it makes progress toward the goal while preserving the invariants. In fact, it is sometimes possible to derive the transitions formally because transitions often contain two kinds of assignments: assignments to independent variables that make progress, and assignments to dependent variables that maintain invariants. In typical informal developments, the latter (dependent) assignments are often handled in a hit-or-miss way because programmers must rely on intuition to discover them. When invariants are explicit, dependent assignments can be inferred (for example see Section 9.4.1 below).

In summary, our strategy for using Z is to write strong state invariants, to check every transition against the invariants, and to derive dependent assignments in tran-

---

[4] In Z it is also possible to describe states implicitly. For example, we can specify an integer square root operation by $x' * x' \leq a < (x' + 1) * (x' + 1)$.

sitions from invariants. In the following subsections we illustrate this strategy at two levels of abstraction: an abstract level that expresses overall system safety requirements and a concrete level that expresses the detailed design. In general, the requirements level expresses properties that we might wish to check or prove; the design level is the system to be checked.

System safety invariants. The central idea of the therapy control program is this safety requirement: the beam can only turn on when the actual state or *setup* of the machine is physically safe, and matches a *prescription* that the operator has selected and approved. We must only deliver setups that are physically consistent and reasonable or *safe*. The control program helps ensure that we can only treat a patient when the *measured* machine setup *matches* a *prescribed* setup.

$$[SETTING, VALUE, FIELD]$$

$$SETUP == SETTING \rightarrow VALUE$$

$$
\begin{array}{|l}
safe\_ : \mathbb{P}\, SETUP \\
match\_ : SETUP \leftrightarrow SETUP \\
prescription : FIELD \nrightarrow SETUP
\end{array}
$$

$$
\begin{array}{|l}
\underline{\quad SafeTreatment \quad\rule{7cm}{0pt}} \\
\quad measured, prescribed : SETUP \\
\hline
\quad safe(measured) \\
\quad match(measured, prescribed) \\
\quad prescribed \in \mathrm{ran}\, prescription \\
\end{array}
$$

The whole design arises from elaborating this simple model. The entire purpose of the control program is to establish and confirm the *SafeTreatment* condition. The *prescribed* setup must be selected; the *measured* setup must be achieved; the *safe* and *match* conditions must be tested. The predicates *safe(measured)*, *match(measured, prescribed)*, and *prescribed* ∈ ran *prescription* each act as goals for certain operations or collections of operations.

Essential safety requirements can be expressed at this level. For example, the condition of the machine when the radiation beam is on is expressed by a state schema, *BeamOn* (its predicate acts as another goal). The safety requirement that the beam can only be on when the machine is in a safe condition can be expressed:

$$BeamOn \Rightarrow SafeTreatment$$

Checking or proving this property would be a significant achievement. It would provide additional evidence (besides inspection and testing) for the soundess of our detailed design. It would not be a superficial exercise; it should reveal even low-level errors because our design is so detailed. We have not yet attempted this, but it is a long term goal of our work.

Our formal description includes more than 1000 lines of Z, but each line is motivated by this abstract model and can be traced back to it. We believe that designers should be able to express the central idea of their system formally on a single page, as we have done here.

Detailed design invariants. At the detailed design level Z state variables correspond to data structures in the code and Z operations correspond to procedures in the code. At this level we try again to write strong state invariants. For example our *Session* state models program data structures that represent the prescription database and aspects of the treatment session that are derived from it. At this level we must model the prescription database in greater detail. There are actually two collections of stored setups: one for patients' prescriptions, another for medical physics and radiobiology experiments which are performed with no patient present. The machine can be operated in two modes, one for patients and the other (with fewer safety interlocks) for the experimental studies. The control program maintains a list of names for which the operator can select setups. This list must be kept consistent with the operating mode: patients in therapy mode, studies in experiment mode. This consistency requirement is expressed by an invariant in the *Session* state.

$[NAME]$

$$patients, studies : \mathbb{P}\, NAME$$

$MODE ::= therapy \mid experiment$

$$
\begin{array}{l}
\underline{\quad Session \quad\quad\quad\quad\quad\quad\quad\quad\quad\quad\quad\quad\quad\quad} \\
mode : MODE \\
names : \mathbb{P}\, NAME \\
\dots \\
\overline{\quad\quad\quad\quad\quad\quad\quad\quad\quad\quad\quad\quad\quad\quad\quad\quad\quad} \\
names = \textbf{if } mode = therapy \textbf{ then } patients \textbf{ else } studies \\
\dots
\end{array}
$$

Here the declarations in the Z (above the line) are intended to be translated to declarations of data structures in the code. However the invariant (below the line) does not correspond directly to any code, rather it expresses a property that the program should possess.

The *ExptMode* operation toggles the session from therapy mode to experiment mode or back again. It could be written:

$$
\begin{array}{l}
\underline{\quad ExptMode \quad\quad\quad\quad\quad\quad\quad\quad\quad\quad\quad\quad\quad\quad} \\
\Delta Session \\
\overline{\quad\quad\quad\quad\quad\quad\quad\quad\quad\quad\quad\quad\quad\quad\quad\quad\quad} \\
mode' = \textbf{if } mode = therapy \textbf{ then } experiment \textbf{ else } therapy \\
\dots
\end{array}
$$

The predicate on *mode'* is intended to be translated to an assignment statement. However something is missing. The invariant requires that the list of names must change whenever the mode changes. We should write the operation this way:

$$
\begin{array}{|l}
\underline{\quad ExptMode \underline{\hspace{6cm}}} \\
\Delta Session \\
\hline
(mode', names') = \textbf{if } mode = therapy \textbf{ then } (experiment, studies) \\
\hspace{4.5cm} \textbf{else } (therapy, patients) \\
\dots
\end{array}
$$

Here *mode* is the independent variable; this operation makes progress by changing *mode*. In this operation *names* is the dependent variable; it must be changed to maintain the invariant. The predicate on *names'* instructs the programmer that the code must read the appropriate file contents into control program data structures when the mode changes. This is the kind of thing which is often overlooked when programming from intuition.

In Z both versions of *ExptMode* mean exactly the same thing; writing out the predicate about *names'* is redundant because it is implied by the invariant. We always try to use the second form; we feel strongly that it is important to write out the predicate for each state variable explicitly, even when it could be derived from the invariant. We write our code based on these operation schemas, and we feel it is unreasonable to derive consequences of invariants at coding time — that work should be part of specification, not implementation.

We also believe that it is very valuable to express the same requirement in two places, as an invariant in the state schema and as an assignment in the operation schema. We believe that using redundancy in this way is an important advantage of the Z notation and a key component of good Z style. It encourages specifiers to think about the requirements in a systematic way, and it gives reviewers something to look for.

Perhaps tools could help: given the value of the independent variable, the tool could calculate the value of the dependent variable. For example, given only $S \mathbin{\widehat{=}} [\dots \mid x = a \Rightarrow y = b]$ and $Op \mathbin{\widehat{=}} [\Delta S \mid x' = a]$ with no explicit constraint on y' in Op, the tool should provide a (highly automated) reminder that $y' = b$ in Op.

9.4.2 Partition the Design

Much of the apparent complexity of the therapy machine arises from the interaction of several subsystems which, by themselves, are simpler. We partition the system into subsystems and describe one state schema and several (or many) operation schemas on each. For each operation on the system as a whole, we define a separate operation on each affected subsystem. The complex behaviours of the whole system emerge when we compose these simpler operations together. In Z we perform the composition by schema composition or inclusion.

The advantages of this approach arise because many operations involve only a few of the subsystems, and many complex operations can emerge when simpler operations appear together in different combinations. As a result, the formal description of the partitioned design is shorter and clearer than would be possible with a monolithic design, and is easier to review in sections.

Identifying the best partition requires much exploration; we eventually discovered that the obvious partition corresponding to the hardware subsystems that the users see is not the best one. We settled on a partition that included these subsystems: *Session* models those aspects of the treatment session that are related to the prescription database, *Field* models the many settings (from all hardware subsystems) that characterise a single field, *Intlk* models software interlocks and other flags that indicate readiness, *Console* models the user interface, *TMC* models the process that communicates with the treatment motion controller (one of the embedded computers), etc. This partition can itself be expressed in Z.

┌─ *TherapyControl* ──────────────────────────────
│ *Session*
│ *Field*
│ *Intlk*
│ *Console*
│ *TMC*
│ . . .
├──────────
│ . . .
└──

Each subsystem has its own invariants, and as we combine subsystems we add more. For example the *Console* state schema represents which screen design or *display* is visible on the operator's console. *Console* also includes *nlist*, a list of items which may appear on the display.

$[DISPLAY]$

┌─ *Console* ──────────────────────────────
│ *nlist* : $\mathbb{P}\,NAME$
│ *display* : $DISPLAY$
│ . . .
├──────────
│ . . .
└──

One of the displays is the **Select Patient** display. This display shows the list of patients or experimental studies, so the operator may select one. To express this, we combine *Console* and *Session* and add an invariant.

│ *select_patient* : $DISPLAY$

```
┌─ ConsoleSession ─────────────────────────────────────────┐
│ Console                                                   │
│ Session                                                   │
├───────────────                                            │
│ display = select_patient ⇒ nlist = names                  │
│ ...                                                       │
└───────────────────────────────────────────────────────────┘
```

It is clear from this that if the operating mode is changed when the patient list display is visible, the display contents must change to show the list of experimental studies instead of patients (or vice versa). This is another example of something that might be missed if left to intuition.

9.4.3 What is an Operation?

Z is just mathematics; designers must choose an interpretation for the mathematics that is meaningful for their project. It is necessary to decide what a Z operation schema represents, which entails answering these questions: What occurences in the real system will be modelled by operation schemas in the Z description? How do you know when your formal description is complete; that is, you have written all of the operations? The answers to these questions are not provided by the Z notation itself; designers must answer them for each project.

We decided that our choice of state variables determines what the operations must be: *any* occurence that changes the value of *any* state variable should be modelled by an operation schema. The formal description is not complete until all such operation schemas have been written. As a result of this decision, our description is very detailed: each X window system event (including every keystroke) and transmission or receipt of every message to or from a controller is modelled by a Z operation schema. Many activities that the users see as single operations, which are described as single operations in the prose specification, must be modelled in Z by several, or many, operation schemas. For example the activity described in the prose as the single **Select Field** (from the prescription database) operation is represented in Z by one operation to display the list of available fields, a second operation to move the cursor from one field on the list to the adjacent field, and a third operation to select the field under the cursor and update pertinent state variables with new values copied or derived from the prescription database. Moreover, this third operation is defined by composing several different operation schemas, one for each of the subsystems discussed in Section 9.4.2.

One might ask, is all this low-level detail really necessary? We believe that it is. In order to understand errors that have caused fatal accidents, it is sometimes necessary to descend to this level (Jacky, 1996; Leveson and Turner, 1993; Leveson, 1995). The effort might seem burdensome, but it makes it possible to do analyses that can detect low-level errors.

9.4.4 When is an Operation Invoked?

Having chosen the operations, it is still necessary to decide how and when the implementation of each operation schema should be invoked. Z has no built-in concept of a program or any explicit control structure, and Z users often do not write any formal definition of the "main program" or "top level" that invokes the appropriate operation schemas when they are needed. Nevertheless, we have to implement the top level anyway.

We decided that our program is defined implicitly by the "top-level" operation schemas. We can tell which operation schemas are at the top level because they are not included in any others. The control structure is determined implicitly by the input variables and preconditions of the top-level operations. Each top-level operation should be invoked whenever its input appears and all of its preconditions are satisfied. We had to code the machinery to make that happen. We defined the machinery formally, and the formal definition shows the way to the implementation. If we call the top level schemas $Op1, Op2, \ldots, OpN$ then the formal definition of the main program is just the disjunction of these operations.

$$Main \cong Op1 \vee Op2 \vee \ldots \vee OpN \vee Exception$$

It is a good idea to include an *Exception* operation to handle any cases that might have been overlooked. The precondition for *Exception* is implicit in the program logic: control reaches *Exception* when no other operations are invoked.

An obvious implementation strategy would code the main program as a large case analysis (`switch` or `if ...else if ...` in C.) (Jacky, 1997). We chose instead to build a table-driven dispatcher. To add new operations we do not have to revise the program control structure, we merely add entries to a table and write functions that implement the operations. This code is derived and proved correct in (Jacky and Unger, 1995).

Our program implements a particular interpretation of the meaning of the precondition of an operation. In our view, preconditions are *guards* or *triggers*: an operation is invoked when its input appears and all of its preconditions are satisfied. For example, consider again the *ExptMode* operation that switches between therapy and experiment mode (Section 9.4.1, above). Experiment mode is only permitted to certain privileged operators called *physicists*. We model this by adding another state variable and an invariant to the *Session* state.

$[OPERATOR]$

$\mid$ $physicists : \mathbb{P}\ OPERATOR$

```
┌─ Session ──────────────────────────────────────────────
│  ...
│  operator : OPERATOR
│  ...
├─────────────────────────────────────────────────────────
│  ...
│  mode = experiment ⇒ operator ∈ physicists
│  ...
└─────────────────────────────────────────────────────────
```

A physicist may switch operating modes by pressing a function key (modelled by a value of the *INPUT* type).

[*INPUT*]

```
│  expt_mode : INPUT
```

```
┌─ ExptModeOp ───────────────────────────────────────────
│  ΔConsoleSession
│  ExptMode
│  input? : INPUT
├─────────────────────────────────────────────────────────
│  input? = expt_mode
│  operator ∈ physicists
│  operator' = operator
│  ...
└─────────────────────────────────────────────────────────
```

The precondition of *ExptModeOp* is $input? = expt\_mode \land operator \in physicists$. This is a *trigger*: our program invokes the *ExptModeOp* operation whenever the **Experiment Mode** key is pressed and the operator is a physicist. If the operator is not a physicist, pressing this key does not cause any change of state (in our implementation it does elicit an output: a message indicating that an unprivileged user may not select experiment mode).

In Z, the precondition $operator \in physicists$ is redundant because it can be inferred from the invariant $mode = experiment \Rightarrow operator \in physicists$[5]. Nevertheless, we always try to write out the precondition explicitly. We take advantage of the opportunity to express the same requirement in two places, as an invariant in a state schema and as a guard in an operation schema. We would consider the omission of $operator \in physicists$ from *ExptModeOp* to be an error. A tool that can calculate implicit preconditions such as (Saaltink, 1997) could be used to detect such errors.

Our interpretation of preconditions is a design decision, it is not determined by the Z notation itself. Another interpretation holds that preconditions in Z are

---

[5] This inference is valid in the case where $mode = therapy \land mode' = experiment$ but not vice-versa.

correctness conditions, not triggers (this interpretation may be more common than ours). In this view it is possible to invoke an operation even when the precondition is not satisfied, but in that case the operation may not behave as specified. According to this view, it is valid for the precondition of the implementation of an operation to be weaker than the precondition of its specification. However this not always valid when preconditions are interpreted as triggers.

9.5 Checking the Formal Description

The initial draft of any nontrivial formal description will be full of errors. It is necessary to have some systematic method for detecting and correcting them. In our project we used (subjective) reviews with very little automated support. We discovered a great many errors and eventually produced a much better revised description. We continue to find minor errors almost every time we reread the revised formal description thoroughly; despite this, is quite usable as our primary source for coding and test planning.

We did not do any formal proofs to confirm that the Z texts express the intended behaviours. We did use a type checker (Spivey, 1992b) and we corrected the numerous but trivial errors that it found. We also tried the domain checking capabilities of a theorem prover (Saaltink, 1997). The prover found a few expressions where functions were applied to arguments that could not be proved to lie within their domains, and we corrected these by providing additional predicates to restrict the arguments.

As an alternative to formal proof, we do systematic inspection of specifications presented in tabular format. The following subsections present an extended example to illustrate the method and describe some errors we discovered.

9.5.1 Treatment Motion Controller

Here we consider one subsystem of our control program: the process that communicates with a separate embedded controller called the *treatment motion controller* (TMC). Our program exchanges messages with the TMC and several other controllers to perform operations specific to our application, such as setting up the the therapy machinery to conform to a patient's prescription (Jacky *et al.*, 1990, 1995b).

The TMC controller process handles *events* (in our implementation these are derived from hardware and software interrupts); the process may be *running* or *waiting* for an event. The process and its controller exchange *messages*. Messages can be classified into types called *commands* (from the process) and *responses* (from the controller). Certain events called *command events* are invoked by the user to signal the controller process to issue a whole sequence of commands that accomplish some useful goal, such as automatically setting up machine components to prepare for a treatment. The process responds by sending that sequence of commands to the controller; for each of these commands, a particular sequence of responses is expected. In addition to command events, there is a *receive* event that occurs when a response message appears. It is also possible to arrange for a *timeout* event to signal that a deadline has expired.

9.5.2 Treatment Motion Controller Formal Description

The state of the controller process is the set of unhandled events, the real time clock, a timer to store the deadline when a timeout is pending, the (inferred) status of the controller, the processing state, the sequence of pending commands that have not yet been sent to the controller, and the sequence of responses expected for the most recently sent command that have not yet been received. This is expressed by the *Controller* state schema:

$STATUS ::= ok \mid error$

$PROCESSING ::= wait \mid run$

__ Controller _____
$events : \mathbb{P}\, EVENT$
$clock, timer : TIME$
$status : STATUS$
$processing : PROCESSING$
$pending : \text{seq}\, COMMAND$
$expected : \text{seq}\, RESPONSE$
_____

The environment outside the *Controller* state provides different events, which we model as different values of the input variable $e?$. When an event occurs, it joins the set of unhandled events. No other state variables change when an event is signalled. This state transition is expressed by the *Signal* operation schema:

__ Signal _____
$\Delta Controller$
$e? : EVENT$
_____
$events' = events \cup \{e?\}$
$\dots$

The two basic controller operations are *Wait* and *HandleEvent*. The controller process executes *Wait* to wait for an event. The processing state switches from *run* to *wait*.

__ Wait _____
$\Delta Controller$
_____
$processing = run$
$processing' = wait$
$\dots$

When an awaited event is signalled, the controller process executes *HandleEvent*. *HandleEvent* changes *processing* from *wait* to back to *run*; the controller process alternates executing *Wait* and *HandleEvent*. Specialisations of *HandleEvent* are called *handlers*; most of the work of the controller process is accomplished by handlers.

Each handler waits for a particular event; if this event appears and the handler's other preconditions are also satisfied, the handler will remove this event from the set and execute.

```
┌─ HandleEvent ─────────────────────────────────────
│ ΔController
│ e? : EVENT
├───────────────────────────────────────────────────
│ e? ∈ events
│ processing = wait
│ processing' = run
│ events' = events \ {e?}
│ ...
└───────────────────────────────────────────────────
```

In the initial state, there are no pending commands or expected responses. The controller process waits for a command event.

```
┌─ WaitCmd ─────────────────────────────────────────
│ Controller
├───────────────────────────────────────────────────
│ pending = ⟨⟩
│ expected = ⟨⟩
└───────────────────────────────────────────────────
```

After the user causes a command event to be signalled, *HandleCmd* loads the appropriate sequence of new commands. If the controller is not *ok* this handler is disabled, except for certain *restart* commands which are provided to recover from the error state.

```
┌─ HandleCmd ───────────────────────────────────────
│ HandleEvent
│ c : COMMAND
├───────────────────────────────────────────────────
│ WaitCmd
│ e? ∈ cmd
│ status = ok ∨ e? ∈ restart
│ (let cs == commands e? •
│       c = head cs ∧ pending' = tail cs)
│ status' = status
└───────────────────────────────────────────────────
```

The *Send* operation creates a message from the command and (if appropriate) the data.

Send _____

$\Delta Controller$
$c : COMMAND$
$data? : DATA$
$message! : MESSAGE$

_____

$message! = \ldots$ format msg from c and $data?$
$expected' = responses\ c$

These two operations are combined to send a new command

$$NewCommand \;\widehat{=}\; HandleCmd \wedge Send$$

After executing *NewCommand* the process resets the timer for the appropriate deadline and waits for the controller to respond.

$$WaitReceive \;\widehat{=}\; [\,Controller \mid expected \neq \langle\rangle\,]$$

When a handler detects a possible controller error, it sets the controller state to *error* and abandons any command sequence in progress.

ControllerError _____

$HandleEvent$

_____

$state' = error$
$pending' = \langle\rangle$
$expected' = \langle\rangle$

9.5.3 Tabular Presentation

We defined thirteen Z operations for this subsystem; each defines one state transition. To show how the operations work together we collect the pertinent formulas in a table. Tables 9.3 and 9.4 together form a state transition table, similar to the mode transition tables of the SCR notation (Atlee, 1993) (this format is most effective when space permits all the information to be presented in one table on a single page).

There is one entry in the tables for each Z operation schema. The three columns in Table 9.3 show the operation name, the conjuncts of the precondition that only involve the state variables, and the conjuncts of the precondition that only involve input variables. The first two columns in Table 9.4 are the same as in Table 9.3; the third column shows progress: the conjuncts from the postcondition that indicate a change of state (postconditions of the form $x' = x$ indicating that x does not change are not shown). In addition to the thirteen top-level operations, there are entries for three building-block operations. Each group of top-level operations is headed by the building-block operation whose predicates are conjoined with theirs. For example, *Wait* appears above *StartTimer* so the full state precondition of *StartTimer* is $processing = run \wedge WaitCmd$.

Table 9.3. Controller operations and preconditions

Z operation name	State precondition	Input precondition
Wait	$processing = run$	*true*
StartTimer	*WaitCmd*	*true*
RestartTimer	*WaitReceive*	*true*
HandleEvent	$processing = wait$	$e? \in events$
NewCommand (*HandleCmd* ∧ *Send*)	*WaitCmd* ∧ *p*	$e? \in cmd$
CommandError	*WaitCmd* ∧ ¬ *p*	$e? \in cmd$
ReceiveUnsolicited	*WaitCmd*	$e? = receive$
ReceiveAck	*WaitReceive* $tail\ expected \neq \langle\rangle$	$e? = receive \wedge q$
NextCommand (*ReceivePending* ∧ *Send*)	*WaitReceive* $tail\ expected = \langle\rangle$ $pending \neq \langle\rangle$	$e? = receive \wedge q$
ReceiveComplete	*WaitReceive* $tail\ expected = \langle\rangle$ $pending = \langle\rangle$	$e? = receive \wedge q$
ReceiveError	*WaitReceive*	$e? = receive \wedge \neg q$
ReceiveTimeout	*WaitReceive*	$e? = timeout$
Signal	*true*	*true*
SignalEvent	*true*	$e? \neq timeout$
SignalTimeout	$clock > timer$	*true*
Tick	*true*	*true*

$WaitReceive \Leftrightarrow expected \neq \langle\rangle$
$WaitCmd \Leftrightarrow pending = \langle\rangle \wedge expected = \langle\rangle$
$WaitCmd \vee WaitReceive$ is invariant; $pending \neq \langle\rangle \wedge expected = \langle\rangle$ is forbidden.

$p \Leftrightarrow status = ok \vee e? \in restart$; $\langle cmd, \{receive\}\rangle$ partition $EVENT$
$q \Leftrightarrow message? \in \text{dom}\ response \wedge response\ message? = head\ expected$

Table 9.4. Controller operations, state preconditions and progress postconditions

Z operation name	State precondition	Progress postcondition
Wait	$processing = run$	$processing' = wait$
StartTimer	*WaitCmd*	$timer' = clock + period$
RestartTimer	*WaitReceive*	$timer' = clock + deadline$
HandleEvent	$processing = wait$	$processing' = run$ $events' = events \setminus \{e?\}$
NewCommand *(HandleCmd ∧ Send)*	$WaitCmd \wedge p$	$WaitReceive'$ $expected' = responses\ c$ $pending' = tail\ cs$
CommandError	$WaitCmd \wedge \neg p$	$status' = error$
ReceiveUnsolicited	*WaitCmd*	$status' = error$
ReceiveAck	*WaitReceive* $tail\ expected \neq \langle \rangle$	$status' = ok$ $expected' = tail\ expected$
NextCommand *(ReceivePending ∧ Send)*	*WaitReceive* $tail\ expected = \langle \rangle$ $pending \neq \langle \rangle$	$status' = ok$ $expected' = responses\ c$ $pending' = tail\ pending$
ReceiveComplete	*WaitReceive* $tail\ expected = \langle \rangle$ $pending = \langle \rangle$	$WaitCmd' \wedge status' = ok$ $expected' = tail\ expected$
ReceiveError	*WaitReceive*	$WaitCmd' \wedge status' = error$
ReceiveTimeout	*WaitReceive*	$WaitCmd' \wedge status' = error$
Signal	*true*	$events' = events \cup \{e?\}$
SignalEvent	*true*	
SignalTimeout	$clock > timer$	$timer' = stopped$
Tick	*true*	$clock' > clock$

$WaitReceive \Leftrightarrow expected \neq \langle \rangle$
$WaitCmd \Leftrightarrow pending = \langle \rangle \wedge expected = \langle \rangle$
$WaitCmd \vee WaitReceive$ is invariant; $pending \neq \langle \rangle \wedge expected = \langle \rangle$ is forbidden.

$c = head\ pending \wedge cs = tail(commands\ e?)$
$p \Leftrightarrow status = ok \vee e? \in restart;$ $\langle cmd, \{receive\}\rangle$ partition $EVENT$

9.5.4 Analysis

Many properties of our controller specification can be confirmed by inspecting Tables 9.3 and 9.4.

Generic properties. Generic properties such as completeness and determinism do not depend on the particular features of the application.

Completeness: The controller specification is complete if the response to all events is defined in all states permitted by the invariant. Table 9.3 shows this is true: the disjunction of all the preconditions forms a tautology. For example in the second column, there are two large sections for *processing* = *run* and *processing* = *wait*, together these cover all values of *processing*. Within each section there are subsections for *WaitCmd* and *WaitReceive*, together these cover the invariant *WaitCmd* ∨ *WaitReceive*, etc.

Determinism: The controller specification is deterministic if only one operation is enabled for each input in each state. Table 9.3 shows that all the preconditions are disjoint. For example in the second column we find the disjoint pairs *processing* = *run* and *processing* = *wait*, *WaitCmd* and *WaitReceive*, etc.

Application-specific properties. These invariance and progress properties are particular to this application.

Invariance: Table 9.3 shows that every operation has either *WaitCmd* or *Wait-Receive* in its precondition. If the controller process entered a state where neither predicate were true, no operations would be enabled; the process would deadlock. Therefore *WaitCmd* ∨ *WaitReceive* must be an invariant. The negation of the invariant is the forbidden state where an unsent command is pending but no reply is expected.

Progress (liveness): To make progress, it is necessary to make state transitions from one table entry to another. This is shown in Table 9.4. For example unhandled command events can accumulate in the *WaitReceive* state. However all the operations that begin in *WaitReceive* either end in *WaitCmd* or make progress toward *WaitCmd* by establishing *expected'* = *tail expected* or *pending'* = *tail pending*. Therefore the system will eventually reach *WaitCmd* and pending command events will be handled.

9.5.5 Error Discovery

Z specifications are built up from schemas spread over many pages, so it is easy to introduce errors and outright inconsistencies. For example:

Inconsistent includes: Schema C includes A and B, but A is inconsistent with B. Usually occurs because A was revised after C was written.

Displaced precondition: Operations B and C both include operation A. Precondition P should apply only to B but appears in A, so the precondition of C is too strong. Usually occurs because A was revised by splitting into a new A, plus B and C.

For example we discovered this displaced precondition: $pending = \langle\rangle$, intended to prevent a new command event from pre-empting a command sequence that is already in progress, appeared in *HandleEvent* not *WaitCmd*.

A simple remedy to these kinds of errors is to collect the predicates in one place (Table 9.3); this often reveals the errors. We observe that many of our schemas are inconsistent at first, perhaps as a result of our efforts to make predicates as strong as possible. A tool that could automatically identify obvious inconsistencies in expanded schemas would be quite useful, particularly if it could present its findings informatively, for example $x' = a \wedge x' = b$ or $x' = x \wedge x' = b$.

More subtle errors arise when collections of operations must work together. For example:

- **omitted case:** Sometimes occurs because the author was thinking of a poorly chosen (overly restricted) example. Common variations are *Missing operation* and *Precondition too strong*;
- **overbooked state variable:** Operation A stores a value in state variable x, intending it to be found by operation B. However operation C can store a different value in x before B is invoked;
- **implicit invariant:** The implicit invariant formed by the disjunction of the preconditions of all the operations is stronger than the explicit state invariant. However the postcondition of one operation does not satisfy this implicit invariant. After that operation executes, no operations are enabled and the system deadlocks.

For example we discovered these two missing operations: we forgot *RestartTimer*, and we only provided a single *Receive* operation instead of *ReceiveAck*, *Receive-Complete* and *NextCommand*.

These errors cannot be detected by analysing schemas one at time; it is necessary to consider whether the entire collection of operations satisfies some progress property. Our tabular inspection method provides one way to do this; Evans (1994) proposes another method involving Unity-like proof rules. Model checking provides a third possibility.

9.5.6 An Experiment in Model Checking

We translated the TMC specification presented here into the input language of the SMV temporal logic model checker. SMV is less expressive than Z so we had to create a simpler model that still represents the interesting behaviors. For example in Z we modelled pending commands and expected responses by sequences; in SMV we only modelled the lengths of the sequences. We checked the SMV specification against the application-specific invariance property $WaitCmd \vee WaitReceive$ (AG (WaitCmd | WaitReceive) in SMV) and the simplest possible progress property, that a waiting process will eventually run (AG (!run -> AF run)). The checker detected some seeded errors we had discovered during our inspections, but detected no errors in our latest (corrected) version.

9.6 Other Lessons

We offer some other observations based on our experience so far:

- formal methods can help create novel designs and develop original code. They are not just for documenting existing designs and analysing code that has already been written;
- a detailed and explicit informal specification that has been reviewed by the systems' designers and users (not just software developers) is an indispensable prerequisite to any use of formal methods. Only this can serve as the standard for validation. It is a major portion of the whole project effort, not just a preliminary;
- a useful formal description is not just a paraphrase of the informal specification into mathematical notation. Creating the formal description requires design judgment in addition to understanding the requirements and the formal notation;
- all documents and code require much revision for clarity and organisation, not just content and correctness;
- software developers who have the education and experience needed to work on this kind of project can learn to read, review, and implement Z and even write small amounts of it fairly quickly. Writing a useful formal description of a complex system is much more difficult and requires much experience on progressively harder problems;
- simply having a good formal description does not guarantee that a good implementation will come easily. Diligent ongoing review is required to ensure that the implementation is simple and clear enough to review against the formal description. This is a prerequisite to checking that the implementation is correct;
- inspection and simple paper-and-pencil analyses can detect most, but not all, errors in a large Z specification if it is sufficiently well partitioned to be reviewed in small sections;
- a formal description that contains minor errors can still be useful as a guide for coding and test planning.

Acknowledgments

The author thanks Ruedi Risler, Ira Kalet, Michael Patrick, Stan Brossard and Peter Wootton for contributions to the informal specification; Michael Patrick and Jonathan Unger for contributions to the formal specification and implementation guide; Michael Patrick, David Reid and Jonathan Unger for contributions to the code; and Mark Saaltink for running the domain check.

CHAPTER 10

Using Formal Methods to Develop an ATC Information System

Anthony Hall

10.1 Introduction

The air traffic management system in the UK is being upgraded to handle increasing traffic levels. One of the aspects of this upgrade is the development of the Central Control Function (CCF), a new way of handling terminal traffic. CCF provides controllers in the London Area and Terminal Control Centre (LATCC) with automated support for their new roles. In particular, CCF includes Approach Sequencing, a function for generating and manipulating the sequence of flights inbound to a major airport complex (MAC) such as Heathrow or Gatwick. The automated support is provided by a number of systems, including upgrades to the National Airspace System (NAS), a new radar system, an Airport Data Information System (ADIS), a new digital closed circuit television and a new information system, CCF Display Information System (CDIS).

The CDIS system was developed by Praxis for the Civil Aviation Authority (CAA) and delivered in 1992. We used formal methods extensively to specify, design and verify CDIS. This article reports our experiences on that project, one of the largest applications of formal methods so far attempted.

A system of this size has many different aspects and no single method covers them all. We used different formal methods for the sequential and concurrent aspects of the system, and combined them with more conventional methods where these were appropriate. We also used different notations at different stages of the project, both for technical reasons—for example because one notation gave us bet-

© 1996 IEEE. Reprinted by permission.
Reprinted from *IEEE Software*, March 1996, 13(2):66–76

ter modularity—and for non-technical reasons such as the expertise available within the team.

The next section describes the role of CDIS in CCF and gives an overview of the CDIS architecture. Section 1.3 outlines the structure of the projects which specified, built and integrated CDIS. Section 1.4 describes the use of formal methods during requirements analysis, where we supplemented traditional structured analysis with a formal specification. Section 1.5 describes how CDIS was specified using a formal notation for the functional core and supplementing it with less formal user interface definitions and with notations to describe concurrency. Section 1.6 deals with the many aspects of design where different notations were used including formal module definitions and detailed formal specification, design and proof of critical infrastructure software. Section 1.7 gives some metrics on productivity and defects in CDIS, together with some qualitative assessments of the project and the product, and draws some conclusions about the use of formal methods. There is a list of references and a glossary of acronyms at the end of the paper.

10.2 CCF and CDIS

Figure 10.1 is a picture of a CCF controller's workstation, showing the various sources of information including the CDIS screen and devices. The main display of information from CDIS is on the Electronic Display Device (EDD), a 19 inch colour graphics screen. This displays pages of information. Pages are selected using a Page Selection Device, a custom-built keypad which allows one-keystroke selection of frequently used pages, and also provides extra keys for special functions such as acknowledging changed data and reading broadcast messages. The Approach Sequence Allocator, the controller responsible for managing the inbound approach sequence, has available a Computer Entry and Readout Device (CERD), a touch-sensitive plasma display screen which allows direct manipulation of flights.

CDIS receives information in real time from NAS and from the ADIS systems at the major airports. These are both connected over an X.25 network. In addition, CDIS can send information to the closed circuit television system, also over an X.25 link. CDIS also has its own store of information produced and edited within CDIS itself using administrative workstations provided with a graphical and text editor.

CDIS is responsible for displaying to the controllers information about arriving and departing flights, weather conditions and equipment status at airports and other support information provided by CDIS data entry staff. It also maintains real-time displays of its own status to allow the engineers to control the system.

Since CDIS is a real-time, operational system it has stringent performance and availability requirements. Information must be displayed within one or two seconds of receipt. The system must be available for at least 99.97% of the time and there must be no single point of failure.

The design of the hardware and software of CDIS, and the methods of development, were all driven by these requirements as shown in Table 10.1.

The overall hardware architecture of CDIS is shown in Figure 10.2. One ma-

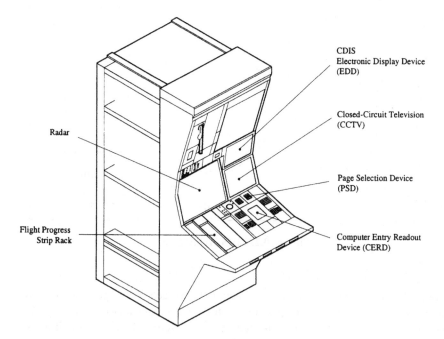

Figure 10.1. The CCF controller's workstation

Table 10.1. Meeting the CDIS requirements

Requirement	Hardware	Software	Development Method
Functionality			Formal specification Prototyping Formal design
Performance	Distributed processing Multi-processor hardware	Data located at point of use Optimized process organisation	Performance calculation
Availability	Dualled hardware Hardware health monitoring	Fail-stop processes Defensive programming	Formal design Precondition checking Proving critical properties

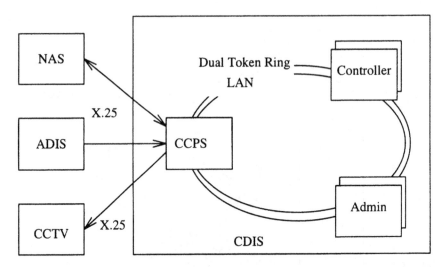

Figure 10.2. CDIS architecture

chine, the CDIS Central Processing System (CCPS), acts as the point of communication with all external systems, provides the central repository of all CDIS data, and controls the system including management of failure and recovery of all workstations. The CCPS is a fault-tolerant computer.

About thirty controller workstations are used by air traffic controllers to display information and manipulate the approach sequence. A further twenty display positions, used by other operational staff, are simplified controller workstations. Six administrative workstations are used by the CCF supervisor, by engineers, and by data entry staff. Each controller workstation uses a pair of computers so that in the case of failure, processing switches from the failed machine to the standby.

Communication between workstations and the CCPS uses a local area network (LAN) consisting of two token rings, acting in main/standby mode. If one ring fails, communications switch automatically to the other ring with no loss or duplication of data.

10.3 The CDIS Projects

Development of CDIS was undertaken in two stages: during 1989, there was a study project to define the requirements, and from late 1989 until 1992 was the main implementation project. From delivery in 1992 until October 1993 CDIS underwent operational system integration with other CCF systems, and it went into operational use in Autumn 1993.

The study project delivered a functional requirements document, together with a preliminary design of the system, a plan for implementation and accompanying analyses including reliability, maintainability and availability. In this article I will concentrate on the functional requirements.

The software implementation project had five major phases: system specification, software design, coding and unit test, system test and acceptance test.

Coding and testing were done in parallel, with two separate teams. One team was responsible for coding and unit testing the software. The other team was responsible for integrating the developed software and carrying out black box system testing. The software was developed in six incremental builds. Each build was the subject of a formal handover from the implementation team to the test team.

Acceptance testing was carried out by running a subset of the system tests which was agreed with the client and covered all aspects including each functional area, all performance requirements and full resilience testing.

The fault management process on CDIS is central to maintaining control of the development and maintenance process. Fault management started with the delivery of software from the implementation team to the test team, and continued through operational system integration and into maintenance. Each fault was analysed to determine its point of introduction. If, for example, the specification was wrong, then the specification, design and code were all fixed. This means that the CDIS specification, design, code and user documents were always in step and we have avoided the common situation where the code is the only real authority on what the system does.

10.4 Functional Requirements

10.4.1 Overview

The functional requirements for CDIS were developed using three techniques. First, a world model was constructed using entity-relationship (ER) analysis to describe the real-world objects that CDIS had to deal with, the properties of these objects, and the relationships between them.

Second, the processing requirements were defined using dataflow diagrams following a real-time structured analysis method (Hatley and Pirbhai, 1988). At the top level the *context diagram* showed CDIS as a single process with dataflows to and from all the external systems and all the different users of CDIS. This was then decomposed into lower level diagrams.

Third, a formal specification language, VDM (Jones, 1986), was used to give a precise definition of the data maintained by CDIS and the operations on the data. As well as being technically suitable, VDM was familiar to the requirements team and had been used on other projects for CAA. At this stage the VDM model was only partial. It included the major data structures and some of the most critical operations.

10.4.2 Formal and Semi-Formal Notations

We changed our ideas of how to use formal specification during the study. Initially we expected that we would define operations of the system using dataflow diagrams to represent the processing for each operation, and that we would use formal specifications to define the lowest level processes on these dataflow diagrams. This is similar to the method suggested by Plat *et al.* (1991). However, we found that this approach was not giving useful results, for two reasons. First, decomposing an operation into lower level processes is not really specifying the operation at all—rather, it is giving a sketch of its design. Second, specifying the processes on a dataflow diagram does not give a clear specification of the diagram as a whole, since the meaning of the dataflows themselves is left undefined. We therefore decided to carry out the formal specification at the top level. We defined a VDM state which was the whole state of the CDIS system, and VDM operations each of which corresponded to a single user-level operation of the system, an *event* in the structured model. For example, receipt of a message from an external system is an event, and there is a corresponding VDM operation. The structured model is still primary in the sense that the context diagram defines *what* operations are needed and identifies their inputs and outputs; however, we did not use dataflow diagrams at all for defining the *effects* of the operations.

The state in the VDM specification is closely related to the ER model. In principle, indeed, it is possible to derive a VDM state directly from an ER model. However, this is not the best way to proceed because the VDM is richer than the ER model. It is therefore better to *replace* some ER constructs by simpler and more direct formal representations. It is also possible to make the model more precise by adding more detailed constraints than the simple cardinalities of the ER model.

The following example illustrates the different kinds of specification. One of the functions of CDIS is to receive messages from NAS about the Approach Sequence and to update the screen displays with the new information. The corresponding piece of state is shown as an ER diagram in Figure 10.3.

A typical dataflow diagram for the operation is shown in Figure 10.4. This shows that a message from NAS is first validated. Then the data from the message is stored in the *Arrival Data* store. An update is sent to a process which broadcasts a message over the local area network, and this message, together with the stored arrival data, is used to compute the new value of the display.

These two diagrams are typical of a structured requirements analysis. However, the dataflow diagram in particular is unsatisfactory as a requirement statement. First, it is not clear from the diagram what, for example, the validation process does, nor what happens if the validation fails. Second, the fact that a message is broadcast, and that computation of the display uses stored data rather than the LAN message contents are design decisions. They are of no interest to the user and anyway at the requirements stage it is premature to assume an implementation strategy. Third, if we specify the processes on the diagram, we find that the resulting low level specifications do not help the user to understand the overall effect of processing the message.

To write a VDM specification of the operation we first modelled the state from the ER diagram in VDM. Figure 10.5 shows the main notations used in the VDM

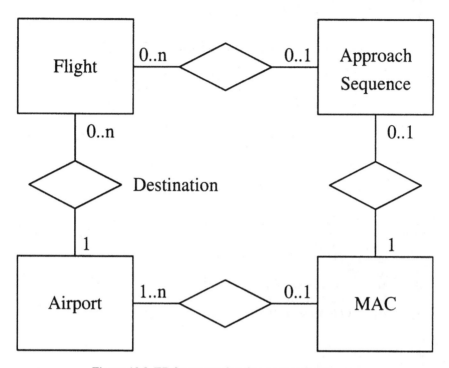

Figure 10.3. ER fragment showing approach sequence

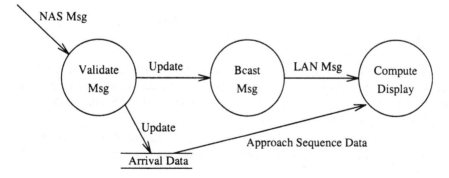

Figure 10.4. Dataflow diagram for approach sequence update

specification, apart from the usual logical and set-theoretic symbols. Figure 10.6 is a simplified version of the VDM state.

state	Declaration of state components
inv	Constraints on the state
operations	Operations on the state
ext	External state affected by an operation
post	Postcondition defining effect of operation
$\overleftarrow{data}$	Value of *data* before operation

Figure 10.5. VDM notation

state
airports : set of *Airport*
flights : set of *Flight*
MACs : set of *MAC*
airport_MACs : map *Airport* to *MAC*
approach_seqs : map *MAC* to seq *Flight*
destination : map *Flight* to *Airport*

inv
dom *destination* = *flights* $\wedge$
ran *destination* $\subseteq$ *airports* $\wedge$
dom *airport_MACs* $\subseteq$ *airports* $\wedge$
ran *airport_MACs* = *MACs* $\wedge$
dom *approach_seqs* $\subseteq$ *MACs* $\wedge$
$\forall m \in$ dom *approach_seqs* $\bullet$
    elems *approach_seqs*$(m) \subseteq$
        $\{f \in flights \mid airport\_MACs(destination(f)) = m\}$

Figure 10.6. The state in VDM

The mathematics in Figure 10.6 corresponds closely to the ER diagram in Figure 10.3. The use of functions and the constraints on their domains and ranges represent the cardinality constraints expressed in the ER diagram. However, the VDM is an improvement in the following ways:

– it represents the approach sequence directly by a *sequence* of flights associated with the MAC. The ordering of flights in the sequence is not expressed in the ER at all;
– the last part of the invariant expresses the fact that for a flight to be in the approach sequence for a MAC, it must be bound for an airport associated with that MAC (although not all such flights need be in the sequence). That fact is not expressible at all in ER notation.

To define the effect of an update message we need some more state, because we need to represent the information about each flight and also the displays on the screens.

```
state
arrival_data : map Flight to Data
edd_displays : map EDD to EDD_display
edd_pages : map EDD to Page

operations
AS_MSG(msg : Approach_Sequence_Message)
      ext
            wr arrival_data
            wr approach_seqs
            wr edd_displays
            rd edd_pages
      post
      if can_update_arrival_data(msg, arrival_data⃖)
      then arrival_data_updated(msg, arrival_data⃖, arrival_data,
                approach_seqs⃖, approach_seqs) ∧
            arrival_data_displayed(edd_pages, arrival_data,
                approach_seqs, edd_displays)
      else arrival_data = arrival_data⃖ ∧
            approach_seqs = approach_seqs⃖ ∧
            edd_displays = edd_displays⃖
      fi
```

Figure 10.7. Operation specification in VDM

As shown in Figure 10.7, the definition of this operation can be understood in small pieces each of which is understandable in terms of user concepts. The validation is encapsulated in the definition of *can_update_arrival_data*, the way the data are updated is encapsulated in *arrival_data_updated* and the effect on the screens is encapsulated in the function *arrival_data_displayed*. Each function is defined elsewhere in the specification. For example *arrival_data_displayed* defines how a given collection of arrival data appears on the screens. It is defined in terms of a lower level function which describes how arrival data appear on a particular page; that in turn is based on the internal definition of how a page is set up and encapsulates the rules for how arrivals are selected and ordered for display.

10.4.3 Issues in Formal Requirements Specification

We used a formal method as one of our requirements analysis techniques because we believed that the precision of the formal notation would help to clarify our understanding of the requirements and to make the requirements unambiguous and complete. This belief was borne out in practice: we asked a lot of questions during the study, many of them as a result of trying to formalise certain requirements, and as a result we gained a good understanding of what the system was intended to do. However, there are a number of problems with using this style of specification at the requirements stage.

First, this kind of functional specification, whether formal or informal, cannot distinguish requirements which are essential from those that are only desirable.

Second, the first-order logic used allows us to write down properties of each individual operation, but often requirements are expressed in more global terms as properties of *all* operations—for example, that all operations must be reversible. Such higher-order properties cannot be directly expressed using VDM.

Similarly, any specification based on a system model and a specific set of operations has already committed to a considerable level of detail. The user might like to specify, for example that "there should be a complete set of query operations" without having to specify anything about what form these operations might take.

Finally, only functional requirements can be captured using this kind of specification; usability, performance, aspects of safety and reliability are all outside its scope.

10.5 The System Specification

10.5.1 The Three Specifications

At the beginning of the implementation project we decided that we should produce a complete specification of CDIS to serve as a basis for design. Based on our experience in the study, we abandoned the use of dataflow diagrams and based the specification primarily on the formal notation. However, a specification entirely in VDM would not have been adequate, for two main reasons:

– one of the most important aspects of CDIS is its user interface. VDM provides no real help in specifying the details of the user interface;
– CDIS processes many inputs concurrently. The VDM specification only describes sequential aspects of behaviour. In practice it was important to know what operations could occur concurrently and how they could interfere with each other.

We therefore produced the system specification in three parts:

1. a formal *Core Specification*;
2. a set of *User Interface Definitions*;
3. a *Concurrency Specification*.

These three specifications were three different views of the system rather than specifications of different parts of the system. Figure 10.8 shows how they were related to each other.

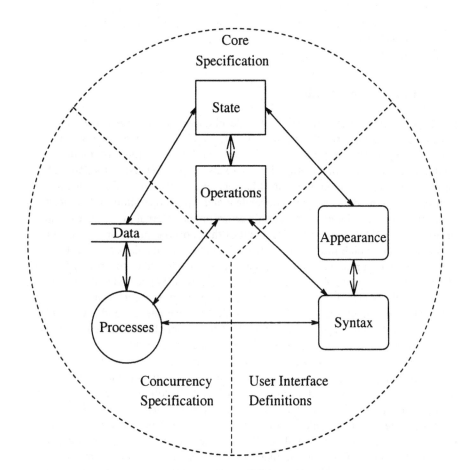

Figure 10.8. The three CDIS specifications

The core specification described the data managed by CDIS and every operation that CDIS could perform. Each operation was specified at a semantic level by defining its inputs, outputs and effect on the state. For each operation in the core specification, there was a corresponding user interface definition. This described the operation at a syntactic and lexical level by describing the dialogue between user and machine to effect the operation, the physical keystrokes or mouse actions that were necessary and the appearance of the screen during the dialogue. The concurrency specification showed what processes in the real world could carry out the operations. The data accesses and possible sequences of operations of each process were identified.

10.5.2 The Core Specification

CDIS, which has about 150 specification-level operations, is larger than most systems that have been formally specified to date, and one issue we faced was how to structure the specification into understandable modules. The top level modules are related to major areas of functionality: Arrivals, Departures, Airports, Page Management, Displays, Communications Management, Engineering Management. Unfortunately, the modules are not independent and typical operations affect the state of several modules. For example, certain errors on the external links cause communications with NAS to be lost. As a result of this, portions of the arrivals database become invalid, which in turn means that the controllers' displays are affected. We therefore needed a modularisation mechanism which allowed us to write operations affecting the state of several modules in a natural way. We considered three alternatives: VDM, which did not have a useful modularisation mechanism; Z (Spivey, 1992), which seemed to offer the kind of structuring we needed; and VVSL (Middleburg, 1989), a language which has a VDM-like syntax but has a well developed module structure which gave us most of the facilities we needed.

Because we had used VDM during the requirements analysis we were reluctant to change to Z even though we considered the schema calculus ideal for the kind of modularisation we wanted. Furthermore, the error-handling conventions in Z are clumsy compared with those of VVSL. We therefore decided to use VVSL.

When one VVSL module imports another it imports the constructs which are exported from the imported module. Unfortunately, there is no way of importing operations in this way because, unlike Z, VVSL has no calculus for combining operations. This caused problems in building up the specification. For example, receipt of an arrival update message affects the state in the Arrivals module and also in the Displays modules. We would like to be able to write the update as the conjunction of an operation UPDATE_ARRIVAL_DATA in the ARRIVAL_DATA module and an operation UPDATE_ARRIVAL_DISPLAYS in the various DISPLAY modules. In Z this is exactly what we would do. In VVSL this was not possible, so we had to write two *functions*: *can_update_arrival_data* and *arrival_data_updated*. The first corresponds to the error checking that UPDATE_ARRIVAL_DATA would do, and the second to the actual updates that would be carried out. Then the operation in the top level module uses these two functions to describe the effect in the arrivals module. This convention is the one that was used in Figure 10.7. It does unfortunately lead to clutter in the specification and means that operations are often not defined where one would expect to find them. This makes the specification less readable than we would have liked.

In preparing the core specification we did not use any tools other than some document preparation macros for LATEX. At the time, the only typechecking tools available would not have allowed us to generate easily readable output, nor would they have supported VVSL and its module constructs. Subsequent experience with other formal methods tools suggests that we would have eliminated a lot of syntactic errors in the specification if we had had a suitable typechecker available. On the other hand, we made several extensions to the notation to allow ourselves to write the specification in a more compact and understandable way, and tools might have prevented us from doing that.

10.5.3 The User Interface Definitions

The user interface definitions contained two kinds of information. They described the physical appearance of the interface using pictures and text, and the syntax of the user dialogues using state-transition diagrams. The definitions were developed using throw-away prototypes.

Each operation described at an abstract level in the core specification had a concrete specification in a user interface definition. However, the level of abstraction was not uniform; rather, it depended on the complexity and criticality of the operation. At one extreme, there is a single operation in the core specification, EDIT_PAGE, which corresponds to a complete document, the Editor's User Interface Definition. At the other extreme, the operations in the core specification describing how the approach sequence allocator manipulates flights are at the level of individual keystrokes, since the behaviour of this interface is critical and subtly related to the information being received from NAS while the operations are in progress.

10.5.4 The Concurrency Specification

The concurrency specification describes the *inherent* concurrency of the CDIS environment: that is, the processes which could run concurrently in the real world. There was one such process for each user input device of CDIS, one for each connection to an external system, and one for each of the hardware devices in CDIS whose health was monitored and which could therefore fail or recover.

We used two notations for the concurrency specification. Each process was described by a CSP (Hoare, 1985) process whose alphabet was the set of operations available to that process. This served as a check that the operations were correctly defined in the core specification.

We also drew dataflow diagrams showing all the processes and all the state variables they read and wrote. These DFDs, unlike those used in structured analysis, had a precise semantics: a circle represented a concurrent process, a data store represented a state variable, and dataflows represented read and write access to state variables by processes. This showed us where there was shared data which needed to be accessed by several processes simultaneously.

10.5.5 Successes and Problems in the Specification

Overall I believe the specification phase was successful. It defined the functionality of CDIS precisely and was a firm foundation for the rest of the project. We were using well understood techniques and although they had not been used before in this combination or on this scale, we understood the strengths and limitations of what we were doing and did not have major unexpected difficulties.

However, the specification is far from perfect and there are some problems remaining and lessons to be learned.

First, it is hard to get an overview of the system from the specification. The formal specification is not top down—indeed, because we followed a declaration-before-use style, it is almost completely bottom up. We also failed to write enough English commentary in the core specification, which makes it even more difficult to read.

The second issue is that there were, inevitably, problems at the boundaries between the three kinds of specification. One problem is that the user interface definitions were not as complete as the core specification. This is because the concrete representations in the user interface definitions were necessarily *examples* of the appearance, not exhaustive definitions. For example we failed to specify the colours of all aspects of the engineer's display under all circumstances, leading to uncertainties as to what the behaviour was meant to be. We also did not manage to separate concerns as much as we would have liked: an example is that during the design phase our idea of the user interface changed from an "enquire and get a snapshot" style to a continuous update style. This had a major effect on the core specification which it would have been nice to avoid.

A third issue which is always difficult was choosing the right level of detail. For example, we did not specify the validation of messages well: some of the checking for internal consistency was left to the design phase when it should logically have formed part of the specification.

Finally there is an interesting sense in which the specification is only an approximation to the real behaviour of CDIS. That is the pervasive assumption that operations are atomic. In practice, an operation can take several seconds to execute, giving ample time for other operations to interfere. There are therefore observable states of CDIS (where, for example, only some of the screens have updated in response to a message) which are definitely not allowed by the specification. Intuitively it is obvious that these deviations from the specification are "harmless" but it is not obvious how to decide what is and what is not really allowable behaviour. It may be that work on refinement of shared systems (Jacob, 1988) can illuminate this question.

Writing the specification was a useful exercise in its own right. The process of defining the functionality and the reviews which were conducted with the CAA served to clarify and make precise exactly what was needed. The formality of the notation certainly helped to focus this process. Once complete, the specification then became the foundation for the rest of the project.

First, it was the basis for change control. Like any large project, CDIS suffered a large number of requirements changes during its implementation. The existence of a clear and complete definition was invaluable in deciding what was and was not a real change, and in evaluating the impact of proposed changes.

Second the specification was, of course, the basis for the design and implementation of the system. The next section discusses that in more detail.

Third, the specification was the basis of system testing and acceptance. For this purpose the system specification superseded the original functional requirements, since it included everything they contained and more. The system tests were derived by the test team from the system specification together with the non-functional requirements. In particular, the formal specification was used to derive black box tests by equivalence partitioning and boundary value analysis in a systematic way. Every test was traced back to the part of the specification which was being tested, giving complete visibility of test coverage.

Finally the specification was used as the basis of the user documentation, which was, inevitably, prepared before the system was complete. Again the precision and completeness of the specification minimised the extent to which the user documentation had to be revised once the real system was available.

10.6 Design

10.6.1 Overview of the CDIS Design

The CDIS design consisted of five major parts:

1. Design Overview
   System architecture, design rationale and guidelines.
2. Functional Design
   Design of the application modules, primarily derived from the core specification.
3. Process Design
   Processes, tasks, inter-process communication and data sharing. Derived primarily from the concurrency specification together with the non-functional requirements (especially performance) and characteristics of the machines and operating systems we were using.
4. User Interface Design
   Derived from the user interface definitions and knowledge of the services offered by the application modules.
5. Infrastructure
   Mainly the LAN software design. A definition of the required LAN protocol

and of the interface between the LAN software and the rest of CDIS was developed as part of the overall design, then a design was produced for the LAN software itself.

There is a difference between the partitioning of the design and that of the specification. While the three kinds of specification were three different *views* of the same thing, the four different designs (excluding the overview) were designs for different *parts* of the software. Thus the relationship between the design components, which is shown in Figure 10.9, reflected a division of the software into subsystems and also a division of effort between teams.

Because the different design components required different programming styles and the design issues in each area were different, different notations were used in the four kinds of design.

The functional design was done by devising a module structure for the application code and then specifying, for each module, the internal data and the operations offered by the module. The module structure was derived from the structure of the core specification, with two modifications. First, each module was usually divided into two layers—an operation layer, used by the process or UI software, and a services layer, used by other application modules. Then, each module was divided into three parts for CCPS-specific processing, workstation-specific processing and common code.

Process design was carried out first by identifying the processes and their communications mechanisms and shared data, and documenting these using dataflow diagrams. Then the response of each process to each possible event was defined.

The user interface was implemented using Presentation Manager, which requires a particular programming style. The design of the user interface was expressed as specifications of Presentation Manager window classes, defining the messages each could process and the response to each one.

The LAN software was a difficult area because the requirements were stringent: in-order delivery of all messages without duplication, over two token rings with automatic and invisible switch in case of failure. Performance considerations dictated that the unreliable broadcast service provided by Netbios had to be used as the basis of most communications, so a complex layer of CDIS software had to be built on top.

Formal methods were used in three places in the design: the application modules, the processes and the LAN software.

10.6.2 Application Modules

The application modules were specified in VVSL. They were intended to be refinements of the corresponding specification modules. That is, the specification data types would be transformed into more concrete, computer-oriented types, and the operations redefined to use these types.

At first we intended to use VVSL only for the more critical modules, and to develop those quite formally, writing down the refinement relations and the corresponding proof obligations. For less critical modules we intended to write more

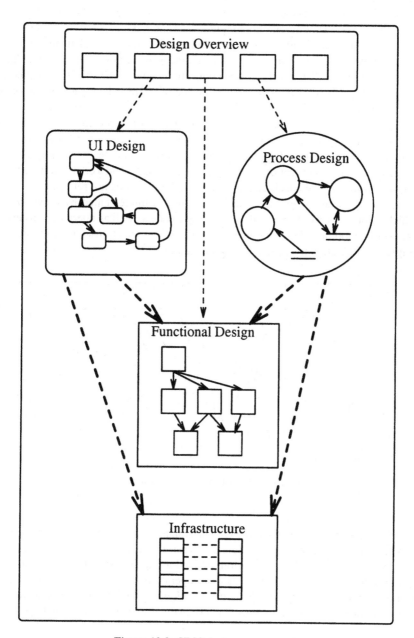

Figure 10.9. CDIS design components

code-oriented specifications. Neither of these intentions was carried out in practice. First, it proved awkward to use different notations, so we decided to specify almost everything in VVSL although for simple cases we did not give the full specification of each operation, but only its signature. Conversely, it turned out that the refinement relations were extremely large and cumbersome to write down, and we abandoned the attempt to establish a fully formal connection between the specification and the design. One problem was the large state-space of CDIS, where each operation affected a large part of the state.

There was also a more basic reason for our inability to write down the refinement relation. Although the set of data in a design module was a concrete form of the data in the corresponding specification modules, the design module as a whole was not a refinement of the specification module, because it usually had a completely different set of operations. The specification of a user operation was not refined by a single operation on an application module; rather, it was implemented by a *transaction* which involved process code and user interface code as well as operations in several application modules. For example, Figure 10.10 shows the transaction involved in a single user operation to set an airport data value.

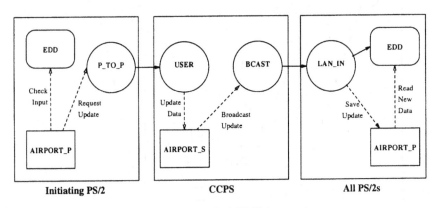

Figure 10.10. A typical CDIS transaction

No single operation in the AIRPORT design modules corresponds to the specification operation - instead, the module offers services which allow the user interface to check the validity of the operation, to send a request to the CCPS to make the change and to broadcast the new data, an operation to accept the new data at the workstation and many query operations to allow display of the new data. It is an open question how, formally, these operations are related to the formal specification.

10.6.3 Process Design

We used finite state machines (FSMs) for process design. The only novel thing we did was to use VVSL predicates as a way of characterising states when these were complex. Also, the actions in the FSM were operations of the application modules, specified in VVSL. In the more complex machines we did have difficulty relating the machines back to the specification they were implementing. In fact, FSMs could be encoded in VVSL and this might have been a better approach, giving us a better integration with the module specifications.

10.6.4 LAN Software Design

The requirements for the LAN software were initially expressed using VVSL. This was not entirely successful, because VVSL did not easily capture the dynamic behaviour of the protocol and the relationship between the behaviours at the two ends of the communication. For that purpose a notation supporting concurrency proved necessary and later parts of the requirements, and all the design, was expressed using Milner's Calculus of Communicating Systems (CCS) (Milner, 1989). The CCS processes were translated directly into the code of the implementation. We used a form of value-passing CCS in which we incorporated VVSL definitions of data types and message structures.

The LAN software design was the one area of CDIS where we made any use of proofs. Since the LAN was such a critical component, and its design was so complex, we were concerned about its correctness. We attempted proofs of correctness in two areas.

The first was at the interface between the LAN and the engineering part of the CDIS application. The LAN software detects failed machines and connections and either takes appropriate action or passes information to the rest of CDIS, which then makes decisions about stopping and starting failed machines. Since machines at each end of the link can fail at any time, even during restart after a previous failure, it is far from obvious that there is no possibility of deadlock. To verify the protocol we wrote a simplified version and used the Edinburgh Concurrency Workbench (Cleaveland *et al.*, 1993) to establish temporal formulae representing facts such as "Following a failure it is always eventually possible to recover". This gave us some confidence in the correctness of the protocol.

The second area was recovering from message loss. We wrote a CCS process representing a specification of the desired behaviour and another CCS process which was intended to implement that behaviour. We tried to prove that the implementation was correct even when a loss was suffered during recovery. This was not possible, because the protocol suffered from a subtle concurrency problem. It would have been almost impossible to find that bug during testing, so attempting the proof allowed us to correct the design rather than put into service a system which could have exhibited an incomprehensible fault at some time in the future. Details of this work have been published elsewhere (Bruns, 1994).

10.6.5 Issues in Formal Design

In my opinion, the use of formal methods in the design of large systems is less well understood than their use in specification. We had some difficulties in carrying out the design of CDIS as formally as we would have liked.

One difficulty is that design is many-dimensional. We were forced to use different methods for designing different parts of the system and there was no unifying way we could formalise the design as a whole—no theory of software architecture that we could use to validate the design. In particular, conventional refinement rules do not apply when the structure of the design is different from the structure of the specification, as it will inevitably be in any large, distributed system. Our initial misunderstanding of this point led to problems at the interface between the application modules and the user interface, and a lot of necessary operations were missed in our first attempts to specify the application modules.

It was difficult to decide on the right level of formality because the design was large and it was impractical to formalise all of it. We did not always make the right decisions. Formalising too much gave us unnecessary work; in some pathological cases, the formal specification was more complicated than the code itself. Not formalising enough meant that developers were sometimes faced with operations for which they had signatures but no clear definition of what was required. We should probably have adopted a simple rule: specify all update operations.

In spite of these problems, the functional design was largely successful in generating a sound design satisfying the specification. Few of the faults in CDIS can be attributed to an incorrect relationship between the specification and the functional design. The main benefit of the formal application design was that the interface of each module was precisely defined so clients of the module knew exactly what they could rely on. We also found that, starting from the VVSL module specifications, the implementation of the application modules was relatively straightforward and the code usually reflected the specification in a fairly direct way. This has given us good traceability between the code and the design. In some cases the code was developed using rigorous correctness arguments.

The CCS design the LAN software was particularly successful in mastering the complexity of a difficult area and generating extremely reliable code.

We were unable to use a really formal process, such as carrying out proofs, to any large extent. This does not mean that such a process is always impractical; however, one has to balance the cost of using formality against the cost of *not* using it. From the point of view of a developer, the purpose of a formal step such as a proof is to discover errors [1]. The expected cost of not carrying out a proof depends on the probability of there being an error which the proof would have discovered and other techniques would not, and on the cost of that error. In the case of refinement proofs we believe that expected cost is small compared with the cost of actually doing the

---

[1] From other points of view the purpose may be different—for example from the point of view of a regulatory authority or customer the purpose of a proof may be to gain *assurance*, which has different costs and benefits.

proofs; in the case of the LAN we believe it is large and easily justified our modest proof effort.

10.7 Qualitative and Quantitative Conclusions

10.7.1 Some Numbers

The operational CDIS software contains about 197,000 lines of non-blank, non-comment C code. In addition a comparable amount of code was written for test harnesses, emulators and other non-operational software. The specification documents were about 1,200 pages long and the design documents about 3,000 pages.

The total effort on the implementation project was about 15,500 person days, distributed as shown in Table 10.2. Overall the effort, at about 13 lines of code

Table 10.2. Effort distribution on CDIS implementation project

Activity	Days	%
Requirements	270	2
Specification	1,274	8
Design	1,556	10
Code & Unit Test	5,219	34
Test and Integration	2,458	16
Acceptance	723	5
User Documentation	405	3
Project Management	2,137	14
Development Environment	549	4
Others	945	6
Total	15,536	

per day, seems comparable with or better than other projects of the same size and kind (it is better than a simple CoCoMo (Boehm, 1981) prediction, for example). We do not believe that the use of formal methods cost us anything on the project compared with not using them — if anything, they saved effort. The distribution of effort is not very different from the standard CoCoMo model although a slightly higher percentage of time is spent on requirements and specification.

During development, about 11 faults per thousand lines of code (KLOC) were delivered from the developers into the integration and system test team. In the first twenty months after delivery CDIS manifested about 150 faults, that is about 0.75 faults per KLOC. We believe this figure is significantly better than that on comparable projects. Furthermore, few of these faults are specification or requirements problems. Such faults are often the ones that persist into the delivered system and prove costly to eliminate.

10.7.2 Impressions of Formal Methods

As far as CAA was concerned, the main impact was our use of formal methods for the system specification. This had both advantages and disadvantages. The main advantages were:

1. The specification was comprehensive. The CAA team could answer essentially any question about what CDIS would do by referring to the specification.
2. The specification was precise. There was rarely any doubt about what it meant and how CDIS would behave.
3. The use of the specification to derive the system tests meant that CAA had good visibility of the level of testedness of CDIS at any time.

On the other hand, there were some drawbacks:

1. It was difficult to get an overview from the formal specification, because it was not top-down and did not have a hierarchical structure.
2. The core specification was a poor aid to internal communication with CAA, because the notation was only understandable to the CAA team directly working on CDIS, so they had to interpret the specification to other people within CAA.
3. The user interface specification was not as precise and complete as the core specification and therefore the user interface was not as well defined as it should have been. Furthermore the relationship between the two specifications was not always clear.
4. The specifications were not clear about certain timing issues, in particular the point at which events became visible on the user interface.

The lessons that should be drawn for any future use of formal methods are two. First, the formal specification should be accompanied by much more informal explanation using English text, diagrams and any other convenient notation. Second, more emphasis should be placed on making the user interface specification precise and complete.

For Praxis, the benefits of formal methods covered the whole lifecycle:

1. The formal specification helped clarify key requirements. CDIS had few requirements or specification faults after delivery.
2. The formal specification was a precise definition of what had to be developed, leading to verifiable design and code.
3. The formal specification was a precise baseline for change control.
4. The formal specification was a sound basis for testing and led to a highly testable system.
5. The formal application design was a precise definition of module interfaces for clients and implementers leading to a simple, reliable design.
6. Formal notations helped master the complexity of difficult design areas.

The main limitations were:

1. Only functional behaviour was covered by the formal specifications.

2. Formal specifications do not distinguish necessary from desirable requirements or allow very high level requirements to be expressed.
3. Care is needed when integrating formal and informal specifications.
4. There are many aspects of design which formal methods do not address, and integrating all the aspects can be hard.
5. More research is needed on the formal basis of large-scale design.
6. Some uses of formal methods, such as proof, are expensive and can only be justified in critical areas.

10.7.3 Conclusion

CDIS was a large and complex project and many factors contributed to its eventual success. I believe that one important factor was our use of formal methods combined with other good software engineering practices. We have evidence that using formal methods helped us to build the right system, and helped us to build it right. We think they improved the quality of the system at no extra cost.

I would not hesitate to use formal methods for the system specification in any similar project, and I think we have learned lessons about making that effective by combining formality with more comprehensible explanations and better specification structure.

Formal methods also contribute to the design process, but it is clear that there are many other aspects of good design as well. Carrying out formal design requires more work on understanding the different dimensions of design and on formal understanding of large-scale architectures.

CDIS shows that the use of formal methods on real, large scale projects is not only practicable but beneficial. The question software engineers should now be asking about formal methods is not *whether* to use them, but *how* best to benefit from them as part of a complete software engineering approach.

Acknowledgements

This paper should really have as named authors all my colleagues in Praxis who worked on CDIS. It is their work which led to the results reported here. I hope that the opinions here, which are of course my own, do some justice to their efforts. I am also grateful to the CAA CDIS team who supported our use of unfamiliar methods on a critical and difficult project.

I should like to thank David Isaac who contributed the CAA's impressions of formal methods to an early version of this paper, and Glenn Bruns from the Laboratory for the Foundations of Computer Science at Edinburgh who helped us with the CCS proof work.

CHAPTER 11
Rigorous Review Technique

Lesley Semmens and Tony Bryant

11.1 Introduction

The Rigorous Review Technique (RRT) emerged from a research project established between Leeds Metropolitan University (at that time called Leeds Polytechnic) and British Telecom (BT). In the late 1980s a small group of researchers at LMU started work on the integration of formal and structured approaches, with the objective of finding ways in which the two forms could complement each other. This would allow the strengths of the differing approaches to be combined within an integrated method. The strength of the structured methods derived from their concern for software management and productivity; stressing the planning, monitoring and control aspects of software production on a large scale. Formal methods on the other hand emanated from a focus on reliability and correctness; stressing production of error-free code, developed through use of formal languages and specification techniques, incorporating proofs based on mathematical models. Our aim and intention was to harness the reasoning power of the mathematically-based specification to the management and project-based discipline of structured development.

At the outset the enormous conceptual and pragmatic obstacles confronting any use of mathematically-based specification in industrial software production became immediately obvious; and were made more so once our collaboration with BT was started. No simple-minded concoction of the two approaches would be practical: It had taken many years to persuade developers to make any attempt to use the informal, superficially user-friendly, graphical techniques of the structured methods. The only way to persuade developers to employ any sort of formality in their specifications would be as adjuncts to existing practices.

Any attempt to refine existing working practices must contend with the accrued experience and prejudices of the target community. They will not simply abandon or even revise their own skills and expertise without good cause, even if that comes in the form of both positive inducement and potential chastisement. Furthermore any attempt to persuade developers of the benefits of formal specification had to be accessible to their idiosyncratic approaches, with a minimal cost in terms of resources or discomfort to those involved.

These factors led us to develop the Rigorous Review Technique as part of our objective of seeking to establish ways to incorporate formal modelling notations in an intelligent and effective manner, using the constraints of existing development methods. Within BT the vehicle selected for this exercise in technology transfer was their own in-house development method TELSTAR. At the time TELSTAR drew upon many of the key techniques used on methodologies such as SSADM, Information Engineering, and Yourdon; in addition it incorporated a range of management, planning and quality techniques.

BT were keen to accomplish the controlled transfer of this technology into its own organisational practice, recognising that every user organisation must continue to develop and maintain its own systems harnessing the rigour of formal methods; and as a supplier organisation, it could not ignore the growing demand for formal verification of client systems.

The technique itself was one component of a larger framework that distinguishes between four main levels of use of formal specification — respectively termed formal review, enhancement, convergence, and automated support.

- formal review involved provision of a platform for the use of formal methods as a quality review mechanism in systems projects;
- enhancement concerned the incorporation of formal notations within development methods, aiming to enhance and augment the quality and decrease the production costs of systems products;
- convergence sought to use both formal review and enhancement as a basis to assist the transfer of the technology of formal notations and methods into wider use among systems practitioners;
- automated support outlined the necessity of developing a model for assessment and specification of tools designed to support integrated methods.

The RRT was an attempt to harness the power of formal notations. It was also, critically, a way of applying context and method to formal approaches themselves. Initially that context was provided by the BT TELSTAR framework; but the technique as such can be used in conjunction with many similar development approaches. The technique permits developers to establish requirements based in their conventional manner. They produce their standard models, which are then translated into Z. The translation process itself operates on a number of levels, and the operation of the technique can be used to clarify aspects of the specification, expose inconsistencies and contradictions, highlight omissions and ambiguities.

The translation process can be carried out by a small number of (formal specification) specialists, who need not be fully involved in the project itself. On the other hand RRT has been designed to be readily usable by non-expert project personnel with relatively common skills. (Experience demonstrated that it was easier to teach an experienced analyst the fundamentals of the restricted Z notation, than it was to teach a mathematically competent person to understand the skills of analysis.)

11.2 The Technique

The RRT may be applied to any specification developed using Structured Systems Analysis. The only requirement is that suitable mappings from the elements of the structured specification techniques to a formal notation have been defined. In principle, specifications developed using Object Oriented Analysis (OOA) are also suitable candidates for the application of the technique. However, the semantics of some OOA notations are not clear and work is ongoing to define these formally (Evans *et al.*, 1997). OOA techniques to which the RRT could currently be applied are the Object Model and Object Life Histories.

The primary reason for carrying out the translation is not to produce a Z specification to be used in place of the structured system specification, though this remains an option, but rather to use the translation process itself to expose hidden errors, specifically those associated with ambiguity, incompleteness and inconsistency, which may be missed by conventional review techniques.

Here we describe in detail the application of the Rigorous Review Technique to a structured system specification consisting of:

- an entity relationship model;
- data flow diagrams;
- English text supporting the diagrams and forms.

Instructions for reviewing a structured system specification using the rigorous notation Z are given. The steps should be followed in the given order, but some backtracking and rewriting may be necessary if serious errors are found. The technique is subdivided, for convenience, into three sequential stages as follows:

1. translation of the entities (see Section 11.3.1);
2. translation of the datastores (see Section 11.3.4);
3. translation of the data flow model (see Section 11.3.6).

A simple "security specification" is used as a vehicle for the example translations given at each stage of the technique. This specification is relatively small but serves to illustrate the essence of the technique. Appendix A outlines the requirements for the security subsystem.

11.2.1 Objectives

The objectives of the rigorous review technique are:

- to identify errors in a system specification, thereby reducing the cost of finding those errors later in the lifecycle;
- to supplement, or replace, conventional review techniques; especially where a (business) critical system or system component is involved.

The Z specification resulting from the use of this technique should consist of mathematics and English text. The mathematics will be in the form of Z paragraphs. The main function of the English text is to describe the intended behaviour of the system, and not simply to explain the (mathematical) Z; however, if it is thought useful, the English can be used to clarify unusual or complex constructions.

It must be stressed that the primary goal of the technique is to expose errors in a structured system specification; however, it remains as an option to make use of the resulting Z specification, either in place of or in combination with the existing structured system specification.

The diagrams and text which are input are:

- the entity relationship model:
  - an entity relationship diagram,
  - entity and relationship descriptions;
- the entity/datastore cross-reference showing which entities are contained within each datastore;
- the DFDs (data flow diagrams);
- supporting English text including process descriptions.

The technique will often, in practice, be used on selected, important parts of the system; usually these will be complex or (business) critical parts.

A list of the type of errors uncovered is given for each stage of the technique. Most errors should be found just by going through the translation process or by *type checking* the resulting Z specification. Although typical errors are listed in the sections to which they relate, many of them may not be noticed until a later stage, e.g., a deficiency in an entity may not be found until a process using it is specified.

It is useful to adopt a naming convention for Z identifiers to avoid clashes. The one used here is: upper case for Z data types, lower case for Z variables derived from entity attributes, and mixed case for schema names (for entities, datastores and processes). The identifiers used in the System Specification, such as entity names and datastore names, can often be used as the corresponding Z variable/schema names (if they are put in the correct case). It may be useful to add a suffix such as "-ds" to the names of datastore schemas, to distinguish them from entity schemas. The work will be easier if meaningful identifiers are used whenever possible.

On completion of this process, there will be a (perhaps partial) Z specification of the system and a list of problems/errors. These errors will refer to the System Specification, but problems with the original requirements may also be noted.

11.3 The Stages of the RRT

11.3.1 Translation of the Entities

The translation of the entity model is almost an automatic process and consists largely of choosing names for variables and types.

- this stage requires the outputs from entity relationship modelling. The essential diagrams and text are:
  - entity relationship diagram;

– entity descriptions;
– attribute descriptions;
– The following Z will be produced:
  – a set of Z type definitions;
  – a Z schema for each entity;
  – English text supporting the schemas.

An entity is represented in Z by a schema. The translation is quite simple. Each attribute of the entity is declared, as a variable, in the schema. It is sensible to use the entity's name for the schema name, and to use the attribute names, or something similar, for the Z variable names. In Z, each variable must have a type, so these must be declared first.

The System Specification may specify precisely how attributes are to be stored (e.g. a simple flag may be a 1 or 0, and a name might be 20 alphabetic characters), but this is not usually appropriate or necessary in a Z specification. Unless the structure of an attribute is important to the system operations, (e.g. earlier/later comparisons may be necessary on dates, and some attributes may be combinations of other data items), then it is easiest to just define a *basic type* for each attribute.

The best approach is to consider all the attributes of all the entities together, and, having decided which are distinct and what relationships, if any, exist between them, to define types for them all.

Each entity will have one or more *keys*. Often *foreign keys* will also have been identified. These keys are important for specifying the datastores.

If an entity has subtypes, then each subtype must be given a separate Z *type*. However, it sometimes proves useful to combine several types into a single *super-type*; this can be achieved by using a *free type definition*. See Appendix B for further details of subtyping.

Experience shows that the English descriptions for entities and attributes are often brief or non-existent, which causes problems in an unfamiliar work area and should be highlighted as an omission.

Check, at least, that:

– the key for each entity is unique for each entity occurrence;
– if foreign keys have been identified, each relationship shown between entities is valid; i.e., if there is a many-to-one relationship between entities A (many) and B (one), then a key for an occurrence of B should be derivable from each occurrence of A;
– there is no redundant or missing data.

11.3.2 The Entity Relationship Model

Figure 11.1 shows the complete entity relationship diagram for the computer security system. Figure 11.2 shows an extract from the data dictionary giving the attribute lists for each entity.

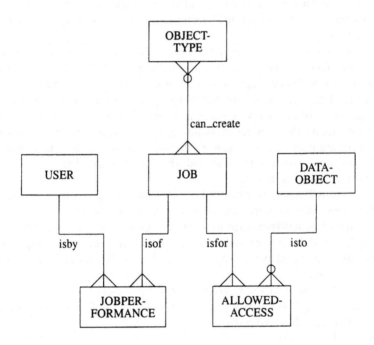

Figure 11.1. Entity relationship diagram for access security system

Entity Name:	USER	
Datastore:	Users	
Attributes:	UserId	key
	Password	
	SecurityLevel	topsecret, secret, classified, unclassified

Entity Name:	JOB	
Datastore:	Jobs	
Attributes:	JobId	key
	SecurityLevel	topsecret, secret, classified, unclassified

Entity Name:	OBJECTTYPE	
Datastore:	ObjectTypes	
Attributes:	ObjectTypeId	key
	ObjectType	

Entity Name:	DATAOBJECT	
Datastore:	Permissions	
Attributes:	DataObjectID	key
	ObjectTypeId	
	SecurityLevel	topsecret, secret, classified, unclassified

Entity Name:	JOBPERFORMANCE	
Datastore:	JobPerformances	
Attributes:	JobId	key
	UserId	key
	Status	loggedin, loggedout

Entity Name:	ALLOWEDACCESS	
Datastore:		
Attributes:	JobId	key
	DataObjectId	key
	AccessMode	read, update, create

Figure 11.2. Data dictionary extract showing entity descriptions

11.3.3 The Entity Relationship Model in Z

The following Z paragraphs are a direct translation of (part of) the System Specification of the entity model.

[*USERID, PASSWORD*]
SECURITYLEVEL ::= *topsecret* | *secret* | *classified* | *unclassified*
[*JOBID*]
[*OBJECTTYPEID, OBJECTTYPE*]
[*DATAOBJECTID*]
STATUS ::= *LoggedIn* | *LoggedOut*
ACCESSMODE ::= *read* | *update* | *create*

Next a schema type is defined for each entity.

```
┌─ User ──────────────────────────────────
│ userid : USERID
│ password : PASSWORD
│ clearance : SECURITYLEVEL
└──────────────────────────────────────────
```

```
┌─ Job ───────────────────────────────────
│ jobid : JOBID
│ clearance : SECURITYLEVEL
└──────────────────────────────────────────
```

```
┌─ ObjectType ────────────────────────────
│ objecttypeid : OBJECTTYPEID
│ objecttype : OBJECTTYPE
└──────────────────────────────────────────
```

```
┌─ DataObject ────────────────────────────
│ dataobjectid : DATAOBJECTID
│ classification : SECURITYLEVEL
│ objecttypeid : OBJECTTYPEID
└──────────────────────────────────────────
```

```
┌─ JobPerformance ────────────────────────
│ jobid : JOBID
│ userid : USERID
│ status : STATUS
└──────────────────────────────────────────
```

```
┌─AllowedAccess ──────────────────────────────
│  jobid : JOBID
│  dataobjectid : DATAOBJECTID
│  accessmode : ACCESSMODE
└──────────────────────────────────────────────
```

11.3.4 Translation of the Datastores

– This stage requires the entity relationship model, the datastore/entity cross-reference and the outputs from the first stage of the technique.
The essential text and diagrams are:
  – entity descriptions;
  – entity attribute descriptions;
  – datastore/entity cross-reference;
  – Z entity schemas and other output from the previous stage.
– The following Z will be produced:
  – a Z schema for each datastore;
  – a Z schema for the whole entity model;
  – English text supporting the schemas.

The datastores are given on the datastore/entity cross-reference, which simply shows how the set of entities is partitioned into datastores.

A datastore contains all occurrences of one or more entities. This is represented in Z by defining a datastore schema which contains a set for each of the entities in that datastore. Additionally, since each entity has a primary key, a function is defined for each entity, which maps an instance of the key to the unique entity occurrence. The fact that this function is injective ensures that no two keys map to the same entity occurrence.

If the datastore contains more than one entity, then the master-detail relationships are given by declaring a partial function from detail to master in the signature of the datastore schema. The function reflects optional and mandatory relationships in the predicate part of the datastore schema. All the relationships internal to the datastore are given in this way.

If any other functions or relationships between entities or attributes are considered necessary (these may not be noticed until the process descriptions are translated), then these may also be specified. Also, any invariants (predicates) on the data may be included.

At the end of this stage the relationships between entities in different datastores are given in a final schema modelling the whole of the entity model.

Most errors in the entity model will probably be discovered when it is found that a DFD process does not make sense, but some may become apparent whilst translating the entity model. More errors may be found as a better understanding of the system develops.

Check, at least, that:

- the entity model matches the English description of the system;
- the set of entities is consistent (e.g., if an entity occurs on the datastore/entity cross-reference, then it should have an Entity Attribute Description).

The Datastores in Z

The following, illustrates the translation of the (system) datastores shown in Figure 11.3 to their Z equivalents.

Datastore:	Users
Entities:	USER
Datastore:	Jobs
Entities:	JOB
Datastore:	ObjectTypes
Entities:	OBJECTTYPE
Datastore:	JobPerformances
Entities:	JOBPERFORMANCE
Datastore:	Permissions
Entities:	DATAOBJECT
	ALLOWEDACCESS

Figure 11.3. The datastore/entity cross-reference

$$
\begin{array}{l}
\underline{\ UserDS\ }\\
user\_set : \mathbb{P}\, User\\
\\
user\_key : USERID \rightarrowtail User\\
\hline
user\_key = \{u : user\_set \bullet u.userid \mapsto u\}
\end{array}
$$

$$
\begin{array}{l}
\underline{\ JobDS\ }\\
job\_set : \mathbb{P}\, Job\\
\\
job\_key : JOBID \rightarrowtail Job\\
\hline
job\_key = \{j : job\_set \bullet j.jobid \mapsto j\}
\end{array}
$$

ObjectTypeDS

$objecttype\_set : \mathbb{P}\, ObjectType$

$objecttype\_key : OBJECTTYPEID \rightarrowtail ObjectType$

$objecttype\_key = \{ot : objecttype\_set \bullet ot.objecttypeid \mapsto ot\}$

JobPerformanceDS

$jobperformance\_set : \mathbb{P}\, JobPerformance$

$jobperformance\_key : (JOBID \times USERID) \rightarrowtail JobPerformance$

$jobperformance\_key = \{jp : jobperformance\_set \bullet$
$\qquad\qquad\qquad (jp.jobid, jp.userid) \mapsto jp\}$

PermissionsDS

$dataobject\_set : \mathbb{P}\, DataObject$
$dataobject\_key : DATAOBJECTID \rightarrowtail DataObject$

$allowedaccess\_set : \mathbb{P}\, AllowedAccess$
$allowedaccess\_key : (JOBID \times DATAOBJECTID) \rightarrowtail$
$\qquad\qquad\qquad AllowedAccess$

$aa\_isto\_do : AllowedAccess \twoheadrightarrow DataObject$

$dataobject\_key = \{do : dataobject\_set \bullet$
$\qquad\qquad\qquad do.dataobjectid \mapsto do\}$
$allowedaccess\_key = \{aa : allowedaccess\_set \bullet$
$\qquad\qquad\qquad (aa.jobid, aa.dataobjectid) \mapsto aa\}$

$\mathrm{dom}\, aa\_isto\_do = allowedaccess\_set$
$aa\_isto\_do = \{aa : allowedaccess\_set;\ do : dataobject\_set \mid$
$\qquad\qquad\qquad aa.dataobjectid = do.dataobjectid\}$

11.3.5 The Complete State

The complete system state can then be defined by including the entity and relationship schemas and stating the constraints on the domains and ranges of the relationships.

Compulsory and optional participation in a relationship is specified by including constraints on the domain and range of the relation, in the predicate of the state schema. *Job* is an optional participant in the relationship *cancreate* so the domain of *cancreate* is a subset of *job_set* whereas *ObjectType* is a compulsory participant in the same relationship and so the range of *cancreate* is equal to *objecttype_set*.

$$
\begin{array}{l}
\underline{\quad SecurityData\quad}\\
\quad ObjectTypeDS\\
\quad JobDS\\
\quad UserDS\\
\quad JobPerformanceDS\\
\quad PermissionsDS\\
\\
\quad j\_cancreate\_ot : Job \leftrightarrow ObjectType\\
\quad jp\_isby\_u : JobPerformance \twoheadrightarrow User\\
\quad jp\_isof\_j : JobPerformance \twoheadrightarrow Job\\
\quad aa\_isfor\_j : AllowedAccess \twoheadrightarrow Job\\
\rule{5cm}{0.4pt}\\
\quad \mathrm{ran}\, j\_cancreate\_ot = objecttype\_set\\
\quad \mathrm{dom}\, j\_cancreate\_ot \subseteq job\_set\\
\\
\quad \mathrm{dom}\, jp\_isby\_u = jobperformance\_set\\
\quad \mathrm{ran}\, jp\_isby\_u = user\_set\\
\quad jp\_isby\_u = \{jp : jobperformance\_set;\ u : user\_set \mid\\
\qquad\qquad\qquad\qquad jp.userid = u.userid\}\\
\\
\quad \mathrm{dom}\, jp\_isof\_j = jobperformance\_set\\
\quad \mathrm{ran}\, jp\_isof\_j = job\_set\\
\quad jp\_isof\_j = \{jp : jobperformance\_set;\ j : job\_set \mid\\
\qquad\qquad\qquad\qquad jp.jobid = j.jobid\}\\
\\
\quad \mathrm{dom}\, aa\_isfor\_j = allowedaccess\_set\\
\quad \mathrm{ran}\, aa\_isfor\_j = job\_set\\
\quad aa\_isfor\_j = \{aa : allowedaccess\_set;\ j : job\_set \mid\\
\qquad\qquad\qquad\qquad aa.jobid = j.jobid\}
\end{array}
$$

11.3.6 Translation of the Data Flow Diagrams

- all the available information such as English text, ELHs, etc., can be referred to at this stage, but the following items are fundamental:
  - Z entities and datastores (from previous stages);
  - DFDs (Data Flow Diagrams);
  - DFD Process Descriptions;
  - data flow descriptions.
- the following Z will be produced:
  - a Z schema for each data flow which does not begin or end at a datastore;
  - a Z specification of each bottom-level process;

– English text supporting the schemas.

The top-level DFDs are not translated directly. It is the lowest level DFDs which contain the most detailed information. The higher level DFDs are not totally ignored, however, as they give a larger view of the system, and can be used to check the correctness of the bottom-level DFDs and process descriptions.

It is usually unprofitable to attempt to use the Z versions of low-level processes to construct higher level processes. The information about how the processes relate to each other (apart from the data flows) can be given in the English description which accompanies the Z. However is is possible to use the schema calculus to combine lower level processes.

The data flow schemas and the signature part (top half) of the process schemas are translated almost automatically. Only the predicate parts of the process schemas should require significant effort.

Bottom-level processes sometimes represent more than just one simple operation. They may carry out two or three tasks, or have to deal with error cases. It is easiest to translate such a process into more than one Z operation schema, and then combine these using the schema calculus. If this is not possible, it may be an indication that the process has not been sufficiently decomposed.

Data flows may be divided into the following 3 types :

1. flows between a process and another process;
2. flows between a process and an external entity;
3. flows between a process and a datastore.

The last type is not needed in Z, because a Z operation schema (representing a process) simply includes the datastore if it needs to access or update it. The other two types are translated as follows :

All of the attributes of a data flow are copied into a Z schema, in exactly the same way as entities are translated. This schema will be included in the appropriate operation schema(s), and will be used in a *decorated* form; if the schema name is decorated with '?' for input or '!' for output, then all identifiers within it will be similarly decorated.

When specifying the signature, data flows to or from datastores are not explicitly modelled; the datastore is *included* in the operation schemas instead. The datastore's name will be prefixed with Ξ if the process is just reading from the datastore, or Δ if the datastore is being updated.

It is sometimes necessary to specify *global variables* which are not included in any of the datastores (e.g., time/date).

The data flows are specified as described in Section 11.3.4.

The predicate specifies what the outputs and *after* state variables are, in terms of the inputs and *before* state variables. The process description should give all the necessary information, but in practice this is often vague and incomplete.

Problems with the data that may be found at this stage, include the following :

- processes and data flows may be inadequately or ambiguously defined;
- a data flow may contain insufficient or redundant information, or may contain information that its source does not have;
- processes may be trying to use information they do not have, for example, a process may try to access an entity without knowing its key;
- the data flows described may not correspond to those on the diagrams;
- comparisons between data items may not be defined;
- the process descriptions may not agree with the user's requirements.

It can be fruitful to check that the preconditions for a process do not place impossible requirements on the data.

The following examples illustrate the translation of parts of the data flow model to their Z equivalents.

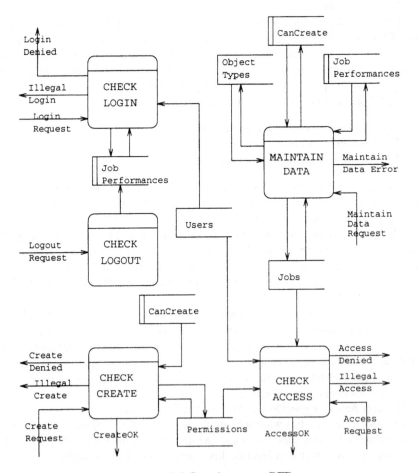

Figure 11.4. Security system DFD

Flow:	Create Request	
Attributes:	UserId	
	JobId	
	ObjectTypeId	
	JobId	May occur more than once
	AccessMode	Occurs same number of times as JobId
	DataObjectId	
	SecurityLevel	
Flow:	Create OK	
Attributes:	UserId	
	DataObjectId	
	ObjectTypeId	
Flow:	Access Request	
Attributes:	UserId	
	JobId	
	DataObjectId	
	AccessMode	
Flow:	Access OK	
Attributes:	UserId	
	DataObjectId	
	AccessMode	

Figure 11.5. Data dictionary extract showing dataflows to and from processes Check-Create and CheckAccess.

Each flow is described by a schema which specifies the constituents of the data flow. The data flows which start or end in a datastore are not specified explicitly. Looking at the flows to and from a successful *CheckCreate* operation, only *CreateRequest* and *CreateOK* have to be translated into Z schemas.

$$
\begin{array}{l}
\text{\_\_\_\_\_} CreateRequest \text{_____} \\
userid : USERID \\
jobid : JOBID \\
objecttypeid : OBJECTTYPEID \\
accesspermissions : \mathbb{P}(JOBID \times ACCESSMODE) \\
dataobjectname : DATAOBJECTID \\
classification : SECURITYLEVEL
\end{array}
$$

$$
\begin{array}{l}
\text{\_\_\_\_\_} CreateOK \text{_____} \\
OKowner : USERID \\
OKdataobjectname : DATAOBJECTID \\
OKobjecttype : OBJECTTYPEID
\end{array}
$$

The signature of the *CheckCreate* operation can then be specified.

```
┌─ CheckCreate ──────────────────────────────────────────
│ ΔSecurityData
│
│ Ξ UserDS
│ Ξ JobDS
│ Ξ ObjectTypeDS
│ Ξ JobPerformanceDS
│
│ create_req? : CreateRequest
│ create_ok! : CreateOK
└────────────────────────────────────────────────────────
```

The Complete CheckCreate Operation

The complete CheckCreate operation is given in Figure 11.6

The process takes as input the dataflow Create Request. The outputs of a successful operation will be the contents of the dataflow Create OK.

For a successful operation the user should be logged in performing that job, the job is allowed to create the object type requested and the data object name should not already exist. The contents of the output dataflow Create OK are *OKowner*, *OKdataobjectname* and *OKobjecttype* and are equal to the corresponding inputs, *cr?.userid*, *cr?.dataobjectname* and *cr?.objecttypeid* from the flow Create Request. The relation *j_cancreat_ot* is unchanged. The data object name is added to the set of data objects, the data object details are updated, and the access permissions are added to *CanAccess*. The other state variables are unaffected.

11.3.7 Process Check Access

The process Check Access takes as input the contents of the dataflow AccessRequest and if the request is valid passes on the request to the system via the dataflow AccessOK. The schema for a valid access request includes *Ξ SecurityData* as the operation does not affect the state of the security system. The inputs correspond to the attributes of the AccessRequest dataflow. The outputs correspond to the attributes of the dataflow AccessOK.

The user should be allowed to perform the job and should be logged in performing that job, the job being performed must have access rights to the data object concerned, and the access right gives right to the type of access requested. Both the user's and the job's clearances should dominate the classification of the data object.

It is sometimes necessary to define functions and relations ouside the operation schemas in order to simplify the specification.

CheckCreateOK _____
$\Delta SecurityData$

$\Xi UserDS$
$\Xi JobDS$
$\Xi ObjectTypeDS$
$\Xi JobPerformanceDS$

$cr? : CreateRequest$

$cr\_ok! : CreateOK$

$(cr?.jobid, cr?.userid) \in \text{dom}\, jobperformance\_key$

$(jobperformance\_key(cr?.jobid, cr?.userid)).status =$
$\qquad\qquad\qquad LoggedIn$

$cr?.objecttypeid \in \text{ran}\, objecttype\_key$

$\forall jid : JOBID;\ a : ACCESSMODE\ |$
$\qquad (jid, a) \in cr?.accesspermissions \bullet$
$\qquad\qquad \exists j : job\_set \bullet job\_key(jid) = j$

$(job\_key(cr?.jobid), objecttype\_key(cr?.objecttypeid)) \in$
$\qquad\qquad\qquad j\_cancreate\_ot$

$dataobject\_key(cr?.dataobjectname) \notin dataobject\_set$

$cr\_ok!.OKowner = cr?.userid$
$cr\_ok!.OKdataobjectname = cr?.dataobjectname$
$cr\_ok!.OKobjecttype = cr?.objecttypeid$

$j\_cancreate\_ot' = j\_cancreate\_ot$

$dataobject\_set' = dataobject\_set \cup$
$\qquad \{do : DataObject\ |$
$\qquad\qquad\qquad do.dataobjectid = cr?.dataobjectname \wedge$
$\qquad\qquad\qquad do.classification = cr?.classification \wedge$
$\qquad\qquad\qquad do.objecttypeid = cr?.objecttypeid\}$

$allowedaccess\_set' = allowedaccess\_set \cup$
$\qquad \{j : JOBID;\ a : ACCESSMODE;\ aa : AllowedAccess\ |$
$\qquad\qquad\qquad (j, a) \in cr?.accesspermissions \wedge$
$\qquad\qquad\qquad aa.jobid = j \wedge$
$\qquad\qquad\qquad aa.dataobjectid = cr?.dataobjectname \wedge$
$\qquad\qquad\qquad aa.accessmode = a \bullet aa\}$

Figure 11.6. The complete CheckCreate operation.

$\_$ dominates $\_$: *SECURITYLEVEL* $\leftrightarrow$ *SECURITYLEVEL*
$\_$ givesrightto $\_$: *ACCESSMODE* $\leftrightarrow$ *ACCESSMODE*

$\forall s1, s2 : SECURITYLEVEL \bullet$
    $((s1 \text{ dominates } s2) \Leftrightarrow$
        $((s1 = topsecret \wedge s2 \in$
            $\{topsecret, secret, classified, unclassified\}) \vee$
        $(s1 = secret \wedge s2 \in \{secret, classified, unclassified\}) \vee$
        $(s1 = classified \wedge s2 \in \{classified, unclassified\}) \vee$
        $(s1 = unclassified \wedge s2 = unclassified)))$

$\forall am1, am2 : ACCESSMODE \bullet$
    $((am1 \text{ givesrightto } am2) \Leftrightarrow$
        $((am1 = create \wedge am2 \in \{create, update, read\}) \vee$
        $(am1 = update \wedge am2 \in \{update, read\}) \vee$
        $(am1 = read \wedge am2 = read)))$

$\_$*AccessRequest*$\_$
user : *USERID*
job : *JOBID*
dataobjectname : *DATAOBJECTID*
accessmode : *ACCESSMODE*

$\_$*AccessOK*$\_$
user : *USERID*
dataobjectname : *DATAOBJECTID*
accessmode : *ACCESSMODE*

CheckAccessOK
ΞSecurityData

ar? : *AccessRequest*

a_ok! : *AccessOK*

$(ar?.job, ar?.user) \in$ dom *jobperformance_key*
$(jobperformance\_key(ar?.job, ar?.user)).status = LoggedIn$
$(ar?.job, ar?.dataobjectname) \in$ dom *allowedaccess_key*
$(((allowedaccess\_key(ar?.job, ar?.dataobjectname)).accessmode)$
         givesrightto *ar?.accessmode*)
$((user\_key(ar?.user)).clearance$ dominates
         $(dataobject\_key(ar?.dataobjectname)).classification)$
$((job\_key(ar?.job)).clearance$ dominates
         $(dataobject\_key(ar?.dataobjectname)).classification)$

$a\_ok!.user = ar?.user$
$a\_ok!.dataobjectname = ar?.dataobjectname$
$a\_ok!.accessmode = ar?.accessmode$

11.4 Conclusions

The main benefits derived from the use of RRT include the following:

– RRT provides an additional level of confirmation to any existing techniques used for assessment of adequacy, correctness and completeness. Even if the strength and power of the formal notation are of no further use, and merely confirm the existing system's models, this is an important factor in substantiating the progress of the project. This is particularly important in mission-critical and highly visible development projects;
– given the range of views developed in most structured approaches, it is essential that some form of integration is provided. In existing environments this is accomplished through the construction of a large number of cross-references or matrices. If the rules underlying each cross-reference or matrix can be expressed meaningfully, the details can be stated formally and hence assessed for compatibility with other consolidated products or models;
– the information contained in different models — e.g., data, process, event — can be transformed into a common notation to ensure consistency and completeness. The common notation will also provide an infrastructure against which changes and enhancements can be assessed for overall compatibility, not only with other aspects of the specific project, but also with organisational objectives and constraints;

- items in data dictionaries, repositories or encyclopaedias concerned both with project data, organisational data, and meta-data can be reviewed for consistency and completeness;
- the results from application of RRT can be fed into later design stages constraining the models produced in these later stages;
- the results from RRT also provide a foundation for the development of test specifications for eventual application against the implemented system;
- the process of preparing the input for RRT, and its application itself, ensure an added level of understanding and clarity is achieved by some project personnel. Formal notations are not universal panaceas, but their use obliges practitioners to elucidate certain key systems properties at an early stage of development.

RRT has continued to be used in systems development; and in addition the underlying principles of methods integration have received increasing attention in the 1990s.

Appendix A

Security Requirements

The Requirements

In secure computer systems access to information needs to be controlled. Each user should only be able to access a restricted set of data. In addition user/password validation at login, control of the creation of new data objects and the maintenance of the security data are included in the requirements for our secure system.

The system has four major functional areas: login/logout control, checking requests to access data, checking requests to create data objects, and maintenance of security data.

Login/Logout

At Login the user should enter a personal identifier, a job title and a password. For a valid access, the password should be the correct one for the personal identifier, and the job should be one that the user is allowed to perform. If the access is valid and no one is already logged in using that identifier then login is allowed and the fact that the user is logged in, performing that job, is recorded. If the access is invalid then an invalid access attempt should be reported to the system manager and the user should be informed that the login has failed. At Logout the fact that the user is no longer logged in should be recorded.

Check Access Request

When an access request is made, the user identifier, the job title, the access mode and the name of the data object are entered. For a request to be valid the security clearance of the user performing that job should *dominate* the security classification of the data object, the user should be logged in to perform that job, and the job being performed should have the right to access the data object using the requested access mode. If the request is valid then it is passed on to the system, otherwise a report of an invalid access attempt is sent to the system manager and the user is informed that access has been denied.

Check Create Request

A create request comprises a user identifier, a job title, a data type, a data object name and a set of access permissions for the jobs which may access the data object. Each access permission is a tuple, the first member of which is a job and the second an access mode. The jobs which may access the data object and the modes which may be used are thus defined by the access permissions. The request is valid if the user performing the job has create permission for that data type. If the request is valid then the new data name is recorded together with its owner, and all the access permissions associated with that object are also recorded. The create request is then transmitted to the system. If the request is invalid a report is sent to the system manager and the user is informed that create permission has been denied.

Maintain Security Data

The data that must be maintained is that relating to individuals registered on the system, their passwords, the jobs they may perform, the security clearances of individuals and jobs, and the data types for which jobs have create permission. The system manager performs all maintenance functions.

Appendix B

Translating Subtypes

Subtyping allows a classification hierarchy to be set up within an entity model, in which subtypes represent specialisations of their supertypes, and supertypes represent generalisations of (all) their subtypes.

This hierarchical classification structure can easily be expressed in Z. Schema inclusion suffices to describe the basic relationships between supertypes and (their) subtypes, and free type definitions allow a simple description of the associated data-stores.

The subtypes of a supertype inherit both the attributes and the relationships of the supertype. They will also have their own, additional, attributes (and relationships) which relate only to them, and not to the supertype. This inheritance property of subtypes can increase the descriptive richness of the model, but it can also lead to problems; eg when *unintended* inheritance occurs.

A model which uses subtyping can be considerably more complex than one which does not, and therefore subtyping should be used cautiously and only where strictly necessary.

Basic Subtypes

Subtyping is a way of partitioning an entity into smaller entities called subtypes. These subtypes are:

- mutually exclusive;
- collectively exhaustive.

Thus, for a given supertype occurrence, precisely one of the subtypes is used to describe/distinguish it; and, together, the subtypes make up the whole of the supertype.

More Complex Subtyping

Multiple partitions are necessary when there are several different ways of partitioning an entity. In this case, subtypes within the same partition are mutually exclusive but all the partitions are necessary, i.e., they are mutually obligatory.

A subtype itself may be partitioned into smaller subtypes. This *nesting* of subtypes further extends the model's expressive power, but can also increase complexity and must be used with great care if problems, e.g., unintended inheritance are to be avoided. The translation into Z of a subtype hierarchy is a straightforward process.

Details are not included here for reasons of space but may be found in (Semmens, 1996).

The Translation Process

The translation of a subtype structure into Z is in two parts:

- translating the individual entity supertypes and subtypes into Z schemas, using schema inclusion to show inheritance and nesting;
- writing the Z datastore schema(s) using free type definitions to help describe relationships between the subtypes and supertypes.

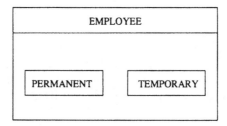

Figure 11.7. Simple subtyping

Example of Basic Subtyping

The following example illustrates the translation into Z of an elementary subtyping structure.

EMPLOYEE has two subtypes, PERMANENT and TEMPORARY, which partition the supertype. The subtypes inherit all the attributes of the supertype.

The inheritance property of subtypes is expressed in Z using schema inclusion.

$[EMPLOYEEID, NAME, SEX, GRADE, BENEFITS, RATE]$

```
┌─ Employee ──────────────────────────────
│ EmpId : EMPLOYEEID
│ Name : NAME
│ Sex : SEX
│
└─────────────────────────────────────────
```

```
┌─ Permanent ─────────────────────────────
│ Employee
│ Grade : GRADE
│ Benefits : BENEFITS
│
└─────────────────────────────────────────
```

```
┌─ Temporary ─────────────────────────────
│ Employee
│ Rate : RATE
│
└─────────────────────────────────────────
```

Free type definitions are used in Z to describe recursive structures such as lists and trees. The following expression introduces a new type, EMPLOYEE, and also lists the two unique functions (Perm and Temp) by which members of that type can be accessed. These two functions (injections) are identified with the leaf nodes (permanent and temporary) of the entity subtype diagram expressed as a tree.

$EMPLOYEE ::= Perm\langle\langle Permanent \rangle\rangle \mid Temp\langle\langle Temporary \rangle\rangle$

The following datastore schema is used to model the function of a primary key; ie, a means to accessing a data record.

The first three variables declared in the signature part of the schema represent successively: the subset of all employees under consideration; the subset of permanent employees; and the subset of temporary employees. The "employee_pkey" function is then declared, which maps an employee's ID to the associated employee data record.

The predicate part of the schema restricts the set of permanent employees under consideration (permanent_set) to being a subset of those employees which can be identified with an ID number. The set of temporary employees (temporary_set) is similarly restricted. The predicate part also describes the partitioning of the set of all employees into two subsets: temporary and permanent. This partitioning means that the two subsets are disjoint and, together, comprise the whole of employee_set.

The final paragraph of the predicate part relates the fact that if an employee is a member of employee_set then he can be uniquely identified by his ID number.

Employee_ds

$employee\_set : \mathbb{P}\,EMPLOYEE$
$permanent\_set : \mathbb{P}\,EMPLOYEE$
$temporary\_set : \mathbb{P}\,EMPLOYEE$

$employee\_pkey : EMPLOYEEID \rightarrowtail EMPLOYEE$

$permanent\_set \subseteq \mathrm{ran}\,Perm$
$temporary\_set \subseteq \mathrm{ran}\,Temp$
$\langle permanent\_set, temporary\_set \rangle$ partition $employee\_set$
$employee\_pkey = \{e : employee\_set;\ eid : EMPLOYEEID\ |$
$\qquad (e \in permanent\_set \wedge eid = (Perm^{\sim}e).EmpId) \vee$
$\qquad (e \in temporary\_set \wedge eid = (Temp^{\sim}e).EmpId) \bullet$
$\qquad\qquad eid \mapsto e\}$

CHAPTER 12

Analysing Z Specifications with Z/EVES

Dan Craigen, Irwin Meisels and Mark Saaltink

12.1 Introduction

This chapter illustrates the use of the Z notation in a formal specification (of the Sliding Window protocol), and shows how Z/EVES (Saaltink, 1997b; Saaltink and Meisels, 1995) can be used to analyse and validate the specification.

12.2 Summary of Z

Z is a specification notation originally developed at Oxford University in the early 1980s. Z is based on conventional discrete mathematics and first-order logic, and uses conventional mathematical notations as much as possible.

Z specifications describe systems using collections of variables to represent various attributes of the system, and mathematical predicates to describe sets of states. The declaration of the variables and any predicates expressing constraints on the state can be combined into a named structure called a *schema*. Schemas can be written horizontally, *e.g.*, $S \cong [x, y : \mathbb{Z} \mid x < y]$, or in boxes, *e.g.*,

$$
\begin{array}{|l}
\hline
\!\!\_S \underline{} \\
\; x, y : \mathbb{Z} \\
\hline
\; x < y \\
\hline
\end{array}
$$

The *declaration part* of the schema, appearing before the vertical bar or above the horizontal line, declares the variables that represent the state of a system. The *predicate part* of the schema gives any constraints on the state variables.

Operations on a system are described by a predicate on two states—the state before the operation and the state after the operation. By convention, the final state is described by primed variable names. So, the specification of an operation on the above schema S where x must increase would include the predicate $x' > x$.

A schema name can be "decorated" (*e.g.*, S'), which stands for the schema with all the component names decorated (so S' is the same as $[x', y' : \mathbb{Z} \mid x' < y']$). By convention, ΔS is the schema $[S; S']$, giving a before and after state and representing an arbitrary change of state. ΞS constrains this schema by adding a predicate expressing that no variables have changed; it specifies the null operation that changes nothing. Using these conventions, we can describe the above operation of increasing x by the schema $[\Delta S \mid x' > x]$.

Schemas can be used to structure specifications, by allowing a complex system to be described as a composition of smaller systems. Schemas can be built from other schemas in several ways. First, a schema name can be used as a declaration; in this case, it is equivalent to the declarations and predicates in its definition. Second, a schema can be used as a predicate; in this case it is (usually) equivalent to the predicate in its definition. Finally, schemas can be combined using Boolean connectives (the so-called *schema calculus*), which we will not have occasion to use in this chapter.

The Z notation defines a number of familiar operations, and a standard "Mathematical Toolkit" further defines most of the basic notions of discrete mathematics. Only a small part of this rich repertoire is used in this chapter. Besides some standard notions of set theory, we use $\mathbb{Z}$ for the integers; $\mathbb{N}$ for the natural numbers (0 and above); $\mathbb{F}X$ for the set of finite subsets of a set X, $\operatorname{dom} R$ for the domain of relation or function R; $X \nrightarrow Y$ for the set of partial functions from X to Y; and $f \oplus \{x \mapsto y\}$ for functional overriding (which gives a new function f' that agrees with f for all arguments except x, and with $f'(x) = y$).

The Z notation supports the industrial application of formal methods in several ways. First, Z strongly supports the integration of formal specifications into project documentation. Z specifications do not need to be separate specification source files with a few comments (if the reader is lucky); instead, Z is designed to have a specification's paragraphs interspersed through a document. This allows extensive commentary on the specification, the use of traditional document structures (e.g., tables of contents, chapters, sections, figures, and indices), and allows the Z paragraphs to be included in the normal project documentation.

Second, Z provides powerful features (in the schema calculus) for composing specifications. There are ways of combining descriptions of subsystems into descriptions of whole systems, and also ways of composing specifications of operations from the specifications of separate cases. This allows, for example, the normal case to be specified separately from the various error cases, and allows specifications of error cases to be reused in the specifications of several different operations.

Finally, the draft Z Standard (Nicholls, 1995) proposes a "sections" mechanism, that addresses some of the needs of very large specifications. This proposal allows a specification to be divided into a collection of sections, each of which specifies the sections it uses. Like module constructs in programming languages, this facility helps divide a specification into parts whose interdependence is made explicit, and so reduces the amount of work needed in reading or revising a specification[1].

There have been numerous applications of Z. Some of these applications are reported in (Craigen *et al.*, 1992) and (Hinchey and Bowen, 1995). There are also numerous tools for, and books on, Z. The Oxford University Z Web page, edited by Jonathan Bowen, is an excellent source of pointers to tools, books, conferences and expertise. At present, Z is undergoing an international standardisation process. A draft document (Nicholls, 1995) is available.

12.3 Tool Support for Z

Early developers of Z were indifferent, or even hostile, to the idea of tools for Z specifications. There were several reasons for this. First, the notation was developed originally as a style for using conventional mathematics in a formal specification, and not as a language in its own right. Thus, the rules were informal guidelines that could not be enforced or checked by a tool. Second, as described in (Hayes, 1995), the notational conventions were developed over a period of years, with frequent extensions and modifications in response to experiences with its application to various systems. During this stage, the language was too fluid to be supported by sophisticated tools. Third, the semantics of some aspects of the notation have been the subject of some study and debate; without clear decisions on these areas, it is difficult to write trustworthy tools.

For serious industrial use of Z, however, the situation is different. Tools such as type checkers can help new users understand the language rules. Cross-reference tools, schema expanders, and type annotaters can help readers of a specification (especially of a large specification). Finally, experience with Z and with other formal notations has shown how easy it is to write incomplete or inconsistent specifications. Tools can help writers and reviewers test specifications to ensure that cases have not been ignored or that the specification is satisfiable.

In an industrial setting, a formal methods tool needs to be integrated with an existing environment for the development, review, and maintenance of documentation or software; otherwise, it can be difficult to get developers to adopt the tool or to maintain consistency between the formal specification and other documents. For example, a widely used representation for Z specifications is based on the LATEX markup language. Few companies, however, use LATEX for their documentation, and find the integration of tools based on it with Word, Framemaker, or WordPerfect to be awkward or impossible.

---

[1] At present, however, the sections proposal offers only minimal features, and does not, for example, allow for the selective "export" of names defined in a section. So, one section sees all or none of another.

12.4 Z/EVES

Z/EVES (Saaltink, 1997b; Saaltink and Meisels, 1995) is a tool for analysing Z specifications. We will not describe it in full detail here, but instead give a short summary of its capabilities.

Z/EVES supports the analysis of Z specifications in several ways:

- syntax and type checking;
- schema expansion;
- precondition calculation;
- domain checking (i.e., are functions applied only on their domains?);
- refinement proofs, and
- general theorem proving.

Z/EVES integrates a leading specification notation with a leading automated deduction capability. Z/EVES supports almost the entire Z notation; only the unique existence quantifier for schema expressions is not currently supported. The Z/EVES prover provides powerful automated support (e.g., conditional rewriting, heuristics, decision procedures) with user commands for directing the prover (e.g., instantiate a specific variable, introduce a lemma, use a function definition). We have automated much of the Z Mathematical Toolkit and include this extended version with the Z/EVES release.

The range of analysis supports an incremental introduction of Z/EVES capabilities. For example, very little knowledge of the theorem prover is required for syntax and type checking, and schema expansion. Even with domain checking, many of the proof obligations are easily proven; and for those that are not, often the generation of the proof obligation is a substantial aid in determining whether a meaningful specification has been written.

Z/EVES accepts its input in the markup format used by the LaTeX system and by Spivey's "fuzz" typechecker. Work is in progress towards a Microsoft Word interface that will allow users to include Z paragraphs in their Word documents, and interact with Z/EVES using the typeset representation.

In the Appendix, we provide a brief description of the system commands used in this chapter.

12.4.1 Analysing a Specification

Before showing the main example, we will illustrate the use of Z/EVES in analysing a specification by applying it to the specification of a simple user logging system from (Potter *et al.*, 1995), Exercise 6.2, where it is described as follows:

> In order to use the facilities of a shared computer system each user must be registered and must have a password which is to be supplied when requested by the system. The system LogSys [...] must maintain information about registered users and their passwords, and must also keep track of which users are currently active on the system.

Z/EVES can be used incrementally, adding a paragraph at a time, and correcting any errors as they arise. This is how we will show it being used. Input to Z/EVES can be a Z Paragraph, shown here in typeset form, or a command, shown here in typewriter font preceded by the prompt =>.

We begin by declaring the given types, one for users and one for passwords. At this level of detail, we are not concerned with any internal structure of these types (e.g., whether passwords are strings or numbers):

[*User, Word*]

The logging system records passwords for a set of *registered* users, allows people to try to log on, and records the set of *active* users (who are successfully logged on and are using the system):

$$
\begin{array}{l}
\rule{3cm}{0.4pt}\ LogSys \rule{8cm}{0.4pt} \\
password : User \nrightarrow Word \\
reg, active : \mathbb{F}\ User \\
\rule{10cm}{0.4pt} \\
active \subseteq reg = \mathrm{dom}\ password \\
\end{array}
$$

Initially, there are no active or registered users:

$$
\begin{array}{l}
\rule{3cm}{0.4pt}\ InitLogSys \rule{7cm}{0.4pt} \\
LogSys \\
\rule{10cm}{0.4pt} \\
password = \emptyset \\
active = reg = \emptyset \\
\end{array}
$$

Z/EVES accepts these three paragraphs without comment; there are no type errors and no possible domain errors.

At this stage, we can use Z/EVES to ensure that the initialisation schema is satisfiable, by proving $\exists LogSys \bullet InitLogSys$:

Theorem InitLogSysIsSatisfiable:
$\exists LogSys \bullet InitLogSys$

When this "theorem" paragraph is entered, Z/EVES establishes it as a goal in need of proof. The user can enter proof commands to work on this goal (or can defer the proof to a later time). We will work on it immediately with the following prover command:

```
=> prove by reduce;
```

This command directs Z/EVES to apply its full power to the goal, and to expand defined schemas while doing so. The result is the predicate *true*, so the stated theorem is valid.

New users can be registered:

```
┌─ Register ─────────────────────────────────────────────
│ ΔLogSys
│ u? : User; p? : Word
├────────────────────────────────────────────────────────
│ password' = password ∪ {u? ↦ p?}
│ active' = active
└────────────────────────────────────────────────────────
```

Schema *Register* specifies the operation of registering a user; this schema declares *ΔLogSys*, which declares the initial and final states of the operation, and two inputs: *u?* is the new user, and *p?* the initial password for this user. Readers unfamiliar with the Z conventions can use Z/EVES to expand this schema as follows:

```
=> try Register;
```

This first command establishes the predicate *Register* as a proof goal. Subsequent proof steps will transform it to equivalent predicates. In particular, the invoke command will use the definitions of schemas *Register*, *ΔLogSys*, and *LogSys* to fully expand the goal:

```
=> invoke;
```

gives

$password \in User \nrightarrow Word$
$\wedge\ reg \in \mathbb{F}\,User$
$\wedge\ active \in \mathbb{F}\,User$
$\wedge\ active \subseteq reg$
$\wedge\ reg = \text{dom}\,password$
$\wedge\ password' \in User \nrightarrow Word$
$\wedge\ reg' \in \mathbb{F}\,User$
$\wedge\ active' \in \mathbb{F}\,User$
$\wedge\ active' \subseteq reg'$
$\wedge\ reg' = \text{dom}\,password'$
$\wedge\ u? \in User$
$\wedge\ p? \in Word$
$\wedge\ password' = password \cup \{u? \mapsto p?\}$
$\wedge\ active' = active$

This can be further simplified by the prove command to remove some.of the redundant or trivial conjuncts:

$password \in User \nrightarrow Word$
$\wedge\; reg = \mathrm{dom}\, password$
$\wedge\; active \in \mathbb{F}\, User$
$\wedge\; u? \in User$
$\wedge\; p? \in Word$
$\wedge\; password' = password \cup \{(u?, p?)\}$
$\wedge\; reg' = \{u?\} \cup \mathrm{dom}\, password$
$\wedge\; active \in \mathbb{P}\,\mathrm{dom}\, password$
$\wedge\; active' = active$
$\wedge\; \mathrm{dom}\, password \in \mathbb{F}\, User$
$\wedge\; (u? \in \mathrm{dom}\, password \Rightarrow password\, u? = p?)$

The Z style of specifying operations as a relation between initial and final states leaves the *precondition* of the operation implicit. Z defines the precondition of an operation *Op* over a state *S*, with outputs $o1 : T1$ and so on, by the predicate $\exists S', o1 : T1, \ldots \bullet Op$; this predicate can be referred to as pre *Op*. This predicate determines those initial states and inputs for which the operation's predicate can be satisfied. As we may assume the initial state satisfies the state schema, and that inputs lie in their declared sets, in Z/EVES we analyse the precondition by working on the goal $\forall S; i1 : T1 \bullet$ pre *Op*. This shows us any additional assumptions needed to ensure that the operation can succeed.

Before stating a theorem about the precondition of the *Register* operation, we can simply explore it by establishing a goal:

```
=> try ∀LogSys; u? : User; p? : Word • pre Register;
```

Using the `prove by reduce` command gives

$u? \in User$
$\wedge\; p? \in Word$
$\wedge\; password \in User \nrightarrow Word$
$\wedge\; reg = \mathrm{dom}\, password$
$\wedge\; active \in \mathbb{F}\, User$
$\wedge\; active \in \mathbb{P}\,\mathrm{dom}\, password$
$\wedge\; u? \in \mathrm{dom}\, password$
$\wedge\; \mathrm{dom}\, password \in \mathbb{F}\, User$
$\Rightarrow password\, u? = p?$

Evidently, there is a constraint here: if the user is already registered, then the given password must be the user's current password. (Otherwise, $password' = password \cup \{u? \mapsto p?\}$ would not be a function, in violation of the constraints of *LogSys*.) In fact, we only intend to use this operation when the user is not already registered, and we can easily show:

Theorem PreRegister:
$\forall LogSys; u? : User; p? : Word \mid u? \notin reg \bullet$ pre *Register*

using the command:

```
=> prove by reduce;
```

which results in the formula *true*.

Simple conjectures can be used to validate a specification. For example, we can show that the Register operation adds a user:

Theorem RegisterAddsToReg:
$Register \Rightarrow reg' = reg \cup \{u?\}$

```
=> prove by reduce;
```

Again, this results in the formula *true*; the conjecture is a theorem.
Users who are not already logged in can try to log in, giving a password:

```
┌─ LogIn ─────────────────────────────────────
│ ΔLogSys
│ u? : User
│ p? : Word
├─────────────────────────────────────────────
│ u? ∉ active
│ p? = password(u?)
│ password' = password
│ active' = active ∪ {u?}
└─────────────────────────────────────────────
```

When this paragraph is added, Z/EVES generates a domain check and establishes it as a goal:

Beginning proof of *LogIn$domainCheck*...

$\Delta LogSys$
$\wedge\ u? \in User$
$\wedge\ p? \in Word$
$\wedge\ u? \notin active$
$\Rightarrow u? \in \mathrm{dom}\,password$

When we try to prove this:

```
=> prove by reduce;
```

we get the formula:

$$password \in User \nrightarrow Word$$
$$\wedge \ reg \in \mathbb{F}\,User$$
$$\wedge \ active \in \mathbb{F}\,User$$
$$\wedge \ active \in \mathbb{P}\,reg$$
$$\wedge \ reg = \mathrm{dom}\,password$$
$$\wedge \ password' \in User \nrightarrow Word$$
$$\wedge \ reg' \in \mathbb{F}\,User$$
$$\wedge \ active' \in \mathbb{F}\,User$$
$$\wedge \ active' \in \mathbb{P}\,reg'$$
$$\wedge \ reg' = \mathrm{dom}\,password'$$
$$\wedge \ u? \in User$$
$$\wedge \ p? \in Word$$
$$\wedge \ \neg \ u? \in active$$
$$\Rightarrow u? \in \mathrm{dom}\,password$$

which is obviously not a theorem. Z/EVES has helped us uncover a domain error in the specification: the expression $password(u?)$ might be undefined since $password$ is a partial function and $u?$ might not be in its domain.

The treatment of off-domain function applications in Z is a contentious issue; different authors use different conventions. As explained in detail in (Saaltink, 1997a), the conditions generated by Z/EVES are enough to guarantee that a specification has a meaning that is independent of the conventions used for "non-denoting" terms. We therefore prefer to write specifications with provable domain checks. So, we will undo the schema declaration:

```
=> undo;
```

and enter a revision that explicitly requires the user to be registered:

LogIn

$\Delta LogSys$
$u? : User$
$p? : Word$

$u? \in reg \setminus active$
$p? = password(u?)$
$password' = password$
$active' = active \cup \{u?\}$

This time, the domain check is easily proved; the `prove by reduce` command results in the predicate *true*.

We will not continue this small example, as we have already shown most of the analyses possible with Z/EVES. (Our main omission here has been refinement proofs, which are difficult to show in a short presentation.)

12.5 Sliding Window Protocol

In this section, we present a more substantive example through which we elaborate upon the capabilities of Z/EVES. In particular, we present an abstraction of the Sliding Window Protocol (SWP). The SWP was brought to our attention by Michael Ferguson (INRS-Telecommunications, Université du Quebec) who then produced an EVES proof of SWP behaviour (Craigen *et al.*, 1991). Dan Craigen reworked Ferguson's solution and the current authors used the later version as a basis for the work reported here.

In our model of the SWP, the SWP consists of four processes: *Sender*, *Channel1*, *Receiver* and *Channel2*. *Channel1* is the link for sending messages from *Sender* to *Receiver*. *Channel2* is the link for sending acknowledgements from *Receiver* to *Sender*. In our model, we treat the two communication channels as distinct entities. However, a physical realisation might consist of a single multiplexed channel.

In the SWP, a message is assigned both a message identifier (*mid*) and a sent sequence number (*ssn*). The *ssn* records that the *Sender* process is transmitting for the *ssn*'th time. The *Receiver* will acknowledge to the *Sender* the set of *mid*s and the highest *ssn* (*maxssn*) it has received. As *ssn* is monotonically increasing with every transmission, any unacknowledged *mid* with corresponding *ssn* less than *maxssn* is deemed to have been lost. Consequently, the *Sender* will need to retransmit *mid* with a new *ssn*. While, in our model, we do not concern ourselves with the content of the messages, we will concern ourselves with the possible loss of data on *Channel1*.

Our approach to specifying the SWP varies only slightly from conventional Z practice for specifying state machines. Our variation is that we ignore extending the partial operations to total operations, where the extension only specifies that the system state is left unchanged.

We start our specification by defining the states of each of the processes and then combine the process states into an overall SWP system state. Some simple properties of the states are proven. We then define the state changing operations that form the functionality of the SWP and prove various properties.

12.5.1 SWP System State

For each of the process states, we follow the same pattern of definition:

– introduce a schema that defines the components of the process;
– introduce a schema that describes the initial state of the process;
– discharge a conjecture that demonstrates that the initial state is, in fact, a valid process state.

To conserve space, we will provide all of the above information for the *Sender* process, but will omit the initial state conjecture from the subsequent process state descriptions.

Sender State. The *SenderState* consists of five components: the set of message identifiers known to the *Sender* process as having been received by the *Receiver* process; the maximum sent sequence number known to the *Sender* process as having been received by the *Receiver* process; the next message identifier that can be assigned; the next sent sequence number that can be assigned; and a function relating each assigned message identifier to the latest sent sequence number associated with the identifier.

We define the Sliding Window as $(\operatorname{dom} s\_sent) \setminus s\_rcvd$; this is the set of message identifiers that the *Sender* process has sent but for which acknowledgement has not been received from the *Receiver* process. Our abstraction of the Sliding Window differs from convention in two ways: (i) there is no explicit inclusion of a "lower" and "upper" window edge, and (ii) there is no bound on the size of the window.

$$
\begin{array}{|l}
\hline
\_\_SenderState _____ \\
\; s\_rcvd : \mathbb{P}\,\mathrm{N} \\
\; s\_maxssn : \mathrm{N} \\
\; s\_mid\_n : \mathrm{N} \\
\; s\_ssn\_n : \mathrm{N} \\
\; s\_sent : \mathrm{N} \nrightarrow \mathrm{N} \\
\hline
\end{array}
$$

$$
\begin{array}{|l}
\hline
\_\_InitialSenderState _____ \\
\; SenderState \\
\hline
\; s\_rcvd = \{\} \\
\; s\_maxssn = 0 \\
\; s\_mid\_n = 0 \\
\; s\_ssn\_n = 1 \\
\; s\_sent = \{\} \\
\hline
\end{array}
$$

Theorem ValidInitialSenderState:
$\exists\, SenderState \bullet InitialSenderState$

All of the conjectures regarding valid initial states are proven by a `prove by reduce` command.

Channel1 State. The *Channel1State* consists of two components: the message identifier and the related sent sequence number of the message being transmitted. However, to model the absence of data on the channel, we permit both components to be assigned to -1. As -1 is neither a valid message identifier nor a sent sequence number, no ambiguity arises.

$$
\begin{array}{|l}
\hline
\_\_Channel1State _____ \\
\; ch1\_mid : \mathbb{Z} \\
\; ch1\_ssn : \mathbb{Z} \\
\hline
\end{array}
$$

```
┌─ InitialChannel1State ──────────────────────────────
│ Channel1State
│ ┌─────────────────────────────
│ │ ch1_mid = -1
│ │ ch1_ssn = -1
└─┴───────────────────────────────────────────────────
```

Receiver State. The *ReceiverState* consists of two components: the set of received message identifiers and the maximum sent sequence number received.

```
┌─ ReceiverState ─────────────────────────────────────
│ r_rcvd : $\mathbb{P}\,\mathrm{N}$
│ r_maxssn : N
└─────────────────────────────────────────────────────
```

```
┌─ InitialReceiverState ──────────────────────────────
│ ReceiverState
│ ┌─────────────────────────────
│ │ r_rcvd = {}
│ │ r_maxssn = 0
└─┴───────────────────────────────────────────────────
```

Channel2 State. The *Channel2State* consists of two components that reflect the data in the *ReceiverState*. In our model, acknowledgement is modelled by transmitting the *ReceiverState* back to the *Sender* process.

```
┌─ Channel2State ─────────────────────────────────────
│ ch2_rcvd : $\mathbb{P}\,\mathrm{N}$
│ ch2_maxssn : $\mathbb{Z}$
└─────────────────────────────────────────────────────
```

```
┌─ InitialChannel2State ──────────────────────────────
│ Channel2State
│ ┌─────────────────────────────
│ │ ch2_rcvd = {}
│ │ ch2_maxssn = -1
└─┴───────────────────────────────────────────────────
```

System State. We now define the overall state of the SWP through the *SystemState* schema. The initial SWP state is defined by the initial states of each of the four processes.

```
┌─ SystemState ───────────────────────────────────────
│ SenderState
│ Channel1State
│ ReceiverState
│ Channel2State
└─────────────────────────────────────────────────────
```

```
┌─ InitialSystemState ─────────────────────────────────
│ SystemState
├──────────────────────────────────────────────────────
│ InitialSenderState
│ InitialChannel1State
│ InitialReceiverState
│ InitialChannel2State
└──────────────────────────────────────────────────────
```

12.5.2 SWP Operations

Having defined the SWP state, we are in a position to start defining the operations that may modify the state. For our version of the Sliding Window Protocol, there are six operations:

— *ResendMessage*: the *Sender* process resends a previous message.
— *NewMessage*: the *Sender* process transmits a new message.
— *LoseChannel1*: the *Channel1* process loses its data.
— *ReceiveMessage*: the *Receiver* process receives a message.
— *SendAcknowledgement*: the *Receiver* process sends an acknowledgement.
— *ReceiveAcknowledgement*: the *Sender* process receives an acknowledgement.

For pedagogical purposes, we start our discussion with the simple *LoseChannel1* operation and then move through the remaining operations in order.

LoseChannel1. Our model of the SWP supports the loss of messages over the communication channel between the *Sender* and *Receiver* processes. As described above, we model the absence (loss) of data by corrupting the components with the magic number -1.

Our approach to defining the effect of an operation on the system state will be to define a sub-operation, for each of the four process states, that describes the effect on the specific process state. We will then combine the effects to obtain the overall system level view.

For the operation of losing data on *Channel1*, there is no effect on the *Sender*, *Receiver* and *Channel2* states. Consequently, we need only define one sub-operation (*LoseChannel1OnChannel1State*), which modifies the *Channel1* state. The following schema describes the appropriate effect.

```
┌─ LoseChannel1OnChannel1State ────────────────────────
│ ΔChannel1State
├──────────────────────────────────────────────────────
│ ch1_mid' = −1
│
│ ch1_ssn' = −1
└──────────────────────────────────────────────────────
```

Having defined the effect on the state of *Channel1*, we combine it with conjuncts specifying the invariance of the other process states to obtain a specification of the *LoseChannel*1 operation. A process state preceded by Ξ (*e.g.*, Ξ*SenderState*), specifies the invariance of the process state.

```
┌─ LoseChannel1 ──────────────────────────────────
│ ΔSystemState
├──────────────────────────────────
│ Ξ SenderState
│
│ LoseChannel1OnChannel1State
│
│ Ξ ReceiverState
│
│ Ξ Channel2State
└──────────────────────────────────
```

All our operation specifications will follow the above template of defining sub-operations and then appropriately combining the sub-operations.

ResendMessage. Our specification of the *ResendMessage* operation starts by describing the predicate that is used to determine if we need to resend a message. *ResendIdentifiers* formalises the idea that a transmitted message identifier has been lost if it is not known to be received and its sent sequence number is less than the current maximum sent sequence number.

```
┌─ ResendIdentifiers ──────────────────────────────
│ SenderState
│ mid? : N
├──────────────────────────────────
│ mid? ∈ dom s_sent ∧
│ s_sent mid? < s_maxssn ∧
│ ¬ mid? ∈ s_rcvd
└──────────────────────────────────
```

In our entire specification, this is the only place where a domain proof obligation is generated and not proven immediately by Z/EVES. The proof obligation is trivial, however, and is easily proven.

> **Theorem** WF_ResendIdentifiers:
> *SenderState* $\wedge$ *mid?* $\in$ N $\wedge$ *mid?* $\in$ dom *s_sent*
> $\Rightarrow$ *mid?* $\in$ dom *s_sent*

```
=> trivial simplify;
```

To define the *ResendMessage* operation, we will initially describe how the operation effects the two relevant processes: *Sender* and *Channel*1.

To resend a message identifier, we relate the current send sequence number with the message identifier. The current send sequence number is incremented.

```
┌─ ResendMessageOnSenderState ──────────────────
│ ΔSenderState
│ mid? : N
├──────────────────────────────────────────────
│ s_rcvd' = s_rcvd
│
│ s_maxssn' = s_maxssn
│
│ s_mid_n' = s_mid_n
│
│ s_ssn_n' = s_ssn_n + 1
│
│ s_sent' = s_sent ⊕ {mid? ↦ s_ssn_n}
└──────────────────────────────────────────────
```

The *Channel*1 process state obtains the message identifier and the corresponding send sequence number.

```
┌─ ResendMessageOnChannel1State ────────────────
│ ΔChannel1State
│ SenderState
│ mid? : N
├──────────────────────────────────────────────
│ ch1_mid' = mid?
│
│ ch1_ssn' = s_ssn_n
└──────────────────────────────────────────────
```

Having described the component effects of resending a message, we can now combine the effects on the two process states to a system-wide operation as follows:

```
┌─ ResendMessage ───────────────────────────────
│ ΔSystemState
├──────────────────────────────────────────────
│ (∃ mid? : N • ResendIdentifiers ∧
│                 ResendMessageOnSenderState ∧
│                 ResendMessageOnChannel1State)
│
│ ΞReceiverState
│
│ ΞChannel2State
└──────────────────────────────────────────────
```

The only real subtlety with *ResendMessage* is in the use of the existential quantifier to limit the scope of the *mid?* component of the three Resend schemas. *mid?* is bound by the quantifier and is not a component of *ResendMessage*.

NewMessage. Sending a new message is almost the same as above except that the message identifier component is also incremented. Note that *NewMessage* will have an effect only if there are no messages needing retransmission.

NewMessageOnSenderState
_____

$\Delta SenderState$

$s\_rcvd' = s\_rcvd$

$s\_maxssn' = s\_maxssn$

$s\_mid\_n' = s\_mid\_n + 1$

$s\_ssn\_n' = s\_ssn\_n + 1$

$s\_sent' = s\_sent \oplus \{s\_mid\_n \mapsto s\_ssn\_n\}$

NewMessageOnChannel1State
_____

$\Delta Channel1State$

$SenderState$

$ch1\_mid' = s\_mid\_n$

$ch1\_ssn' = s\_ssn\_n$

NewMessage
_____

$\Delta SystemState$

$\neg\, (\exists mid? : \mathbb{N} \bullet ResendIdentifiers)$

$NewMessageOnSenderState$

$NewMessageOnChannel1State$

$\Xi ReceiverState$

$\Xi Channel2State$

ReceiveMessage. If there is data in *Channel1State*, the *Receiver* process reads the message identifier, adds it to the set of received message identifiers, and updates the maximum sent sequence number with the new sent sequence number.

ReceiverReceivesData
_____

$Channel1State$

$\Delta ReceiverState$

$r\_rcvd' = r\_rcvd \cup \{ch1\_mid\}$

$r\_maxssn' = ch1\_ssn$

ReceiveMessage
ΔSystemState
___
$ch1\_mid \neq -1$

$ch1\_ssn \neq -1$

ΞSenderState

LoseChannel1OnChannel1State

ReceiverReceivesData

ΞChannel2State

SendAcknowledgement. The *SendAcknowledgement* operation specifies that an acknowledgement is on its way from the *Receiver* process. In this model, no loss of information is assumed. The only process state to change is that of *Channel2*.

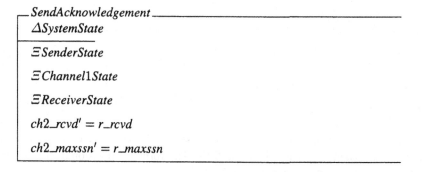

SendAcknowledgement
ΔSystemState
___
ΞSenderState

ΞChannel1State

ΞReceiverState

$ch2\_rcvd' = r\_rcvd$

$ch2\_maxssn' = r\_maxssn$

ReceiveAcknowledgement. Finally, we model the transmission of an acknowledgement from *Channel2* to the *Sender*. We define the operation for when data is present in the channel. Note that, as part of the operation, the channel data is, in effect, nulled as the *Sender* process successfully receives the data.

─── *ReceiveAcknowledgement* ───────────────────────────
$\Delta SystemState$
───

$ch2\_rcvd \neq \{\}$

$ch2\_maxssn \neq -1$

$s\_rcvd' = ch2\_rcvd$

$s\_maxssn' = ch2\_maxssn$

$s\_mid\_n' = s\_mid\_n$

$s\_ssn\_n' = s\_ssn\_n$

$s\_sent' = s\_sent$

$\Xi Channel1State$

$\Xi ReceiverState$

$ch2\_rcvd' = \{\}$

$ch2\_maxssn' = -1$

12.5.3 SWP State Invariant

Having defined the Sliding Window Protocol state and operations, we now focus on proving invariant properties about the SWP. The formal expression of the system invariant is defined by the *Invariant* schema.

Of all the *Invariant* conjuncts, probably the most interesting are the first two, $r\_rcvd \subseteq \text{dom } s\_sent$ and $s\_rcvd \subseteq r\_rcvd$, which state that the *Receiver* has received only messages that the *Sender* has sent and that the *Sender* has received acknowledgement for messages that *Receiver* has received. Most other aspects of the *Invariant* are in support of the above two conjuncts or are demonstrating monotonicity properties.

```
┌─ Invariant ─────────────────────────────────────
│ SystemState
├─────────────────────────────────────────────────
│ r_rcvd ⊆ dom s_sent
│
│ s_rcvd ⊆ r_rcvd
│
│ ch2_rcvd ⊆ r_rcvd
│
│ ch1_ssn ≤ s_ssn_n
│
│ ch2_maxssn ≤ r_maxssn
│
│ ch2_maxssn ≤ s_ssn_n
│
│ s_maxssn ≤ r_maxssn
│
│ r_maxssn ≤ s_ssn_n
│
│ ch2_rcvd ≠ ∅ ⇒ s_rcvd ⊆ ch2_rcvd
│
│ ch1_mid ∈ {−1} ∪ dom s_sent
│
│ ch1_ssn ≠ −1 ⇒ ch1_ssn ≥ r_maxssn
│
│ ch2_maxssn ≠ −1 ⇒ ch2_maxssn ≥ s_maxssn
└─────────────────────────────────────────────────
```

12.5.4 Proving the SWP Invariant

Our proof of the SWP *Invariant* follows normal practice: (i) prove that *Invariant* holds for the initial state and (ii) that for each of the six operations, if *Invariant* holds for a state, it holds for the state resulting from application of the operation. Here, we show (i) and two examples of (ii).

Summaries of the Z/EVES commands used to prove the theorems on invariance are presented in the Appendix. To conserve space, in addition to showing only three of the seven theorems here, we do not include the resulting Z/EVES output in this chapter.

Theorem InvariantOnInitialState:
InitialSystemState ⇒ Invariant

```
=> prove by reduce;
```

Theorem NewMessagePreservesInvariant:
NewMessage ∧ Invariant ⇒ Invariant'

```
=> prove;
```

Theorem SendAcknowledgementPreservesInvariant:
SendAcknowledgement $\wedge$ *Invariant* $\Rightarrow$ *Invariant'*

```
=> invoke;
=> prove;
=> equality substitute ch2_rcvd';
=> equality substitute r_rcvd';
=> rewrite;
```

12.6 Exploring the Specification

Having developed the formalism, we thought it would be interesting to explore the specification both by (i) modifying some aspects of it, and (ii) calculating the preconditions of a few of the operations.

The principal purpose of modifying the specifications was to see what sort of information would arise from using Z/EVES on what were expected to be unprovable conjectures. So, for example, our first effort was to redefine the *NewMessage* operations by forgetting to increment s_mid_n.

$$
\begin{array}{l}
\hline
\_\textit{BadNewMessageOnSenderState}_____ \\
\Delta \textit{SenderState} \\
\hline
s\_rcvd' = s\_rcvd \\
s\_maxssn' = s\_maxssn \\
s\_mid\_n' = s\_mid\_n \\
s\_ssn\_n' = s\_ssn\_n + 1 \\
s\_sent' = s\_sent \oplus \{s\_mid\_n \mapsto s\_ssn\_n\} \\
\hline
\end{array}
$$

$$
\begin{array}{l}
\hline
\_\textit{BadNewMessage}_____ \\
\Delta \textit{SystemState} \\
\hline
\neg\,(\exists\,mid? : \mathbb{N} \bullet \textit{ResendIdentifiers}) \\
\textit{BadNewMessageOnSenderState} \\
\textit{NewMessageOnChannel1State} \\
\Xi \textit{ReceiverState} \\
\Xi \textit{Channel2State} \\
\hline
\end{array}
$$

Theorem BadNewMessagePreservesInvariant:
BadNewMessage $\wedge$ *Invariant* $\Rightarrow$ *Invariant'*

Unfortunately, from the perspective of extracting information from failed proof attempts, the above theorem was provable. The proof was longer than that for the original *NewMessage* operation and suggests that our abstraction of the SWP may not be fully adequate. Perhaps, the intentional omission of message data has made this specification too abstract in that there in no clear role for *s_mid_n* and, consequently, the component could be eliminated from this abstraction. (In fact, as we prove the safety properties we will find that the incrementing of *s_mid_n* is important to the correct functioning of the protocol.)

Our second effort was more successful in generating an unprovable conjecture. In this case, we deleted the requirement that valid data must be in the state of the *Channel*1 process.

$$
\begin{array}{|l}
\hline
\_\_BadReceiveOperation_____ \\
\Delta SystemState \\
\hline
\Xi SenderState \\
\\
LoseChannel1OnChannel1State \\
\\
ReceiverReceivesData \\
\\
\Xi Channel2State \\
\hline
\end{array}
$$

Theorem BadReceiveOperationPreservesInvariant:
BadReceiveOperation $\wedge$ Invariant $\Rightarrow$ Invariant'

One of the cases related to the above conjecture is as follows:

$$
\cdots
$$
$$
\wedge\ r\_rcvd' = r\_rcvd \cup \{ch1\_mid\}
$$
$$
\cdots
$$
$$
\wedge\ r\_rcvd \in \mathbb{P}\,\mathrm{dom}\,s\_sent
$$
$$
\wedge\ \mathrm{dom}\,s\_sent \in \mathbb{P}\,\mathbb{Z}
$$
$$
\cdots
$$
$$
\wedge\ r\_rcvd \in \mathbb{P}\,\mathbb{Z}
$$
$$
\cdots
$$
$$
\wedge\ ch1\_mid \in \{-1\} \cup \mathrm{dom}\,s\_sent
$$
$$
\cdots
$$
$$
\Rightarrow
$$
$$
ch1\_mid \in \mathrm{dom}\,s\_sent
$$

where we have removed those hypotheses unrelated to the conclusion. The formula would be provable if $ch1\_mid \neq -1$ was one of the hypotheses. This observation is strongly suggestive that *BadReceiveOperation* is missing a restriction on its initial state.

As we discussed in Section 12.4.1, there is an easy recipe for exploring preconditions using Z/EVES. For the *ReceiveMessage* operation, we work on the following goal:

$SystemState \Rightarrow \exists SystemState' \bullet ReceiveMessage.$

On performing a reduce, followed by a rewrite, the goal is reduced to the form:

$$\cdots$$
$$\land ch1\_mid \in \mathbb{Z}$$
$$\land ch1\_ssn \in \mathbb{Z}$$
$$\cdots$$
$$\Rightarrow$$
$$ch1\_mid \geq 0$$
$$\land ch1\_ssn \geq 0$$

So, a more robust version of our *ReceiveMessage* operation would be:

ReceiveMessage
$\Delta SystemState$

$ch1\_mid \geq 0$

$ch1\_ssn \geq 0$

$\Xi SenderState$

LoseChannel1OnChannel1State

ReceiverReceivesData

$\Xi Channel2State$

12.7 Safety Properties

We analysed two safety properties of the protocol:

- no message should be retransmitted unless it was lost. Hence, the message should not have been received by the *Receiver*, nor should it be in transit (i.e., not in *Channel*1);
- the receiver should never receive a duplicate message.

We start by considering the retransmission requirement. Observe that for a message to be in transit the message identifier must satisfy the *ResendIdentifiers* schema. Consequently, we can prove the "not in transit" requirement by demonstrating the invariance of the following:

ResendIdentifiersNotInTransitInvariant
SystemState

$\neg\, ResendIdentifiers[ch1\_mid/mid?]$

So, for the operations that can affect the *Channel1State*, we proved the above invariant. For example, with regards to the *ResendMessage* operation we have:

Theorem ResendMessageOnResendIdentifierNotInChannel1:

    ResendMessage
    $\wedge$ *ΔInvariant*
    $\wedge$ *ΔChannel1Invariant*
    $\wedge$ *ResendIdentifiersNotInTransitInvariant*

$\Rightarrow$

    ResendIdentifiersNotInTransitInvariant'

```
=> invoke;
=> prove;
```

There are two points to note about the above: firstly, we have introduced a new invariant called *Channel1Invariant*. It turns out that we needed to be more explicit about the relationship between the two components of the *Channel1State*. As a result, we introduced:

Channel1Invariant
    SystemState
    Invariant

    $ch1\_mid \neq -1 \Rightarrow s\_sent\ ch1\_mid = ch1\_ssn$

An interesting aspect of the above schema is that it was necessary to include *Invariant*, for otherwise the domain proof obligation was not provable.

```
=> invoke;
=> prove;
```

An example proof[2] of the property is:

Theorem NewMessageOnChannel1Relationship:

    NewMessage
    $\wedge$ *Invariant*
    $\wedge$ *Invariant'*

$\Rightarrow$

    Channel1Invariant'

```
=> invoke;
=> prove;
```

Secondly, our proofs are not as automated as earlier. While it is almost certain that the number of proof steps could be reduced, it was through the above kind of proof

---

[2] We should note that we mechanised the proofs for only those SWP operations that actually affect *Channel1*.

development that the completed proofs were discovered. In particular, as the automated steps took a reasonable amount of time, it was decided to more carefully control the analysis and invoke automation (normally as a rewrite or simplify) only when one had reasonable certainty that useful results would be achieved.

The second aspect of the retransmission requirement was that the retransmitted message should not have been received by the *Receiver*. Similar to the first aspect, we observe that a message could be retransmitted only if it satisfies the *ResendIdentifiers* predicate. So, we posit that for all received messages, the predicate is not satisfied:

ResendIdentifiersNotReceived
SystemState
___

$\forall x : \mathrm{N} \bullet x \in r\_rcvd \Rightarrow \neg\, ResendIdentifiers[x/mid?]$

Once again, we proved that the above is an invariant of the SWP. So, for example, we have:

Theorem ResendMessageOnResendIdentifierNotAlreadyReceived:
   ResendMessage
   $\wedge$ *ΔInvariant*
   $\wedge$ *ΔChannel1Invariant*
   $\wedge$ *ΔResendIdentifiersNotInTransitInvariant*
   $\wedge$ *ResendIdentifiersNotReceived*
$\Rightarrow$
   ResendIdentifiersNotReceived'

```
=> invoke;
=> prove;
=> instantiate x_0 == x;
=> split x = mid?;
=> reduce;
```

The second safety property is that the receiver should never receive a duplicate message. Our formalism of this property is that *Channel1* should never have a message identifier which belongs to the receiver's *r_rcvd* component.

NoDuplicateMessages
SystemState
___

$\neg\, ch1\_mid \in r\_rcvd$

So, once again using *ResendMessage* as our exemplar, the invariance proof is:

Theorem ResendMessageOnNoDuplicateMessages:
>   *ResendMessage*
> $\wedge$ *ΔInvariant*
> $\wedge$ *ΔChannel1Invariant*
> $\wedge$ *ΔResendIdentifiersNotInTransitInvariant*
> $\wedge$ *ΔResendIdentifiersNotReceived*
> $\wedge$ *NoDuplicateMessages*
> $\Rightarrow$
>   *NoDuplicateMessages'*

```
=> invoke;
=> prove;
=> instantiate x == ch1_mid' ;
=> rewrite;
```

However, to prove *NewMessageIdentifierNotInDomain*, it turns out that we need an additional fact about an invariance relationship between *s_sent* and *s_mid_n*. In particular, we need to show that *s_mid_n* is not in the domain of *s_sent*. To prove the conjecture, we first prove a *DomainInvariant* and then demonstrate that our fact is a consequence of the *DomainInvariant*. (We do not include the proofs here.)

$$
\begin{array}{|l}
\hline
\!\!\_\,\textit{DomainInvariant}\,\rule{6cm}{0.4pt} \\
\quad \textit{SystemState} \\
\rule{3cm}{0.4pt} \\
\quad \forall x : \mathbb{N} \bullet x \in \mathrm{dom}\, s\_sent \Rightarrow 0 \le x \wedge x < s\_mid\_n \\
\hline
\end{array}
$$

Theorem NewMessageIdentifierNotInDomain:
DomainInvariant $\Rightarrow \neg\, s\_mid\_n \in \mathrm{dom}\, s\_sent$

Finally, we can complete the proof of the second safety property by showing its invariance through *NewMessage*.

Theorem NewMessageOnNoDuplicateMessages:
>   *NewMessage*
> $\wedge$ *ΔInvariant*
> $\wedge$ *ΔChannel1Invariant*
> $\wedge$ *ΔResendIdentifiersNotInTransitInvariant*
> $\wedge$ *ΔResendIdentifiersNotReceived*
> $\wedge$ *NoDuplicateMessages*
> $\wedge \neg\, s\_mid\_n \in \mathrm{dom}\, s\_sent$
> $\wedge \neg\, s\_mid\_n' \in \mathrm{dom}\, s\_sent'$
> $\Rightarrow$
>   *NoDuplicateMessages'*

```
=> invoke;
```

```
=> prove;
=> split ch1_mid' ∈ r_rcvd';
=> rewrite;
```

Finally, just to clean up one remaining nicety, we show that the additional invariant properties hold for the *InitialSystemState*.

> **Theorem** SafetyPropertiesOnInitialState:
> > *InitialSystemState*
>
> ⇒
>
> > *Channel1Invariant* ∧
> > *ResendIdentifiersNotInTransitInvariant* ∧
> > *ResendIdentifiersNotReceived* ∧
> > *NoDuplicateMessages* ∧
> > *DomainInvariant*

```
=> reduce;
```

12.8 Conclusions

We have introduced the basic concepts of the Z specification language through the specification of a simple protocol: an abstraction of the Sliding Window Protocol. Our specification approach was to define the protocol using a conventional state-transition approach. Two safety properties of the protocol were successfully proven.

The Z/EVES tool was used, as an example toolset, to analyse the specification. Z/EVES (Saaltink, 1997b; Saaltink and Meisels, 1995) has been released, but is still a bit rough around the edges. For example, some of the proofs reported herein take a few minutes (on a SPARC 2) to complete; we would rather have proof attempts measured in seconds. On the other hand, few Z tools provide analytical capabilities beyond that of simple type checking. It is also likely that the structure of the specification could be modified to enhance analysis. For example, the primary invariant (*Invariant*) contains information that was necessary only to bring ourselves to a point where we had particularly relevant foundational facts about the SWP. We could, therefore, have specified a strengthened invariant and used only the strengthened invariant in subsequent proofs.

The development of Z/EVES is not complete. We are continuing to extend its capabilities, and keep a keen eye on industrial uses of Z to ensure that Z/EVES can be applied to specifications of realistic size and complexity. Our regression testing suite includes the Railtrack specification (King and Rawlings, 1994), part of the draft Posix 1003.21 standard (IEEE, 1996), and Jacky's specification of a radiation therapy machine (Jacky, 1992). We have also experimented with the application of Z/EVES to the DTOS specification (Secure Computing Corp., 1996), which, at several hundred pages of dense schema definitions, is more than Z/EVES can currently handle; we use this specification to encourage us to improve our speed and resource usage.

Some authors has claimed that effective theorem proving support for Z is not possible, because the language design never included this as a design goal. It is true that Z presents some challenges to mechanised proof support, but these are offset by its facilities for the concise and clear specifications. We feel that Z/EVES shows that powerful proof support can, indeed, be provided for Z.

Appendix

Z/EVES System Commands

In this appendix, we provide brief descriptions of the commands used with the Sliding Window Protocol example.

Once a proof has been started, proof steps apply to the goal predicate and result in a new goal that is equivalent to the original. A proof is complete when the goal is the predicate *true*.

Starting Proofs

Named proof goals are established by `theorem` declarations or by domain checking conditions for paragraphs. The `try` command establishes an unnamed proof goal. Named goals can be deferred; at any time, it is possible to begin, or return to, a named goal. The `print status` command can be used to display the status of all named goals.

Try Syntax: `try` *predicate*
The `try` command establishes a new, unnamed, proof goal.

Reduction

The reduction commands traverse the goal, accumulating assumptions and *reducing* predicates and expressions. A command modifier can be used to enable or disable a theorem or definition for a single reduction command.

Reduce Syntax: `reduce`
The `reduce` command traverses the goal, accumulating assumptions and reducing predicates and expressions. As each subexpression or subpredicate is considered, frules and grules are used, as well as the built-in decision procedures for equality and linear arithmetic. If any rewrite rule applies to the considered phrase, one is applied and the result is again reduced. (If the rule is conditional, it is applied only if its conditions can be reduced to *true*.) Finally, if no rewrite rules apply and the considered phrase is a schema reference or generic instance, the definition of the schema or generic symbol will be invoked and the result will again be reduced.

Rewrite Syntax: `rewrite`

The `rewrite` command traverses the goal, accumulating assumptions and *rewriting* predicates and expressions. As each subexpression or subpredicate is considered, frules and grules are used, as well as the built-in decision procedures for equality and linear arithmetic. If any rewrite rule applies to the considered phrase, one is applied and the result is again rewritten. (If the rule is conditional, it is applied only if its conditions can be rewritten to *true*.)

Trivial simplify Syntax: `trivial simplify`

The `trivial simplify` command traverses the goal, accumulating assumptions and *simplifying* predicates. As each subpredicate is considered, if the predicate has been assumed true (or assumed false), it is replaced by `true` (or `false`). Occurrences of `true` and `false` within Boolean connectives are eliminated, by either dropping the occurrence or replacing the containing predicate by its value (*e.g.*, $P \wedge true$ becomes P, $P \wedge false$ becomes *false*).

Prove Syntax: `prove [by reduce]`;

The `prove` command repeatedly applies the sequence `prenex; rearrange; equality substitute; rewrite;` (or `reduce;` for the `prove by reduce` command), until the `rewrite` or `reduce` command has no effect. These are the two most commonly used sequences of prover commands.

Quantifiers

Prenex Syntax: `prenex`

The `prenex` command removes any quantifiers that can be made into leading universal quantifiers. For example, the formula:

$$(\exists x : N \mid x \in S) \Rightarrow (\forall y : S' \bullet y < x)$$

is equivalent to the formula:

$$\forall x : N;\ y : S' \bullet x \in S \Rightarrow y < x.$$

When the quantifiers are removed, the colons become epsilons. Thus, applying `prenex` to the original formula results in the goal:

$$x \in N \wedge x \in S \wedge y \in S' \Rightarrow y < x.$$

Instantiate Syntax: `instantiate` *instantiations*

The `instantiate` command is used to instantiate one or more quantified variables. The variables instantiated must appear together in a quantified predicate (that is, one cannot instantiate for both x and y in $\forall x : \mathbb{Z} \mid x > 1 \bullet \forall y : \mathbb{Z} \bullet \ldots$, but can in $\forall x, y : \mathbb{Z} \bullet \ldots$).

The goal predicate will be rearranged if possible and necessary, so that the variables being instantiated are within the scope of any bound variables used in the instantiations.

Miscellaneous Commands

Invoke Syntax: `invoke` [*name*]

If *name* is the name of a schema or of a name introduced in a definition, any occurrences of the name in the goal are replaced by its definition.

If no name is given, all enabled defined functions in the goal are replaced by their definitions (and all enabled defined functions in the definitions are replaced, and so on).

Equality substitute Syntax: `equality substitute` [*expression*]

If the optional expression is given, and there is a hypothesis in the goal that is an equality between the given expression e and some other expression e', then any subsequent occurrences of e in the goal are replaced by e'.

If no expression is given, some equalities are chosen (if possible) and used as in the above case.

Split Syntax: `split` *predicate*

The `split` command is used to consider two cases. The command `split` P transforms a goal G to the new goal **if** P **then** G **else** G. (The `cases` command can be applied to this new goal to break it into two cases: $P \Rightarrow G$ and $\neg P \Rightarrow G$.)

Rearrange Syntax: `rearrange`

The `rearrange` command changes the order of conjuncts appearing in the goal, heuristically choosing the new order. Membership tests and equalities tend to be moved to the front of the conjunction, and conjuncts involving Boolean connectives are moved to the end. This usually allows the reduction commands to work more effectively.

CHAPTER 13

How to Construct Formal Arguments that Persuade Certifiers

**Andrew P. Moore, J. Eric Klinker
and David M. Mihelcic**

13.1 Introduction

Developers of a critical system must argue that the system satisfies its *critical requirements* — those that, if not satisfied, could result in human injury or death, substantial loss of capital, or the compromise of national security. Documenting an explicit, persuasive *assurance argument* is especially important when the system produced must be evaluated and approved by an independent certifier, as is often the case for safety- and security-critical systems. Past experience developing independently evaluated systems using formal methods (Moore and Payne, 1996a; Payne *et al.*, 1994) demonstrates that the presentation of the assurance argument is as important as the rigor of the *assurance evidence* on which that argument is based. Formal specifications and analyses must be presented coherently in the context of the overall system decomposition or much of their power to persuade may be lost. This chapter describes and illustrates a general framework that supports gathering, integrating, presenting and reviewing the evidence that we can *trust* a system to conform to its critical requirements.

Persuasive assurance arguments must be consistent and complete, both internally (ignoring how the argument is being applied) and externally (with respect to its particular application). Arguments that have these properties must be under-

United States Government work; not subject to US copyright.
Reproduced with permission of United States Naval Research Laboratories.

standable, coherent and relevant. Roughly, understandability ensures an argument's internal consistency in the sense that an inconsistent argument cannot be understood to be valid. Likewise, coherence ensures an argument's internal completeness and relevance ensures its external consistency and completeness. Of course, there is always the danger that a persuasively presented but invalid argument will convince the certifier (incorrectly) that the argument is valid. In this case, the certifier believes the argument to be valid through a misunderstanding. Making arguments easier to understand will reduce the chances of making such mistakes.

Our framework enables a developer to produce understandable, coherent and relevant assurance arguments that use formal methods by:

1. integrating formal specification and verification techniques into a sound software engineering and documentation methodology,
2. maintaining the consistency of the assurance documentation with formal specifications and code that are input to specification, verification and compilation tools,
3. providing an overview of the assurance argument and the process by which it is constructed that serves as an index into the more detailed assurance evidence, and
4. automating and, when appropriate, enforcing the process of assurance argument refinement.

The framework is not a step-by-step guide, but a set of guidelines within which individual organisations can customise or improve their existing software development process to use formal methods as an effective tool for convincing an independent certifier of a system's trustworthiness. The framework is most cost-effective when the system architecture isolates critical function in simple, well-defined and reusable components that are implemented primarily in software.

We have applied the elements of our framework to three significant applications: a network security device called the External COMSEC Adaptor (ECA) (Payne *et al.*, 1994), a software-controlled RS-232 character repeater (Landwehr, 1989; Moore and Payne, 1996b), and a security-critical extension of a Navy command and control system called the Joint Maritime Command Information System (JMCIS) (Froscher *et al.*, 1995). The ECA is a device that permits secure communication between network subscribers by cryptographically protecting the sensitive portions of messages that traverse unprotected transmission media. The ECA development process integrates formal specifications and proofs with structured software documentation to maintain a clear relationship between the ECA's overall refinement and the formal assurance evidence (item 1 above) (Moore *et al.*, 1995). The character repeater application is a much smaller example that demonstrates the utility of the literate programming paradigm and hypertext methods for improving the readability of the assurance argument while maintaining its consistency with formal specifications and code that are input to tools (item 2) (Moore and Payne, 1996a). The JMCIS extension is an ongoing effort to securely replicate SQL database updates from a Secret processing enclave to a Top Secret processing enclave. This effort extends previous work by investigating the graphical depiction of assurance argument overviews (Moore, 1996) and the automation and enforcement the development process (items 3 and 4).

The following sections describe our general framework, instantiate it to use specific publicly-available tools, and demonstrate the instantiated framework as applied to the ECA. We choose the ECA for demonstration purposes since it exemplifies the most thoroughly developed application of the techniques described in this chapter. The ECA assurance argument includes a chain of formal reasoning that spans from a critical requirements model to a low-level program design that was proven to conform to the model. Thirty software modules were identified and implemented resulting in approximately 11 000 lines of Verdi specifications (including proof heuristics), 4 000 lines of proven Verdi code, and 6 000 lines of Ada code mapped from the Verdi. A total of 24 ECA devices were constructed by a contractor from the software implementation and hardware specification produced at NRL during the early 1990s. The real-world examples provided are simple enough to demonstrate concretely and concisely how to put into practice the techniques on which our framework is based.

13.2 Framework

The quality of an organisation's personnel, both technical and management, and its system development process play a large role in determining that organisation's success in building quality products (Boehm, 1981). These factors are even more important in the successful development of systems using formal methods given the increased discipline that those methods require (Craigen *et al.*, 1993). The greatest benefit of tools, whether based on formal or less rigorous methods, can only be obtained if they are used in a well-defined development process by well-trained personnel (Curtis, 1992). This section assumes that these are in place and describes an approach for augmenting the process to include the development of a persuasive and cost-effective assurance argument using tools of varying rigour. A later section describes ongoing work to provide automated support for an example assurance argument development process.

13.2.1 Integrating Formal Arguments into System Refinement

The successful application of formal methods to engineering systems of interest to industry or the military requires their balanced integration with less rigorous methods. Figure 13.1 depicts a framework for refining an assurance argument in the context of a simple, but typical, software development process based on the Software Cost Reduction (SCR) Methodology (Parnas and Clements, 1986; Parnas and Madey, 1992). The primary levels of system refinement and documentation are shown along the left side of the figure. Along the right side are classes of specification languages and tools that contribute to the formal specification and analysis of the system. The result of integrating the use of the languages and tools on the right into the production of the system documentation on the left is the system's assurance argument, which corresponds to the center of the figure (the area between the arrows.) Slanted arrows indicate a refinement of a specification to a more detailed specification or implementation; vertical arrows indicate a translation of a specification from one semantic domain to another at a comparable abstraction level. The increase in the area between the arrows from top to bottom represents additional detail specified and reflected in the assurance argument at the lower levels. For simplicity, the figure abstracts away details regarding the iterative improvement and feedback between levels that inevitably occurs during system refinement.

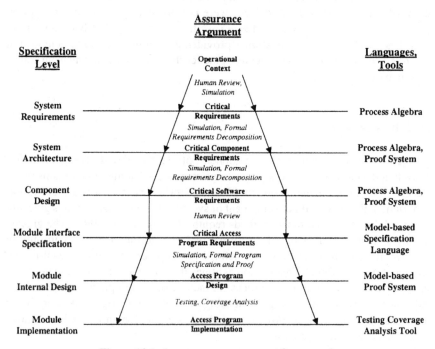

Figure 13.1. An assurance argument framework

Figure 13.1 does not show methods or tools used to refine (informally) the overall system specification because of the wide range of specification paradigms on which existing technology is based. Nevertheless, CASE tools that help trace functional requirements, graphically specify and simulate designs, or record design rationale, for example, are an important part of the development process especially during early design. The assurance argument must weave informal and formal lines of reasoning together into an understandable, coherent and relevant whole. This requires any differences to be resolved among the informal and formal semantic mod-

Table 13.1. Customising the framework: an example

Language, Tool Level of Specification	Statemate	CSP	EVES	Verdi	Ada	VADS
System Requirements	✓	✓				
System Architecture	✓	✓	✓			
Component Design	✓	✓	✓			
Module Interface Specification				✓		
Module Internal Design			✓	✓		
Module Implementation					✓	✓

els on which the argument is based, e.g., state machine versus process algebraic. Resolution will likely be informal and dependent on how the models are used in the context of the argument. In some cases it may be possible to use the less rigorous methods and tools for early discovery, communication and design, but then cast the results in a formal specification language for analysis. This permits the use of less rigorous methods where they are most useful while using formal methods to gain higher assurance that critical requirements are satisfied. The generality of this model of assurance argument refinement promotes its customisation to more complex industrial development processes.

The rest of this section elaborates Figure 13.1. Throughout this description, we incrementally refine an example of how to customise the framework using specific languages and tools. This example uses the Statemate® graphical specification and simulation tools (Harel *et al.*, 1990), the Communicating Sequential Processes (CSP) process algebra (Hoare, 1985), the EVES formal verification system (Craigen *et al.*, 1991) and Verdi programming language (Craigen, 1991), and the Verdix® Ada Development System (VADS®) (Verdix Corporation, 1990). Table 13.1 indicates the specification level in which each language and tool is applied.

Requirements Elicitation. The operational context describes in English the concept of operations for the system, including those responsibilities imposed by the system in which it is embedded. Since systems often involve a number of concurrently executing processes, the requirements specification language of an appropriate process algebra (Hoare, 1985; Milner, 1989; van Eijk *et al.*, 1989) is chosen to specify the critical requirements in the first level of Figure 13.1. This specification, which forms the basis for the formal assurance argument, must be validated to be consistent with its responsibilities described in the operational context and with the overall system requirements. The formal specification of critical requirements and the overall system requirements specification should share the same structure of the system's external interface.

Example. Suppose we use Statemate as the basis for describing the overall system requirements and CSP as the basis for specifying the critical requirements. Statemate has a graphical language called activity charts that permits the specification of the external interface to a system. Requirements for a system can be stated in terms of the primitives set up by that system's activity chart. A CSP process can be defined to reflect the system's activity chart specification. A critical requirement specified in CSP is a restriction on the trace of communications in which that process may engage. If, during later development, we find that the refined CSP process is restricted to these traces, the process is said to satisfy the critical requirement.

System Design. The next two levels of specification in Figure 13.1 involve the design of the system including the derivation of the software requirements. This process draws heavily on the experience of the development team with the past development of similar systems. CASE technology helps capture the developer's understanding of the problem domain in the form of graphical specifications of the system's design (Harel *et al.*, 1990; Nu Thena Systems, 1993; O'Rourke, 1992). Although not typically amenable to formal proof, specifications produced by production-quality CASE tools are valuable during the necessarily informal phase of discovery characterised by early design. The graphical specifications provide a more natural and comprehensible medium for communication among engineers. Simulation helps ensure that this design conforms to the overall system requirements specified earlier.

More rigorous analysis involves reflecting this design in the process algebra used as the basis for the specification of critical requirements. The formal rules of that process algebra help decompose the critical requirements onto requirements of the primary concurrently executing components of the design; several model checkers (Cleaveland *et al.*, 1990; Formal Systems Ltd., 1994) and general-purpose theorem provers (Craigen *et al.*, 1991; Gordon and Melham, 1993; Owre *et al.*, 1992) can help prove the correctness of this decomposition. Identifying the components that are implemented in software allows refinement of the design and formal derivation of the software requirements.

Example. Extending the example from last section, we can use Statemate to specify and verify the design and CSP to decompose the critical requirements onto the primary components of the design. In addition to activity charts for refining the data flow structure of a system, Statemate supports state charts, which present a behavioural view akin to state machine diagrams. The design combines activity and state charts to refine the activity chart that forms the basis of the requirements specification. The formal decomposition of the system-level critical requirements in CSP traces follows the approach outlined in (Moore, 1990), using EVES to perform the proofs as in (Moore and Payne, 1996b). Derivation of the software requirements proceeds by refining the Statemate and CSP specifications, in parallel, to distinguish those components implemented in software from those implemented in hardware. CSP proof rules permit deriving the critical software requirements from the system-level critical requirements and the CSP process structure.

Module Refinement. Further system refinement requires the modularisation of the system – the mapping of the functions previously specified into distinct and relatively small modules based on the criteria of information hiding (Parnas, 1972). This mapping will not be direct, and probably not one-to-one, since the module structure is very different from the structure of system designs previously specified. An information hiding module is a logical grouping of system functions that share (and hide) some secret. Secrets of a module include those characteristics of the system most likely to change in future updates of the system. Each such characteristic is hidden in some module so that developers of other modules do not rely on it.

An effective modularisation is extremely important for cost-effective software development, particularly where formal methods are used. Structuring the module decomposition hierarchically helps designers and maintainers quickly find the modules affected by a change. If the change is among those recognised as likely during earlier phases of development, modification to the existing software will be confined to a minimal number of modules. These benefits are magnified when formal methods are used since changes to a formal argument due to changes in design or implementation can be very expensive, perhaps resulting in changes to the overall structure of the argument. Information hiding modularisation also often protects the formal argument from change during the iterative process of design and implementation of the system.

The last three levels of specification in Figure 13.1 involve the refinement of the modules identified. Each module's interface consists of a set of access programs, the behavioural specification of which is restricted to externally visible information. The critical requirements for the access programs derive from the critical requirements of the process algebraic designs specified earlier. They are cast in terms of a model-based specification language that permits the design and verification of individual software programs (Craigen *et al.*, 1991; Guaspari *et al.*, 1990). This specification provides the oracle to which the implementation must conform. Verification proceeds either through formal proof or by structured testing. The type of verification performed depends on the complexity and type of the requirement and the complexity of the code. Testing tools (Reliable Testing Technologies, 1996) can help analyse the coverage of tests conducted using the module interface specification as the oracle. If the model-based specification language serves also as the implementation language for the system, the last two levels of specification of Figure 13.1 can be collapsed into one.

Example. Continuing the example, we map the functions of the Statemate design into an information hiding module structure. The components that are implemented in software should correspond to an access program on one of the module's interfaces. We map each critical requirement of each such component, represented as a CSP trace specification, to a post-condition (and invariant) of a Verdi (access) program as follows:

> We define Verdi Get and Put procedures that reflect the semantics of CSP input and output communication operators, respectively. A Verdi program that communicates with other concurrently executing Verdi programs using these procedures builds up a trace of its execution that is recorded in a variable used only for specification purposes. CSP trace specifications translate to Verdi program specifications as restrictions on this specification-only variable.

We derive the critical requirements for subroutines called by each Verdi access program and refine the module interfaces appropriately. The module internal design implements each access program in Verdi and verifies that it conforms to its critical requirements using EVES. The implementation of the Verdi Get and Put procedures is below the CSP trace model of abstraction and, as such, is not subject to EVES verification. We translate all programs to Ada and test their conformance to their specification using VADS.

13.2.2 Maintaining Documentation Consistency

The development of an assurance argument for a complex system involves constructing specifications using disparate notations, both formal and informal, that must be interwoven in a comprehensible way. An approach called Literate Programming (LP) (Knuth, 1984) allows the improvement of an assurance argument's readability while maintaining consistency with specifications and code that are input to specification, verification and compilation tools. Extending the concept slightly, a literate specification is a description of a system from which both intuitive documentation and analysable specifications can be extracted. LP tools typically process literate programs in two phases: a *tangle* phase produces the tool-ready specifications and a *weave* phase produces the human-ready documentation. As shown in Figure 13.2, language-generic LP tools (Ramsey, 1994; Williams, 1992) permit a literate specification to be written that tangles into a set of specifications, each of which is processed by an appropriate analysis tool. The weave phase produces cross-referenced documentation that can be fed into a typesetter for hard- or soft-copy formatting. Developers must incorporate verification results into the documentation, extending the assurance evidence provided. Generating both the documentation and input to analysis tools from a single source helps to ensure their consistency.

The LP paradigm fits well with the example assurance argument refinement process described in the last section. FunnelWeb (Williams, 1992) can be used as the LP tool from which readable module interfaces, designs and implementations are generated. FunnelWeb tangles Verdi specifications and Ada code from the literate specification of the module refinement, which can then be processed using EVES and VADS, respectively. LaTeX (Lamport, 1994) serves as the typesetter for Funnel-Web. The LaTeX2HTML HTML generator (Drakos, 1993) can be used to produce

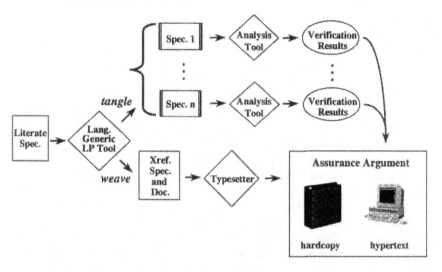

Figure 13.2. Flow of literate specification

hypertext versions of the argument, in addition to the hard copy, for ease of navigation. Although LP tools do not work well with graphical specifications, intuitive documentation integrating the most current Statemate specifications can be generated from a single source using the Statemate Documentor. Generating FunnelWeb compliant literate specifications permits the inclusion of Statemate charts, Verdi and Ada code all in the same document while maintaining their consistency with input to tools. As an example, this chapter was generated using the Statemate Documentor to maintain the consistency of Statemate charts that appear later in the chapter with the ECA Statemate development database.

13.2.3 Defining the Assurance Strategy

As seen above, an assurance argument is a complex chain of reasoning that developers refine throughout system development. The detail inherent in rigorous assurance evidence can obscure the logical structure of the argument unless that structure is explicitly defined and central to its documentation. The assurance strategy documents this logical structure with the goal of demonstrating coherence of the argument. It defines a "road-map" into the assurance argument, tracing meaningful threads between different pieces of assurance evidence and helping certifiers gain an accurate and complete understanding of how the evidence contributes to the overall argument.

The assurance strategy must also explain and motivate the process to be used to develop the assurance evidence. It documents assumptions of formal models used and resolves any conflicts between the assumptions or between an assumption and the system being modelled. Because system requirements often pull the design in different directions, tradeoffs may have to be made. The assurance strategy documents and justifies the choices made during the design process with a discussion of any residual risk that remains, e.g., the vulnerability due to a covert channel through which classified information may leak but, for reasons of performance, is left in place. An approach to define information security-specific assurance strategies described in (Payne *et al.*, 1993) maps security assumptions in one security discipline (e.g., computer security, personnel security or physical security) to security assertions in other disciplines; a gap in this mapping indicates a vulnerability.

Many notations and tools support certain aspects of the definition of assurance strategies, such as tracing requirements (Chung and Nixon, 1995; Gotel and Finkelstein, 1994; O'Rourke, 1992) and recording design rationale (MacLean *et al.*, 1989; Potts and Bruns, 1987). CASE tools usually focus on a specific method involving design decomposition or code analysis that is too narrow to document a complete assurance strategy. They may support requirements traceability, but not usually for non-functional requirements such as security or performance. A graphical notation flexible enough to support many classes of process- and product-oriented requirements and to record detailed design rationale is essential to promote understanding of complex logical arguments of non-trivial critical systems. Such notations often structure arguments similar to that described in (Toulmin, 1957). We focus on one in particular called the Goal Structuring Notation (GSN) (Wilson and McDermid, 1995) that is having significant application.

GSN is a graphical notation originally designed to manage the complexity of developing arguments about the safety of systems. GSN can be used to represent the assurance strategy and its evolution into a full-scale assurance argument for critical systems in general. Distinct graphical elements representing goals (requirements), assumptions (basis for sufficiency of goals), strategies (means of achieving goals), justifications (basis for sufficiency of strategies) and choices (alternative design options) combine to form assurance strategies. The notation is flexible enough to represent assurance gained through the development process, e.g., the use of particular verification techniques, and design decomposition, e.g., the separation of critical and non-critical aspects of the system. The notation leaves the level of abstraction of the assurance strategy up to the user. Other graphical elements representing solutions (that which satisfies a goal), models (representations of the system) and contexts (other contextual information) provide links to the assurance evidence, thus, refining the assurance argument. A tool called the Safety Argument Manager (SAM) (McDermid, 1994) is available for building GSN graphs.

13.3 Application

The detailed refinement of the ECA's assurance argument makes it a good example for demonstrating the techniques described in this chapter. This section summarises the ECA assurance strategy and argument in the context of the overall system refinement and documentation. A family of devices, called the Selective Encryption Domain, provides a framework for identifying the critical requirements for the ECA, which is a member of that family. Details of particular portions of the ECA assurance strategy and argument illustrate the application of the techniques. Although we keep these illustrations relatively simple, understanding certain details of the problem domain will make the examples more comprehensible. A detailed description of the notations used can be found in (Wilson and McDermid, 1995) for GSN, (Harel *et al.*, 1990) for Statemate, (Hoare, 1985) for CSP, and (Craigen, 1991) for Verdi.

13.3.1 Characterising the Problem

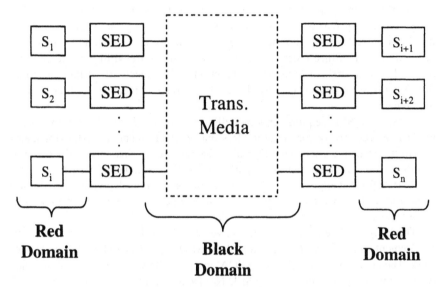

Figure 13.3. The SED's environment

The Selective Encryption Domain contains applications responsible for providing cryptographic protection of information, based on rules that determine the sensitivity of that information. We refer to a particular member of the domain as a Selective Encryption Device (SED). SEDs reside in a network that supports secure communication between subscribers of the network service. As shown in Figure 13.3, every subscriber (S_i) is connected to a unique SED, and all communication between subscribers must pass through the subscribers' SEDs. Subscribers range from simple PCs to multi-level secure systems and are accredited to process information up to a particular classification level. The SED encrypts the sensitive portions of messages that traverse the transmission media between subscribers. The rules for determining whether data is sensitive – and thus in need of encryption – may, due to the complexity of the task, only coarsely determine the actual sensitivity of the information, e.g., a dirty word check. The policy for distributing cryptographic key enforces a network-wide communications plan defining which pairs of subscribers may communicate over the transmission media.

Achieving information security as described above is most closely related to Sutherland's definition of multi-level security based on non-deducibility (Sutherland, 1986): although low level users may be able to view encrypted data, they will not be able to deduce its higher level meaning. We, therefore, define an interpretation of non-deducibility for members of the Selective Encryption Domain:

> SED NonDeducibility: It is not possible to deduce sensitive information by analysing communications over the transmission media.

Unfortunately, in many environments, this "perfect" security would place unnecessary processing burdens on the network as a whole, e.g., it would require all messages be padded to a constant length, completely encrypted, and transmitted at a constant rate. Since most operational environments are willing to accept some minimal security risk to improve the function and connectivity of their information systems, we consider SED NonDeducibility to be an ideal, rather than a strict, requirement.

A paper on SED requirements modelling (Payne *et al.*, 1994) describes a parameterised framework for defining "less-than-perfect" security models for members of the Selective Encryption Domain. The parameters characterise the range of members of the domain, each of which enforces SED NonDeducibility to a degree appropriate for that application. The framework also permits delaying the definition of security-critical parameters until details of the operating environment are known and a realistic risk assessment can be made.

The ECA is a member of the Selective Encryption Domain since its security requirements model is an instantiation of the SED parameterised modelling framework. The environment in which the ECA operates, shown in Figure 13.4, justifies relaxing the constraints imposed by SED NonDeducibility. Although the ECA's environment has the same structure as an SED's environment generally, the transmission media are more complex than Figure 13.3 suggests. A partially protected LAN and link encryptor separates the ECA from the completely unprotected part of the media. The LAN is physically protected only to a level that permits certain control data to bypass encryption; all subscriber data must still be fully encrypted. Messages being sent to remote subscribers must pass through a link encryptor which encrypts the entire message, resulting in doubly encrypted subscriber data. This approach has the benefit that communication over the LAN is not slowed by requiring the router to decrypt and re-encrypt the routing data; the router has all the information it needs in the clear to send the message to its final destination, be it local or remote.

13.3.2 Defining the Assurance Strategy

A segment of the assurance strategy that documents the derivation of the ECA's critical requirements is shown in Figure 13.5 as a GSN graph produced using SAM. The top-level goal (Goal 0) requires that the ECA satisfy SED NonDeducibility so

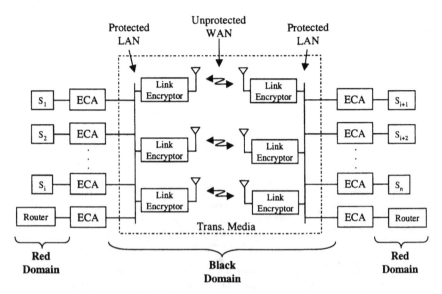

Figure 13.4. The ECA's environment

that the derivation and justification of the relaxed requirements can be made explicit. As shown, Goal 0 can be refined into three subgoals requiring padding of messages to constant length, encryption of all data, and transmission at a constant rate. The protections provided on the LAN obviate the need for the closing of covert channels provided by Goal 1 and Goal 3, although the link encryptor may be required to perform these functions over the unprotected WAN. Our strategy relaxes the encryption requirement to apply only to subscriber data (Strategy 0); we bypass header data containing routing data to improve throughput on the protected LAN. Three sub-goals, Goal 4 through Goal 6, describe the requirements for bypassing header data and encrypting non-header data. As is generally the case with GSN graphs, goals are vague at the top of the hierarchy and become increasingly detailed as they are elaborated at lower levels.

Figure 13.6 elaborates the requirements that discharge the constraint that certifiers be convinced that the ECA implementation conforms to its requirements (Constraint 1), shown in Figure 13.5. The general strategy conforms to the example refined in Section 13.2. We refine the ECA requirements and design using Statemate while formally tracing the critical requirements through this design using CSP (Strategy 2). We identify and refine the software modules using the SCR methodology, map the CSP trace requirements onto this module structure in Verdi, and formally refine the module design and implementation using EVES (Strategy 3). The structure of the GSN graph in Figure 13.6, in particular Goal 7 through Goal 12,

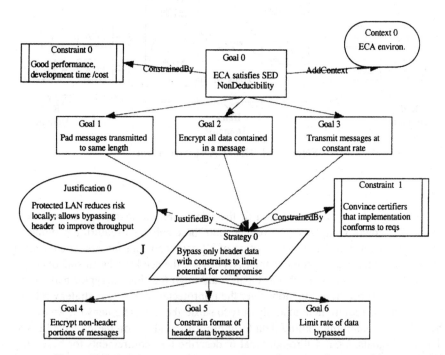

Figure 13.5. Assurance strategy excerpt: requirements decomposition

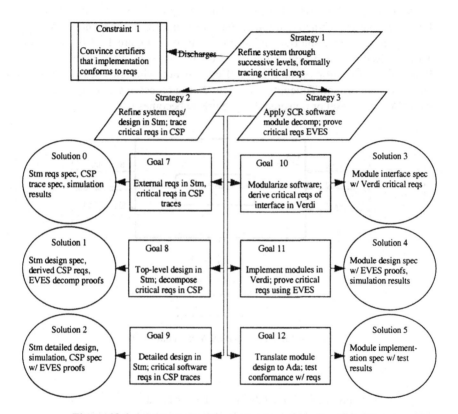

Figure 13.6. Assurance strategy excerpt: process decomposition

illustrates use of the assurance strategy as a "road-map" to the assurance argument and reflects the structure of the rest of this section.

13.3.3 Elaborating the Requirements

We partition the ECA requirements to isolate behaviour that is most likely to change: the details of the protocol for exchanging data with the network. The activity chart in Figure 13.7 and its controlling state chart in Figure 13.8 construct a framework for stating the core functional requirements for the ECA, independent of its network interface.[1] This interface is abstracted away in Figure 13.7 by the external activities RedInt and BlkInt. Figure 13.8 distinguishes between processing in the Red-to-Black direction or the Black-to-Red direction with priorities set through an unspecified algorithm. Timeouts may occur during processing causing a hard fail. If the ECA is ever reset or powered down, SysRdy becomes false.

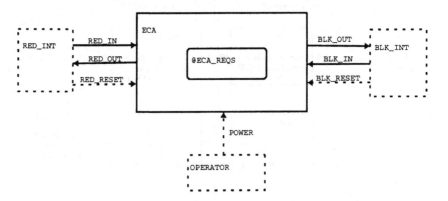

Figure 13.7. The core ECA external interface

We state requirements in a tabular format inspired by (van Schouwen *et al.*, 1993). For example, an entry in a table specifying requirements for values of the BlkOut queue is shown in Table 13.2 where SET is the Selective Encryption Transform applied to messages. This is read "If the ECA is in the state ProcessingRed-ToBlk, RedIn is not empty, BlkOut is not full, and the first element in RedIn passes the format check, then the SET-transformed message must be sent over BlkOut." Table 13.3 requires that status messages be sent over RedOut whether the message format checks or not.

---

[1] Activity charts distinguish two types of flows between activities: flows of data (represented by solid arrows) and flows of control (represented by dashed arrows). Dashed boxes represent activities external to the activity being refined. Arrows between flows in a state chart must be labelled with a trigger that has the general form E[C]/A, where E is an (instantaneous) event, C is a (Boolean) condition, and A is an action; any specific trigger must have either an event or a condition and may not require any action.

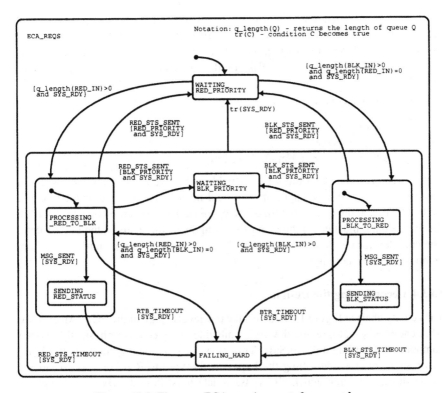

Figure 13.8. The core ECA requirements framework

Table 13.2. Example BlkOut requirement assuming SysRdy

State	Triggering Event	BlkOut =
Processing-RedToBlk	¬Empty(RedIn) ∧¬Full(BlkOut) ∧ FmtOK(Byp(Next(RedIn)))	EnQ(SET(Next(RedIn)), BlkOut)

Table 13.3. Example RedOut requirements assuming SysRdy

State	Triggering Event	RedOut =
Sending-RedStatus	¬Empty(RedIn) ∧¬Full(RedOut) ∧ FmtOK(Byp(Next(RedIn)))	EnQ(StsMsg(Next(RedIn)), TranSucc), RedOut)
Processing-RedToBlk	¬Empty(RedIn) ∧¬Full(RedOut) ∧¬FmtOK(Byp(Next(RedIn)))	EnQ(StsMsg(Next(RedIn)), FmtFail), RedOut)

To facilitate formal analysis of lower levels of refinement, we cast the critical requirements as CSP trace specifications (Payne *et al.*, 1992). Using Figure 13.7 as the basis, the bypass format requirement, ProperFormat, requires that the bypass portion of every message sent over BlkOut (that occurs in the system trace *tr*) satisfy FmtOK:

ECA **sat** ProperFormat

ProperFormat
$\equiv \forall m \in$ Message :
    BlkOut.m **in** $tr \Rightarrow$ FmtOK(Byp(m))

FmtOK requires that the value of each field of the bypass data must be within a predetermined range; the length of each field must match a predetermined length for that field; and the overall length of the bypass data, as specified by a field within the bypass data, must equal the sum of the lengths of the fields of the bypass data. The complex formal definition is omitted here since it does not significantly help demonstrate the techniques.

13.3.4 Decomposing the Design

The activity chart in Figure 13.9 depicts the top-level design of the ECA. An existing NSA-endorsed cryptographic device is embedded between two physically distinct components: RedSide and BlkSide. This physical separation centralises the function responsible for controlling the bypass and crypto to RedSide and provides a single channel through which all bypassed data must flow (RBBypass). Crypto is fed plaintext through the PTxt channels and ciphertext through the CTxt channels. The purpose of the remaining control channels will be elaborated in later refinement. Notice that the Power control flow of Figure 13.7 has been decomposed into one control flow for each component.

The following describes a typical scenario in which a message is transmitted from a local subscriber to some remote subscriber. Let us assume that the message passes all checks, e.g., format and bypass rate. The local subscriber's ECA receives the message from the Red Domain. RedSide splits it into the bypass data and crypto data portions, sends the crypto data to Crypto and the bypass data to BlkSide. Crypto encrypts the crypto data using the appropriate key and sends the result to BlkSide. BlkSide then recombines the message and transmits the result over the message interface to the Black Domain. The intended recipient's ECA must reverse this procedure using the corresponding decryption key to restore the original message. The link encryption/decryption that occurs, as shown in Figure 13.4, is transparent to the subscribers.

The CSP process specification for the ECA top-level decomposition shares the structure of the Statemate specification in Figure 13.9. The alphabet of the process contains all possible communications over channels shown. Communication over control channels are modelled as single-bit transmissions. Applying the approach in Moore (1990) derives critical requirements for RedSide and BlkSide as follows (Crypto has no responsibilities in this case):

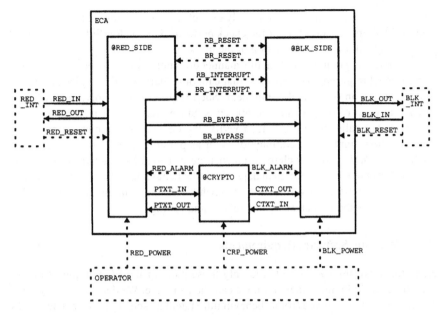

Figure 13.9. ECA top-level internal structure

$\text{ProperFormat}_{\text{RedSide}}$
$\equiv \forall b \in \text{BypData} :$
$\quad \text{RBBypass}.b \text{ in } tr \Rightarrow \text{FmtOK}(b)$

$\text{ProperFormat}_{\text{BlkSide}}$
$\equiv \forall outm \in \text{Message} :$
$\quad \text{BlkOut}.outm \text{ in } tr$
$\quad \Rightarrow \exists inm \in \text{Message} :$
$\quad\quad (\text{RBBypass}.\text{Byp}(inm) \text{ in } tr$
$\quad\quad \wedge outm = \text{BlkSET}(inm)$
$\quad\quad \wedge (\text{FmtOK}(\text{Byp}(inm)) \Rightarrow \text{FmtOK}(\text{Byp}(outm))))$

where BlkSET is the BlkSide transformation performed on messages sent to the Black Domain. Conditions sufficient to verify this decomposition of ProperFormat requires showing that:

- the truth of ProperFormat depends only on the ECA's external communications;
- the truth of $\text{ProperFormat}_{\text{RedSide}}$ and $\text{ProperFormat}_{\text{BlkSide}}$ depends only on their respective alphabets; and
- the conjunction of $\text{ProperFormat}_{\text{RedSide}}$ and $\text{ProperFormat}_{\text{BlkSide}}$ implies Proper-Format.

The first two conditions involve showing that the components do not interfere with each other in regards to satisfying the requirements; they are trivial to prove in this case. The last condition is proven easily as well by recognising that BlkSide's requirement simply ensures the format check performed by the RedSide is maintained through any BlkSide transformation of the message.

Decomposing requirements in this manner does not always proceed so smoothly. System-level requirements may exist that cannot be partitioned completely into requirements on an individual component. Such requirements involve the synchronised behaviour of two or more components. Since these synchronisation requirements are typically more difficult to verify, the decomposition method promotes reducing their number and complexity as far as possible. The set of these requirements is *minimal* if, when each requirement is described in conjunctive normal form, each conjunct of each requirement depends on the behaviour of two or more components. The cost-effective verification of synchronisation requirements may involve less rigorous methods such as human review and testing.

13.3.5 Deriving Software Requirements

Henceforth, we refer to as software only those parts of the ECA implemented in Ada; the rest of the implementation we call the firmware. We derive the critical requirements of the software from a behavioural Statemate specification that describes the interactions between the software and the firmware. If the firmware is consistent with the behavioural specification and the assumptions of the modelling and decomposition process, the critical software requirements derived will be sufficient to guarantee that the ECA system satisfies its critical requirements.

The decomposition of RedSide illustrates this approach. Figure 13.10 shows the two primary software functions for RedSide: the initialisation procedure called RedInit and the message traffic processing procedure called RedMain. The controlling state chart RedCtl describes the firmware context in which these procedures operate. This context describes the effect that power cycles, resets, interrupts and crypto alarms have on processing. Of course, this context is in addition to the firmware supporting execution of the software. This firmware is transparent to the logical level at which we are currently working.

Figure 13.11 refines RedCtl. After power invocation and successful initialisation, RedMain starts processing traffic. Five events can suspend processing: a power cycle, a reset from RedInt, a reset from BlkSide, an alarm from Crypto, or an interrupt from BlkSide. Resets simply cause the ECA to re-initialise. An alarm causes execution to be suspended until the alarm goes off and the ECA is re-initialised. An interrupt causes the ECA to halt until it is power cycled or reset.

The specification of RedSide is modelled in CSP as four processes:[2]

RedSide
$\equiv \text{RedPower?} \rightarrow \mu X.(\text{RedOnline}(AllOK) \triangle \text{RedResetMntr}); X$

RedOnline(*status*)

---

[2] We use the abbreviation "*ch*?" and "*ch*!" to represent an input and output, respectively, of *any* value over channel *ch*.

$\equiv$ if *status=AllOK*
  then RedInit(*status*);
    (if *status=AllOK*
      then ((RedMain;(RBInterrupt! $\rightarrow$ RedOut!*HaltMsg*
                             $\rightarrow$ *status:=HardFail*)
         $\triangle$ RedInterruptMntr)
      else RedOut!*HaltMsg* $\rightarrow$ *status:=HardFail*
      end if);RedOnline(*status*)
  else *Stop*
  end if

RedResetMntr

$\equiv$ RedReset? $\rightarrow$ RBReset! $\rightarrow$ *Skip*
 | BRReset? $\rightarrow$ *Skip*
 | RedPower? $\rightarrow$ RedPower? $\rightarrow$ *Skip*

RedInterruptMntr

$\equiv$ RedAlarm? $\rightarrow$ RBInterrupt! $\rightarrow$ RedOut!*AlarmMsg*
            $\rightarrow$ RedAlarm? $\rightarrow$ *status:=AllOK*
 | BRInterrupt? $\rightarrow$ RedOut!*HaltMsg*
            $\rightarrow$ *status:=HardFail*

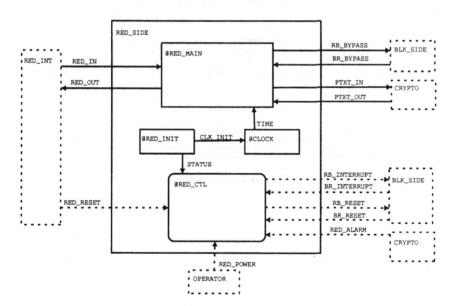

Figure 13.10. Data flow of RedSide

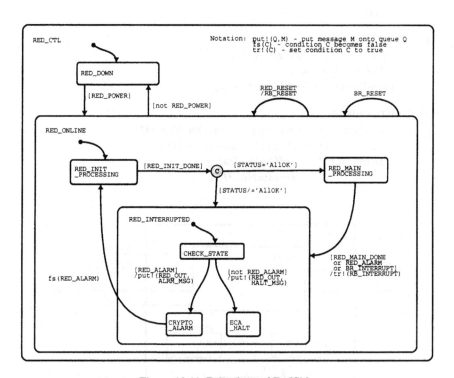

Figure 13.11. Behaviour of RedSide

These processes describe the RedSide as a process that must first be turned on. Once on, it iteratively behaves like RedOnline interruptable by RedResetMntr. Just as in Figure 13.11, RedOnline processes message traffic. RedResetMntr can interrupt this process if the ECA is reset – either external to the ECA or from the Black Side – or powered down. If an external reset occurs RedResetMntr signals the Black Side and terminates. Turning the power off simply causes it to wait for it to be toggled on before proceeding.

Upon successful initialisation, RedOnline behaves like RedMain interruptable by RedInterruptMntr. Just as the exit transition from the state RedMainProcessing in Figure 13.11, interrupts include an alarm signal from the crypto – in which case the Black Side and the external Red Domain are alerted – or an interrupt signal from the Black Side – in which case the Red Domain is alerted. If RedMain stops for any reason, an interrupt is sent to the Black Side, the Red Domain is notified, and the process hangs until RedResetMntr responds to a reset or power cycle. The Red Side can be re-initialised if a crypto alarm caused the interrupt; otherwise, it hangs until a reset or power cycle.

Showing that RedSide satisfies its critical requirements requires it to be shown that the firmware context in which the software runs does not violate these requirements. To do this we need some idea of what the software components are supposed to do. We state their required behaviour as axioms below since they are assumptions of the argument that the firmware context does not violate the critical requirements.

Axiom 1: RedMain **sat** ProperFormat$_{\text{RedSide}}$

Axiom 2: RedInit(*status*) **sat** ProperInit$_{\text{RedSide}}$
where ProperInit$_{\text{RedSide}} \equiv (tr \upharpoonright \text{RBBypass}) = \langle \rangle$

Axiom 1 is straightforward; RedMain must satisfy the same requirements as RedSide. Axiom 2 simply states that RedInit cannot send any data over the RBBypass channel.

While there are many details of the formalisation that, given Axioms 1 and 2, RedSide satisfies ProperFormat$_{\text{RedSide}}$, the argument is fairly straightforward and easy to prove using EVES. Intuitively, ProperFormat$_{\text{RedSide}}$ depends only on the presence (or absence) of certain events in the trace, namely outputs over RBBypass. The only arguments needed are that the following processes satisfy ProperFormat$_{\text{RedSide}}$:

- RedInit;
- the sequential composition of RedInit and RedMain, and
- the iteration of the composition of RedInit and RedMain.

These requirements are derived by analysing the definition of RedSide and noticing that RedResetMntr and RedInterruptMntr involve no communications over RBBypass. Axiom 2 implies that no bypass of data occurs in the Red-to-Black direction during initialisation. Thus, RedInit satisfies ProperFormat$_{\text{RedSide}}$, as does the sequential composition of RedInit with RedMain by Axiom 1. The argument that the iteration of the composition of RedInit and RedMain also satisfies the critical requirement proceeds by induction on the trace of the composition.

13.3.6 Modularising the Software

Table 13.4 shows selected portions of the ECA software module structure. At the top of the hierarchy are three modules. The Hardware Hiding Module (HwHd) contains modules that hide the details of the primary ECA interfaces. The Control Flow Module (CntlFlw) contains modules that hide the sequencing of major activities and the algorithm for establishing the direction of traffic flow. The Object Processing Module (ObjProc) contains modules that hide the algorithms used to process the primary data objects – e.g., messages (and parts thereof), format check and bypass rate parameters – and the internal representation of those objects.

Table 13.4. Software modularisation excerpt

1 Hardware Hiding Module (HwHd)
  1.1 Machine Interface Module (MchInt)
  1.2 Red Side Interface Module (RSInt)
  1.3 Red/Black Interface Module (RBInt)
  1.4 Red/Crypto Interface Module (RCInt)
  ...

2 Control Flow Module (CntlFlw)
  2.1 Red Master Control Module (RedMstrCntl)
  2.2 Red Black Crypto Decomposition Module (RBCDecomp)
  2.3 Flow Direction Module (FlwDir)
  2.4 Error Handler Module (ErrHndlr)
  ...

3 Object Processing Module (ObjProc)
  3.1 Global Utilities Module (GlobUt)
  3.2 Message Processing Module (MsgProc)
    3.2.1 Message Partition Utilities Module (MsgPrtUt)
    3.2.2 Message Format Requirements Module (MsgFmtReq)
      3.2.2.1 Format Requirement Storage Module (FmtReqStr)
      3.2.2.2 Format Checker Module (FmtChkr)
    3.2.3 Bypass Crypto Partition Module (BypCrpPrt)
  3.3 Bypass Rate Checker Module (BypRtChkr)
  ...

HwHd contains programs that implement the interface between the ECA and the network in which it is embedded, and the interfaces among the three primary components of the ECA – RedSide, BlkSide and Crypto. This module provides the basis for stating the ECA's critical requirements by setting up the framework by which the trace of the system is generated. For example, RBInt presents an abstract view of the internal data channels used for the bypass of data. The Verdi access program RBBypassPut on this interface transmits bypass data over the RBBypass channel if it returns a successful status code:

```
type RqstSts = (AllOK,SoftFail,HardFail);
```

```
procedure RBBypassPut(mvar mstate : MchInt!MState,
                      lvar byp_data : MsgPrtUt!BypData,
                      pvar rqst_sts : GlobUt!RqstSts) =
initial mstate'0=mstate
pre true
post if rqst_sts = AllOK then
        MchInt!Hist(mstate) = MchInt!Hist(mstate'0)
                                     ^ RBBypass.byp_data
     else MchInt!Hist(mstate) =
                              MchInt!Hist(mstate'0)
     end if
```

The post-condition reflects success by appending the corresponding communication event to the end of the system trace. Notice that objects called from other modules are prepended with the module name.

The specified behaviour of the access programs in HwHd permit specifying the CSP software requirements in CntlFlw. This module contains programs that sequence the major activities performed in the ECA, such as message traffic flow in the Red-to-Black or Black-to-Red direction. RedMstrCntl contains the primary RedSide software programs, RedInit and RedMain, specified as follows:

```
procedure RedMain(mvar mstate : MchInt!MState) =
pre RSProperFormat(MchInt!Hist(mstate))
post RSProperFormat(MchInt!Hist(mstate));

procedure RedInit(mvar mstate : MchInt!MState) =
pre true
post (MchInt!Hist(mstate) |^ RBBypass) = <>
```

These program specifications are the Verdi counterparts to the CSP specifications given in Axioms 1 and 2 previously. The derived requirements for RedMain reside in the RBCDecomp module:

```
function RSProperFormat(tr) =
begin
  all byp_data:
     RBBypass.byp_data in tr
     -> FmtChkr!FmtOK(byp_data)
end;
```

13.3.7 Designing the Modules

The design of RedMstrCntl and its counterpart BlkMstrCntl drive the elaboration of the requirements of the access programs of other module interfaces (Clements, 1986), particularly those in ObjProc. For example, an overview of a segment of RedMain for processing messages in the Red-to-Black direction follows:

```
procedure RedMain(mvar mstate : MchInt!MState) =
pre RSProperFormat(mstate)
post RSProperFormat(mstate)
begin
  loop
    invariant RSProperFormat(mstate)
    FlwDir!RedFlowCntl(mstate,flw_dir)
    if flw_dir = RedToBlk then
      RSInt!RedInGet(mstate,msg_data,rqst_sts)
      BypCrpPrt!BypCrpSplit(msg_data,byp_data,
                                       crp_data)
      FmtChkr!FmtChk(byp_data,fmt_chk_sts)
      if fmt_chk_sts=ValidMsg then
        BypRtChkr!BypRtChk(mstate,byp_data,
                                       rate_sts)
        if rate_sts=AllOK then
          RCInt!PTxtInPut(mstate,crp_data,rqst_sts)
          RBInt!RBBypassPut(mstate,byp_data,
                                       rqst_sts)
        else ErrHndlr!RedHndlErr(mstate,RateFail)
        end if
      else ErrHndlr!RedHndlErr(mstate,FmtFail)
      end if
    else ...
  end loop
end RedMain
```

By abstracting away much of the internal structure, error handling, and handshaking protocol, we can trivially see that, in the Red-to-Black direction, bypass data is only sent over RBBypass if the format check returns valid message. RSProperFormat requires that FmtChk satisfy the following specification:

```
procedure FmtChk(lvar byp_data : MsgPrtUt!BypData,
                 pvar fmt_chk_sts : FmtChkSts) =
pre true
post fmt_chk_sts = ValidMsg
     -> FmtOK(byp_data)
```

Of course, the difficult part is specifying the details of FmtOK and showing that the implementation of FmtChk satisfies this specification. Once done, however, FmtOK can be used to determine the actual security provided by quantifying the leakage of sensitive information possible.

13.3.8 Implementing the Modules

We translate the (executable) Verdi module design into a relatively small subset of Ada (a Verdi analog) using strict coding standards. This approach avoids many of the problematic portions of Ada; tasking, for example is not needed since the concurrently executing components are implemented on distinct processors. Access programs below the CSP trace model of abstraction, which are not implemented in Verdi, are implemented independently in Ada. Compiler optimisations performed by VADS are disabled since their correctness is difficult to assess in general. The software undergoes several levels of testing for conformance to the module specification. Unit and integration testing takes place on a Unix workstation that emulates the ultimate hardware configuration. Finally, integration testing takes place on the hardware platform constructed by E-Systems.

At the time that we applied our framework to the ECA, there was no strong basis for deciding how to combine software assurance techniques in an effective and affordable manner. A recently developed technique called testabilitity (Voas and Miller, 1995) provides a foundation for deciding how to combine the use of testing and formal verification to achieve the desired assurance at lowest cost. A fault in a program may or may not lead to a failure of the program when executed with a given set of inputs. Testability measures the probability that a failure will occur if the program contains a fault. Knowing the testability of a program permits significantly reducing the amount of random testing (based on an assumed input distribution) required to meet a specified reliability goal. Testing is an effective assurance technique for highly testable programs since, by definition, testing is likely to find any existing faults. However, formal verification (or other less rigorous methods such as human review) is needed for lowly testable programs since testing is unlikely to reveal certain problems. Testability thus permits developers to use testing and formal verification in proportion to the benefits that accrue from their application.

13.4 Automation

Creating and maintaining an assurance argument requires an organised means to update and access diverse specifications and analyses. Developers need to be able to construct and evolve assurance evidence as the system refinement progresses with concurrency control for simultaneous updates; certifiers need to be able to access and review the evidence and make suggestions on the coherence of the assurance argument. Although a particular tool may provide some of this function for the products of that tool, an application-independent database is needed to store and coordinate the diverse assurance artifacts generated during development of a system assurance argument. This assurance database provides a common and consistent interface to store, update and review specifications, proofs, and simulation, model-checking and test results, for example. The artifacts captured in the database reflect the current development status of the assurance argument, providing a window into the process for both developers and certifiers.

Certifiable assurance arguments require the management of the development process as well as the assurance evidence. A well-defined process permits a focused view of system refinement in which certifiers and developers can track the evolution of the system and assess when, where and why progress is hampered. Many tools can help define, (partially) automate, and, when appropriate, enforce the development process (Lonchamp *et al.*, 1990; Sutton *et al.*, 1995). Primarily, developers benefit from process automation, through the integration/federation of development tools, and certifiers benefit from process enforcement by ensuring that the process is applied completely and consistently. However, certifiers also gain from process automation when application of their assessment and analysis tools can be automated, and developers also gain from prudent process enforcement when their progress can be guided in proper directions.

We are building support for developing and evaluating an assurance argument using Columbia University's OzWeb tool (Kaiser *et al.*, 1996). In general, OzWeb is a tool for constructing development environments that automate and enforce a particular development process within a WWW-based context. OzWeb requires the definition of three models to characterise this environment: a data model, which defines the structure and relationship between the development artifacts, a process model, which defines a set of user-invokable operations that manipulate the development artifacts, and a coordination model, which controls access to the development artifacts. Operations of the process model are defined in terms of a set of rules; forward- and backward-chaining enable customising process automation and enforcement. Ozweb organises the development artifacts associated with a project as a sub-web of the WWW. The data can be accessed using standard Web browsers with all the advantages of distributed access and sub-web search that the browser provides. Documenting the assurance argument in hypertext improves its navigability and ultimate certifiability.

We are using OzWeb to construct the Support Environment for Security Assurance Management and Evaluation (SESAME). As shown in Figure 13.12, SESAME maintains an object-oriented database containing the assurance artifacts (e.g., specifications, proofs, test suites and coverage results) and the status of the validation and verification effort (as attributes of the assurance artifacts). A user's role determines that user's view of SESAME. Developers can construct and modify assurance artifacts. Certifiers can assess their status through detailed examination, as appropriate. Users can execute system specifications to determine their appropriateness. These operations invoke various development and certification tools, which return some execution status. SESAME then updates the assurance database and modifies object attributes appropriately. Although we are in the early phases of this work, initial application of SESAME technology to the JMCIS extension described in the introduction appears promising.

13.5 Conclusions

This chapter describes a general framework that integrates existing formal methods with less rigorous methods to develop an understandable, coherent and relevant assurance argument as a basis for the independent certification of critical systems. The framework enables a developer to produce persuasive assurance arguments that use formal methods by:

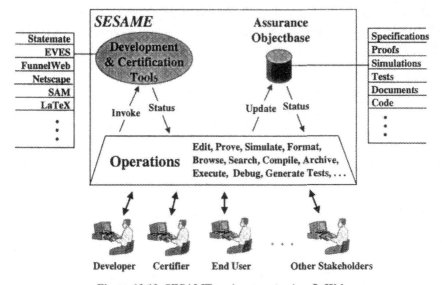

Figure 13.12. SESAME environment using OzWeb

- integrating formal specification and verification techniques into a sound software engineering and documentation methodology;
- maintaining the consistency of the assurance documentation with formal specifications and code that are input to specification, verification and compilation tools;
- providing an overview of the assurance argument and the process by which it is constructed that serves as an index into the more detailed assurance evidence, and
- automating and, when appropriate, enforcing the process of assurance argument refinement.

The generality of this approach to assurance argument refinement promotes its customisation to more complex industrial processes. We demonstrated how to apply the framework using specific, publicly available tools by formally tracing a critical requirement through the refinement of an assurance argument for an operational network security device. The examples provided show how to put the techniques into practice and can help readers decide how to apply the approach in other contexts. Future evolution of the SESAME environment will facilitate the development and certification of assurance arguments using the framework.

Acknowledgments

We wish to thank Charles Payne, Jr. for insights on applying literate programming to formal specifications; Carl Landwehr for valuable comments on earlier drafts;

and the other ECA development team members — Eather Chapman, Ken Hayman, David Kim, Charles Payne, Jr. and Maria Voreh — for their contribution to the ECA development.

CHAPTER 14

Formal Methods Through Domain Engineering

Mark Ardis and Peter Mataga

14.1 Introduction

It is almost an article of faith among advocates of formal methods that the major benefits should be most evident for large, complex software systems — yet there are few examples of the use of formal specification and analysis techniques in such systems. This is in large part because of the lack of attention paid by the formal methods community to the technology transfer process and the realities of large software development.

We believe that the application of formal methods technology in large software development hinges upon two key characteristics: the technology must be adapted to each specific application; and technology transfer must be incremental. These are not, of course, novel technology transfer principles. For example, in adapting Everett Rogers's framework (1983) for diffusion of innovations to apply to software design methodologies, Raghavan and Chand (1989) made several recommendations, including the following:

- extend the methodologies with domain-specific knowledge;
- develop techniques by which you can incrementally introduce these methodologies and by which you can seamlessly bridge the incompatibilities among the past, current, and future development practices.

In this chapter, we discuss how informal domain analysis can provide a mechanism for enabling both strategies.

The goal of formal specification is a precise description of the behaviour of the specified system. If the semantics of the specification are well enough understood (e.g., the specification can be automatically translated into code), this can be thought of as a specification of the system itself. However, it is more accurate to say that it is a description of an abstraction of the system. This distinction raises an important issue: how is this abstraction arrived at?

In the real world, software is rarely written from scratch; the documentation, code, and expertise from an existing system is essential to the production of a new (or re-engineered) component. Moreover, the new component will still typically have to interact with a legacy system. This domain knowledge must be gathered from many sources (including many people) and brought to a state of precision and abstraction sufficient to begin formalisation. Any attempt to introduce formal methods on an industrial scale must therefore inevitably deal with the technical and the social processes of domain analysis.

Properly managed as part of the software engineering process, informal but structured domain analysis can be used to gradually introduce new paradigms, tools, and skills, in particular those of formal methods. The process of attempting to describe a complex domain offers many opportunities to teach the skills of abstract modelling. As concepts become more precise they can be described in notations that are progressively more formal. The tools needed to support these notations can evolve as the notations mature, and as opportunities to take advantage of the resulting automation possibilities become apparent.

The members of our research group have been involved in several industrial projects involving domain analysis. These projects have used the FAST software engineering process, which is described in more detail in Section 14.3, in which domain commonality analysis plays a primary role. In this chapter, we describe our experiences in applying FAST in an experimental project whose long-term goal is to re-engineer a critical software component of Lucent's 5ESS switch. Our main role was to facilitate discussion between and document the ideas of a group of experts from the development organisation. The descriptions were originally composed as narrative and structured text, but have evolved into a formal language. We are now building technology to support the use of this language in future software development.

The project and the lessons we learned from our participation in it are described in Sections 14.4 and 14.5, but we first present some general remarks on strategies for technology transfer to a large software production environment.

14.2 Technology Transfer Strategies

There are two general approaches one could use for the introduction of formal methods into software development:

- Big-bang: The change to new technology is made all at once. All the users receive training, the technology is installed, and a project uses the technology.
- Evolutionary: The technology is introduced gradually, with incremental changes to the existing process and technology.

There are other strategies that one could imagine, but an important requirement of any strategy is that it eventually includes all the participants in software development.

We have found that it is easy to introduce new technology to individuals. Not all individuals embrace change, but there are enough early adopters (Rogers, 1983) willing to try anything new. On the other hand, changing the behaviour of individuals is not enough. The benefits of formal methods are often realised only after an entire project team has used them. For example, precise descriptions of designs may help to resolve inconsistencies between refinements of parts of those designs. This is only effective when all the participants in the design process use the same notation.

14.2.1 Problems with a Big-Bang Approach

There are several problems with the big-bang approach to technology transfer, especially for the introduction of formal methods.

Software engineering differs from programming in its application of many people to many tasks. It is almost impossible to change the behaviour of a group of people without their willing cooperation, and this cooperation is usually only forthcoming if the new technology makes their job easier. If new technology increases immediate overheads (though perhaps reducing it in the future or for someone else), the technology is unlikely to gain grass-roots support.

Even if people could adapt to sudden change, the software they create cannot. Any new technology must prove before adoption that it can deal comprehensively with legacy problems in code and in production process.

The handle of a hammer has been molded by the hands of generations of users. The technology of most formal methods has only been touched by a handful of users, and has usually been developed with a specific class of applications in mind. The big-bang approach does not allow information transfer from development to research to improve the toolset.

14.2.2 Benefits of an Evolutionary Approach

Social change is best accomplished through the willing participation of volunteers. Early adopters will soon convert the early majority through existing social processes. No amount of advertising or management force can compete with this approach, although grass-roots efforts will also fail without sufficient management support.

Interaction with early adopters has the important feature that the real needs of the technology's customers are pointed out. Technology that adapts to its use can be optimised for productivity and for ease of adoption. The danger here is proliferation of one-of-a-kind tools, but we are in no danger of that yet. Adaptation also demonstrates deficiencies that need to be addressed; rigid technology will often fail because it cannot acmmodate the constraints under which its customers must operate.

Just as people can learn to change, software can be revitalised. This takes patience and some trial-and-error, since for complex systems neither the technology provider nor the customer knows enough to do the job alone. Incremental introduction of technology ensures that it matches its application domain.

In general, successful technology transfer requires both management and grassroots support. Incremental introduction usually helps with both, because of the much smaller resources necessary to begin, and the opportunity to carry out the introduction with a group of early adopters. (It is worth pointing out an interesting anomaly: the big-bang approach is often easier to sell to high-level management; without grass-roots support and an appreciation of the true difficulties of process change, such efforts are rarely successful.) We believe that domain analysis provides an avenue to introduce new technology that accommodates the needs of the end user, development management, and the technology provider.

14.3 Domain Engineering

In order to introduce technology in an evolutionary way, it is important to carefully choose a domain for application. The abstractions within a domain should be stable, so that the concepts expressed in the analysis are of continuing use. The domain must be broad enough that the abstraction is applicable in more ways than one specific example.

At the same time, the domain must be restricted enough that it has some coherence, and that the resources available to analyse it are adequate. Often this restriction emerges during the analysis itself.

Domain analysis is likely to be worthwhile only if the domain and its boundaries are expected to be stable over a long period of time. This ensures that the results of the analysis will be reused enough to recover the effort involved in the analysis. (Typically this requires that the domain correspond to an organisational unit of some kind.)

The benefits of a reusable domain analysis and of increased formality of description (though not necessarily "formal methods" as the term is usually used) are the cornerstone of the FAST process for software engineering. This is not a new idea—the use of formal methods to specify reusable domain knowledge has been successfully demonstrated in several domains (Heninger, 1980; Hayes, 1985; Garlan and Delisle, 1990). A significant finding of our project is the success of a collaborative approach in selecting and adapting formalisms to describe the domain.

14.3.1 Overview of FAST

The Family-Oriented Abstraction, Specification, and Translation (FAST) process is an alternative to the traditional waterfall software development process. Recognising that most software production is iterative and produces over time a family of similar software products or components, FAST proposes that such software should be constructed by a two stage process (see Figure 14.3.1):

1. A domain engineering process builds an environment that can generate software from a compact parameterisation of a specific family member.
2. This application engineering environment is used many times to generate a sequence of customised products.

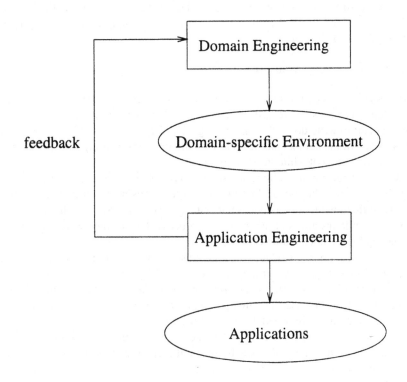

Figure 14.1. FAST process

Unanticipated requirements may necessitate modification of the environment, but such domain engineering activity should occur on a different time scale from the application engineering cycle. Specifications of family members are intended to be easily writable and updatable, and can be carried out by application engineers who may be unaware of the details of the underlying machinery.

The domain engineering stage of FAST includes a domain commonality analysis. The objectives of the analysis are:

– establishment of a common technical vocabulary;
– identification and precise description of the common characteristics of the family;
– identification and precise description of the variabilities between family members;
– formalisation of the variabilities as simple parameters.

This analysis is used to build the application engineering environment, typically by constructing a compiler for an application-oriented language that embodies the parameterisation of the family members.

The FAST process has evolved from work originally done by Parnas and his colleagues at the Naval Research Laboratory in the 1970s and 80s. A derivative version, called Synthesis, was developed by David Weiss and others at the Software Productivity Consortium. A short description and an example of the use of Synthesis is reported in (O'Connor *et al.*, 1994).

14.3.2 Commonality Analysis

The domain analysis phase of FAST is a social process that extracts knowledge from domain experts and records it in a document. We have found that these experts are reluctant to write down their knowledge, but they enjoy talking about it (Ardis, 1994). Each of the authors has acted as a facilitator in these discussions, composing the written document while the experts spoke.

Over several commonality analyses we have observed some general patterns in the discussions that occur. During early discussions many terms were defined, mostly so that the facilitators could understand the experts. Most of these terms described specific instances of technology or process. That is, they were often simple names of objects, not abstract concepts.

Later discussions introduced abstractions that had no common names, even though the experts agreed that the ideas were shared by many. In some cases there were competing names for the same thing, while in other cases there were no names. It was also often the case that attempts at precise definition of a concept exposed fundamental conflicts between the users of the concept.

As abstractions were clarified and refined, we experimented with many different representations. There was usually no single representation that adequately described all the concepts of interest. The process of expressing the representation formally often led to new insights and revision of the abstraction.

Examples were later cast in the languages of the newly-described abstractions. For example, a set of illustrative scenarios might be expressed in the abstract framework. The process of formalising the examples often yielded new insights for the experts, resulting in a new iteration of the abstraction cycle.

We believe FAST, and domain analysis in general, to offer a vehicle for formal methods technology because it addresses the critical step of determining the right abstractions. Conversely, we believe that a modicum of formal specification and analysis assists in the determination of those abstractions, but must come as part of an iterative interaction with the domain experts.

14.4 Case Study

The 5ESS (Martersteck and Spencer, 1985) is an extremely reliable system. Some reliability comes from duplication of components. Other reliability derives from the internal fault detection and recovery that is an integral part of the design. A third form of reliability comes from the fault prevention work of switch maintenance.

Configuration control is that part of the switch maintenance software that ensures that the switch is in a valid *configuration*. That is, it prevents actions that might reduce the functionality of the switch, and it compensates for dangerous configurations by taking actions that will restore safety.

Components, or *units* of the switch, may be in different states of readiness or use. Typical states are *active, standby*, and *out of service*. Any attempt to change the status of a unit is first checked by configuration control to see if it should be allowed. This checking is called *validation* of the *request*. Determining the necessary steps that should be taken to satisfy a request and carrying them out is called *realisation* of the request.

14.4.1 Objectives

The development organisation with which we worked had observed that there was an opportunity for automation of some of their work. Each year brought new desired modifications to the switch, and they needed to update the software in similar ways for each modification. The developers wanted to automate the repetitious parts of their job, so that those steps would proceed faster and with a high degree of reliability.

To get the benefits of automation, the developers realised that some restructuring of the software would be needed. Such re-engineering is a desirable process for any software that undergoes several cycles of modification. This looked like a good opportunity to achieve two goals at once.

14.4.2 History

At the beginning of the project research suggested several options for exploration. One approach was to experiment with a specific formal method on a small project. Another approach was to conduct a domain analysis, followed by development of an application-oriented language and technology to support that language. The development organisation decided to try both approaches.

Accordingly, two efforts were started at the same time:

- the domain analysis worked top-down from generalities about the area to specific details;
- a second project sought to introduce a formal notation as a substitute for traditional coding. This project worked bottom-up from details of coding to abstract states of a finite-state machine.

Each project helped the other. The second project used an early version of the domain analysis as part of their design. Experience gained from that first use helped clarify some issues for the domain analysis team.

We are now developing an application-oriented language from the domain analysis. Specifications written in this new language will be translated into the finite-state machine notation (Wagner, 1992) used by the other project, but writers of the specification will not need to see this translation. The creators of the language get the benefits of the formalism as a descriptive device — simplifying maintenance of the tools for the language. The users of the language get the benefits of performance and reliability.

14.4.3 Example abstractions

Domains. As the project started it became obvious that some bounds would need to be precisely drawn. We needed to identify which parts of the software were going to be included in our analysis, and which would be left for later. We did not have enough resources to describe all of switch maintenance in the time allotted to us. Our first attempts at this division into subdomains did not do much more than achieve this objective. After discussing our subdomain structure with some experts outside the project, we refined it to better describe the relationships between each of the subdomains.

Maintenance states. An abstraction that evolved slowly throughout the project was a generalisation of maintenance states. The standards for switching name some of these states, namely those states that technicians observe in operating the switch. There are other states that the software needs to understand, but that are not visible to the technicians.

As the 5ESS has evolved, these extra states have increased in number and type. As part of the restructuring, we wanted to identify those states that were equivalent. We introduced a mapping from a more abstract notion of state, which we called *condition*, to the specific states used in the existing software. At first this mapping was incomplete, as it did not seem to include all the information necessary to understand the exact state of some units.

As we made progress describing validation and realisation we identified precisely which pieces of information were missing from our mapping. By the end of the project we were able to precisely describe the mapping, and to ensure that all the analysis could use the condition abstraction. As new projects modify the software, we hope to simplify more and more cases by the use of this abstraction.

Relationships. A key abstraction that we discovered early in the project was the set of relationships between units. This started as a partially-vague concept, and matured to a precisely-defined abstraction.

Some of the relationships between units, such as the mate relationship, had been used by domain experts for years. It was not clear, however, whether all the connections between units could be expressed in terms of static relationships. Some units seemed to have transient relationships with other units. For example, a unit might serve as a helper for diagnosis of another unit, but that relationship did not seem to persist after the diagnosis was completed.

Also, there were units that did not seem to have any clearly-defined relationship with one another, but which were involved in one another's requests for change of status. An example of this is a unit that will become active if another unit is taken out of service. It is not obvious that all such units can be identified in terms of static relationships, since this seems to depend on the status of several units at the moment the action is performed.

Gradually, we found relationships that dealt with all these cases, and more. It became clear that many things could be based on the relationships, such as the order of validation checks to perform for a request. The relationship structure became a key structuring mechanism for several parts of our analysis. As it did, we became more and more precise in our definitions of relationship types and instances. This was helped by several iterations of informal review.

Validation/Realisation split. Another concept that was not precisely expressed at the beginning of the project was the separation of validation and realisation. The existing implementation did not make such a separation, though it was suggested by some of the structures. There were some members of the team who believed that such a separation was possible and desirable, while others did not think it possible. In this case we tested the hypothesis by examples.

As more and more examples were accumulated to support the division, we looked for mechanisms that would guarantee that this would work in all cases. Again, an iterative approach was used to find the right mechanism. Also, we continued to bring in outside reviewers informally to test our idea in wider and wider subdomains.

Denial reasons. Whenever a request is denied by validation, a reason is reported to the requester. Since there may be several reasons for denying a request, it makes sense to report only the most important reason. Otherwise, the requester might try another action that gets denied for some of the same reasons.

It is tempting to perform validation checks in the order of importance, and report the first denial. Unfortunately, we discovered several examples where this would not work. Rather than waste too much time looking for the optimal ordering for all cases, we deferred this issue until we had an ordering that was easy to understand and check. Then we tried several examples to see how many denial reasons were generated, and in which order. We discovered that there was no appreciable improvement in performance by stopping early, and there were cases where all the checks would always need to be performed. On the other hand, it turned out to be easy to assign priorities to reasons, as we had worked out a scheme for specifying each check. As we developed the mechanism for storing and reporting reasons we optimised it to avoid storing any more than the highest priority reason.

14.4.4 Example Formalisations

Validation. One of the phases of processing that takes place for each input request is validation. During this phase the intended action is checked against the current configuration to see if it can be allowed. For example, a request to remove a unit might be denied if that unit is the only available unit performing some critical function of the switch. Or, removing a unit might require that some related unit also be removed, and *that* unit might be performing a critical function.

On the other hand, some requests are more urgent than others, especially if they are made by the fault detection software of the switch. In those cases the request should almost always be allowed, even if it appears to violate normal constraints. The philosophy is that fault detection knows more about the consequences of its requests than configuration control does. For example, fault detection might request that a critical unit be removed in order to fix some more important problem.

Our first attempt at describing validations used a simple language based on relationships between units. A template containing all possible checks was constructed. Within the template we ordered the checks by relationships, such as checks of the children before checks of the parent. Individual validations would specialise the template by removing checks for relationships that did not exist, or for reasons that were not important to the request.

Since the type of validation performed depends on the requester, we started with a model that used the source of the request as a parameter to validation. This was adequate for our first version of the validation routines, but it proved unwieldy as we expanded the set of requester types.

At the same time we were trying to decide how to determine which units were critical for validation purposes. There seemed to be a conflict between deciding that a unit was (always) critical, and deciding that some requests (from certain sources) could ignore that criticality. To complicate this further, it seemed that criticality could be an attribute of a group of units, when they back up one another.

These issues were finally separated by observing that urgent requests ignored almost all the validation checks, including all the critical unit checks. We were only able to determine that after careful study of all the possible validations. We then proceeded to place criticality with groups of units, which might be a single unit in some cases.

Realisation. One part of our domain that we needed to describe precisely was the sequence of steps taken to change the configuration of the switch. We called this part of satisfying a request, "realisation." Although we knew that the atomic events that would be used in a realisation came from a small set, we struggled with the right representation of the control flow.

We started with a restricted description of control flow based on the relationships between units. Since the validation steps followed these relationships, we were tempted to describe realisation steps the same way. We tried several different orderings of steps, but none of them worked, so we abandoned this strategy.

Our second strategy was to use flowcharts. We knew that we could describe any possible sequence of events that way, and we hoped to discover a more regular pattern after making a first pass through all the realisations. This worked, and in the process of writing the flowcharts we discovered a useful abstraction. Realisations were originally proposed as responses to input requests, but we discovered that they were also useful as subroutines to be called by other realisations. In fact, they were often recursively called to traverse the parent-child hierarchy of units.

There were other sequences of steps that were logically coherent as separate units, but which did not correspond to realisations. That is, they did not satisfy input requests. We decided to treat these as macros, rather than subroutines, with the usual substitution semantics.

After several iterations of realisation descriptions in flowchart form, we started to recognise some simplifying abstractions. This made it possible to change our language to a form of pseudocode, with the standard structured programming control structures (while loops, if-then-else, and subroutine calls). In this new form we were able to build a simulator, so that we could experiment with our descriptions.

Once we were confident that the descriptions were accurate, we refined the pseudocode further so that it could be translated into a finite-state-machine language. The key step here was to reduce the complexity of the tests in the while loops and if-then-else constructs. That made it possible to use simple events to trigger transitions that corresponded to the control flow.

14.4.5 An Example Domain Engineering Process: Reviews

One of the complications of building our model was the need to bring several minds to bear on the problem. In some cases we were able to gather all the experts we needed in one place to discuss the problem. In other cases we needed to use a review process.

Formal reviews were helpful in widening the applicability of the analysis. We asked a group of experts from a related area to review our document to see if it could be used to describe their systems. We thought that many modifications would be needed to do this, but it turned out to be easier than we expected.

Informal reviews were even more valuable, as we could schedule these more often. We asked colleagues to review our work whenever we proposed a solution that needed review by experts with a broader background than we represented. These reviews often provided the simplifying assumptions we needed to propose more general abstractions.

14.5 Lessons Learned

From this and other projects that we have been involved in, some general lessons can be drawn for application of formal methods to large scale industrial software. These apply to both areas identified in the introduction: the ways in which the technology is introduced, and the ways in which it must be adaptable.

In our experience, an informal domain analysis is a critical step on the road to any level of formality. A formal paradigm cannot be introduced to what is in large part an oral culture (Ardis, 1994) without first establishing the utility of writing down the abstractions that software craftspeople actually employ.

Some of the abstractions identified in the domain analysis were simple generalisations of existing ideas, like the maintenance states. One important effect in this case was that by introducing new terminology, we were able to avoid much of the baggage that the existing terms carried for the intended audience, forcing a focus on the common abstraction rather than specific examples.

Other abstractions emerged from the interaction between the various developers' individual points of view (as well as the formal methods participants'). In the case of relationships, for example, we found the right abstraction by gradual refinement of an idea that was already familiar to the experts, though not precisely defined. Rather than attempt to formalise it at the beginning, we used working definitions to discuss other parts of our analysis. This process revealed flaws and suggested obvious improvements to the definitions. As we improved the definitions, the abstraction became more formal. For this reason, and because there was a variety of abstractions that emerged, no single preconceived formalism would have worked. Most formalisms we used were adapted in one way or another (e.g., extension, restriction, syntax modification, or non-standard semantics). The domain analysis should drive the choice of formalism.

At the same time, attempting to formalise the abstractions was clearly helpful, even when we later abandoned the formalisation in favour of a different one. Provided this flexibility is maintained, encouraging formalisation of the abstractions introduced speeds up the discovery process. Formalisation forces precise thinking about the abstractions, and makes it easier to examine the test cases to ensure that the abstractions are indeed generally applicable. Much of the validation and realisation discussion displayed this iteration of abstraction, formalisation, and testing.

The adaptability of the formalism is especially important because the formalisation is driven by the development participants. In parameterising the realisations, we tried several iterations of what amounts to language design. Parameterisation of complex variabilities in FAST is a natural application of formal methods; in retrospect we could have benefited from an earlier emphasis on formalisation. In fact, much of the formality in FAST is usually directed toward application-oriented language development. An AOL is a much more familiar (and acceptable) idea to developers than a formal specification language. Note that an essential feature of an AOL is that it may be used to generate the application; a formal description that does not support this will not be thought of as useful.

This project reveals some of the advantages of an incremental approach. First, we were able to focus our attention on problems that were small enough to solve with the resources available to us. Second, we did not attempt to involve all the domain experts at once, but gradually added more experts as we needed them, usually by asking them to review some aspect of our current analysis. This process itself was incremental; as concepts evolved, we discussed the changes with the informal reviewers. This gave them a greater sense of participation in the process, and helped them keep up with our progress.

Third, success on a small but real project is critical to both grass-roots and management support of new technology. This means dealing with legacy problems of constrained design and implementation, and with the existing development process. Even if the eventual goal is to eliminate part of the development cycle entirely, technology transfer must accommodate the evolutionary approach.

Domain analysis is a necessary prerequisite to formalisation, but is valuable without formalisation. The document produced in our analysis provided important and immediately useful reference documentation and educational material for the organisation responsible for the domain. This re-engineering aspect of domain analysis is important in selling its use. To convince development management to invest the personnel necessary to carry out domain analysis requires an intermediate pay-off. Precisely because the commonality analysis produced in the FAST process is mostly informal, it is an immediately useful and socialisable document. Once it exists, it is much easier to explain the potential benefits of a more formal approach.

14.6 Closure

As advocates of formal methods, we believe that there is much to be gained by including formal models and notations in the software engineering process. It is encouraging to see recent efforts to embed formalisms such as extended finite state machines into traditional structured analysis (Polack *et al.*, 1993) and objected-oriented methodologies (Carrington, 1992). We note that a multi-paradigm approach has already been proposed by others (Nielsen *et al.*, 1989). Our experiences indicate the dangers of a methodology that is too rigid, however; care must be taken to ensure that an appropriate formalism or range of formalisms is available for each domain. The need for accommodation of a range of abstractions suggests that multi-paradigm specification techniques might be a fruitful research area (Mataga and Zave, 1995; Zave and Jackson, 1993).

By the same token, formal methods technology developers must consider the process by which their techniques are introduced into large-scale development. It is important to recognise the gap that often exists between the form in which domain knowledge exists and the corresponding formal version. The standard researcher's approach of "throwing the tools over the wall" may work for small systems where the abstractions are well understood, but is not likely to make much impact on a large legacy system.

A structured domain analysis process provides a bridge for technology introduction, but also for the gathering of information for technology adaptation. As one might expect, one benefit from our point of view as industrial researchers is that we better understand the industries we are supporting. More generally, however, our experiences have helped us understand the needs of software developers, as well as to accumulate the beginnings of what we hope will be a specification library for our own group and the wider formal methods community.

Acknowledgments

It is a pleasure to acknowledge the colleagues whom we helped carry out the domain analysis described in the chapter: Paul Iverson, Andrew Kranenborg, Bob Olsen, and Paul Pontrelli. We thank David Weiss for introducing us to FAST, and Barbara Hornbach, Lee Stecher, Michael Merritt, and Mary Zajac for their support in conducting the project.

CHAPTER 15

Formal Verification in Railways

Arne Borälv and Gunnar Stålmarck

15.1 Introduction

The motive for adopting a formal method is an improved development process with resource savings, a reduced number of errors, and reduced time-to-market. That formal methods potentially can give these benefits is not very controversial since formal methods consider software construction just like construction in any other traditional engineering discipline: by model building and model analysis before construction and production takes place. A model is an abstraction of a system to be constructed with the advantage that it can be analysed thoroughly for its intended, and also unintended, design characteristics. This prior-to construction analysis is used in many traditional engineering disciples, e.g., in mechanics of materials in order to establish the solidity of constructions. It seems very likely that, with the appropriate methodology and tool support, prior-to construction analysis based on mathematics and logic is equally beneficial to use in software development as related methods are in traditional engineering disciplines.

Most potential formal methods users are experts not in logic and mathematics, but in specific application domains such as the railway signalling, avionics or process industries. Because of this, they are seeking formal methods that can be used in the same fashion as, for instance, the author uses a word processor. The author is not aware of how the functionality of the word processor is achieved, but invokes it as needed in order to be a productive writer. The algorithms and representations used in, for instance, string matching and spell-checking, are not of interest to the user of the word processor. He wants to use them transparently in order to improve efficiency and increase the quality of his work. The same approach is expected in formal methods tools; application domain experts ideally want to use formal methods tools that hide as much as possible of the underlying techniques giving the required support for system specification, validation and verification. Of course, since the technical challenges in formal methods are much harder than the algorithms used in a word processor, one cannot automate all formal methods. Some parts will always require expert knowledge in formal methods, whereas many industrial problems can be solved in the word processor fashion using existing formal methods. For instance, see the case study in Section 15.4.1, or consider the success of many existing circuit equivalence checkers. Both industry and the formal methods community would gain from finding and solving these industrial problems, since industry would get a fast return on its investment in formal methods, and would be encouraged to take an interest in more advanced formal methods.

This chapter presents formal methods used in Swedish railway signalling, developed by the formal methods company Prover Technology (see Section 15.1.2). The formal methods are tailored for the development of software-based interlocking systems from ABB Daimler-Benz Transportation Signal (ADtranz), and are designed for experts in railway signalling, not experts in formal methods. The formal methods include: (1) tool support for formal verification of safety requirements in the generic interlocking software used by ADtranz; (2) automatic formal modelling of complete interlocking systems in a commercial formal verification tool; (3) implementation independent formal specification of system-level safety requirements reflecting the Swedish safety regulation (Swedish National Rail Administration, 1996); and (4) automatic translation of implementation independent specifications into specifications of the system level safety requirements for a specific interlocking implementation. All steps are integrated in the development environment of ADtranz and are based on commercial standard software: the verification tool Prover[1] (see Section 15.3.3).

From the point of view of industrialising methods, the most important question is how to develop formal methods that are usable by application engineers, and that are so powerful that they will give users a return on their investment. The methods and tools applied to railway interlocking presented here are used in Sweden by industry (ADtranz) as well as by the Swedish National Rail Administration. All steps above ((1)—(4)) are used regularly in production today. The four studies reported here will illustrate the successful use of this approach, though the industrial use today differs somewhat from the descriptions given here.

The tool or verification of safety properties of ADtranz's generic interlocking software has been in use since 1989 at both ADtranz and the Swedish National Rail Administration. ADtranz reports that the introduction of this tool has reduced their software development costs by more than 30%, and significantly improved quality (see Section 15.4.1).

15.1.1 Chapter Outline

This chapter is organised as follows. In Section 15.1.2 we introduce the company, Prover Technology. In Section 15.1.3 we argue that basing automated formal methods on a low-level language such as propositional logic does not preclude the use

---

[1] Prover is a trademark of Prover Technology.

of high-level system description languages, nor does it limit the possibility of proving safety properties. On the contrary, it gives some advantages when it comes to making formal methods industrially applicable. In Section 15.2, we briefly present ADtranz's interlocking system development and the formal methods used. In Section 15.3, the underlying theorem proving techniques used by Prover Technology are presented (this may be omitted by readers not interested in verification techniques and system modelling). Studies illustrating applied formal methods are presented in Section 15.4. The chapter is summarised in Section 15.5.

15.1.2 Prover Technology

Prover Technology AB, founded in 1989, is a company working exclusively with formal methods, specifically based on a patented proof procedure (Stålmarck, 1989). The company develops computer-based tools[2] for automated formal verification, performs formal methods R&D (Carlsson *et al.*, 1997), and formal methods consultancy. The company currently has 30+ employees. Prover Technology focuses on the industrialisation of formal methods within five major industries: avionics (Åkerlund *et al.*, 1996), automotive, railways (Borälv, 1997), process control (Widebäck and Ekenberg, 1996) and hardware verification (Sheeran and Borälv, 1997; Borälv and Östberg, 1997).

15.1.3 Propositional-Level Verification

Consider again the author's use of a word processor. Ideally, potential formal methods users want to use formal methods tools in the same fashion, where as much as possible of the underlying technique is hidden. This claim is not meant to be derogatory regarding the intellectual capacity of the potential user; instead, we are striving to construct rugged, easy-to-use tools liberating the user from having to understand underlying techniques. It does not make any sense to teach a writer how a string matching algorithm works in order to use the word processor. Nor does it make any sense to teach an application engineer to become an expert in model checking algorithms.

Hence, automation becomes crucial and therefore must influence the specification and proof techniques that are chosen. Figure 15.1 illustrates the trade-off between expressiveness and automated proof power.

For instance propositional logic has several advantages as a modelling and specification language: it allows for a high degree of automation in the proof process; it is sufficiently expressive for modelling relevant aspects of many industrial problems; and the language is known by engineers. However, it is not very convenient to specify systems directly in propositional logic. Hence, a suitable (with respect to the application domain) higher level language can be used in the specification of systems; it can then be compiled into a low level representation before verification takes place (see Figure 15.2).

---

[2] Currently distributed in Sweden (by Prover Technology), in France (by Teuchos) and in the UK (by the National Physical Laboratory).

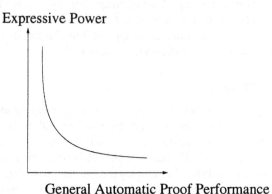

Figure 15.1. Trade-off between proof power and expressive power

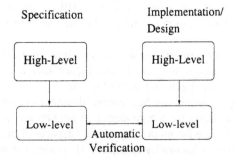

Figure 15.2. Compilation of high-level descriptions into a low level

Prover Technology's formal methods tools are based on an efficient theorem-prover for propositional logic together with compilers from various design and specification languages down to the level of propositional logic. Of necessity, this limits the range of problems that can be addressed, but many important industrial problems can be solved. The approach of low-level verification with input generated from higher-level descriptions is similar to the compilation of high-level programming languages into a low-level representation before execution takes place, or model checking using BDDs.

15.2 Railways Formal Methods

ADtranz's computerised interlocking systems are based on Sternol[3] (Ericsson Dansk Signalindustri, 1989), a programming language for *generic* interlocking programs. Generic means that any interlocking system can be built from one and the same Sternol program. The generic program consists of a number of logical objects corresponding to physical railyard objects such as points and signals. A logical object specifies the behaviour of all objects of the same type. The individual behaviour of an object instance is set using individualised values. For instance, an individualised value determines the number of lights of a signal object. Similar values are set for all properties that are not common to all objects of the same type.

The complete interlocking instance is specified in the *site file*, containing information about the physical objects in the interlocking, which logical object each physical object should be controlled by, the connections between objects and the individualised values for each object.

Figure 15.3 describes the steps in the formal methods that we, the formal methods technology supplier, the customer (ADtranz), and the relevant authority (the Swedish National Rail Administration), have produced for the development and certification of Sternol-based railyard interlockings:

1. a formal verification tool is used in the development of the generic Sternol program in order to prove that the Sternol program satisfies a set of safety requirements, and an equivalence checking feature is used for inspection of new revisions of Sternol code and also for strengthening the confidence in the Sternol compiler (see Section 15.4.2);
2. formal methods consultants and railway interlocking experts produce an implementation independent specification of the safety requirements for arbitrary interlockings (for a specific railway administration[4]);
3. a tool generates a formal model of an interlocking implementation, based on the Sternol program and the information in the site file;

---

[3] The <u>S</u>terner and <u>N</u>ordenfors <u>L</u>anguage.

[4] In Sweden, the safety regulation is set by the Swedish National Rail Administration (1996).

4. the implementation independent specification is automatically instantiated using the interlocking information in the site file, producing the specification for the interlocking instance;
5. the formal model of the interlocking implementation is automatically proved to fulfil its specification and the proof is logged onto a file;
6. the proof is checked separately by a proof checker in order to strengthen confidence in the correctness of the proof[5].

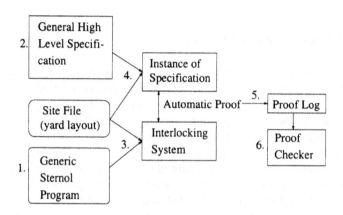

Figure 15.3. Formal methods for railway interlockings

Since the automatically generated proof may be inspected separately, in principle even manually, the critical parts in this model are the translators for producing the system model and the specification instance. Producing the implementation independent specification requires expert knowledge in both formal methods and railways. The extra effort is worthwhile since the general specification allows the automatic generation of specifications for each specific interlocking instance. The model in Figure 15.3 allows for a high degree of industrialisation, since most of the formal methods expertise is needed only in step 2, and the remaining steps can be automated to a great extent. Currently all the steps above are applied in production at ADtranz in the development of new interlockings. The studies in Section 15.4 illustrate each step. Furthermore, the studies illustrate the efficiency of the verification technology, and that the results of using it are measurable by industrial users in a quantitative way: significant resources are saved and errors are reduced.

ADtranz reports that using the formal methods described above has reduced the verification phase by 90%.

Problems and failures that occurred in early efforts at system-level verification (Peterson, 1996) have been eliminated by coding rules and structure in interlocking

---

[5] This is a requirement from ADtranz in order to replace parts of the system-level test phase with formal proofs.

software coding, introduced in order to make systems provable. The customer identifies the introduced *design for verifiability* as an advantage, since it facilitates the use of automated verification.

15.3 Technical Description

In this section we briefly describe the technique underlying the case studies in Section 15.4: the computation model for synchronous systems; the formal language used to model synchronous systems; the reduction to a simplified version of the formal language; and the automated proof procedure.

The techniques presented are not aimed at general-purpose specification and verification. The techniques are rather simple but highly automated, and fit well into a number of industrial application areas where the problems can actually be reduced to propositional logic and integer constraint problems.

15.3.1 Modelling Synchronous Systems

We will consider a simple version of synchronous systems (Halbwachs, *et al.*, 1991). We assume systems to be executed in discrete steps. In each step a combinational function f is computed. The function f is applied to input values and values of the internal memory cells and computes output values and updated system memory.

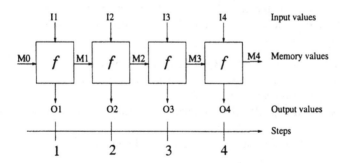

Figure 15.4. The synchronous system model

The above approach is sufficient to describe systems with finite memory, e.g., Turing machines with finite tape. Our aim here is not to give natural, readable and easy to understand system models, but only to represent the various system functions formally. System functions and system requirements are axiomatised in a first order language, a timed propositional arithmetic (see Section 15.3.2). We only consider discrete linear time: the natural numbers N are used as the step domain. Quantification is restricted to the step type N. Furthermore, we only consider systems with variables (input, output and memory) of type Boolean (B) and type integer (Z).

In our modelling language, each system variable is treated as a function from steps to its data type, i.e., a Boolean variable will be treated as a monadic predicate on N and an integer variable as a function from N to Z.

The system functions are represented by axioms defining the initial state and the transition function of the system.

The transition diagram in Figure 15.5 will be used to illustrate our modelling language before it is defined in Section 15.3.2.

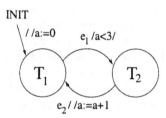

INIT

Figure 15.5. A small transition diagram

Informally the transition diagram is interpreted as follows::

1. initially (at step 0) the system is in state T_1 and a is assigned the value 0;
2. a transition takes place from T_1 to T_2 at a given step t+1 if e1 is true (has occurred) at t+1 and the value of a at t is lower than 3;
3. a transition will take place from T_2 to T_1 at a given step t+1 if e2 is true at t+1. Furthermore, when a transition from T_2 to T_1 occurs, the value of a is increased by one.

e1 and e2 are considered as Boolean input variables that are true at a given step t iff[6] the corresponding event has occurred. e1 and e2 are assigned their values outside the system. The Boolean variables T_1 and T_2 are true at step t if, and only if, they evaluate to true at step t. Finally, a is an integer variable evaluated to an integer value at each step.

The interface to the transition function for Figure 15.5 is illustrated by Figure 15.6.

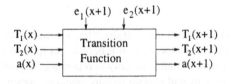

Figure 15.6. The sample system model interface

---

[6] If, and only if.

In our modelling language we treat T_1 and T_2 as one-place predicates with a step argument. $T_i(t)$ expresses that T_i holds at t. Also e1 and e2 are treated as one-place predicates on steps and a will be considered as a one-place function from steps to integers; a(t) is interpreted as the value of a at t. Our modelling language also includes the function symbols s (for successor) and +, and relation symbols < and = operating on steps.

The system function model will consist of axioms for the initial state and axioms for the transition function. Initially T_1 holds and a has the value zero:

$$T_1(0) \land \neg T_2(0) \land a(0) = 0 \qquad (15.1)$$

T_1 holds at s(x) iff either a transition is taken from T_2 or if T_1 holds at x and no transition is taken to T_2 at s(x):

$$\forall x(T_1(s(x)) \leftrightarrow ((T_2(x) \land e2(s(x))) \lor (T_1(x) \land \neg(e1(s(x)) \land a(x) < 3)))) \qquad (15.2)$$

T_2 holds at s(x) iff either a transition is taken from T_1 or if T_2 holds at x and no transition is taken to T_1 at s(x):

$$\forall x(T_2(s(x)) \leftrightarrow ((T_1(x) \land e1(s(x)) \land a(x) < 3) \lor (T_2(x) \land \neg e2(s(x))))) \qquad (15.3)$$

a is assigned a+1 iff a transition is taken from T_2 to T_1 at s(x):

$$\forall x(a(s(x)) = a(x) + 1 \leftrightarrow (T_2(x) \land e2(s(x)))) \qquad (15.4)$$

a is assigned a iff no transition is taken from T_2 to T_1 at s(x):

$$\forall x(a(s(x)) = a(x) \leftrightarrow \neg(T_2(x) \land e2(s(x)))) \qquad (15.5)$$

The above example illustrates our modelling language and how it is used to formalise system functionality.

15.3.2 Modelling Language

Assume that we are given a system S with input variables $P_1, \ldots, P_j$ of type B and $a_1, \ldots, a_k$ of type Z, output variables $Q_1, \ldots, Q_l$ of type B and $b_1, \ldots, b_m$ of type Z, and memory variables $R_1, \ldots, R_n$ of type B and $c_1, \ldots, c_o$ of type Z. We then give the following first order signature in our modelling framework, here called TPA for Timed Propositional Arithmetic:

Step part:
Individual step variables: $x, y, z, \ldots$
Individual step constants: $0, 1, 2, \ldots$
Step function symbols: s and $+$
Step relation symbols: $<$ and $=$
Quantifiers: $\forall$ and $\exists$

System part:
For each P_i a monadic predicate symbol P_i

For each Q_i a monadic predicate symbol $\mathsf{Q_i}$
For each R_i a monadic predicate symbol $\mathsf{R_i}$
For each a_i a one place function symbol $\mathsf{a_i}$
For each b_i a one place function symbol $\mathsf{b_i}$
For each c_i a one place function symbol $\mathsf{c_i}$
Individual integer constants: $-1, 0, 1, \ldots$ (for integers)
Functional symbols: $+, -$ and $\times$
Relation symbols: $<$ and $=$
Connectives: $\neg, \wedge, \vee, \rightarrow$ and $\leftrightarrow$
Brackets: (and)

We define the following categories of expressions.
Time terms:

1. individual step variables and step constants are time terms;
2. if t and u are time terms then so are s(t) and (t+u).

Integer terms:

1. integer constants are integer terms;
2. if t is a time term and a is a one place function symbol then a(t) is an integer term;
3. if w and v are integer terms then so are (w+v), (w−v) and (w × v).

Step expressions:

1. if t and u are time terms then (t<u) and (t=u) are step expressions;
2. if T and U are step expressions then so are $\neg T$, $(T \wedge U)$, $(T \vee U)$, $(T \rightarrow U)$ and $(T \leftrightarrow U)$.

Formulas:

1. step expressions are formulas;
2. if w and v are integer terms then $(w < v)$ and $(w = v)$ are formulas;
3. if t is a time term and P is a monadic predicate symbol, then $P(t)$ is a formula;
4. if A and B are formulas then so are $\neg A$, $(A \wedge B)$, $(A \vee B)$, $(A \rightarrow B)$ and $(A \leftrightarrow B)$;
5. if A is a formula and x is a step variable then $\forall x A$ and $\exists x A$ are formulas.

We only consider structures of the signature where the step and integer constants are assigned their intended values in N and Z respectively, the usual arithmetic function and relation symbols are interpreted according to their intended meaning, each monadic predicate symbol is assigned a subset to N and each one place function symbol is assigned a total function from N to Z. A structure fulfilling the above conditions will be called a TPA structure.

A formula A is said to be *TPA-valid*, $\vdash_{TPA} A$, iff A is true in all TPA structures according to the standard definition of true in a first order structure. We also say that a TPA formula A is a *TPA consequence* of a set Δ of TPA formulas, $\Delta \vdash_{TPA} A$, iff each TPA structure satisfying all formulas in Δ also satisfies A.

The synchronous system structure and the TPA language is used as a semantical basis for system modelling. However, most TPA problems arising from system verification are reducable to problems in weak sub-theories of TPA.

In the general case, TPA is undecidable. Expressiveness and computational complexity issues of real-time logics similar to TPA are treated in (Alur and Henzinger, 1993).

Reduction to Quantifier-free problems. TPA is used as a modelling language. However, to actually verify properties of systems axiomatised in TPA, we reduce the problems to quantifier-free propositional arithmetic and apply Prover (see Section 15.3.3 below). This reduction can be performed automatically for some particular types of requirement formulas. However, these mathematically very simple forms are sufficient to express most safety requirements.

Prover is capable of finding proofs in a rather weak quantifier-free subsystem of TPA. We use the notation $\Delta \vdash_P A$ to express that A is derivable from Δ in the proof system of Prover.

The reduction relies on the shape of the system axioms as well as the shape of the requirement formulas. System axiomatisations can always be expressed by quantifier-free formulas. The initial values are given by ground formulas and the transition function as formulas in one single step variable. In what follows, let $S(x) = A(0) \wedge A_1(x) \wedge \ldots \wedge A_n(x)$ be an axiomatisation of a system S.

In the case studies below in Section 15.4, all requirements can be put on the form $\forall x B(x)$, where $B(x)$ is quantifier-free and contains x as its single free variable. Hence, our verification obligations will always have the form $\forall x\, S(x) \vdash \forall x B(x)$. In order to establish $\forall x\, S(x) \vdash \forall x B(x)$, we perform P-derivations using one of the following approaches (see Figure 15.7):

1. $\{S(t_1), \ldots, S(t_n)\} \vdash_P B(x)$, for suitable choices of time terms $t_1, \ldots, t_n$.
2. $\{S(t_1), \ldots, S(t_n)\} \vdash_P B(0)$, and $\{S(t_1), \ldots, S(t_n)\} \vdash_P B(x) \rightarrow B(s(x))$, for suitable choices of time terms $t_1, \ldots, t_n$.

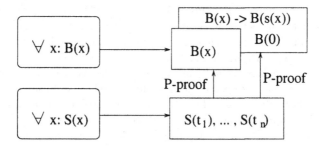

Figure 15.7. Verification of TPA requirements using reduction to quantifier-free formulas

15.3.3 Prover — The Stålmarck Method Implementation

Prover is an automated theorem prover which is used as the proof engine in the tools by Prover Technology. Prover is based on a proof system for propositional integer arithmetic. The propositional part of the proof procedure was invented and patented by (Stålmarck, 1989) and is further described in, for example, (Harrison, 1996). The method is based on refutation graphs similar to Mondadori's proof trees (Mondadori, 1988), (D'Agostino, 1990). Stålmarck's proof graphs extend Mondadori's proof trees with a more efficient set of propagation rules, a restricted use of lemmas, resulting in series parallel graphs instead of trees, and a weak extension of the subformula principle. However, the efficiency of Stålmarck's method is essentially due to the so called saturation procedure, an exhaustive search procedure for shallow proof graphs. Stålmarck defines a notion of proof depth, corresponding to the maximum number of simultaneously free assumptions in a proof. The saturation procedure then exhaustively searches for proofs up to a given depth n. The saturation procedure for a given n is polynomially time bounded in the length of the input formulas.

The saturation procedure has an obvious advantage over well-known proof techniques such as BDD based methods (Bryant, 1995) in applications with very large formulas and where shallow proofs can be expected. Shallow proofs can often be expected in verification and validation applications as opposed to, for instance, combinatorial optimisation. In a recent study the Stålmarck method proved very efficient compared to BDD based methods and the Otter prover for the verification of formulas originating from the Dutch railway field (Groote *et al.*, 1994).

The Prover implementation extends Stålmarck's method with propagation rules for integer constraints. A similar extension of the method is described in (Carlsson *et al.*, 1997).

15.4 Industrial Formal Methods Studies

This section presents four studies illustrating the application of the formal methods in Figure 15.3 in railway interlocking at ADtranz and the Swedish National Rail Administration. In the first study, we show how automated formal verification has been used to eliminate a major problem in the development process of Sternol, ADtranz's generic interlocking software. In the second study, a formal method for comparing interlocking software is presented. The third study presents a tool for automated formal modelling of ADtranz's Sternol-based interlockings, and illustrates how safety breaches have been eliminated. The last study shows how an implementation independent specification for small railway interlockings was produced, and how it was instantiated and used to verify a relay-based interlocking implementation. Taken together, the studies cover all steps in the formal methods application model in Figure 15.3.

The technical description given in Section 15.3 is intended to be used as a framework for understanding the case studies that follow, though the techniques are used implicitly. For example, the language TPA is not used. Instead the propositional logic level is used directly.

15.4.1 Finding Double Values

Around 1988-89, ADtranz changed the language used in their computerised railway interlocking systems. Instead of using a subset of Fortran, a new language called Sternol was adopted. At that time, a major headache for the development of Sternol software was to ensure that a run-time error known as *double values* could not occur. When a double value occurs the interlocking is forced to enter a safe state in which all signals show the aspect stop, and thereafter the system has to be restarted manually. Obviously this error led to reduced availability of the interlocking functionality each time it occurred, and furthermore cost significant resources to correct. Even a very long software test phase could not guarantee the absence of potential double values in the software.

The Problem. The proprietary language Sternol used for ADtranz's computerised interlockings is a generic declarative language. A Sternol program consists of a set of logical object types such as points and signals, corresponding to physical objects in the railyard. That the Sternol software is generic means that each object in the railyard of the same type, for instance all signal objects, are controlled by the same piece of software. The individual behaviour of an object instance is set using individualised values, e.g., one individualised value determines the number of lights on a signal object. Each logical object consists of a set of finite domain integer variables, and the value of a variable V is determined by its equation group. The equation group is a sequence of equations, each consisting of an expression (V_i) and a guard (C_i):

$$V := V_1 : C_1;$$
$$V := V_2 : C_2;$$
$$\vdots$$
$$V := V_n : C_n;$$

The variable is assigned the integer expression if the guard, a Boolean condition on finite domain constraints, is true. Sternol is executed in the target machine by two separate systems; the first system evaluates the guards starting with the first guard in the group, and the second system starts with the last guard. If the two systems should find different guards to apply, we have a double value.

The Solution. A sufficient condition for ensuring that double values do not occur is that *at least one* of the guards in the group applies:

$$\vdash C_1 \vee \ldots \vee C_n \tag{15.6}$$

and that *at most one* guard applies ($\forall i, j : i \neq j$):

$$\vdash \neg(C_i \wedge C_j) \tag{15.7}$$

Finding double values using Prover Technology's automated verification was more efficient than any other method known to ADtranz, so the special-purpose tool CVT was developed (Stålmarck and Säflund, 1990; Widebäck, 1993). The CVT tool reads a Sternol program, generates the double value specification (15.6 and 15.7 above) and automatically verifies it against an automatically generated formal model of the program. If the program does not fulfil the specification, all countermodels can be inspected graphically.

Figure 15.8 illustrates a potential double value when a variable can be assigned two values simultaneously (where the true arithmetic constraints are highlighted).

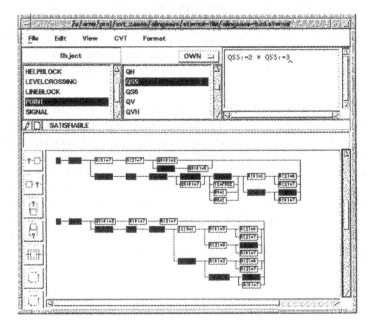

Figure 15.8. A double value model displayed in CVT

The double value check for a complete Sternol program is performed automatically by pushing a button, and typically takes half a minute CPU time (on a Sparc 10 work-station). CVT was commercially released in 1990 and has been part of ADtranz's development environment since then. After the introduction of CVT at ADtranz, no run-time errors due to double values have occurred (with one interesting exception, see Section 15.4.2). ADtranz estimates that using the CVT tool has reduced the software test phase time by at least 60%, and the overall software development cost by at least 30%.

15.4.2 Comparing Interlocking Software

Swedish interlocking systems are inspected by the Swedish National Rail Administration. The main supplier of interlockings in Sweden is ADtranz and most of the interlockings delivered are based on the Sternol language. In order to facilitate inspection of new revisions of Sternol interlocking packages, the Swedish National Rail Administration needed a tool for comparing Sternol programs. Earlier inspections of new revisions were performed manually. An equivalence checker for Sternol programs would make the inspection safer and more efficient, since the tool could point out the parts that needed to be inspected further.

ADtranz too could make use of such a tool in the development of Sternol. In spite of the use of CVT for finding and eliminating double values, a double value once occurred in a railway yard. A closer inspection revealed that the double value was caused by an error in the Sternol compiler. At that point ADtranz wrote a decompiler, which generated a second Sternol program that should have been equivalent to the original program. However, it was not possible to inspect the decompiled version manually (since it was based on a 2-complement representation). Proving that the original Sternol program is equivalent to the decompiled version would increase the confidence in the correctness of the Sternol compiler, since it is not very likely that both the original compiler and the decompiler would exhibit the same error.

Since both ADtranz and the Swedish National Rail Administration could make use of an equivalence checker tool for Sternol, a comparison functionality was developed as an extension to CVT in 1991. The comparison functionality first reports all static differences in the set of object types, variables, equations and assignments in two Sternol programs. Next, for all common variables in common objects, the guards in the corresponding equations are compared pairwise by the following two analyses:

$$\vdash C_{i_1} \rightarrow C_{i_2}$$
$$\vdash C_{i_2} \rightarrow C_{i_1}$$

The differences are reported based on the results of the two analyses above and any static differences in the two Sternol programs.

In the beginning of the 1990s, when Sternol-based interlocking systems were still rather new, as many as 10 revisions per year were made by the Swedish National Rail Administration. The financial benefits of using the CVT tool for inspection have not been estimated, but the Swedish National Rail Administration reports that the equivalence checker has clearly made inspection easier, safer and more efficient. CVT is still used for inspection of new Sternol program revisions (only one or two inspections are done per year nowadays) and for checking compiler correctness.

15.4.3 Automatic System Modelling

ADtranz puts a significant effort into system-level test and simulation for each delivered interlocking package[7]. Replacing parts of this inefficient and incomplete veri-

---

[7] A typical system-level safety requirement states that two facing signals should never be able to show a green light simultaneously.

fication procedure with formal proofs could potentially save a lot of time and also improve quality as given by formal proofs. In 1995 the SVT tool was developed[8] (Borälv, 1997), which includes a translator from a Sternol interlocking system into a formal model in NP-Tools[9]. NP-Tools is Prover Technology's general-purpose formal verification toolbox. SVT also includes all functionality of the CVT tool (See Sections 15.4.1 and 15.4.2). SVT and NP-Tools are currently used in the development of new interlocking systems at ADtranz.

Madrid Subway Station Lago. In 1997, ADtranz was given an assignment to supplement the validation phase of the Madrid subway station Lago using a formal approach with NP-Tools and SVT. The Lago system was already in test use. The interlocking system consists of approximately 30 coded track sections with an electronic signalling function, six ordinary light signals and four border sections handling the interaction with neighbouring interlockings (see Figure 15.9).

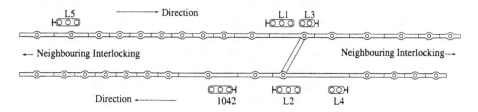

Figure 15.9. The Lago subway interlocking layout

The assignment was not specified in detail concerning requirements to be proven, so ADtranz produced formal requirements for the system in an ad-hoc fashion. Requirements were formulated only for the top-most track line (see Figure 15.9) covering only a subset of all safety requirements. The methodology for producing the safety requirements was quite simple (see Figure 15.10). Firstly, each logical object with safety-critical output values is identified. Secondly, when a certain value of the safety-critical signal is output, the safety condition (*safe*) that should hold for the objects positioned after the object in the direction of travel is identified. The safety condition was divided into two parts: the object should not be occupied; and if the object is a point object, it should be locked in the direction of travel. The safety requirements produced from Figure 15.10 (the last track object has a point object connected to it) are to be read as "if TRACK0 emits signal S with value 1, the next track object in the direction of travel should be *safe*, if TRACK0 emits signal S with value 2 the next two track object should be *safe*", and so on. Similar safety requirements were produced for similar object segments in the station topology.

Some of the requirements could be proven falsifiable and countermodels were given in NP-Tools. Understanding the countermodels required expert knowledge of

---

[8] SVT (Sternol Verification Tool) is a trademark of ADtranz Signal.
[9] NP-Tools is a trademark of Prover Technology.

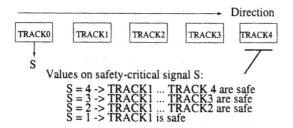

Values on safety-critical signal S:
S = 4 -> TRACK1 ... TRACK 4 are safe
S = 3 -> TRACK1 ... TRACK3 are safe
S = 2 -> TRACK1 ... TRACK2 are safe
S = 1 -> TRACK1 is safe

Figure 15.10. A model for producing safety requirements

the Sternol language, since countermodels are given as values on the Sternol variables (see Figure 15.11). However, for a person with this competence, the countermodels were not hard to interpret. The countermodels were due to a single type of error, namely that the point did not need to be locked in the direction of travel even if the value of the signal indicated that this was the case. Points can actually be in three states: left, right or out of control, i.e. somewhere between left and right. In this case, the point was only guaranteed not to be in the *wrong* direction.

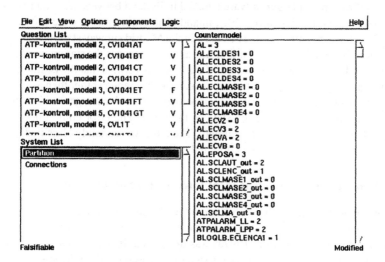

Figure 15.11. A countermodel for one of the safety requirements

The error found was not considered very safety-critical by ADtranz Sweden for two reasons. Since the point was not a facing point but a trailing point, passing it when it is not in control would have forced it into control, possibly with some minor damage caused to train and track, and since the point was close to the station platform, the train speed would not be very high when passing it. If the point in question had been a facing point, the error could have caused the train to de-rail in the extreme case. The corrected software could be proven to fulfil all requirements, and the error was reported to the Spanish ADtranz division.

All in all some 65 safety requirements were produced. Producing the requirements and performing the verification took about 40 man hours in total, the analysis being done by one person at ADtranz Sweden. The NP-Tools analysis consisted of about 36 000 subformulas, and used 6 MB of memory (including the memory overhead for NP-Tools, about 1.2 MB). The total analysis time for disproving the requirements was 19 seconds[10].

In order to replace parts of ADtranz's extensive system-level test phase with formal proofs, ADtranz requires that proofs can be checked separately. Therefore Prover, the Stålmarck Method implementation which is used as the proof engine in CVT, SVT and NP-Tools, is augmented with the possibility of logging proofs (Jonasson, 1996). Prover-generated proofs are human-readable due to their simple structure, and can be checked by a relatively simple proof checker program. This strengthens confidence in the proofs generated, especially since the proof checker can be written using a rigorous formal approach.

Other Interlocking Studies Using SVT and NP-Tools. A similar approach to the Lago station analysis was used by Prover Technology in a recent (1997) system-level verification of a larger railyard situated in Finland between Vasa and Helsinki. The system was developed by VR, Finland. The requirements were produced according to the same methodology as used in the Madrid subway station analysis, but were more involved due to the station size and also because the station was based on a different design principle. One part of the analysis verified that the positions of the points that are part of a locked train route cannot be changed other than as specified. A counter-example showed a situation in which a control message was lost, thereby making it possible to change the state of the point. The error could under certain circumstances have caused a de-railment. The error was certainly classified as being safety-critical, and is now being corrected at the station in question.

15.4.4 Implementation Independent Interlocking Specification

In a recent project for the Swedish National Rail Administration, an implementation independent formal specification of the functional safety requirements for small railyard interlockings (Eriksson, 1997a) was developed. In a second step, the specification was instantiated for verification of a relay-based interlocking system in Sweden. The interlocking implementation was modelled using the graphical editor of NP-Tools. Using NP-Tools' automated formal verification, it was possible to prove that the interlocking, with one exception (Eriksson, 1997b), did satisfy the specification. The objective of this project was to investigate if it was possible to produce an implementation independent specification for interlockings, and whether it could be used as the basis for inspection of new interlocking systems. A formal specification can significantly improve efficiency in inspection, and since automated inspection would increase efficiency even more, it was also interesting to investigate if it was

---

[10] The machine used was an Hewlett-Packard 9000/715 workstation.

feasible to automatically translate the implementation independent specification to a specification for the interlocking instance, and use this in the analysis. As we will show, this was indeed the case. The small railyard type was selected as the target for the specification since a new generation of small railyard interlockings (Alister) is to be procured by the Swedish National Rail Administration in the near future.

The Specification in Predicate and Propositional Logic. The formal specification is, within the given framework, a complete formal specification of the functional safety requirements of the interlocking function for small railyards. The restrictions imposed on the specification within this project (Eriksson, 1997a) do not preclude the inclusion of requirements for larger railyards, or a larger set of functional safety requirements. The formal specification was developed using the Delphi tool. Delphi (Ericsson Utvecklings AB, 1993) is a prototype tool designed for high-level formal specification of telecommunication services, developed by Prover Technology and Ericsson Utvecklings AB[11]. Delphi includes Prover Technology's verification module Prover, and offers formal verification and formal simulation of Delphi specifications.

A Delphi specification contains two parts: a conceptual model and a set of transition rules. The conceptual model is a first-order axiomatisation of invariants, time independent facts about the application domain. The transition rules define system change. The Delphi tool provides a graphical language to simplify modelling. The graphical language is automatically translated to first-order logic. The graphical language contains entity types with associated states and relations. The conceptual model for this study was made graphically as shown in Figure 15.12 (in Swedish).

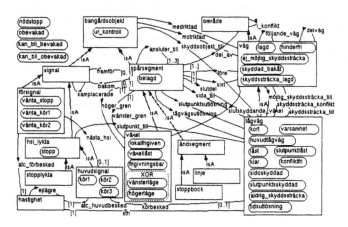

Figure 15.12. The graphical part of the Delphi specification

When a specification is instantiated into a specification of a particular railyard, the entity types are given finite domains. For instance, the entity type *signal* is asso-

---

[11] Ericsson has developed the Eclare tool, which is an extension and new implementation of Delphi. Eclare version 1.0 was released in mid 1997.

ciated with the set of signal names appearing in the interlocking system. The conceptual model is taken further down to the level of propositional logic by replacing universal quantifiers by iterated conjunction and existential quantifiers by iterated disjunction.

Given the general specification and a list of all objects in the railyard (signals, points, and so on), the translation outlined above can be performed automatically.

The transition rules in Delphi specify change of state. In the translation from rules to propositional logic, variable names are distinct for previous and next state. For example, the Delphi transition rules

```
WHEN e1(x) IS DETECTED
    IF p1(x) CONCLUDE a(x)
END;
WHEN e2(x) IS DETECTED
    IF p2(x) CONCLUDE NOT a(x)
END;
```

generates the intermediate formula in 15.8, provided that no other rules change the value of a(x). !a(x) denotes the new value of a(x).

$$!a(x) \leftrightarrow (e1(x) \land p1(x) \lor a(x)) \land \neg(e2(x) \land p2(x)) \qquad (15.8)$$

Translating the intermediate formula down to propositional logic is done by iterated conjunction of the formula, where the variable x is replaced with names of the elements in the appropriate entity types.

In this study, the specification was both produced and automatically instantiated in the Delphi tool. In addition, Delphi was used for formal validation of the specification using the built-in theorem-proving and simulation capability.

Since the Delphi specification is implementation independent, the notions in the specification must be related to the notions in the interlocking system in order to verify that it is satisfied by a specific interlocking implementation. Consider an expression locked(TrainRoute1), expressing that the train route instance TrainRoute1 is locked. In the interlocking implementation considered here, there is no single object carrying this information. Instead, the information is given by the three relays L21, L31 and Vs101. Thus *integration formulas* expressing the mapping of concepts need to be added. The integration formula for the expression locked(TrainRoute1) becomes:

$$trainrount\_1\_locked \leftrightarrow \neg L21 \land \neg L31 \land \neg Vs101$$

The integration formulas were produced manually. However, for a family of interlocking systems, the integration formulas can be re-used.

In order to perform the analysis of the system represented as a state transition system (see Section 15.3), some unreachable states had to be excluded. An unreachable state is, for example, a combination of memory values that can never be reached. Two such assumptions were added in this study, after they had been verified to hold for the system.

The Interlocking Implementation in Propositional Logic. The interlocking considered in this study was a small relay-based interlocking system. The formal model of the interlocking was constructed in NP-Tools using its graphical editor, based on the topology and the schemata for the hardware components in the interlocking implementation (Eriksson, 1997a). The relay-based interlocking system was made to fit into the synchronous system model. In order to do this a number of items such as sequential circuits, short and long time delays, and failure of hardware components had to be considered. For a description of the modelling, see (Eriksson, 1997b).

Failure modes were not covered in the formal specification (Eriksson, 1997a), but were introduced in the model of the interlocking implementation for external equipment like points and signals, since the safety requirements in the specification should also hold for a set of component failures. For instance, lights were firstly modelled with ideal lights that cannot malfunction and then the model was extended with models for the case of the lights malfunctioning. Similar failure modes were modelled for other hardware components.

The formal specification covers time delays, and so can specify that an action is to be taken within a specified time interval. The model of the system needs to consider time in the same way. Due to the synchronous hypothesis, time delays within one time step (cf. Section 15.3.1) were ignored. Time delays over several time steps can be handled by extending the propositional language with explicit time (see Section 15.3.1), but since this makes the task of verification harder it should be avoided if possible. A simple way of modelling delays over several time steps, which was used here, is to express the delay with a propositional variable as

$$timeout \rightarrow action$$

That is, if the time delay *timeout* has expired, *action* takes place. The delay variables were connected to the delay circuits used for measuring time delays in the implementation. This handling of delays over several steps does not allow verification of length of time delays which has to be checked separately. However, the model was sufficient for our purposes.

Verifying the Interlocking System. In order to perform the verification of this system, the specification instance, the formal system model, the integration formulas, the assumptions (excluding unreachable states) and the failure modes were collected in an NP-Tools system analysis (Ekenberg *et al.*, 1996).

All requirements could be either proved or disproved (by supplying countermodels) in less than a minute, requiring less than 6 MB of memory (the analysis contained about 13 000 subformulas). This made it possible to perform the verifications on an ordinary portable notebook computer. One of the falsifiable requirements was considered to be an unacceptable error, which will lead to a change in the interlocking implementation (Eriksson, 1997b). The remaining falsifiable requirements were due to over-specified safety requirements in the original specification which led to changes. After changing the specification, all requirements could be proven in less than 10 minutes. Changing the specification as a result of the actual verification (Eriksson, 1997b) illustrates the complexity of validating a specification in the first place, even though it was produced by experts in formal methods and railways.

The major steps in the study were done automatically, and most of the manual steps were due to the translations between the tools involved (NP-Tools and Delphi). Translators between these tools would reduce the manual work needed. Two other tasks that required manual modelling were producing the integration formulas and the inductive assumptions. Tool support for these two tasks would reduce the manual work to a minimum. Detailed knowledge of the interlocking type in question was necessary in order to interpret the countermodels in case of requirements being falsified.

Two technical reports give a detailed description of this study's formal specification (Eriksson, 1997a) (104 pages) and formal verification (Eriksson, 1997b) (162 pages).

The Swedish National Rail Administration successfully repeated the system modelling and verification procedure using the same specification but for another hardware interlocking implementation. All safety requirements could be proved to hold. Being able to repeat the verification procedure shows that the approach can be successfully applied even by non-experts in formal methods.

15.5 Summary

The motives for adopting formal methods are reduced costs and increased quality of produced systems. In order to achieve this, formal methods must be adopted by application engineers in various application areas. Most application engineers care about theorem provers and model checking algorithms as little as authors care about the string matching algorithms used in word processors. The creative phases in the development process, for instance producing the requirement specification, should be emphasised, but the validation and verification process should be hidden as much as possible.

The formal methods advocated here consist of a number of steps, of which many have been made fully automatic. A number of studies from railway interlocking applications demonstrate that they can be successfully applied by railway application engineers, and that they result in quantitative benefits; significant resources are saved and errors are reduced.

We argue that we have reached a level of automation where only the essentially creative phases, such as requirements capture, require expert knowledge and manual steps. Essentially, only expert knowledge in the application area of concern is required.

We briefly described the underlying techniques, Prover and the Stålmarck method. A low-level verification is used as the basis of the formal methods. High-level specifications are compiled down to an equivalent low-level description.

The studies presented are the result of collaboration begun in 1988 with ADtranz and the Swedish National Rail Administration. The experience has given us, the tool supplier, the necessary application domain understanding to be able to develop suitable formal methods of commercial quality.

CHAPTER 16

Cleanroom Software Engineering: Theory and Practice

Richard C. Linger and Carmen J. Trammell

16.1 Cleanroom Software Engineering

16.1.1 Overview

Cleanroom software engineering is a rigorous engineering discipline for the development and certification of high-reliability software systems under statistical quality control (Mills, 1992; Linger, 1993, 1994). The Cleanroom name is borrowed from hardware cleanrooms, with their emphasis on process control and focus on defect prevention rather than defect removal. Cleanroom combines mathematically-based methods of software specification, design, and correctness verification with statistical usage testing to certify software fitness for use.

16.1.2 Science Base

Engineering is the application of science to produce useful artifacts. Cleanroom software engineering is a collection of software practices that are explicitly based in science: the basis for Cleanroom management is engineering process control theory, the basis for Cleanroom development is mathematical function theory, and the basis for Cleanroom testing is statistical science.

The Cleanroom process embeds software development and testing within a statistical quality control framework. The value of a process under statistical quality control is well illustrated by modern manufacturing processes where the sampling of output is directly fed back into the processes to control quality. Once the discipline of statistical quality control is in place, there is objective visibility into the software development process; the relationship between process changes and product quality can be measured and evaluated.

Mathematically-based software development processes are employed to create software that is correct by design. Software requirements, traditionally given as a list of "shalls," are recast as a mathematical function specification in which the domain of all possible input sequences is mapped to the range of correct responses. Team correctness verification is used to ensure that the function definition is preserved as the specification is implemented in design and code.

Statistical usage testing processes are employed to enable valid inferences about software reliability. An engineering formalism — usually a finite state, discrete parameter Markov chain — is used to represent the population of all possible operational uses, and test cases randomly generated from the model form a statistically correct sample for testing.

16.1.3 Engineering Practices

The key Cleanroom engineering practices are incremental development under statistical process control; functional specification, design, and verification; and statistical testing based on a usage model.

An incremental development lifecycle provides the iterative process needed for the ongoing assessment of product quality and process control. Each increment is a complete iteration of development and certification activity, producing product and process measures used to determine whether or not the development process is under control.

The development lifecycle starts with a specification that not only defines function and performance requirements, but also identifies the expected operational usage profile of the software. The Box Structure method for top-down, stepwise design and verification provides the engineering discipline required to create correct software. Correctness verification by development teams, used to identify and eliminate defects prior to any execution of the software, can eliminate the need for unit testing.

Software testing is performed by an independent certification team that uses statistical testing methods to evaluate software quality. Statistical testing is conducted according to a formal experimental protocol, resulting in objective quality certification of software at delivery and an estimate of expected operational reliability in the field.

The Cleanroom processes can be applied to development of new software systems and evolution of legacy systems. For new systems, Cleanroom processes provide a rigorous management and technical framework for developing new software systems under intellectual control. Theory-based processes for specification, design, and verification produce software that exhibits very high quality at the inception of testing. Incremental development permits early quality assessment through statistical testing and user feedback on system function, and avoids risks associated with component integration late in the lifecycle. Modifications and extensions to legacy systems can be developed with the Cleanroom processes as well. Components of legacy systems can be re-engineered to Cleanroom quality through use of structuring, design abstraction, correctness verification, and statistical testing techniques.

16.1.4 Field Experience

Cleanroom has been used to develop and evolve a variety of systems, including real-time, embedded, host, distributed, workstation, and client-server. Cleanroom supports prototyping and object-oriented development (Ett and Trammell, 1996), and enables reuse through precise definition of common services and component functional semantics, and certification of component reliability.

The Cleanroom process has been demonstrated in software development projects in industry, as well as in NASA and the DoD STARS (Software Technology for Adaptable, Reliable Systems) program. Experience has shown substantial improvements over traditional quality and cost (Basili and Green, 1994; Hausler *et al.*, 1996, Linger, 1996):

- IBM developed a COBOL structuring product that exhibited just seven minor errors in the first three years of field use, all simple fixes, with a corresponding drop in maintenance costs compared to baselines for similar products (Linger and Mills, 1988);
- the AT&T International Definity project (a PBX switching system) combined Cleanroom development with testing based on an operational profile, and reported a factor of 10 reduction in customer-reported problems and program maintenance costs (Lyu, 1995);
- IBM developed an embedded, real-time, bus architecture, multiple-processor device controller product that exhibited no failures in three years use at over 300 customer locations (Linger, 1994);
- in its program of experimental investigations in software engineering, the NASA Goddard Space Flight Center Software Engineering Laboratory (SEL) conducted a series of flight dynamics ground support projects using Cleanroom on which quality and productivity compared favourably with the SEL baseline (Basili and Green, 1994);
- an Ericsson Telecom project to develop a 374 KLOC operating system reported gains of 1.7X in development productivity (Hausler *et al.*, 1996);
- a large, complex IBM project to develop a network management and outage avoidance product reported a 2X improvement in development productivity (Hausler *et al.*, 1996);
- the US Army Picatinny Arsenal STARS demonstration project reported a 4.6X productivity gain. A 21-to-1 return-on-investment in Cleanroom technology introduction was also reported for the project (Sherer *et al.*, 1993);
- a US Department of Defense report entitled *A Business Case for Software Process Improvement* compared Cleanroom with a number of traditional approaches and found an 80% advantage for Cleanroom in cost savings and a dramatic decline in rework for systems of increasing size (McGibbon, 1996).

16.2 Cleanroom Management by Incremental Development

Cleanroom management is based on development and certification of a pipeline of user-function software increments that accumulate into the final product (Linger, 1993). Incremental development enables early and continual quality assessment and user feedback, and facilitates process improvements as development progresses. The incremental approach avoids risks inherent in component integration late in the development cycle. Incremental development permits systematic management and incorporation of requirements changes over the development cycle.

The technical basis for incremental development in Cleanroom is the mathematical property of referential transparency. In the context of software development, this property requires that a specification and its design decomposition define the same mathematical function, that is, the same mapping from the domain of input histories to the range of correct outputs. When this property holds, a design can be shown to be correct with respect to its specification.

In practice, the requirement for referential transparency places constraints on the functional content and order of design decomposition of a system. User functions are organised into a sequence of verifiable and executable software increments, each providing additional function. The functional content of the increments is defined such that they accumulate into the complete set of functions required for the final system. Architectural requirements and risk avoidance strategies place additional constraints on increment content.

For verifiable correctness, each increment must satisfy its parent specification through the functions it provides combined with the subspecifications it contains for future increments. For statistical testing and certification, each increment can contain stubs as placeholders for future increments to permit execution in the system environment. Each new increment replaces stubs in the evolving system and satisfies the subspecifications associated with it. In this way, referential transparency is maintained throughout system development. Referential transparency in incremental development is important for maintaining intellectual control in Cleanroom project management.

16.2.1 Mathematical Foundations of Incremental Development

Referential transparency is defined as follows in Denotational Semantics by Joseph Stoy (1977).

> We use [referential transparency] to refer to the fact of mathematics which says: The only thing that matters about an expression is its value, and any subexpression can be replaced by any other equal in value. Moreover, the value of an expression is, within certain limits, the same wherever it occurs.

Referential transparency is the property of arithmetic that allows one to evaluate lengthy arithmetic expressions one subexpression at a time and still be guaranteed of getting the right answer. For example, the expression $(6 + 2) \times (5 - 3)$ is equivalent to $8 \times (5-3)$ because $6+2 = 8$; and because $5-3 = 2$, it is also equivalent to 8×2; and finally, because $8 \times 2 = 16$, the original expression is equivalent to 16.

Referential transparency guarantees that one can replace $(6+2)$ by 8 unconditionally; without worrying, for example, about whether the result will go on to be multiplied by $(5-3)$, or subtracted from 17, or whatever. Referential transparency is a property of arithmetic, and is proved once and for all in the mathematics of arithmetic. Referential transparency does not need to be checked or rechecked for each individual expression.

Pleszkoch has described and exemplified the application of referential transparency in a wide range of areas, e.g., in computer science, linguistics, mathematics, and logic (Trammell *et al.*, 1996). In general, referential transparency means that the relevant lower-level details of an entity are abstracted rather than omitted in a particular system of higher-level description, so that the higher-level description contains everything needed to understand the entity when placed in a larger context. Examples are given in Table 16.1.

Table 16.1. Referential transparency in various systems

System	Entity	Description	Larger Context	Referentially transparent?
Arithmetic	(Sub)-expressions	Value	Expressions	Yes
English	Nouns	Real Objects	Sentences	No
λ calculus	λ-terms	Beta-reduced λ-term	λ-expressions	Yes
Program Design Language	Programming	Functions	Programs	Yes*
'C' Language	'C' integer expressions	Integer-valued functions	Programs	No

A traditional illustration that English is not referentially transparent is the following:

"William Rufus" and "King William II" refer to the same historical person. However, the first sentence can be understood while the second sentence makes no sense.

1. William Rufus was so called because of his red beard.
2. King William II was so called because of his red beard.

C programming language expressions are not referentially transparent because of side-effects relative to their values. For example, the following two C statements both print out 1 plus the current value of *x*, but they are definitely not interchangeable in any program that subsequently requires the value of *x*:

```
1.    printf("%d",x+1);
```

2.   `printf("%d",++x);`

If the current value of x is 4, then $x + 1$ returns the value 5 but leaves x unchanged. However, $++x$ returns the value 5 and has the side-effect of setting the new value of x to be 5.

The lack of referential transparency in the C programming language does not mean that Cleanroom development cannot be applied using C. Cleanroom has indeed been applied very successfully with C. The lack of referential transparency described above is a mismatch between entity and description. To restore referential transparency, one can either restrict the entity or enhance the description.

Referential transparency can be restored in the first case (i.e., restricting the entity) by using a well-behaved subset of the C language. In the second case (i.e., enhancing the description), referential transparency can be restored by using two functions to describe a C expression: one function for the return value, and another function for the new state in terms of the old state.

In the Cleanroom method, referential transparency must be established for a programming or design language and corresponding functional description. This is done at the outset of a project using the precepts of mathematical function theory. Once referential transparency has been established for a particular programming or design language, Cleanroom incremental development and verification techniques are guaranteed to work for any application that is developed in that language. In particular, just as $(6 + 2)$ can be replaced by 8 without regard to the larger context, so can any component of the application be verified with respect to its functional context without regard to any other component of the application, and furthermore, need not be reverified if and when other components of the application change. Referential transparency is the key to the validity of Cleanroom specification and development techniques.

16.2.2 Referential Transparency in System Design

The basis for incremental development lies in the view of programs and program parts as rules for mathematical functions (Linger *et al.*, 1979), that is, as mappings from domains to ranges. This view regards program development as top-down refinement of functions (specifications) into control structures and subfunctions (subspecifications), rather than bottom-up aggregation of programming statements into programs. Such refinement may result in object-based or functional decompositions, or a combination of the two. For example, a given function (specification) f could be refined into:

sequence: $[f] = \text{do } [f1]; [f2] \text{ od}$
alternative: $[f] = \text{if } p \text{ then } [f1] \text{ else } [f2] \text{ fi}$
iteration: $[f] = \text{while } p \text{ do } [f1] \text{ od}$

where $[f1]$ and $[f2]$ represent subfunctions (subspecifications) for further refinement. The successive function refinements must maintain functional equivalence for correctness verification at each step. For example, in the sequence refinement above, the composition of subfunctions f1 and f2 must be equivalent in net effect on data to the original function f. Referential transparency requires that any function (f, f1, or f2 above) completely specify the required net effect of processing at the point it appears in the design, and no further information or reference to other design parts be required for its independent refinement. This crucial property is a key to successful incremental development.

Because of referential transparency, the verification of any refinement step can be conducted independently of any other refinement step. This means that the system architecture can be verified in the first increment, before most of the system components have been written, and that the architecture need not be reverified in later increments. Note, however, that the specifications of system components enter into the architecture verification, and in fact provide the precise interface documentation required to guarantee that the system as a whole will perform as required when coding is complete.

A simple illustration of function refinement with referential transparency is shown in Figure 16.1. The two-step refinement on the right side of the figure maintains function equivalence at each step. First, the initial sequence f is refined into loop initialisation code g and subspecification k, where k completely specifies interfaces and the required net effect of processing at that point in the design. Next, subspecification k is refined into an iteration in a second step. These expansion steps are referentially transparent, and represent possible increment definitions. In this case, the first increment would contain the loop initialisation code represented by g, with the subspecification k defined and connected in the sequence for verification against f, but stubbed off in the code. A crucial point is that the sequence of code g followed by subspecification k is functionally equivalent to the original specification f. The second increment would refine k into the whiledo iteration, which is functionally equivalent to k. Other design strategies, such as the one given on the left side of the figure, would violate referential transparency and forfeit intellectual control of top-down design. The difference between these approaches may seem minor in this simple example, but if g and k represent 50 KLOC and 500 KLOC respectively, with a complex interface between them, referentially transparent increments could mean the difference between success and failure of the project.

16.2.3 Engineering Process Control

Incremental development affords customer feedback on the evolving system, intellectual control of the technical work, and management control of the schedule and budget. User feedback on each increment is a gauge on whether the right system is being built, and quality measures in each increment are a gauge on whether the system is being built right. Product quality and process control are both supported. Incremental development has sound mathematical foundations, but has been reduced to a highly practical engineering process.

A more extensive explanation of incremental development is given in (Trammell *et al.*, 1996).

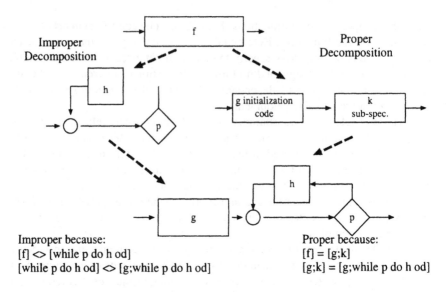

Figure 16.1. Referential transparency in stepwise refinement

16.3 Cleanroom Specification, Design and Verification

The foundation for Cleanroom specification, design, and verification is that a program can be regarded as a rule for a mathematical function (or relation). That is, programs carry out transformations from input (domain) to output (range) that can be precisely specified as function mappings. Programs can be designed by decomposing their function specifications, and can be verified by abstracting and comparing their designed functions to their function specifications for equivalence. This approach is scale-free, with application ranging from large specifications for entire systems down to individual control structures, and to every intermediate decomposition and verification along the way.

Three forms of mathematical functions are important in Cleanroom development because of their correspondence to useful system views, and their interrelationships in a stepwise decomposition and verification process. These forms are known as black box, state box, and clear box and, collectively, as box structures (Mills *et al.*, 1986). Box structures are used extensively by Cleanroom specification and development teams. Other methods may also be used to implement the Cleanroom principles of mathematically-based software specification and development; the box structure method is most prominent in Cleanroom practice.

16.3.1 Black Box

Box structures map system stimuli (inputs) and stimulus histories (previous inputs) to responses (outputs). A black box defines the required external behaviour of a software system or system part in all possible circumstances of use. The transition function of a black box is:

((current stimulus, stimulus history) → response).

That is, a black box maps the current stimulus to a response that also depends on the history of stimuli received. For example, given a stimulus of 5, a hand calculator will produce a response of 175 if the stimulus history is C 1 7 (C for Clear), but a response of 5 if the history is C 1 7 +. The stimulus is the same in both cases, but the histories of stimuli are different, leading to different responses. A black box definition is state-free and procedure-free, referencing only externally-observable stimuli and responses. Black box definitions are often given in tables with columns for current stimulus, conditions on history, and responses. Abstraction techniques are used to enable scale-up to large systems.

In the conceptual representation of a black box in Figure 16.2, *S* represents a stimulus and *R* represents a response.

SSS...S → R

Figure 16.2. Conceptual view of a black box

16.3.2 State Box

A state box is derived from and verified against a corresponding black box. The state box transition function is:

((current stimulus, current state) → (response, new state)).

That is, a state box maps the current stimulus and the current state to a response and a new state. In the state box, the stimulus history of the black box is replaced by retained state data necessary to achieve black box behaviour. A state box definition is procedure-free, and isolates and focuses on state invention. State box definitions are often given in tables with columns for current stimulus, current state, response, and new state.

In the conceptual representation of a state box in Figure 16.3, the necessary stimulus history in Figure 16.2 has been encapsulated as state data.

16.3.3 Clear Box

A clear box is derived from and verified against a corresponding state box. The clear box transition function is:

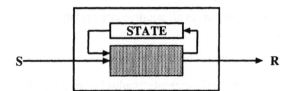

Figure 16.3. Conceptual view of a state box

((current stimulus, current state)→ (response, new state)) by procedures.

In the clear box, the procedures required to implement the state box transition function are defined, possibly introducing new black boxes for further decomposition into state and clear boxes. That is, a clear box is a program, or set of programs, that implements the state box and introduces and connects operations in a program structure for decomposition at the next level. Such connections are critical to maintaining intellectual control in large-scale software development.

Figure 16.4 depicts the full procedural clear box, including new black boxes to be decomposed as development continues.

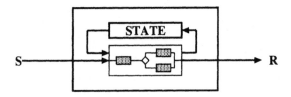

Figure 16.4. Conceptual view of a clear box

16.3.4 Decomposition

Box structures can be applied to a variety of decomposition strategies, including functional, object-oriented, etc. In the object-oriented case, the black box defines the behaviour specification of an object, the state box defines its data encapsulation, and the clear box defines its procedural services or methods (Ett, 1996).

Box structures also provide a systematic framework for incorporating reused and COTS software. Clear boxes may contain new black boxes that represent either subcomponents to be further decomposed, or common services (reusable components) from internal or external sources. Incorporation of a pre-existing component requires a precisely specified interface between the clear box context in the target system and component to be reused.

A full explanation of box structure specification and design is given in (Mills *et al.*, 1986).

16.3.5 Correctness Verification

All Cleanroom-developed software is subject to function-theoretic correctness verification by the development team prior to release to the certification test team. The function-theoretic approach permits development teams to completely verify the correctness of software with respect to specifications. A *Correctness Theorem* defines conditions to be met for achieving correct software . These conditions are verified in correctness arguments during development team reviews.

Programs contain an infinite number of paths that cannot all be checked by path-based inspections or software testing. However, the Correctness Theorem is based on verifying individual control structures (sequence, if-then-else, whiledo, etc.) rather than tracing paths. Because programs contain a finite number of control structures, the Correctness Theorem reduces verification to a finite number of checks, and permits all software logic to be verified in possible circumstances of use. The verification step is remarkably effective in eliminating defects, and is a major factor in the quality improvements achieved by Cleanroom teams.

The correctness conditions defined by the Correctness Theorem for fundamental control structures are given in Figure 16.5. On the left, each control structure is preceded by a function definition, f, that defines its net effect on data. The sequence correctness question involves function composition; the if-then-else, case analysis; and the while-do, case analysis and function composition combined.

A full explanation of function-theoretic verification is given in (Linger *et al.*, 1979).

16.3.6 Re-engineering and Design Recovery

Non-Cleanroom-developed software may require re-engineering to enable developers to maintain intellectual control and to achieve Cleanroom levels of quality and reliability.

Unstructured software can be transformed into a structured form for improved understandability and maintenance through application of the *Structure Theorem* (Linger *et al.*, 1979). The constructive proof of the theorem defines a systematic procedure for transforming unstructured logic into function-equivalent structured form. The procedure can be carried out manually, or fully or partially automated if large quantities of software must be structured.

Missing or incomplete designs and specifications for existing structured programs can be recovered and documented as well through systematic analysis and abstraction based on function-theoretic techniques.

A full explanation of program structuring and function abstraction is given in (Linger *et al.*, 1979).

Sequence

```
[f]
do
    g;
    h
enddo
```
Does g follow by h do f?

If-then-else

```
[f]
if p
then
    g
else
    h
endif
```
When p is true
        does g do f,
and when p is false
        does h do f?

While-do

```
[f]
while p
    g
end do
```
Does the loop terminate,
and when p is true
        does g followed by f do f,
and when p is false
        does doing nothing do f?

Figure 16.5. Correctness questions for basic control structures

16.4 Cleanroom Statistical Testing and Certification

The set of possible executions of a software system is an infinite population. All testing is really sampling from that infinite population. No testing process, no matter how extensive, can sample more than a minute fraction of all possible executions of a software system. If the sample embodied in a set of test cases is a random sample based on projected usage, valid statistical estimates of software quality and reliability for that usage can be obtained. Statistical usage testing of a software system produces scientific measures of product and process quality for management decision-making, just as has been done in hardware engineering for decades.

16.4.1 First Principles

When a population is too large for exhaustive study, as is the case for all possible uses of a software system, a statistically correct sample must be drawn as a basis for inferences about the population. In statistical testing of software, testing is treated as an engineering problem to be solved by statistical methods. Figure 16.6 shows the parallel between a classical statistical design and statistical software testing.

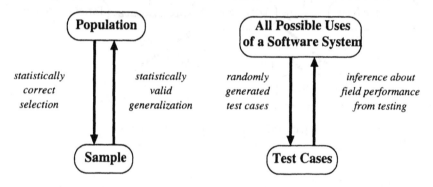

Figure 16.6. Parallel between a statistical design and software testing

Under a statistical protocol, the environment of use can be modelled, and a statistically valid statement can be made about the expected operational performance of the software based on its test performance. Statistical testing was originally developed as part of Cleanroom software engineering, and is also used now to test software produced by non-Cleanroom methods as well.

16.4.2 Operational Usage Modelling

A usage model characterises the infinite population of scenarios of use of a software system. Usage models are built from specifications, user guides, or even existing systems. More than one model might be constructed for a single system if there is more than one environment of interest, such as routine and non-routine use. The "structure" of a usage model represents the possible use of a system, and the "transition probabilities" imposed on the structure represent the expected use of the system.

16.4.3 Model Structure

The basic task in model building is to identify the states-of-use of the system and the possible transitions among states-of-use. This information is encoded into Markov chains in the form of directed graphs and stochastic matrices. Every possible scenario of use, at the chosen level of abstraction, is represented by the model and potentially generated from the model as a test case. Figure 16.7 portrays a simple Markov chain usage model as a directed graph with transition probabilities on the arcs; Table 16.2 contains the corresponding stochastic matrix.

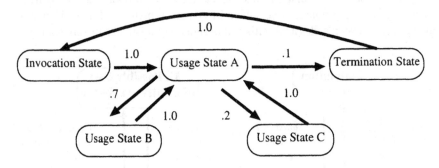

Figure 16.7. Markov Chain usage model

Table 16.2. Stochastic matrix for the usage model in Figure 16.7

From State	To State				
	Invocation	A	B	C	Termination
Invocation	0	1	0	0	0
A	0	0	0.7	0.2	0.1
B	0	1	0	0	0
C	0	1	0	0	0
Termination	1	0	0	0	0

Models should be designed in a standard form consisting of connected sub-models with a single-entry and single-exit. States and arcs can be expanded like macros. Sub-models of canonical form can be collapsed to states or arcs. This permits model validation, specification analysis, test planning, and test case generation to occur on various levels of abstraction. The structure of the usage models should be reviewed with the specification writers, real or prospective users, the developers, and the testers.

Most usage modelling experience to date is with embedded real-time systems, application program interfaces (APIs) and graphical user interfaces (GUIs). Models as small as 20 states and 100 arcs have proven very useful. Typical models are on the order of 500 states and 2 000 arcs; large models of more than 2 000 states and 20 000 arcs are in use. Even the largest models developed to date are small in comparison to similar mathematical models used in other fields of science and engineering, and are manageable with available tool support.

16.4.4 Transition Probabilities

Transition probabilities among states in a usage model come from historical or projected usage data for the application. Because transition probabilities represent classes of users, environments of use, or special usage situations, there may be several sets of probabilities for a single model structure. Moreover, as the system progresses through the lifecycle the probability set may change several times, based on maturation of system use and availability of more information.

When extensive field data for similar or predecessor systems exists, a probability value may be known for every arc of the model (i.e., for every nonzero cell of the stochastic matrix of transition probabilities). For new systems, one might stipulate expected practice based on user interviews, user guides, and training programs. This is a reasonable starting point, but should be open to revision as new information becomes available.

When complete information about system usage is not available, it is advisable to take an analytical approach to setting the transition probabilities. Usage models can be represented by a system of constraints and, with the aid of mathematical programming, the matrix of transition probabilities can be generated as the solution to an optimisation problem.

Under the analytical approach, three forms of constraints are used to define a model: structural, usage, and test management constraints. In the explanations that follow, P denotes the transition matrix and $P_{i,j}$ represents the probability of a transition between usage state i and usage state j.

16.4.5 Structural Constraints

Structural constraints are so named because they define model structure: the states themselves and both possible and impossible transitions among the usage states.

Structural constraints are of four types:

- $P_{i,j} = 0$ defines an impossible transition between usage state i and usage state j;
- $P_{i,j} = 1$ defines a certain transition between usage state i and usage state j;

- $0 < P_{i,j} < 1$ defines probabilistic transition between usage state i and usage state j, i.e., a transition that is possible but not certain to occur;
- Each row of P must sum to one.

16.4.6 Usage Constraints

If one has no information about the expected usage of the software, one should generate uniform probabilities for the possible transitions from each state. As new information arises, it is recorded in the form of constraints:

- $P_{i,j} = c$ may be used for known usage probabilities, i.e., probability values that are exactly known on the basis of historical experience or designed controls;
- $a \leq P_{i,j} \leq b$ defines estimated usage probabilities as a range of values. Defining an estimate as being within a range allows information to be given without being overstated;
- $P_{i,j} = P_{k,m}$ defines equivalent usage probabilities, values that should be the same whether or not one knows what the value should be;
- $P_{i,j} = d \times (P_{k,m})$ defines proportional usage probabilities, where one value is a multiple of another.

Probability values can be related to each other by a function to represent what is known about the relationship, without overstating the data and knowledge. More complex constraints may be expressed as:

- $P_{i,j} = f(P_{k,m})$, where one value is a function of another;
- $a \leq f(P) \leq b$, where the value of a function of the matrix P is bounded, for example, to constrain the average test case length to a certain range.

Most usage models can be defined with very simple constraints.

16.4.7 Test Management Constraints

Finally, constraints may be used to represent test management controls. Management constraints are of the same forms as usage constraints. A limitation on revisiting previously tested functions, for example, may be represented in the form of a "known usage probability"(defined above) — a constant that limits the percentage of test cases entering a certain section of the model.

Objective Functions. When mathematical programming is used to generate transition probabilities, the solution generated is optimised for some objective function (e.g., greatest testing value, least testing cost) while satisfying all constraints.

Model Analysis and Validation. A Markov chain is a thoroughly studied mathematical model for which a standard set of statistics exists. In this application, the standard analytical results calculated for the usage model have important interpretations for resource allocation, safety analysis, test planning, and field support. Statistics that are routinely calculated from the model and used for these purposes include the following:

- **long-run occupancy of each state:** the usage profile as a percentage of time spent in each state;
- **occurrence probability:** probability of occurrence of each state in a random use of the software;
- **occurrence frequency:** expected number of occurrences of each state in a random use of the software;
- **first occurrence:** for each state, the expected number of uses of the software before it will first occur;
- **expected sequence length:** the expected number of state transitions in a random use of the software; the average length of a test case.

These and other statistics describe the behaviour that can be expected in the long run, i.e., in ongoing field use of the software.

Analytical results are studied during model validation, and surprises are not uncommon. Parts of systems thought to be unimportant might get surprisingly heavy use while parts that consume a large amount of the development budget might see little use. Since a usage model is based on the software specification rather than the code, it can be created early in the life cycle to inform the development process as well as testing and certification.

Test Case Generation. Random test cases may be automatically generated from the usage model. Each test case is a "random walk" through the stochastic matrix, from the initial state to the terminal state. Test cases may be generated as scripts for human testers or as input sequences for automated testing. Post-processing of test cases often further facilitates human or automated evaluation. One may generate a large a set of test cases and perform "what-if" analyses to establish bounds on test outcomes before incurring the cost of performing the tests.

Product and Process Measurement. The usage model from which the test cases are generated is called the *usage chain*. A chain of initially identical structure, called the *testing chain*, is developed to record actual testing experience. The progress of testing is monitored by tracking measures calculated from these two chains.

Product Measures. A reliability measure is calculated from the testing chain along with confidence intervals. This reliability is defined strictly in terms of the failure experience recorded in the testing chain; there are no other mathematical assumptions. This definition of reliability is applicable whenever testing has revealed one or more failures. When testing reveals no failures, distributional models should be used, e.g., (Poore *et al.*, 1996).

Process Measures. An information-theoretic comparison of the usage and testing chains is computed to assess the degree to which the testing experience has become representative of expected field use. Its graph will have a terrace-like appearance of declines and plateaus. The trend in the measure reveals the rate at which the usage and testing chains are becoming indistinguishable. As the two converge, it becomes less likely that new information will be gained by further testing.

Certification. Certification is always relative to a protocol, and the protocol includes the entire testing process and all work products. An independent audit of testing must be possible to confirm the correctness of reports. An independent repetition of the protocol should produce the same conclusions, to within acceptable statistical variation.

The Cleanroom certification process involves ongoing evaluation of the merits of continued testing. Stopping criteria are based on statistical measures of reliability, confidence, and convergence between expected and tested use. Decisions to continue testing are based on an assessment that the goals of testing can still be realized within the schedule and budget remaining.

Engineering practices for statistical testing are being used to improve allocations of test resources in many domains. Tool support is available for usage model development, model analysis, test case generation, and monitoring stopping criteria.

A more extensive discussion of statistical certification testing can be found in (Walton, 1995), (Walton *et al.*, 1996), (Whittaker and Poore, 1996), and (Whittaker and Tomason, 1996).

16.5 The Cleanroom Reference Model

The Software Engineering Institute has defined a Cleanroom Reference Model (Linger and Trammell, 1996), comprised of a set of 14 individual processes for Cleanroom management, specification, development, and certification. These processes form a comprehensive guide to Cleanroom project performance for software teams trained in Cleanroom operations. They embody the Cleanroom technologies described above. The 14 processes and their 20 associated work products are described in the appendix. Work product names are shown in italics.

The Cleanroom processes are intended to be tailored and adapted for specific organisation and project environments and contexts. Existing organisational policies and standards should be taken into account in defining the tailored processes. For example, if an organisational requirement exists to program in a specific language, the relationship of that language to box structure specification and design forms should be elaborated, and the specific correctness conditions for verifying language constructs should be defined and documented.

The Software Engineering Institute has mapped the Cleanroom Reference Model to the CMM[1] for Software, as defined in (Linger *et al.*, 1996). The mapping de-

---

[1] CMM is a servicemark of Carnegie Mellon University. CMM is registered with the US Patent and Trademark Office.

fines the integration of Cleanroom technology with the management processes of the CMM. The integration shows that Cleanroom and the CMM are fully compatible and mutually reinforcing.

Appendix

Cleanroom Management Processes

Cleanroom Process: Project Planning

Process Description: Define and document plans for a Cleanroom project, and revise as necessary to accommodate changes. Review plans with the project team, peer groups, and the customer for agreement.

Principal Work Products:
- *Cleanroom Engineering Guide:* Tailored process for a project, including work product definitions, policies, protocols, and standards.
- *Software Development Plan:* Management plan for a Cleanroom project: mission, organisation, work products, schedule and resources, meeasurement, risk, standards, training, CMM.

Cleanroom Process: Project Management

Process Description: Manage the Cleanroom incremental development and certification process to deliver software and associated work products on schedule and within budget. Establish and train Cleanroom teams and define quality objectives and team performance expectations. Initiate and track Cleanroom processes. Meet process performance standards and product quality objectives, and improve team performance. Use the quantitative measurements of product and process performance produced by statistical testing and certification of successive increments for objective management decision-making.

Principal Work Products:
- *Project Record:* Documentation of actions, reviews, decisions, measures, and other events throughout a project.

Cleanroom Process: Performance Improvement

Process Description: Continually evaluate and improve Cleanroom team performance based on conformance with the *Software Development Plan*, process control standards, and causal analysis of software failures. Analyse and pilot prospective improvements in software processes and tools, and introduce them as appropriate.

Principal Work Products:
- *Performance Improvement Plan:* Documentation of plans to refine the current Cleanroom process and/or introduce new software processes and tools.

Cleanroom Process: Engineering Change

Process Description: Correct and change the evolving software system and associated work products under a protocol that preserves correctness and integrity. Implement engineering change control for all changes.

Principal Work Products:

– *Engineering Change Log:* The record of engineering change proposals, evaluations, impacts, and status.

Cleanroom Process: Requirements Analysis

Process Description: Analyse and define initial customer requirements for the software system, as well as requirements changes arising from customer assessment of evolving increments. Express requirements in user terms and review with the customer for agreement.

Principal Work Products:

– *Software Requirements:* The functional, usage, performance, and environment requirements for a software system to be developed under the Cleanroom process.

Cleanroom Process: Function Specification

Process Description: Define the required external behaviour of a software system in all possible circumstances of use based on the *Software Requirements*. Express the specification in box structure form. Create complete, consistent and correct specifications, and review with the customer for agreement.

Principal Work Products:

– *Function Specification:* A complete representation of the external view of a system, typically expressed in terms of the mapping of all possible stimuli to their corresponding responses in all possible circumstances of use; the top-level black box in the box structure usage hierarchy.

Cleanroom Process: Usage Specification

Process Description: Define all classes of users, major patterns of usage, and usage environments for a software product based on the *Software Requirements*. Create complete, consistent, and correct usage specifications, and review with the customer for agreement.

Principal Work Products:

– *Usage Specification:* A definition of the expected users, uses, and environments of the software system.

Cleanroom Process: Architecture Specification

Process Description: Analyse architectural assets and define the architecture strategy for the software product, including major components, high-level structure, and software design strategies and conventions. Review with the customer for agreement.

Principal Work Products:

– *Software Architecture:* The overall structure of the software, typically expressed as a top-level state box and clear box in the box structure usage hierarchy, together with design strategies, and conventions to be used throughout development.

Cleanroom Process: Increment Planning

Process Description: Create an incremental development and certification plan for the software product such that the increments implement user function, accumulate into the final system, execute in the system environment, and permit systematic feedback on process control and product function and quality. Maintain referential transparency bewteen increment specifications and their design decompositions. User incremental development to reduce or eliminate risks and to maintain intellectual control.

Principal Work Products:

- *Increment Construction Plan:* A plan that specifies the number of increments into which a Cleanroom project will be divided, the functions that will be implemented in each increment, and the schedule and resources allocated to development and certification of each increment.

Cleanroom Process: Software Re-engineering

Process Description: Prepare re-used software for incorporation into a software product. Restructure and document the functional semantics of the re-used software as necessary to maintain intellectual control and avoid unforeseen failures in execution. Determine the fitness for use of re-used software as necessary through statistical testing in order to achieve project certification goals.

Principal Work Products:

- *Re-engineering Plan:* A technical plan for evaluation and/or modification of components that may be re-used.
- *Re-engineered Software Specification:* Re-used components that have been re-engineered to meet Cleanroom specification requirements.

Cleanroom Process: Increment Design

Process Description: Design and code the increments for a software product through stepwise decomposition of box structures, typically from stimulus-history-based black box specifications into state-based state box specifications and then into procedure-based clear box designs containing lower-level black boxes for further refinement. Prepare designs for correctness verification by embedding intended function definitions that specify the effect on data of corresponding control structure decompositions.

Principal Work Products:

- *Increment Design:* The complete specification, design and code for a software increment represented in black box, state box, and clear box forms.

Cleanroom Process: Correctness Verification

Process Description: Carry out function-theoretic correctness verification of designs, typically trough verbal proofs of correctness in team reviews, to identify and correct software faults prior to first execution. Document all faults founds and re-review their corrections.

Principal Work Products:

– *Increment Verification Report:* The record of correctness verification reviews, including staff members participating, time spent, number of verification sessions, enumeration and classification of faults found during each session, and any other information relevant to assessment of the correctness of the design and code.

Cleanroom Process: Usage Modelling and Test Planning

Process Description: Create the usage models to be used for software testing and certification. Express the models in terms of software usage states and probabilities of transitions between them. Develop the models to satisfy objectives such as certification for expected operational use, or certification of infrequently used functions with high consequences of failure. Use usage model statistics to provide insight into system complexity and the testing effort required to meet quality objecctives. Develop a statistical test plan, prepare the test environment, and generate the statistical test cases.

Principal Work Products:

– *Usage Models:* The models to be used to generate test cases for software certification.
– *Increment Test Plan:* All information needed for statistical testing, including schedules, staffing, training, hardware and software environment, test case evaluation procedures, certification goals, and statistical models.
– *Statistical Test Cases:* Test cases randomly generated from usage models.

Cleanroom Process: Statistical Testing and Certification

Process Description: Demonstrate the fitness for use of the software in a formal statistical experiment. Execute statistical test cases under experimental control, evaluate results, and initiate engineering change activity if failures are encountered. Compare the values of certification measures obtained in statistical testing to certification goals to assess the software's fitness for use. Compare measures of testing progress to process control standards to assess the likelihood of reaching certification goals with planned schedules and resources.

Principal Work Products:

– *Executable System:* The executable load modules for testing.
– *Statistical Testing Record:* The record of statistical testing, including test cases run in each session, failures observed, and any other information relevant to assessing correctness of the executing software.
– *Increment Certification Report:* Includes values for measures of software fitness for use.

References

Åkerlund, O, Stålmarck, G. and Helander, M. (1996) Safety and Reliability Analysis of Integrated Hard- and Software Systems at Saab using a Formal Method. In *Industrial Track Proceedings of 7th International Symposium on Software Reliability Engineering (ISSRE'96)*, pp 67–75.

Aagaard, M. and Leeser, M. (1994) Reasoning about Pipelines with Structural Hazards. In Ramayya Kumar and Thomas Kropf, editors, *Theorem Provers in Circuit Design, TPCD '94*, Lecture Notes in Computer Science **901**, Springer-Verlag, pp 13–32.

Abadi, M. and Lamport, L. (1993) Composing specifications. *ACM Transactions on Programming Languages and Systems*, **15**:73–132.

Abadi, M. and Lamport, L. (1995) Conjoining specifications. *ACM Transactions on Programming Languages and Systems*, **17**(3):507–534.

Abrial, J.-R. (1994) *Introduction à la méthode de spécification formelle B.* Video cassette lecture series, Teknea, Toulouse.

Abrial, J.-R. (1996) Extending B without changing it (for developing distributed systems). In *Proc. B Confernece*, IRIN, Nantes, November.

Abrial, J.-R. (1997) *The B-Book: Assigning Programs to Meanings*, Cambridge University Press, Cambridge, UK.

Abrial, J.-R., Börger, E. and Langmaack, H., editors (1996) *Formal Methods for Industrial Applications: Specifying and Programming the Steam Boiler Control*, Lecture Notes in Computer Science **1165**, Springer-Verlag, Heidelberg.

Alsop, N., Camillocci, L., Sanchez, A. and Macchietto, S. (1996) Synthesis of Procedural Controllers – Application to a Batch Plant, *Computers and Chemical Engineering*, **29**:S1481–S1486.

Alur, R. and Henzinger, T.A. (1993) Real-time Logics: Complexity and Expressiveness. *Information and Computing*, **104**(1):35–77.

Anderson, R.J. (1992) UEPS — a second generation electronic wallet, In *Computer Security — ESORICS'92*, Lecture Notes in Computer Science **648**, Springer-Verlag, Heidelberg, pp 411–418.

Anderson, R.J. (1994) Why cryptosystems fail, *Communications of the ACM*, **37**(11):32–40, November.

Anderson, R.J., Beame, P., Burns, S., Chan, W., Modugno, F., Notkin, D. and Reese, J. (1996) Model-checking large software specifications, In D. Garlan, editor, *SIGSOFT '96: Proceedings of the Fourth ACM SIGSOFT Symposium on the Foundations of Software Engineering*, ACM Press, pp 156–166; also published in *ACM Software Engineering Notes* **21**(6), November.

Anderson, R.J. and Bezuidenhoudt, S.J. (1996) On the reliability of electronic payment systems', *IEEE Transactions on Software Engineering*, **22**(5):294–301, May.

Anderson, R.J and Kuhn, M.G. (1996) Tamper Resistance — a Cautionary Note", In *Proceedings of the Second Usenix Workshop on Electronic Commerce*, pp 1–11, November.

Anderson, R.J. and Needham, R.M. (1995) Programming satan's computer, In *Computer Science Today*, Lecture Notes in Computer Science **1000**, Springer-Verlag, Heidelberg, pp 426–441.

Archinoff, G.H., Hohendorf, R.J., Wassyng, A., Quigley, B. and Borsch, M.R. (1990) Verification of the shutdown system software at the Darlington nuclear generating station. In *Proceedings of the Internation Conference on Control and Instrumentation in Nuclear Installations*, THe Institution of Nuclear Engineers, Glasgow, UK, May.

Ardis, M. (1994) Software engineering as oral culture, In *Proceedings Fourth IEEE Computer Society Workshop on Software Engineering Technology*, April, IEEE Computer Society Press.

Aristotle (1976) *Ethics*, Translated by J.A.K. Thomson, Penguin Books, London.

Atlee, J.M. and Gannon, J. (1993) State-based model checking of event-driven system requirements, *IEEE Transactions on Software Engineering* **19**(1):24–40, January.

Austin-Seymour, M., Caplan, R., Russell, K., Laramore, G., Jacky, J., Wootton, P., Hummel, S., Lindsley, K. and Griffin, T. (1994) Impact of a multileaf collimator on treatment morbidity in localized carcinoma of the prostate, *International Journal of Radiation Oncology, Biology and Physics*, **30**(5):1065–1071, December.

Barton, P.I., Smith, E. and Pantelides, C.C. (1991) Combined Discrete/Continuous Process Modelling Using gPROMS. In *Proc. 1991 AIChE Annual Meeting: Recent Advances in Process Control*, Los Angeles, CA.

Barringer, H. and Kuiper, R. (1985) Hierarchical development of concurrent systems in a temporal logic framework. In S.D. Brookes, A.W. Roscoe, and G. Winskel, editors, *Proc. of Seminar on Concurrency*, Lecture Notes in Computer Science **197**, Springer-Verlag, Heidelberg.

Basili, V.R. and Green, S.E. (1994) Software process evolution in the SEL, *IEEE Software*, **11**(7):58–66, July.

Birtwistle, G., Graham, B., Simpson, T., Slind, K., Williams, M. and Williams, S. (1990) Verifying an SECD Chip in HOL. In *Proceedings of the IFIP TC10/WG10.2/WG10.5 Workshop on Applied Formal Methods for Correct VLSI Design*. Elsevier Science Publishers, Amsterdam, 1990.

Bjørner, N, Browne, I.A., Chang, E., Colón, M., Kapur, A., Manna, Z, . Sipma, H.B. and Uribe, T.E. (1995) *STeP: The Stanford Temporal Prover, User's Manual*. Technical Report STAN-CS-TR-95-1562, Computer Science Department, Stanford University, November.

Boehm, B.W. (1981) *Software Engineering Economics*. Prentice Hall, Englewood Cliffs, NJ.

Borälv, A. (1997) A Fully Automated Approach for Proving Safety Properties in Interlocking Software Using Automatic Theorem-Proving. In S. Gnesi and D. Latella, editors, *Proceedings of the Second International ERCIM Workshop on Formal Methods for Industrial Critical Systems*, pp 39–62, Consiglio Nazionale Ricerche, Pisa, July.

Borälv, A. and Östberg, K. (1997) VHDL and Formal Verification — An Evaluation of Concepts, Tools, and Use in Electronic Design. Technical report, Logikkonsult NP AB, June.

Bowen, J.P. (1993) Formal methods in safety-critical standards, In *Proc. 1993 Software Engineering Standards Symposium, SESS'93*, Brighton, UK, 30 August – 3 September, pp 168–177, IEEE Computer Society Press.

Bowen, J.P. (1994) *Towards Verified Systems*, Elsevier Real-Time Safety Critical Systems Series, Amsterdam.

Bowen, J.P., Fett, A. and Hinchey, M.G. (1998) *ZUM'98: The Z Formal Specification Notation*, Lecture Notes in Computer Science **1493**, Springer-Verlag, Heidelberg.

Bowen, J.P. and Hall, J.A., editors (1994) *Z User Workshop, Cambridge 1994*, Springer-Verlag, Workshops in Computing, London.

Bowen, J.P. and Hinchey, M.G. (1994) Formal methods and safety-critical standards, *IEEE Computer*, **27**(8):68–71, August.

Bowen, J.P. and Hinchey, M.G. (1995a) Ten commandments of formal methods, *IEEE Computer*, **28**(4):56–63, April.

Bowen, J.P. and Hinchey, M.G. (1995b) Seven more myths of formal methods, *IEEE Software*, **12**(4):34–41, July.

Bowen, J.P. and Hinchey, M.G., editors, (1995c) *ZUM'95: The Z Formal Specification Notation*, Lecture Notes in Computer Science **967**, Springer-Verlag, Heidelberg.

Bowen, J.P. and Hinchey, M.G. (1997) Formal models and the specification process, In A.B. Tucker Jr., editor, *The Computer Science and Engineering Handbook*, Chapter 107, pp 2302–2322, ACM/CRC Press, Boca Raton, FL.

Bowen, J.P. and Hinchey, M.G. (1999) *High-Integrity System Specification and Design*, Springer-Verlag FACIT, London.

Bowen, J.P., Hinchey, M.G. and Till, D., editors (1997) *ZUM'97: The Z Formal Specification Notation*, Lecture Notes in Computer Science **1212**, Springer-Verlag, Heidelberg.

Bowen, J.P. and Stavridou, V. (1993) Safety-critical systems, formal methods and Standards, *IEE/BCS Software Engineering Journal*, **8**(4):189–209, July.

Bowen, J.P. and Stavridou, V. (1994) Formal methods: epideictic or apodeictic?, *IEE/BCS Software Engineering Journal*, **9**(1):2, January.

Boyer, R.S. and Moore, J S. (1998) *A Computational Logic Handbook, 2nd edition.* Academic Press, London..

Boyer, R.S., Goldschlag, D., Kaufmann, M. and Moore, J S. (1991) Functional Instantiation in First Order Logic. In *Artificial Intelligence and Mathematical Theory of Computation: Papers in Honor of John McCarthy.* Academic Press, pp 7–26.

Brilliant, S., Knight, J.C. and Leveson, N.G. (1989) The consistent comparison problem in N–version programming. *IEEE Transactions on Software Engineering*, **15**(11), November.

Brilliant, S., Knight, J.C. and Leveson, N.G. (1990) Analysis of faults in an N-version software experiment. *IEEE Transations on Software Engineering*, **16**(2), February.

Brock, B.C., Kaufmann, M. and Moore, J S. (1996) ACL2 Theorems about Commercial Microprocessors. In *Formal Methods in Computer-Aided Design*, Lecture Notes in Computer Science **1166**, Mandayam Srivas and Albert Camilleri, editors, Springer-Verlag.

Brock, B.C. and Hunt, Jr., W.A. (1997a) The DUAL–EVAL Hardware Description Language and Its Use in the Formal Specification and Verification of the FM9001 Microprocessor. *Formal Methods in System Design*, **11**(1):71–104, July.

Brock, B.C. and Hunt, Jr., W.A. (1997b) Formally Specifying and Mechanically Verifying Programs for the Motorola Complex Arithmetic Processor DSP. In *1997 IEEE International Conference on Computer Design*, 13–15 October, IEEE Computer Society Press, pp 31–36.

Brock, B.C., Hunt, Jr., W.A. and Kaufmann, M. (1994) *The FM9001 Microprocessor Proof*, Technical Report 86, Computational Logic, Inc., December.

Bruns, G. (1994) *Applying process refinement to a safety-relevant system.* Technical Report ECS-LFCS-94-287, University of Edinburgh Laboratory for the Foundations of Computer Science, March.

Bruun, P.M. (1995) *RAISE Tools User Guide*, Technical Report LACOS/CRI/DOC/4, Computer Resources International A/S, Birkerod, Denmark.

Bryant, R.E. (1986) Graph-based algorithms for boolean function manipulation. *IEEE Transactions on Computers*, **35**(8):677–691, August.

Bryant, R.E. (1989) Verification of Synchronous Circuits by Symbolic Logic Simulation. In *Hardware Specification, Verification and Synthesis: Mathematical Aspects*, Lecture Notes in Computer Science **408**, pp 14–24, Springer-Verlag.

Bryant, R.E. (1995) *Binary Decision Diagrams and Beyond: Enabling Technologies for Formal Verification.* Technical report, Carnegie Mellon University, November.

Burch, J.R. and Dill, D.L. (1994) Automatic verification of pipelined microprocessor control. In David Dill, editor, *Computer-Aided Verification, CAV '94,* Lecture Notes in Computer Science **818**, Springer-Verlag, pp 68–80.

Burnet, J. (1892) *Early Greek Philosophy,* A & C Black, London.

Burrows, M., Abadi, M. and Needham, R.M. (1989) A logic of authentication, In *Proceedings of the Royal Society of London A* **426**, pp 233–271.

Card World Indpendent (1996) *Pre-authorised, off-line debit card launched,* pp 1–2, September.

Cadence Design Systems, Inc., Alta Group (1994) *Signal Processing WorkSystem(r) Hardware Design System(tm) User's Guide,* Foster City, CA, December.

Carlsson, B., Carlsson, M. and G Stålmarck, G. (1997) . *NP(FD): A proof System for Finite Domain Constraints.* Technical report, Xerox Parc, SICS and Logikkonsult.

Carrington, D. (1992) ZOOM workshop report, In J.E. Nicholls, editor, *Z User Workshop,* pp 352–364, Workshops in Computing, Springer-Verlag, London.

Chiu, C.K., Chou, C.M., Lee, J.H.M., Leung, H.F. and Leung, Y.W. (1996) A Constraint-Based Interactive Train Rescheduling Tool, In *Proc. Second International Conference on Principles and Practice of Constraint Programming,* LNCS **1118**, pp 104–118, Springer-Verlag, Heidelberg.

Chung, L. and Nixon, B.A. (1995) Dealing with non-functional requirements: Three experimental studies of a process-oriented approach. In *Proc. of International Conference on Software Engineering,* pages 25–37, Seattle, Washington, ACM Press.

Clarke, E. and Wing, J. (1996) Formal methods: state of the art and future directions, *ACM Computing Surveys,* **28**(4):626–643, December.

Clarke, E.M., Grumberg, O. and Long, D.E. (1996) Model checking. In *Model Checking, Abstraction and Composition, Nato ASI Series F* **152**, pp 477–498. Springer-Verlag.

Cleaveland, R., Parrow, J. and Steffen, B. (1990) A semantics-based verification tool for finite-state systems. In E. Brinksma, G. Scollo, and C.A. Vissers, editors, *Protocol Specification, Testing, and Verification,* pp 287–302. Elsevier Science (North-Holland).

Cleaveland, R., Parrow, J. and Steffen, B. (1993) The Concurrency Workbench: a semantics-based tool for the verification of concurrent systems. *ACM Transactions on Programming Languages and Systems,* **15**(1):36–72, January.

Clements, P.C. (1986) Using information-hiding as a design discipline: Techniques and lessons. In *Proc. Structured Development Forum VIII,* Seattle, WA, August.

Coe, M.L. (1994) *Results from Verifying a Pipelined Microprocessor.* Master's Thesis, University of Idaho, October.

Collete, P. and Cau, A. (1995) Parallel composition of assumption-commitment specifications: A unifying approach for shared variables and distributed message passing concurrency. *Acta Informatica.*

Craigen, D. (1991) *Reference Manual for the Language Verdi.* Technical Report TR-91-5429-09a, ORA Canada, Ottawa, Ontario, September.

Craigen, D., Gerhart, S. and Ralston, T. (1993) *An International Survey of Industrial Applications of Formal Methods.* NRL Formal Report 5546–93-9582, Naval Research Laboratory, Washington, D.C., September 1993.

Craigen, D., Kromodimoeljo, S., Meisels, I., Pase, W. and Saaltin, M. (1991) EVES: An Overview. In *Proceedings of VDM '91 (Formal Software Development Methods),* Noordwijkerhout, The Netherlands, October. Lecture Notes in Computer Science **551**, Springer-Verlag, Berlin, 1991.

Crivelli, P. (1996) The argument from knowing and not knowing in Plato's *Theatetus* (187E5–188C8), *Proceedings of the Aristotelian Society,* **XCVI**(VII):177–196.

Curtis, B. (1992) The case for process. In K.E. Kendall, editor, *The Impact of Computer Supported Technologies on Information Systems Development*, Elsevier Science (North-Holland).

D'Agostino, M. (1990) *Investigations into the Complexity of some Propositional Calculi.* Ph.D. thesis, Oxford University, Programming Research Group; also available as Technical Monograph PRG-88.

Dalesio, L.R., Kraimer, M.R. and Kozubal, A.J. (1991) EPICS architecture, In C.O. Pak, S. Kurokawa and T. Katoh, editors, *Proceedings of the International Conference on Accelerator and Large Experimental Physics Control Systems*, Tsukuba, Japan, pp 278–282.

Dandanell, B., Gørtz, J., Zierau, E. and J. Storbank Pedersen (1993) Experiences from Applications of RAISE. In *FME'93: Industrial Strength Formal Methods*, LNCS 570, Springer-Verlag, Heidelberg.

Dean, C.N. and Hinchey, M.G., editors (1996) *Teaching and Learning Formal Methods*, Academic Press International Series in Formal Methods, London.

Dehbonei, B. and Mejia, F. (1995), Formal development of safety-critial software systems in railway signalling, In M.G. Hinchey and J.P. Bowen, editors, *Applications of Formal Methods*, Prentice Hall Interntaional Series in Computer Science, Hemel Hempstead.

Dong, Y. (1996) *Basic Specification of PRaCoSY*, Technical Report, United Nationasl University, International Institute for Software Technology, Macau, March.

Drakos, N. (1993) Text to hypertext conversion with LaTeX2HTML. *Baskerville*, 3(2):12–15, December 1993.

Dürr, E., Plat, N. and de Boer, M. (1995) CombiCom: Tracking and Tracing Rail Traffic using VDM^{++}. In Hinchey and Bowen (1995).

Ekenberg, L. et al. (1996) *Reference Manual, NP-Tools 2.2.* Logikkonsult NP AB, NPT-01-07-02 2.0, October.

Ericsson Dansk Signalindustri A/S (1989) *The Sternol Programming Language.* Technical Report 1/155 17-LXA 108 10 Uen, April.

Ericsson Utvecklings AB (1993) *Delphi Self-Study Reading Material.* Technical Report F920892, April.

Ericsson Utvecklings AB (1997) *Introducing CLARE and ECLARE*, White paper UAB/U-96:080, October.

Eriksson, L.-H. (1997a) *Formalisering av krav på ställverk.* Technical Report 1997:1, Swedish National Rail Administration.

Eriksson, L.-H. (1997b) *Formell verifiering av ställverk.* Technical Report 1997:2, Swedish National Rail Administration.

Ett, W.H. and Trammell, C.J. (1996) *A Guide to Integration of Object-Oriented Methods and Cleanroom Software Engineering*, Available via the WWW at URL: *http://source.asset.com/stars/loral/cleanroom/guide.html.*

Evans, A.S. (1994) Specifying and verifying concurrent systems using Z, In Naftalin *et al.* (1994)

Evans, A.S., Clark, T., Lai, L. and Byrant, T. (1997) Formalising the Unified Modelling Language. In *Proc. Northern Formal Methods Workshop*, University of Bradford, UK.

Faser, M.D., Kumar, K. and Vaishnavi, V.K. (1994) Strategies for incorporating formal specifications in software development, *Communications of the ACM*, 37(10):74–94, October.

Fitzgerald, J.S., Jones, C.B. and Lucas, P., editors (1997) *FME'97: Industrial Application and Strengthened Foundations of Formal Methods*, Lecture Notes in Computer Science **1313**, Springer-Verlag, Heidelberg.

Formal Systems (Europe) Ltd. (1994) *Failures Divergence Refinement: User Manual and Tutorial*, January.

Froscher, J.N., Goldschlage, D.M., Kang, M.H., Landwehr, C.E., Moore, A.P., Moskowitz, I.S. and Payne, C.N. (1995) Improving inter-enclave information flow for a secure strike planning application. In *Proc. 11th Annual Computer Security Applications Conference*, pp 89–98, New Orleans, LA, December, IEEE Computer Society Press.

Garlan, D. (1995) Making formal methods effective for professional software engineers, *Information and Software Technology*, **37**(5–6):261–268, May–June.

Garlan, D. and Delisle, N. (1990) Formal specifications as reusable frameworks. In D. Bjorner, C.A.R. Hoare and H. Langmaack, editors, *VDM'90: VDM and Z — Formal Methods in Software Development*, pp 150–163, Springer-Verlag.

Garon, G. and Outerbridge, R. (1991) DES watch: an examination of the sufficiency of the data encryption standard for financial institution information security in the 1990's, *Cryptologia* **XV**(3):177–193, July.

Gaudel, M.-C. and Woodcock, J.C.P., editors (1996) *FME'96: Industrial Benefit and Advances in Formal Methods*, Lecture Notes in Computer Science **1051**, Springer-Verlag, Heidelberg.

George, C. (1995) *A Theory of Distributing Train Rescheduling*. Research Report International Institute for Software Technology, United Nations University, Macau.

German, S. (1996) Research goals for formal methods, *ACM Computing Surveys*, **28**(4es), pp 118, December.

Gilfeather, S., Gehman, J. and Harrison, C. (1994) Architecture of a Complex Arithmetic Processor for Communication Signal Processing. In *SPIE Proceedings, International Symposium on Optics, Imaging, and Instrumentation*, Volume 2296, Advanced Signal Processing: Algorithms, Architectures, and Implementations V, pp 624–625, July.

Glass, R.L. (1997) Revisiting the industry / academe communication chasm, *Communications of the ACM*, **40**(6):11–13, June.

Gligor, V.D., Kailar, R., Stubblebine, S. and Gong, L. (1991) Logics for cryptographic protocols — virtues and limitations, In *Proceedings of Computer Security Foundations Workshop IV*, IEEE Computer Society Press, pp 219–226.

Gong, L. (1990) *Cryptographic Protocols for Distributed Systems*, Ph.D. dissertation, University of Cambridge Computer Laboratory.

Gong, L., Needham, R.M. and Yahalom, R. (1990) Reasoning about belief in cryptographic protocols, In *Proceedings of the 1990 IEEE Computer Security Symposium on Research in Security and Privacy*, IEEE Computer Society Press, pp 234–248.

Gordon, M.J.C. (1985) *Why Higher-order Logic is a Good Formalism for Specifying and Verifying Hardware*. Technical Report 77, University of Cambridge Computer Laboratory, September.

Gordon, M.J.C. (1995) The Semantic Challenge of Verilog HDL. In *Proceedings of the Tenth Annual IEEE Symposium on Logic in Computer Science (LICS'95)*.

Gordon, M.J.C. and Melham, T.F., editors (1993) *Introduction to HOL: A Theorem Proving Environment for Higher Order Logic*. Cambridge University Press, Cambridge, UK.

Gotel, O.C.Z. and Finkelstein, A.C.W. (1994) An analysis of the requirements traceability problem. In *Proc. International Conference on Requirements Engineering*, pp 94–101, Colorado Springs, CO, May, IEEE Computer Society Press.

Griffin, T.W., Pajak, T.F., Laramore, G.E., Duncan, W., Richter, M.P., Hendrickson, F.R. and Maor, M.H. (1988) Neutron vs photon irradiation of inoperable salivary gland tumors: Results of an RTOG-MRC cooperative randomized study, *International Journal of Radiation Oncology, Biology and Physics*, **15**:1085–1090.

Groote, G., Koorn, J. and van Vlijmen, S. (1994) *The Safety Guaranteeing System at station Hoorn-Kersenboogerd*. Technical Report 121, Logic Group Preprint series, Department of Philosophy, Utrecht University, The Netherlands.

Guaspari, D., Marceau, C. and Polak, W. (1990) Formal verification of Ada programs. *Transactions on Software Engineering*, **16**(9):1058–1075, September.

Halbwachs, N., Caspi, P., Raymond, P. and Pilaud, D. (1991) The synchronous data flow programming language LUSTRE. *Proceedings of the IEEE*.

Hall, J.A. (1990) Seven myths of formal methods, *IEEE Software*, **7**(5), 11–19, September.

Hall, J.A. (1994) Specifying and interpreting class hierarchies in Z. In J.P. Bowen and J.A. Hall, editors, *Z User Workshop, Cambridge 94*, Workshops in Computing, pp 120–138, Springer-Verlag, London.

Hansen, K.M. (1994) Validation of a Railway Interlocking Model. In Naftalin *et al.* (1994).

Harel, D. (1987) Statecharts: a visual formalism for complex systems. *Science of Computer Programming*, **8**:231–274.

Harel, D., Lachover, H., Naamad, A., Pnueli, A., Politi, M., Sherman, R., Shtull-Trauring, A. and Trakhtenbrot, M. (1990) Statemate: A working environment for the development of complex reactive systems. *IEEE Transactions on Software Engineering*, **16**(4):403–414, April.

Harrison, J. (1996) The Stålmarck Method as a HOL Derived Rule. In *Theorem Proving in Higher Order Logics*,Lecture Notes in Computer Science, **1125**. pp 221–234, Springer-Verlag, Heidelberg.

Hatley, D.J. and Pirbhai, I.A. (1988) *Strategies for Real-Time System Specification*. Dorset House, 1988.

Hausler, P.A., Linger, R.C. and Trammell, C.J. (1996) Adopting cleanroom software engineering with a phased approach, In J.H. Poore and C.J. Trammell, editors, *Cleanroom Software Engineering: A Reader*, Blackwell, Oxford.

Hayes, I.J. (1985) Applying formal specification to software development in industry, *IEEE Transactions on Software Engineering*, **11**(2):169–178, February.

Hazards Forum (1995) *Safety-related Systems: Guidance for Engineers*, The Hazards Forum, 1 Great George Street, London SW1P 4AA, UK.

Heimdahl, M.P.E. (1995) *Experiences and Lessons from the Analysis of TCAS II*, Technical Report CPS-95-25, Michigan State University, June.

Heimdahl, M.P.E. and Czerny, B.C. (1996) Using PVS to analyze hierarchical state-based requirements for completeness and consistency. In *Proceedings of the IEEE High Assurance Systems Engineering Workshop*.

Heimdahl, M.P.E. and Leveson, N.G. (1995) Completeness and consistency analysis of state-based requirements, In *Proceedings of the 17th International Conference on Software Engineering*, IEEE Computer Society Press, pp 3–14.

Heimdahl, M.P.E. and Leveson, N.G. (1996) Completeness and consistency analysis of state-based requirements. *IEEE Transactions on Software Engineering*, **22**(6):363–377, June.

Heimdahl, M.P.E. and Thompson, J.M. (1997) Specification and analysis of system level inter-component communication. In M.G. Hinchey and S. Liu, editors, *Proceedings of the First IEEE International Conference on Formal Engineering Methods*, Hiroshima, Japan, 10–12 November 1997, IEEE Computer Society Press, Los Alamitos.

Heimdahl, M.P.E. and Whalen, M.W. (1997) Reduction and slicing of hierarchical state machines. In *Proceedings of the Fifth ACM SIGSOFT Symposium on the Foundations of Software Engineering*, September.

Heitmeyer, C.L. (1997) Formal methods: panacea or academic poppycock?, In J.P. Bowen, M.G. Hinchey and D. Till, editors, *ZUM'97: The Z Formal Specification Notation*, Lecture Notes in Computer Science **1212**, Springer-Verlag, Heidelberg, pp 3–9.

Heninger, K. (1980) Specifying software requirements for computer systems: new techniques and their application, *IEEE Transactions on Software Engineering*, **6**(1):2–13, January.

Henzinger, T.A. (1996) Some myths about formal verification, *ACM Computing Surveys*, **28**(4es):119, December.

Hernandez, D. (1993) Reasoning with qualitative representations: exploiting the structure of space. In *Proceedings of the International Workshop on Qualitative Reasoning and Decision Technologies*, Barcelona, Spain, June.

Hesse, M. (1974) *Structure of Scientific Inference*, Macmillan, pp 142–146.

Hill, J.V. (1991) Software development methods in practice, In A. Church, editor, *Microprocessor Based Protection Systems*, Routledge, London.

Hinchey, M.G. and Bowen, J.P. (1995) *Applications of Formal Methods*, Prentice Hall International Series in Computer Science. Hemel Hempstead.

Hoare, C.A.R. (1983) Programming is an engineering profession, In P.J.L. Wallis, editor, *Software Engineering*, State of the Art Report **11**(3):77–84, Pergamon Press/Infotech, Oxford. Also issued as Technical Monograph PRG-27, Oxford University Computing Laboratory, May 1982.

Hoare, C.A.R. (1985) *Communicating Sequential Processes*, Prentice Hall International Series in Computer Science, Hemel Hempstead.

Holzmann, G.J. (1991) *Design and Validation of Computer Protocols*. Prentice Hall, Englewood Cliffs, NJ.

Hunt, Jr., W.A. (1994) *FM8501: A Verified Microprocessor*. Lecture Notes in Computer Science **795**, Springer-Verlag.

Hunt, Jr., W.A. and Brock, B.C. (1992) A Formal HDL and Its Use in the FM9001 Verification. In C.A.R. Hoare and M.J.C. Gordon, editors, *Mechanized Reasoning and Hardware Design*, pp 35–48. Prentice-Hall International Series in Computer Science, Englewood Cliffs, NJ.

IEEE P1003.21 Working Group (1996) *Posix 1003.21 Realtime Distributed Systems Communication Application Program Interface (API)*, Draft LIS/V1.0.

International Electrotechnical Commission (1986) *Software for Computers in the Safety Systems of Nuclear Power Plants*, IEC-880.

Jacky, J. (1990) Formal specifications for a clinical cyclotron control system, In M. Moriconi, editor, *Proceedings of the ACM SIGSOFT International Workshop on Formal Methods in Software Development*, 9–11 May, Napa, California, USA, pp 45–54 (Also in *ACM Software Engineering Notes*, **15**(4), September).

Jacky, J. (1992) *Formal Specification and Development of Control System Input/Output*, Technical Report 92-05-02, Radiation Oncology Department RC-08, University of Washington.

Jacky, J. (1993) Formal specification and development of control system input/output, In J.P. Bowen and J.E. Nicholls, editors, *Z User Workshop, London 1992*, Springer-Verlag Workshops in Computing Series, London, pp 95–108.

Jacky, J. (1995) Specifying a safety-critical control system in Z, *IEEE Transactions on Software Engineering*, **21**(2):99–106.

Jacky, J. (1996) Safety-critical computing: hazards, practices, standards, and regulation, In R. Kling, editor, *Computerization and Controversy: Value Conflicts and Social Choices*, Second Edition, Academic Press, San Diego.

Jacky, J. (1997) *The Way of Z: Practical Programming with Formal Methods*, Cambridge University Press, Cambridge, UK.

Jacky, J. and Patrick, M. (1997) Modelling, checking, and implementing a control program for a radiation therapy machine, In R. Cleaveland and D. Jackson, editors, *AAS '97: Proceedings of the First ACM SIGPLAN Workshop on Automated Analysis of Software*, ACM Press, pp 25–32.

Jacky, J., Patrick, M. and Risler, R. (1995b) *Clinical Neutron Therapy System, Control System Specification, Part III: Therapy Console Internals*, Technical Report 95-08-03, Radiation Oncology Department, University of Washington, Seattle, WA, August.

Jacky, J., Patrick, M. and Unger, J. (1995a) *Formal Specification of Control Software for a Radiation Therapy Machine*, Technical Report 95-12-01, Radiation Oncology Department, University of Washington, Seattle, WA, December.

Jacky, J., Risler, R., Kalet, I. and Wootton, P. (1990) *Clinical Neutron Therapy System, Control System Specification, Part I: System Overview and Hardware Organization*, Technical Report 90-12-01, Radiation Oncology Department, University of Washington, Seattle, WA, December.

Jacky, J., Risler, R., Kalet, I, Wootton, P. and Brossard, S. (1992) *Clinical Neutron Therapy System, Control System Specification, Part II: User Operations*, Technical Report 92-05-01, Radiation Oncology Department, University of Washington, Seattle, WA, May.

Jacky, J. and Unger, J. (1995) From Z to code: a graphical user interface for a radiation therapy machine, In J. P. Bowen and M.G. Hinchey, editors, *ZUM'95: The Z Formal Specification Notation*, Lecture Notes in Computer Science **967**, Springer-Verlag, Heidelberg, pp 315–333.

Jacky, J., Unger, J. and Patrick, M. (1996) *CNTS Implementation*, Technical Report 96-04-01, Radiation Oncology Department, University of Washington, Seattle, WA, April.

Jacky, J., Unger, J., Patrick, M., Reid, D. and Risler, R. (1997) Experience with Z developing a control program for a radiation therapy machine, In J.P. Bowen, M.G. Hinchey and D. Till, editors, *ZUM'97: The Z Formal Specification Notation*, Lecture Notes in Computer Science **1212**, Springer-Verlag, Heidelberg, pp 317–328.

Jacky, J. and White, C.P. (1990) Testing a 3-D radiation therapy planning program, *International Journal of Radiation Oncology, Biology and Physics*, **18**:253–261, January.

Jacob, J. (1988) Refinement of Shared Systems. In J.A. McDermid, editor, *The Theory and Practice of Refinement*, pp 27–36, Butterworths.

Jaffe, M.S. and Leveson, N.G. (1989) Completeness, robustness, and safety in real-time software requirements specification. In *Proceedings of the Tenth International Conference on Software Engineering*, pp 302–311, Pittsburgh, PA, May. IEEE Computer Society Press, Los Alamitos.

Jaffe, M.S., Leveson, N.G., Heimdahl, M.P.E. and Melhart, B. (1991) Software requirements analysis for real-time process-control systems. *IEEE Transactions on Software Engineering*, **17**(3):241–258, March.

Johnson, S.D. (1989) Manipulating Logical Organization with System Factorizations. In *Hardware Specification, Verification and Synthesis: Mathematical Aspects.*, Lecture Notes in Computer Science **408**, Springer-Verlag, pp 259–280.

Jonasson, A. (1996) *Proof logging; definition of the log format*. Technical Report U-96025, Logikkonsult NP AB, April.

Jones, C.B. (1980) *Software Development: A Rigorous Approach*. Prentice Hall International Series in Computer Science, Hemel Hempstead.

Jones, C.B. (1983) Tentative steps towards a development method for interfering programs. *ACM Transactions on Programming Languages and Systems*, **5**(4):596–619.

Jones, C.B. (1986) *Systematic Software Development Using VDM*. Prentice Hall International Series in Computer Science, Hemel Hempstead.

Jones, C.B. (1996) Formal methods light, *ACM Computing Surveys*, **28**(4es):121, December.

Jonsson, B. (1994) Compositional specification and verification of distributed systems. *ACM Transactions on Programming Languages and Systems*, **16**(2):259–303.

Jover, P., Conflant, M., Bussac, J.P. (1992) The introduction of computer based systems into instrumentation and control: the approach of the French safety authority. In *Proceed-*

ings of the IAEA International Symposium on Nuclear Power Plant Instrumentation and Control, Tokyo, May.

Kaiser, G.E., Dossick, S.E., Jiang, W. and Yang, J.J. (1997) An architecture for WWW-based hypercode environments. In *Proc. of 1997 International Conference on Software Engineering*, May.

Kalet, I.J., Jacky, J.P., Risler, R., Rohlin, S. and Wootton, P. (1997) Integration of radiotherapy planning systems and radiotherapy treatment equipment: 11 years experience, *International Journal of Radiation Oncology, Biology and Physics*, **38**(1).

Kaufmann, J. and Moore, J S. (1996) ACL2: An Industrial Strength Version of Nqthm. In *Proceedings of the Eleventh Annual Conference on Computer Assurance (COMPASS-96)*. IEEE Computer Society Press, pp 23–34, June.

Keenan, D.J. and Heimdahl, M.P.E. (1997) Code generation from hierarchical state machines. In *Proceedings of the International Symposium on Requirements Engineering*, January.

Kesten, Y. and Pnueli, A. (1998) *Deductive verification of fair discrete systems*. Technical report, Minerva Center for the Verification of Reactive Systems at the Weizmann Institute, Israel.

Kesten, Y., Pnueli, A. and Raviv, L. (1998) Algorithmic verification of linear temporal logic specifications. In K.G. Larsen, S. Skyum, and G. Winskel, editors, *Proc. 25th International Colloquium on Automata, Languages and Programming*, Lecture Notes in Computer Science **1443**, Springer-Verlag, Heidelberg.

King, T. and Rawlings, R. (1994) *Logical Elements of Interlocking Systems*. Railtrack plc, November.

Knight, J.C. and Leveson, N.G. (1986) An experimental evaluation of the assumption of independence in multi-version programming. *IEEE Transactions on Software Engineering*, **12**(1):96–109, January.

Knuth, D.E. (1984) Literate programming. *The Computer Journal*, **27**(2):97–111, May.

Koos, C.D. and Breuer, P.T., editors (1995) *Formal Semantics for VHDL*. Kluwer Academic Publishers, Boston.

Kuipers, B.J. (1986) Reasoning with qualitative models. *Artificial Intelligence*, **59**:125–132, August.

Kurshan, R.P. and McMillan, K.L. (1995) A structural induction theorem for processes. *Information and Computation*, **117**:1–11.

Lamport, L. (1997) Proving the correctness of multiprocess programs. *IEEE Transactions on Software Engineering*, **3**:125–143.

Lamport, L. (1994) *A Document Preparation System LATEX: User's Guide and Reference Manual, 2nd edition*. Addison-Wesley, 1994.

Landwehr, C.E. (1989) The RS-232 software repeater problem. Cipher Newsletter of the Technical Committee on Security and Privacy, Summer.

Lano, K.C. (1996) *The B Language and Method: A Guide to Practical Formal Development*, Springer-Verlag FACIT, London.

Lano, K.C. and Sanchez, A. (1997) *Specification of a Chemical Process Controller in VDM^{++} and B*, Technical Report GR/K68783-11, Department of Computing, Imperial College, London, UK, January.

Larsen, P.G., Plat, N. and Toetenel, H. (1994) A Formal Semantics of Data Flow Diagrams. *Formal Aspects of Computing*, **6**:(6), December.

Leveson, N.G. (1995) *Safeware: System Safety and Computers*, Addison-Wesley, Menlo Park, CA.

Leveson, N.G. (1983a) Software fault tolerance: the case for forward recovery. In *Proceedings of the AIAA Conference on Computers in Aerospace*, Hartford, CT.

Leveson, N.G. (1983b) Verification of safety. In *Proceedings Third International Workshop on Achieving Safe Real Time Systems*, Queen's College, Cambridge, England, September.

Leveson, N.G. (1986) Software safety: why, what, and how. *ACM Computing Surveys*, **18**(2):125–163, June.

Leveson, N.G., Cha, S.S., Knight, J.C. and Shimeall, T.J. (1990) The use of self checks and voting in software error detection: an empirical study. *IEEE Transactions on Software Engineering*, **16**(4), April.

Leveson, N.G., Cha, S.S. and Shimeall, T.J. (1991) Safety verification of Ada programs using software fault trees. *IEEE Software*, **8**(7):48–59, July.

Leveson, N.G. and Harvey, P.R. (1983) Analyzing software safety. *IEEE Transactions on Software Engineering*, **9**(5):569–579, September.

Leveson, N.G., Heimdahl, M.P.E., Hildreth, H. and Reese, J.D. (1994) Requirements specification for process-control systems. *IEEE Transations on Software Engineering*, **20**(9), September.

Leveson, N.G. and Palmer, E. (1997) Designing automation to reduce operator errors. *Systems, Man, and Cybernetics*, October.

Leveson, N.G., Reese, J.D., Koga, S., Pinnel, L.D. and Sandys, S.D. (1997) Analyzing requirements specifications for mode confusion errors. In *Proceedings of the Workshop on Human Error and System Development*.

Leveson, N.G. and Shimeall, T.J. (1983) Safety assertions for process control systems. In *Proceedings 13th International Symposium on Fault Tolerant Computing*, Milan, July, IEEE Computer Society Press, Los Alamitos.

Leveson, N.G., Shimeall, T.J., Stolzy, J.L. and Thomas, J. (1983) Design for safe software. In *Proceedings of the American Institute for Astronautics and Aeronautics Space Sciences Meeting*, Reno, Nevada.

Leveson, N.G. and Stolzy, J.L. (1987) Safety analysis using Petri nets. *IEEE Transactions on Software Engineering*, **13**(3):386–397, March.

Leveson, N.G. and Turner, C.S. (1993) An investigation of the Therac-25 accidents, *IEEE Computer*, **26**(7):18–41, July.

Lewerentz, C. and Lindner, T., editors (1995) *Formal Development of Reactive Systems: Case Study Production Cell*, Lecture Notes in Computer Science **891**, Springer-Verlag, Heidelberg.

Linger, R.C., Mills, H.D. and Witt, B.J. (1979) *Structured Programming: Theory and Practice*, Addison-Wesley, Reading, MA.

Linger, R.C. and Mills, H.D. (1988) A case study in cleanroom software engineering: the IBM COBOL structuring facility, In *Proceedings of the 12th Annual International Computer Software and Applications Conference*, IEEE Computer Society Press, Los Alamitos.

Linger, R.C. (1993) Cleanroom software engineering for zero-defect software, In *Proceedings of the 15th International Conference on Software Engineering*, Baltimore, MD, 17–21 May, IEEE Computer Society Press, Los Alamitos.

Linger, R.C. (1996) Cleanroom process model, In J.H. Poore and C.J. Trammell, editors, *Cleanroom Software Engineering: A Reader*, Blackwell, Oxford.

Linger, R.C., Paulk, M.C. and Trammell, C.J. (1996) *Cleanroom Software Engineering Implementation of the Capability Maturity Model (CMM) for Software*, Technical Report CMU/SEI-96-TR-023, Software Engineering Institute, Pittsburgh, PA, December.

Linger, R.C. and Trammell, C.J. (1996) *Cleanroom Software Engineering Reference Model*, Technical Report CMU/SEI-96-TR-022, Software Engineering Institute, Pittsburgh, PA, November.

Lonchamp, J., Benali, K., Godard, C. and Derniame, J.C. (1990) Modeling and enacting software processes: an analysis. In *Proc. of 14th Annual International Computer Software and Applications Conference*, pp 727–736, Chicago, IL, October, IEEE Computer Society Press.

Luqi and Goguen J.A. (1997) Formal methods: promises and problems, *IEEE Software*, **14**(1):73–85, January.

Lutz, R. (1993a) Analyzing software requirements errors in safety-critical, embedded systems. In *Proceedings of the IEEE International Symposium on Requirements Engineering*, pp 35–46, January, IEEE Computer Society Press, Los Alamitos.

Lutz, R. (1993b) Targeting safety-related errors during software requirements analysis. In *Proceedings of the First ACM SIGSOFT Symposium on the Foundations of Software Engineering*.

Lyu, M.R. (1995) *Handbook of Software Reliability Engineering*, McGraw–Hill, New York.

MacKenzie, D. (1995) The automation of proof: a historical and sociological exploration, *IEEE Annals of the History of Computing*, **17**(3):7–29, Fall.

MacLean, A., Young, R.M. and Moran, T.P. (1989) Design rationale: The argument behind the artifact. In *Proc. of CHI'89*, pages 247–252, Austin, Texas, May, ACM Press.

McDermid, J.A. (1984) Support for safety cases and safety arguments using SAM. *Reliability Engineering and System Safety*, **43**:111–127.

McDermid, J.A., editor (1991) *Software Engineer's Reference Book*, Butterworth Heinemann, Oxford.

McGibbon, T. (1996) *A Business Case for Software Process Improvement*, Report, DoD Data and Analysis Center for Software.

McMillan, K.L. (1993) *Symbolic Model Checking*. Kluwer Academic Publishers, Boston..

Manna, Z. and Pnueli, A. (1990) A hierarchy of temporal properties. In *Proceedings of the 9th ACM Symposium on the Principles of Distributed Computing*, pp 377–408, ACM Press.

Manna, Z. and Pnueli, A. (1992) *Time for Concurrency*, Technical Report, Department of Computer Science, Stanford University, CA.

Manna, Z. and Pnueli, A. (1995) *Temporal Verification of Reactive Systems: Safety*. Springer-Verlag, New York.

Martersteck, K.E. and Spencer, A.E. (1985) Introduction to the 5ESS(TM) switching system, *AT&T Technical Journal*, **64**(6 part 2):1305–1314, July–August.

Martin, R. (1994) Mondex: the way forward?, *Cards International* **104**:9, 24 Febraury 1994.

Mataga, P. and Zave, P. (1995) Multiparadigm specification of an AT&T switching system. In M.G. Hinchey and J.P. Bowen, editors, *Applications of Formal Methods*, Prentice Hall International Series in Computer Science, Hemel Hempstead.

Mei, H. (1995) *A Generic Concurrent Distributed Architecture*, Technical Note, International Institute for Software Technology, United Nations University, Macau, June.

Melhart, B.E. (1990) *Specification and Analysis of the Requirements for Embedded Software with an External Interaction Model*. Ph.D. thesis, University of California, Irvine, July.

Middleburg, C.A. (1989) VVSL: A Language for Structured VDM Specifications, *Formal Aspects of Computing*, **1**(1):115–135, January-March.

Mills, H.D. (1971) Top-down programming in large systems, In R. Ruskin, editor, *Debugging Techniques in Large Systems*, Prentice Hall, Englewood Cliffs, NJ.

Mills, H.D., Linger, R.C. and Hevner, A.R. (1986) *Principles of Information Systems Analysis and Design*, Academic Press, New York.

Mills, H.D. (1992) Certifying the correctness of software, In *Proceedings of the 25th Hawaii International Conference on System Sciences*, Kauai, Hawaii, 7–10 January, IEEE Computer Society Press.

Milner, R. (1989) *Communication and Concurrency*. Prentice Hall International Series in Computer Science, Hemel Hempstead.

Modugno, F., Leveson, N.G., Reese, J.D., Partridge, K. and Sandys, S.D. (1997) Experimental application of safety analysis to a software requirements specification. *Requirements Engineering Journal*.

Mondadori, M. (1988) *Classical analytical deduction (part I and II)*. Annali dell'Universita de Ferrara, Sezione III.

Moore, A.P. (1990) The specification and verified decomposition of system requirements using CSP. *IEEE Transactions on Software Engineering*, **16**(9):932–948, September. Preferrably see:
http://www.itd.nrl.navy.mil/ITD/5540/publications/CHACS.

Moore, A.P. (1996) *The JMCIS Information Flow Improvement (JIFI) assurance strategy*. NRL Technical Memorandum 5540–272a:apm, Naval Research Laboratory, Washington, D.C., September. See:
http://www.itd.nrl.navy.mil/ITD/5540/publications/CHACS.

Moore, A.P., Chapman, E., Kim, D., Klinker, J.E., Mihelcic, D.M., Payne, C.N., Voreh, M. and Hayman, K. (1995) *External COMSEC adaptor software engineering methodology*. NRL Memorandum Report 5542–95-7768, Naval Research Laboratory, August. See:
http://www.itd.nrl.navy.mil/ITD/5540/publications/CHACS.

Moore, A.P. and Payne, C.N. (1996a) Increasing assurance with literate programming techniques. In *Proceedings of the 11th Annual Conference on Computer Assurance*, pp 187–198, Gaithersburg, MD, June, IEEE Computer Society Press.

Moore, A.P. and Payne, C.N. (1996b) *The RS-232 character repeater refinement and assurance argument*. NRL Memorandum Report 5540–96-7872, Naval Research Laboratory, Washington, D.C., July.

Moutrey, G.B. (1992) Equipment and system performance validation: Sizewell B reactor protection systems. In *Proceedings of Forum on Safety RElated Systems in Nuclear Applications*, The Roayl Academy of Engineering, London, October.

Naftalin, M., Denvir, T. and Bertrand, M., editors (1994) *FME'94: Industrial Benefit of Formal Methods*, Lecture Notes in Computer Science **873**, Springer-Verlag, Heidelberg.

Neil, M., Osttrolenk, G., Tobin, M. and Southwark, M. (1998) Lessons from using Z to specify a software tool. *IEEE Transactions on Software Engineering*, **24**(1):15–23, January.

Neumann, P.G. (1995) *Computer Related Risks*, Addison-Wesley, Menlo Park, CA.

Nicholls, J.E., editor (1995) *Z Notation*. Draft Standard Version 1.1, June.

Nielsen, M., Havelund, K., Ritter Wagner, K. and George, C. (1989) The RAISE language, method and tools, *Formal Aspects of Computing*, **1**(1):85–114, January–March.

Nu Thena Systems, Inc. (1993) *Foresight: Modeling, Simulation, and Prototyping*.

O'Connor, J., Mansour, C., Turner-Harris, J. and Campbell, Jr. G.H. (1994) Reuse in command-and-control systems. *IEEE Software*, **11**(5):70–79, September.

O'Rourke, J. (1992) *RDD-100: A System Engineering Support Tool*. Technical report, Ascent Logic Corporation, 180 Rose Orchard Way, San Jose, CA.

Ogino, T. and Hirao Y. (1995) Formal Methods and their Applications to Safety-Critical Systems of Railways *Quarterly Review of RTRI*, **36**(4):198–202, December.

Owre, S., Rushby, J. and Shankar, N. (1992) PVS: A prototype verification system. In *Proc. CADE 11*, Lecture Notes in Artificial Intelligence **607**, pp 748–752, Springer-Verlag.

Owre, S., Shankar, N. and Rushby, J.M. (1993) *User guide for the PVS specification and verification system (draft)*. Technical Report, Computer Science Laboratory, SRI International, Menlo Park, CA.

Palmer, E.A., Hutchins, E.L, Ritter, R.D. and van Cleemput, I. (1993) *Altitude Deviations: Breakdowns of an Error-Tolerant System*, NASA Technical Memorandum 108788, National Aeronautics and Space Administration, Ames Research Center, October.

Pandya, P.K. and Joseph, M. (1991) P-A logic – a compositional proof system for distributed programs. *Distributed Computing*, 5:37–54.

Parnas, D.L. (1972) On the criteria to be used in decomposing systems into modules. *Communications of the ACM*, 15(12):1053–1058, December.

Parnas, D.L, Asmis, G.J.K. and Madey, J. (1991) Assessment of Safety-Critical Software in Nuclear Power Plants. *Nuclear Safety*, 32(2):189–198, April–June.

Parnas, D.L. and Clements, P.C. (1986) A rational design process: How and why to fake it. *IEEE Transactions on Software Engineering*, 12(2):251–257, February.

Parnas, D.L. and Madey, J. (1992) *Functional Documentation for Computer Systems Engineering*. CRL Report 237, Communications Research Laboratory, McMaster University, Ontario, Canada.

Paulson, L.C. (1996) Proving properties of security protocols by induction, In *Proceedings of the 10th Computer Security Foundations Workshop*, in press; also available as Technical Report 409, University of Cambridge Computer Laboratory, UK.

Pavey, D.J. and Winsborrow, L.A. (1995) Formal demonstration of equivalence of source code and PROM contents. In *Proceedings of the IMA Confernce on Mathematics of Dependable Systems*, Oxford University Press.

Payne, C.N., Froscher, J.N. and Landwehr, C.E. (1993) Toward a comprehensive INFOSEC certification methodology. In *Proceedings of the 16th National Computer Security Conference*, pp 165–172, Baltimore, MD, September.

Payne, C.N., Milhelcic, D.M., Moore, A.P. and Hayman, K.J. (1992) *The ECA Critical Requirements Model*. NRL Formal Report 9528, Naval Research Laboratory, Washington, D.C., December.

Payne, Jr., C.N., Moore, A.P. and Mihelcic, D.M. (1994) An experience modeling critical requirements. In *Proceedings of the 11th Annual Conference on Computer Assurance (COMPASS 94)*, pp 245–255, Gaithersburg, MD, June, IEEE Computer Society Press.

Petersen, J.L. (1996) *Formal Requirement Verification of a Swedish Railway Interlocking System*. Technical Report NP-K-JLP-001, Logikkonsult NP AB, September.

Pinnel, D.L. (1997) *Visualizing Requirements Specifications: A Toolkit for Rapid Prototyping of Interfaces*, University of Washington Technical Report, May.

Plat, N., van Katwijk, J. and Pronk, K. (1991) A case for structured analysis/formal design. In S. Prehn and W.J. Toetenel, editors, *Proceedings of VDM 91*, Springer-Verlag LNCS 551, pp 81–105.

Pnueli, A. (1985) In transition from global to modular temporal reasoning about programs. In K.R. Apt, editor, *Logics and Models of Concurrent Systems*, sub-series F: Computer and System Science, pp 123–144. Springer-Verlag.

Polack, F., Whinston, M. and Mander, K. (1993) The SAZ project: integrating SSADM with Z. In J.C.P. Woodcock and P.G. Larsen, editors, *FME'93: Industrial Strength Formal Methods*, pp 541–557, Lecture Notes in Computer Science, Springer-Verlag, Heidelberg.

Poore, J.H., Mills, H.D. and Mutchler, D. (1996) Planning and certifying software system reliability, In J.H. Poore and C.J. Trammell, editors, *Cleanroom Software Engineering: A Reader*, Blackwell, Oxford.

Poore, J.H. and Trammell, C.J., editors (1996) *Cleanroom Software Engineering: A Reader*, Blackwell, Oxford.

Potts, C. and Bruns, G. (1987) *Recording the Reasons for Design Decisions*. MCC Technical Report STP-304-87, MCC.

Prehn, S. (1994) *A Railway Running Map Design*, Technical Report SP/12/3, United Nations University, International Institute for Software Technology, Macau, July.

Pressman, R.S. (1997) *Software Engineering: A Practitioner's Approach*, 4th Edition, McGraw-Hill, New York.

Raghavan, S.A. and Chand, D.R. (1989) Diffusing software engineering methods. *IEEE Software*, **6**(4):81–90, July.

RAISE Language Group (1992) *The RAISE Specification Language*, BCS Practitioner Series, Prentice Hall, Hemel Hempstead.

RAISE Method Group (1995) *The RAISE Development Method*, BCS Practitioner Series, Prentice Hall, Hemel Hempstead.

Ramsey, N. (1994) Literate programming simplified. *IEEE Software*, **11**(5):97–105, September.

Ratan, V., Partridge, K., Reese, J.D. and Leveson, N.G. (1996) Safety analysis tools for requirements specifications. In *COMPASS Proceedings*, June.

Reese, J.D. (1995) *Software Deviation Analysis*. Ph.D. thesis, University of California, Irvine.

Reese, J.D. and Leveson, N.G. (1997a) Software deviation analysis: a "safeware" technique. In *Proceedings of the AIChE 31st Annual Loss Prevention Symposium*, March.

Reese, J.D. and Leveson, N.G. (1997b) Software deviation analysis. In *Proceedings of the International Conference on Software Engineering*, Boston, MA, May, IEEE Computer Society Press, Los Alamitos.

Reliable Software Technologies (1996) *WhiteBox DeepCover: User Reference Manual*, Sterling, VA.

de Roever, W.-P. (1985) The quest for compositionality — a survey of assertion-based proof systems for concurrent programs, part i: Concurrency based on shared variables. In E.J. Neuhold and G. Chroust, editors, *The Role of Abstract Models in Computer Science*, pp 181–206. IFIP, North Holland.

Rogers, E.M. (1983) *Diffusion of Information*, Third edition, The Free Press.

Rotstein, G.E., Sanchez, A. and Macchietto, S. (1997) *Procedural Control of Discrete Event Systems*, draft.

Rushby, J. (1995) *Formal Methods and their Role in the Certification of Critical Systems*, Technical Report SRI-CSL-95-1, SRI International, Menlo Park, CA, USA, March.

Saaltink, M. (1997) The Z/EVES system, In J.P. Bowen, M.G. Hinchey and D. Till, editors, *ZUM'97: The Z Formal Specification Notation*, Lecture Notes in Computer Science **1212**, Springer-Verlag, Heidelberg, pp 72–85.

Saaltink, M. and Meisels, I. (1995) *The Z/EVES Reference Manual (draft)*. ORA Canada Technical Report TR-95-5493-03, December.

Saaltink, M. (1997a) Domain Checking Z Specifications. In Proceedings of the Fourth NASA Langley Formal Methods Workshop, September.

Saaltink, M. (1997b) The Z/EVES System. In Bowen *et al.*, (1997).

Sagan, C. (1997) When scientists know sin, In C. Sagan, *The Demon-Haunted World: Science as a Candle in the Dark*, Ballantine Books, New York.

Sanchez, A. (1996a) *Description of the Tank Case Study*, Technical Report GR/K68783-12, Process Systems Engineering, Imperial College, London, UK, September.

Sanchez, A. (1996b) *Formal Specification and Synthesis of Procedural Controllers for Process Systems*. Lecture Notes in Control and Information Sciences **212**, Springer-Verlag, Heidelberg.

Sanchez, A. and Macchietto, S. (1995) Design of Procedural Controllers for Chemical Processes, *Computers and Chemical Engineering*, **19**:S381–S386.

Sarter, N.B. and Woods, D.D. (1993) *Cognitive Engineering in Aerospace Application: Pilot Interaction with Cockpit Automation*. NASA Contractor Report 177617, National Aeronautics and Space Administration, Ames Research Center, August.

Sawada, J. and Hunt, Jr., W.A. (1997) Trace Table Based Approach for Pipelined Microprocessor Verification. In *Computer Aided Verification 1997*, Lecture Notes in Computer Science **1254**, pp 364–375, Springer-Verlag.

Sherer, S.W., Kouchakdjian, A. and Arnold, P.G. (1993) Experience using cleanroom software engineering, *IEEE Software*, **13**(3):69–76. May.

Schneier, B. (1996) *Applied Cryptography*, John Wiley and Sons, Wokingham.

Secure Computing Corporation (1996) *DTOS Formal Top-Level Specification*. Report 83-0902024A, August.

Seger, C.-J. H. and Bryant, R.E. (1997) *Formal Verification by Symbolic Evaluation of Partially-Ordered Trajectories*. Technical Report 93-8, Computer Science Department, University of British Columbia.

Semmens, L. (1996) *Methods Integration: Rigorous Systems Specification using Structured Analysis and Formal Notations*, Ph.D. Thesis, Leeds Metropolitan University, UK

Sheeran, M. and Borälv, A. (1997) *Verification of Arithmetic Circuits using a Functional Language and Stålmarck's method*. Technical report, Chalmers University of Technology and Prover Technology, October.

Shimeall, T.J. and Leveson, N.G. (1991) An empirical comparison of software fault tolerance and fault elimination. *IEEE Transactions on Software Engineering*, **17**(2):173–183, February.

Simpson, A. (1994) A Formal Specification of an Automatic Train Protection System. In Naftalin *et al.* (1994).

Sommerville, I. (1996) *Software Engineering*, 5th Edition, Chapter 21, Addison-Wesley, Harlow.

Spivey, J.M. (1992a) *The Z Notation: A Reference Manual*, Second Edition, Prentice Hall International Series in Computer Science, Hemel Hempstead.

Spivey, J.M. (1992b) *The ƒUZZ Manual*, Second Edition, J.M. Spivey Computing Science Consultancy, Oxford, UK, July.

Srivas, M.K. and Bickford, M. (1990) Formal Verification of a Pipelined Microprocessor. *IEEE Software*, **7**(5):52–64, September.

Srivas, M.K. and Miller, S.P. (1995) *Formal Verification of an Avionics Microprocessor*. Technical Report CSL–95–04, SRI International Computer Science Laboratory, June.

Stålmarck, G. (1989) *A System for Determining Propositional Logic Theorems by Applying Values and Rules to Triplets that are Generated from a Formula*. Swedish Patent No. 467 076 (approved 1992), U.S. Patent No. 5 276 897 (1994), European Patent No. 0403 454 (1995).

Stålmarck, G. and Säflund, M. (1990) Modelling and Verifying Systems and Software in Propositional Logic. In B. Daniels, editor, *Safety of Computer Control Systems 1990 (SAFECOMP'90)*, pp 31–36, Pergamon Press, Oxford.

Storey, N. (1995) *Safety Critical Computer Systems*, Addison-Wesley, Wokingham.

Stoy, J. (1977) *Denotational Semantics*, MIT Press, Cambridge, MA.

Sutherland, D. (1986) A model of information. In *Proceedings of the 9th National Computer Security Conference*, pp 175–183, September.

Sutton, Jr., S.M., Tarr, P.L. and Osterwell, L.J. (1995) *An Analysis of Process Languages*. CMPSCI Technical Report 95-78, University of Massachusetts, August.

Swedish National Rail Administration (1996) *Säkerhetsordningen* (The safety regulation for Swedish interlockings), May.

TA Group Ltd. (1992a) *ASM86 to IL Translator User Guide, Release 3.0*, August.

TA Group Ltd. (1992b) *Intermediate Language Manual for MALPAS Release 6.0*, December.

TA Group Ltd. (1992c) *User Guide for MALPAS Release 6.0*, December.

Tahar, S. and Kumar, R. (1994) Implementational Issues for Verifying RISC-Pipeline Conflicts in HOL. In Thomas F. Melham and Juanito Camilleri, editors, *Higher Order Logic Theorem Proving and Its Applications, 7th International Workshop*, Lecture Notes in Computer Science, **859**, Springer-Verlag, pp 424–439.

Thomas, M. (1996) Formal methods and their role in developing safe systems, *High Integrity Systems*, 1(5):447–451.

Toulmin, S. (1957) *The Uses of Argument*. Cambridge University Press, Cambridge, UK.

Trammell, C.J., Pleszkoch, M.G., Linger, R.C. and Hevner, A.R. (1996) The incremental development process in cleanroom software engineering, *Decision Support Systems*, 17(1):55–71, April.

UK Health and Safety Executive (1992) *The Tolerability of Risk from Nuclear Power Stations*, Her Majesty's Stationery Office, London.

UK Ministry of Defence (1997) *Defence Standard DEF STAN 00-55, Requirements for safety related software in defence equipment* (Part 1: Requirements; Part 2: Guidance).

University of York (1997) *Modular MSc in Safety Critical Systems Engineering:Prospectus 1997/98*, Department of Computer Science, The University of York, Heslington, York YO1 5DD, UK, March.

van Doren, C. (1992) *A History of Knowledge: Past, Present and Future*, Ballantine Books, New York.

van Eijk, P., Vissers, C. and Diaz, M., editors (1989) *The Formal Description Technique LOTOS*. Elsevier Science Publishing Company B.V. (North Holland), Amsterdam, The Netherlands.

van Schouwen, A.J., Parnas, D.L. and Madey, J. (1993) Documentation of requirements for computer systems. In *Proceedings of the International Symposium on Requirements Engineering*, San Diego, CA, January, IEEE Computer Society Press.

Verdix Corporation (1990) *Verdix Ada Development System (VADS) Version 6.0 Manual Set*.

VISA (1986) VISA Security Module Operations Manual, Visa Credit Card Company.

Voas, J.M. and Miller, K.W. (1995) Software testability: The new verification. *IEEE Software*, 12(3):17–28, May.

Wagner, F. (1992) VFSM executable specification. In *Proceedings of CompEuro'92*, pp 226–231, The Hague, The Netherlands, IEEE Computer Society Press.

Walton, G.H. (1995) *Optimizing Software Usage Models*, Ph.D. dissertation, Department of Computer Science, University of Tennessee, Knoxville, TN.

Walton, G.H., Poore, J.H. and Trammell, C.J. (1996) Statistical testing based on a software usage model, In J.H. Poore and C.J. Trammell, editors, *Cleanroom Software Engineering: A Reader*, Blackwell, Oxford.

Ward, N.J. (1993) The rigorous retrospective static analysis of the Sizewell B Primary Protection System software. In J. Gorski, editor, *Proceedings of SafeComp'93: the 12th International Conference on Computer Safety, Reliability and Security*, Poznan-Kiekrz, Poland, October.

Weinhous, M.S., Purdy, J.A. and Granda, C.O. (1990) Testing of a medical linear accelerator's computer-control system, *Medical Physics*, 17(1):95–102, January/February.

Weiser, M. (1984) Program slicing. *IEEE Transactions on Software Engineering*, 10(4):352–357, July.

Whittaker, J.A. and Poore, J.H. (1996) Markov analysis of software specifications, In J.H. Poore and C.J. Trammell, editors, *Cleanroom Software Engineering: A Reader*, Blackwell, Oxford.

Whittaker, J.A. and Thomason, M.G. (1996) A Markov chain model for statistical software testing, In J.H. Poore and C.J. Trammell, editors, *Cleanroom Software Engineering: A Reader*, Blackwell, Oxford.

Williams, R. (1992) *FunnelWeb user's manual*. Technical report, University of Adelaide, Adelaide, South Australia, Australia, May.

Wilson, S.P. and McDermid, J.A. (1995) Safety case development: Current practice, future prospects. In *Proceedings of the First Annual European Network of Clubs for Reliability and Safety of Software (ENCRESS) Conference*, Bruges, Belgium, September.

Windley, P.J. (1995) Formal Modeling and Verification of Microprocessors. *IEEE Transactions on Computers*, **44**(1):54–72, January.

Windley, P.J. and Coe, M.L. (1994) A Correctness Model for Pipelined Microprocessors. In Ramayya Kumar and Thomas Kropf, editors, *Theorem Provers in Circuit Design, TPCD '94*, Lecture Notes in Computer Science **901**, Springer-Verlag, pp 33–51.

Woodcock, J.C.P. (1996) Software engineering research directions, *ACM Computing Surveys*, **28**(4es):128, December.

Xu, Q.W., de Roever, W.-P. and He, J. (1997) The rely-guarantee method for verifying shared variable concurrent programs. *Formal Aspects of Computing*, **9**(2):149–174.

Yu, Y. (1992) *Automated Proofs of Object Code for a Widely Used Microprocessor*, Technical Report 92, Computational Logic, Inc., May.

Yulin, D. (1995) *The Formal Development of a Railway Station Route Management System*.M.Sc. thesis, University of Macau, May.

Zave, P. and Jackson, M.A. (1993) Conjunction as composition. *ACM Transactions on Software Engineering and Methodology*, **2**(4):379–411.

Zwiers, J. (1989) *Compositionality Concurrency and Partial Correctness*. Lectures Notes in Computer Science **321**, Springer-Verlag, Heidelberg.

Index

9 781852 336400